THE Si
Sta

THE Silver Star

NAVY AND MARINE CORPS GALLANTRY IN IRAQ, AFGHANISTAN, AND OTHER CONFLICTS

James E. Wise Jr. and Scott Baron

NAVAL INSTITUTE PRESS
Annapolis, Maryland

Naval Institute Press
291 Wood Road
Annapolis, MD 21402

Library of Congress Cataloging-in-Publication Data

Wise, James E., 1930–
  The Silver Star : Navy and Marine Corps gallantry in Iraq, Afghanistan, and other conflicts /
James Wise, Jr. and Scott Baron.
     p. cm.
  Includes bibliographical references and index.
  ISBN 978-1-59114-930-9 (alk. paper)
  1. Silver Star. 2. United States. Navy—Biography. 3. United States. Marine Corps—
Biography. 4. Heroes—United States—Biography. 5. United States—History, Military—20th
century. 6. United States—History, Military—21st century. I. Baron, Scott, 1954- II. Title.
  UB433.W57 2008
  359.0092'273—dc22

                                        2008034605

Printed in the United States of America on acid-free paper

14 13 12 11 10 09 08   9 8 7 6 5 4 3 2
First printing

Book layout and composition: David Alcorn, Alcorn Publication Design

For my shipmate, Capt. Robert J. Tolle, USN (Ret.), superb professional,
true gentleman . . . in everlasting friendship.
JAMES E. WISE JR.

Dedicated to Marisela, my wife of more than thirty years.
It is only because you do what you do that I can do what I do.
SCOTT BARON

But we in it shall be remember'd;
We few, we happy few, we band of brothers;
For he today that sheds his blood with me
Shall be my brother.
WILLIAM SHAKESPEARE, *King Henry V*
(1598)

CONTENTS

PREFACE

T*he Silver Star: Navy and Marine Corps Gallantry in Iraq, Afghanistan, and Other Conflicts* is a companion book to *The Navy Cross: Extraordinary Heroism in Iraq, Afghanistan, and Other Conflicts*. The purpose of both books is to record for history the heroism of our young men and women who have fought and continue to fight an enemy bent on destroying America's way of life. Like all wars, the cost of lives in a war zone is a tragedy—yet how blessed this country is to have such people who risk their lives daily for their fellow Americans.

In this ongoing war against global terrorism our servicemen and servicewomen continue to carry out their missions with determination and great courage. They display extraordinary dedication to their tasks and to the military men and women with whom they serve; they are truly inspiring. Can we ever repay them for what they and others before them have done in past wars? Perhaps not, but with these books we can introduce future generations to military heroes and preserve the memory of their gallant individual sacrifice.

As of March 2008, when the authors completed their work on this book, there were approximately 24 Sailors and 73 Marines who had been awarded the Silver Star medal for gallantry in Iraq and Afghanistan. Additionally, as of that time Silver Star medals had been awarded to about 247 Army and 28 Air Force personnel.

ACKNOWLEDGMENTS

Many of the same associates who assisted us with the writing and production of *The Navy Cross: Extraordinary Heroism in Iraq, Afghanistan, and Other Conflicts* again joined us in this endeavor.

Natalie Hall, our superb professional editor, was at the center of the effort. Considering that she resides in Ohio and the authors are located on either coast (Wise in Alexandria, Virginia, and Baron in Watsonville, California), it was her task to ensure that the manuscript was carefully edited for textual continuity and format in accordance with our publisher's guidelines. Even though the authors have collaborated on several books and by now can readily mirror each other's writing style, it was up to Natalie to render advice when the length of a chapter would bog down the flow of an individual's heroic story or when repetitious wording would possibly lessen reader interest. She raised flags, kept us on track, and produced a first-rate manuscript. She's the best.

The authors would like to make a special acknowledgment of the Home of Heroes website (homeofheroes.com) and Douglas Sterner, its owner/publisher/researcher. Doug's invaluable research and personal assistance greatly facilitated the writing of the book. A veteran and patriot, he has created a premier website that is a treasure trove of useful information for researchers, historians, lovers of history, and anyone else interested in America's military heritage. It contains databases on awards of the Medal of Honor, Distinguished Service Cross, Navy Cross, Air Force Cross, and Silver Stars. In his website are sections devoted to different military themes (442nd, Pearl Harbor, Spanish American War, and so on), quizzes, bulletin boards, information on veterans affairs, and instructions for contacting the government, among many other items. There are also downloadable databases at no cost. It is an extraordinary resource.

Doug's gracious assistance in locating obscure facts made writing this book significantly easier and certainly more enjoyable, and for that, the authors are forever indebted. He is an outstanding individual and a down-to-earth good guy. Thanks, Doug.

We would also like to personally thank Ted Altenberg; Robert V. Aquilina; Paul Beauchamp; Col. Walter G. Ford, USMC (Ret.); Jack Green; Michael A. Harris; Catherine Hayden; Glenn Helm; Sharon S. MacDonald; Bruce McIver; Clare L. Mugno; Kara R. Newcomer; George Petersen; Herman Pizzi; Nick Popaditch, USMC (Ret.); Kevin Reem; Capt. Kelly D. Royer, USMC; Diane Dellatorre Stevens; Rob Taglianetti; Xiaoming Zhang; and the editors and production staff of the Naval Institute Press.

ACKNOWLEDGMENTS

ACRONYMS

AAV, amtrac, or track: assault amphibious vehicle
ACR: Armored Cavalry Regiment
AFP: Agence France Presse
Amtrac, AAV, or track: assault amphibious vehicle
ANA: Afghanistan National Army
AO: area of operation
AOP: area of patrol
AT: antitank
BCT: Brigade Combat Team
BLT: Battalion Landing Team
CAAT: Combined Anti-Armor Team
CENTCOM: Central Command
CMC: Commandant of the Marine Corps
COC: Combat Operation Center
CP: Command Post
DPMO: Defense POW/Missing Personnel Office
DSC: Distinguished Service Cross
EOD: explosive ordnance demolition
ETT: Embedded Training Team
FAC: Forward Air Controller
FAO: Forward Artillery Observer
FMF: Fleet Marine Force
FMTU: Foreign Military Training Unit
FOB: forward operating base
HM3: Hospital Corpsman 3rd Class
HMG: heavy machine gun
ICDC: Iraqi Civil Defense Corps
Icom: integrated communications
IED: improvised explosive device
ISF: Iraqi Security Forces
KIA: killed in action

LAR: Light Armored Reconnaissance Battalion
LAV: light armored vehicles
LZ: landing zone
MAG: Marine Air Group
MAP: Mobile Assault Platoon
MarSOC: Marine Forces Special Operations Command
MCAGCC: Marine Corps Air Ground Combat Center
MCB: Marine Corps Base
MEB: Marine Expeditionary Brigade
MEF: Marine Expeditionary Force
MEU: Marine Expeditionary Unit
MEU-SOC: Marine Expeditionary Unit–Special Operations Capable
MIA: missing in action
MOH: Medal of Honor
MSR: main supply route
NAVSCOLEOD: Navy Explosive Ordnance Disposal School
OCS: Officer Candidate School
OIF: Operation Iraqi Freedom
OLC: oak leaf cluster
OMLT: Operational Mentor Liaison Team
OP: observation post
POW: prisoner of war
PPS: personal protection specialist
QRF: quick reaction force
RCT: Regimental Combat Team
RPG: rocket-propelled grenade
SASO: Stability and Support Operations
SAW: squad automatic weapon

SERE: survival, evasion, resistance, escape

SMAW: shoulder-fired multipurpose assault weapon

SOC: Special Operations Command

SOI: School of Infantry

SVBIED: suicide vehicle–borne improvised explosive device

TOW: tube-launched, optically tracked, wire-guided

Track, AAV, or amtrac: assault amphibious vehicle

U.K.: United Kingdom

VT: Navy Torpedo Bombers

XO: Executive Officer

INTRODUCTION

History of the Medal, Criteria for Award, and Early Awards

The Silver Star is the third-highest award given for valor, ranking below the Medal of Honor and the Distinguished Service Cross/ Navy Cross/Air Force Cross. Originally authorized as an Army award, subsequent legislation expanded its award to include any branch of the U.S. Armed Forces as well as civilians.

The Silver Star is awarded for gallantry in action against an enemy of the United States not justifying a higher award. It may be awarded to any person who, while serving in any capacity with the U.S. Armed Forces, distinguishes himself or herself by extraordinary heroism involving one of the following actions:

> In action against an enemy of the United States while engaged in military operations involving conflict with an opposing foreign force
>
> While serving with friendly foreign forces engaged in an armed conflict against an opposing armed force in which the United States is not a belligerent party

The action, while requiring a lesser degree of gallantry than that required for the Distinguished Service Cross, must nevertheless have been performed with marked distinction.[1]

The history of the Silver Star dates back to 9 July 1918 when an act of the 65th Congress authorized the award of the Citation Star, a three-six-teenths-inch silver star device pinned to the World War I Victory medal to denote those who had been cited for extreme heroism or valor. In addition the Citation Star could be awarded retroactively and worn with the Civil War Campaign Medal, Indian Campaign Medal, Spanish Campaign Medal, Philippine Campaign Medal, China Campaign Medal, and Mexican Service Medal. Although the Citation Star was authorized only for the Army, a similar award, the Navy Commendation Star, was authorized for wear by Navy and Marine Corps personnel.

On 19 July 1932 the secretary of war authorized the Silver Star medal to replace the Citation Star. On 7 August 1942 Congress placed into law an act authorizing the award for the U.S. Navy, followed by similar legislation for the Army on 12 December 1942.[2]

The medal itself was designed by Rudolf Freund of Bailey, Banks, and Biddle. It can be described as a gold star, one and a half inches in circumscribing diameter, with a laurel wreath encircling rays from the center and a three-sixteenths-inch diameter silver star superimposed in the center to represent the original Citation Star. The pendant is suspended from a rectangular-shaped metal loop with rounded corners. The reverse has the inscription, "For Gallantry in Action," with space to engrave the awardee's name.

The ribbon is one and three-eighths inches wide, and consists of the following stripes: three thirty-seconds-inch ultramarine blue 67118; three sixty-fourths-inch white 67101; seven thirty-seconds-inch ultramarine blue; seven thirty-seconds-inch white; seven thirty-seconds-inch old glory red 67156 (center stripe); seven thirty-seconds-inch white; seven thirty-seconds-inch ultramarine blue; three sixty-fourths-inch white; and three thirty-seconds-inch ultramarine blue.[3]

Additional decorations of the Silver Star are denoted in the U.S. Army and Air Force by a bronze oak leaf cluster (OLC), while the Navy, Coast Guard, and Marine Corps issue a gold star. A silver OLC or star is worn in lieu of five bronze OLCs or five gold stars.[4]

Five women have been awarded the Silver Star: four Army nurses (2nd Lt. Ellen Ainsworth, 1st Lt. Mary Roberts, 2nd Lt. Elaine Roe, and 2nd Lt. Virginia Rourke, with Ainsworth's awarded posthumously) at Anzio during World War II, and Sgt. Lee Ann Hester during the current war in Iraq.

Although the above women have received recognition for their gallantry and are so noted by military historians, three other women—army nurses who served in France during World War I—were cited for the award. Their names and titles were discovered by a historian with the Army's Office of Medical History in 2007. They had been awarded the Citation Star, which predated the Silver Star, for serving on the front lines in July 1918 in France and caring for wounded despite enemy artillery bombardment. Of the three, only Mary Jane Bolles, the daughter of the late Army nurse Linnie Leckrone, was able to attend an Army ceremony at the Women in Military Service for America Memorial in Arlington, Virginia, on 31 July 2007, where the Silver Star was awarded posthumously to Ms. Leckrone and presented to her daughter.[5] One recipient had died leaving no living kin, and the other recipient's family was unable to attend the ceremony.

Col. David Haskell Hackworth, U.S. Army, holds the record for the most awards with ten Silver Stars (three during the war in Korea and seven during the war in Vietnam).

ENDNOTES

1. *United States Armed Forces Awards, Decorations, Campaign & Service Medals*, Institute of Heraldry, United States Army, Government Printing Office, Washington, DC.
2. Silver Star, sec. 3746, title 10, U.S. Code (10 USC 3746), established by Act of Congress 9 July 1918 (amended by act of 25 July 1963).
3. Silver Star Fact Sheet, Air Force Personnel Center, Randolph AFB.
4. Army Regulation 600–8-22 (Military Awards), Chapter 3, 25 February 1995, Government Printing Office, Washington, DC.
5. Fred W. Baker, "Daughter Accepts Silver Star Her World War I Nurse Mother Earned," *Army News Service*, 2 August 2007.

AFGHANISTAN (2001–PRESENT)

1st Lt. Christopher P. Niedziocha, USMC

*Battalion Landing Team One Six Anti-Armor Platoon,
Commander Assigned to 22nd Marine Expeditionary Unit,
Deployed with Commander, United States Fifth Fleet*

Sandabuz, Afghanistan
8 June 2004

For conspicuous gallantry and intrepidity in action against the enemy
while serving as Battalion Landing Team ONE SIX Combined Anti-Armor
Platoon Commander assigned to 22nd Marine Expeditionary Unit deployed
with Commander, United States FIFTH Fleet on 8 June 2004. When his
convoy came under heavy rocket and small arms fire in an enemy ambush
near the village of Sandabuz, Afghanistan, First Lieutenant Niedziocha
pushed his vehicles through the kill zone as far forward as possible to confront the enemy's main ambush site. With his vehicles caught in a crossfire,
he led his Marines from the front by engaging enemy positions with devastating heavy machine gun and small arms fire. First Lieutenant Niedziocha
aggressively engaged the enemy at a distance of less than one hundred
meters and negated the enemy's advantage of standoff and surprise. Seeking
to regain the initiative, he led his Marines in a bold flanking maneuver,
trapping some enemy forces who were later found and eliminated, causing
others to break contact. He then led his Marines in pursuit of the fleeing
enemy, neutralizing the remaining enemy forces with direct fire and close
air support. By his bold leadership, wise judgment and complete dedication
to duty, First Lieutenant Niedziocha reflected great credit upon himself and
upheld the highest traditions of the Marine Corps and the United States
Naval Service.[1]

Silver Star Citation

IT WAS NOT A GOOD DAY for the Taliban near the village of Sandabuz in
Central Afghanistan on 8 June 2004. They had spotted a convoy of four
American Humvees approaching and had set up what has been said to be the
heaviest, most coordinated, and largest ambush as of that date (June 2004)

to quickly dispatch their enemy. They found themselves suddenly faced with heavily armed U.S. Marines who were driving through the Taliban kill zone and who readily took them on. After dismounting from their vehicles they engaged them on foot, filling the air with gunfire and grenade explosions until the Taliban retreated into the adjacent mountains, leaving behind twenty-three dead fighters. In this fierce encounter the Marines were led by (then) 1st Lt. Christopher P. Niedziocha, USMC, who was to be awarded the Silver Star medal for his bold leadership, wise judgment, and complete dedication to duty.

Niedziocha, twenty-seven, was a platoon commander with the 22d Marine Expeditionary Unit–Special Operations Capable (MEU-SOC) at the time. As the four machine gun– and antitank missile–toting Battalion Landing Team 1st Battalion, 6th Marines' Combined Anti-Armor Team (CAAT) continued forward, Niedziocha noted that the village was nestled in front of high rocky terrain. As the convoy entered the village nothing seemed out of place from the dozens of other villages they had visited during the three months he and his platoon had been in country. In fact they had not encountered any sign of the enemy during that time. The Taliban would attack a convoy and then disappear into the local population. Trying to separate the "good guys" from the "bad guys" was particularly difficult, especially when the local villagers would protect the enemy fighters with their lives.

As the CAAT moved through the village and spread out to assume blocking positions on its far side the lead vehicle noticed three Afghan men attempting to walk nonchalantly out of the village and into the surrounding mountains.

"I saw them walking from the village and up a hill," said Niedziocha, who was serving as the CAAT platoon leader. "We immediately went after them and when we got closer they started running."[2] At the same time the other three CAAT vehicles began converging on Niedziocha's position, fighting through the difficult terrain and confusing village layout to reach their platoon leader.[3]

When Niedziocha's vehicle (dubbed Light Horse 11) caught up with the men and stopped, one of the men drew an AK-47 assault rifle from under his clothes and opened fire on the Marines. Cpl. Curtis Spivey, of Valdosta, Georgia, was the first to respond. "He let go a few bursts with the 240 (M-240G machine gun mounted atop the Humvee) and the three 'bad guys' jumped into a trench and started firing at us," Niedziocha said.[4]

Niedziocha and his driver, LCpl. Ray Colvin, accompanied by radio operator LCpl. Thomas Hyland, leapt out of their vehicle and immediately opened fire with their M-16A4 assault rifles. Spivey also jumped from the vehicle and grabbed the rifle of CAAT's forward air controller, Capt. James "Big Jim" McBride who was busy radioing for air support.

"Beaver [Capt. James Hunt] was controlling some helos for Charlie Company so when we broadcast that we were in contact, they switched over to support us," said McBride, an EA-6B Prowler (USN-USMC Electronic Warfare Aircraft) crew from Butte, Montana.[5]

While McBride and Hyland stayed on the vehicle to provide security the other three Marines pressed forward with rifles in hand, their pockets filled with grenades. The helicopters weren't the only ones to hear the announcement of troops in contact. Driving Light Horse 1–6, Sgt. Dan Trackwell, a machine-gunner from Klamath Falls, Oregon, was already speeding toward Niedziocha's position. Sitting beside Trackwell was his assistant driver, Cpl. Nicholas Marrone of Saranac, New York, and riding on top was his MK-19 heavy machine-gunner, LCpl. Jonathan Freeze of Naples, Florida.

"As soon as I heard them say 'contact' all bets were off," said Trackwell, who "stood" on the gas pedal and plowed over the rough, uneven terrain as the sound of firing began to fill the air.[6]

On the hill Niedziocha, Colvin, and Spivey moved forward firing their weapons as the enemy fighters popped up, fired a few rounds, and then moved right or left inside the trench to repeat the process. When Spivey ran out of ammunition in McBride's rifle, he tossed it aside, pulled his 9-mm pistol, and began tossing hand grenades into the trench, as did Niedziocha. Colvin, carrying an M-203 40-mm grenade launcher, attached his M-16A4 and began accurately lobbing rounds into the trench as well. "When one of the grenades went off," Niedziocha said, "all I saw was a turban and equipment flying so I knew we had gotten at least one of them."[7]

By the time the grenades started flying Light Horse 1-6 had pulled up, and Trackwell and another Marine began moving forward and firing at the enemy while Marrone and Freeze stayed with the vehicle. Taking control of the 40-mm up gun, on Trackwell's command Freeze opened fire and lobbed twenty-five 40-mm grenades onto the hillside directly over the trench where a number of Taliban fighters had taken refuge.

At almost the same instant, spotting the yellow smoke billowing from the signal grenade tossed by McBride, one of the UH-1N Huey helicopters overhead banked sharply and the door gunner, Cpl. Samai Alyassini of San Jose, California, let loose a sustained burst of around one hundred 7.62 rounds into the trench. Between the barrage of grenades, rifle, and machine-gun fire from the air and ground, the enemy fire ceased as dozens of dead

Taliban fighters littered the ground. Others fled into mountain crevasses. A thorough search of the slain enemy fighters revealed, in addition to their personal weapons, a wide array of explosives and bomb-making materials that were commonly used in the construction of improvised explosive devices.[8]

Three Marines were wounded in the engagement. In addition to the twenty-three Taliban fighters killed, two were wounded and captured. Niedziocha reflected, "If it weren't for body armor and some very near misses, we could have had four or five Marines killed that day."[9]

On 12 December 2005 Capt. Christopher P. Niedziocha, USMC, was awarded the Silver Star medal by Lt. Gen. James F. Amos, commanding general, II Marine Expeditionary Force, in a ceremony at Naval Station Norfolk, Virginia, for his gallant actions on 8 June 2004 in Afghanistan. A native of King of Prussia, Pennsylvania, a number of Niedziocha's relatives from Philadelphia and King of Prussia were present at the ceremony.

After receiving the award he said, "I really can't stress enough that I think my role in [the firefight] was very small." He went on to say that he wears his Silver Star "as a reminder of something that I thought was really amazing which was the work my Marines did."[10]

ENDNOTES

1. Silver Star citation, 1st. Lt. Christopher P. Niedziocha, USMC, http://www.homeofheroes. com/valor2/SS/7_GWOT/citations_USMC-M.html.
2. GySgt. Keith A. Milks, USMC. "Dispatch from Forward Operating Base Ripley," *Marine Corps News*, 9 July 2004.
3. Beth Zimmerman, "Platoon Leader Honored for Pushing Through Ambush," *Marine Corps Times*, 16 January 2006.
4. Milks, "Dispatch from Forward Operating Base Ripley."
5. Ibid.
6. Ibid.
7. Zimmerman, "Platoon Leader Honored for Pushing Through Ambush."
8. Milks, "Dispatch from Forward Operating Base Ripley."
9. Ibid.
10. Sgt. Chris R. Berryman, USMC, "Captain Awarded for Battlefield Gallantry," *Marine Corps News*, 12 December 2005.

Pfc. Daniel B. McClenney, USMC

Rifleman, Kilo Company, 3rd Battalion, 6th Marines,
U.S. Marine Corps Forces, Central Command

Konar Province, Afghanistan
24 June 2004

The President of the United States takes pleasure in presenting the Silver Star Medal (Posthumously) to Daniel B. McClenney, Private First Class, U.S. Marine Corps, for conspicuous gallantry and intrepidity in action against the enemy while serving as a Rifleman, Kilo Company, Third Battalion, Sixth Marines, U.S. Marine Corps Forces, Central Command, in support of Operation Enduring Freedom on 24 June 2004. Private First Class McClenney's fire team was part of an ongoing operation to locate and disarm enemy militia in the Konar Province of Afghanistan. While on patrol Private First Class McClenney's fire team came under intense enemy fire from two different ambush positions. The ambush was intended to support a much larger attack, targeting Marines and other Coalition Forces at Firebase Naray. The enemy would have dealt a detrimental blow to Coalition forces had Private First Class McClenney's fire team not reacted in a quick and decisive manner. Private First Class McClenney continued to engage the enemy despite being wounded on the initial burst of enemy fire. After his team leader was killed, he took over radio communications and gave constant situation reports to the firebases and quick reaction forces for thirty minutes. Private First Class McClenney aggressively exchanged fire with the enemy while simultaneously requesting medical evacuation for his entire team. McClenney displayed an indomitable fighting spirit as he fought hand-to-hand, until he was mortally wounded. By his bold leadership, wise judgment, and complete dedication to duty, Private First Class McClenney reflected great credit upon himself and upheld the highest traditions of the Marine Corps and the United States Naval Service.[1]

Silver Star Citation

ON 24 JUNE 2004 Pfc. Daniel McClenney, USMC, and his fire team were returning to base after patrolling an area near the town of Bari-Khout in the mountainous Konar Province, which runs along the border between Afghanistan and Pakistan. McClenney and his good friend LCpl. Juston T. Thacker were part of Camp Lejeune's 3rd Battalion, 6th Marine Regiment,

2nd Marine Division, which had left North Carolina just two months before. Thacker, twenty-one, was from Princeton, West Virginia, and was on his second tour. McClenney, nineteen, born and raised in Shelbyville, Tennessee, was on his first tour. In their off hours they talked about their life after serving four years in the Corps. Though they were deeply dedicated to their country and the Corps, McClenney wanted to be a police officer and Thacker was determined to finish college. Neither one would realize his dreams. They were both killed on that fateful day.[2]

As they approached their fire base they came under intense fire from two enemy positions, both heavily concealed. McClenney's team leader was killed instantly as fire swept down on the Marines. McClenney immediately took control of radio communications and called in for quick reaction ground support and medical evacuation. He fought courageously despite receiving a gunshot to the abdomen and suffering a broken arm. As the battle raged on he found himself engaged in hand-to-hand combat. After suffering additional wounds, the seriousness of his injuries finally proved to be fatal. The Department of Defense announced on 26 June 2004 the deaths of Private First Class McClenney and Lance Corporal Thacker due to hostile fire near Bari-Khout, Afghanistan.

McClenney's fire team members recalled that, due to his valiant action, their lives were saved. One said, "If he didn't work the radio like he did, my fellow Marines would not have gotten to us so fast . . . he was selfless and had amazing heart . . . he was exceptional and fought to the last breath; he did everything he could to stop the terrorists."[3]

Daniel McClenney was a native of Bedford County, Tennessee, the son of the late Lera Smith McClenney and Randy McClenney of Shelbyville. He graduated from Shelbyville Central High School in May 2003; as a teenager he worked at a horse barn and later the Farmer's Co-Op feed store in Shelbyville during and after school. He was known to his family and friends as a quiet, shy, and respectful young man. His mother had passed away in 2001. When he started his tour, he left behind a fifteen-year-old sister. He was buried with full military honors at Rose Bank Cemetery, Flat Creek, Tennessee.[4]

In May 2005 Marines from the 3rd Battalion, 6th Marine regiment, 2nd Marine Division, Camp Lejeune, North Carolina, entered the Shelbyville Court House to present the Silver Star medal (posthumously) to Private First Class McClenney's family and friends. The late morning ceremony included the Nashville Marine Corps Reserve unit that provided a Color Guard and a twenty-one-gun salute.

McClenney's commanding officer, Lt. Col. Julian D. Alford, addressed the crowd before presenting the Silver Star to McClenney's father. Colonel

Alford stated, "His life was lived as an example of decency and his death a costly price for freedom. . . . His fellow Marines continue to feel his absence and they will never be the same. But they are more committed to the causes of liberty." Colonel Alford went on to say, "It is right that Daniel's bust will be displayed in this building, so that generations to follow will stand and ask 'Who is this great man?'" Colonel Alford added, "Monuments do that for us, they provide a type of immortality, and they force us to remember. But Daniel has achieved another type of immortality, the type that lives on in the hearts of men."[5]

Randy McClenney accepted the medal and citation saying, "This medal means so much to me. . . . [I]t's something I can look at every day and think of my son. I'm so proud of what Daniel did that day—he gave it his all and didn't give up."[6]

(Note: Survivors of Servicemen, an organization that raises funds to present bronze busts in the likeness of fallen servicemen and servicewomen had unveiled a bust of Pfc. Daniel McClenney in the Shelbyville Court House a month before the Silver Star ceremony. Regarding the bronze bust, Randy McClenney said, "I am sure my son would have been deeply touched by your gift to his family and the city of Shelbyville.")[7]

ENDNOTES

1. Silver Star citation, Pfc. Daniel B. McClenney, USMC, http://www.homeofheroes.com/valor2/SS/7_GWOT/citations_USMC-M.html.
2. John Frank, "Ambush Ends Marines' Dreams: Two from Lejeune Die in Afghanistan," http://newsobserver.com/news/v-printer/story/1380729p-7504071c.html.
3. Staff Sergeant Fischer, 6th Marine Corps District, "Marines Present Silver Star, Bronze Bust, to Fallen Comrade's Family," *Marine Corps News*, 13 May 2005.
4. "Marine Corps Deaths in the Iraq War," 24 June 2004, http://www.scuttlebutt/smallchow.com/mardeath57bb.html.
5. Ibid.
6. Ibid.
7. Fischer, "Marines Present Silver Star, Bronze Bust."

Capt. Brian G. Cillessen, USMC

Operational Detachment Alpha 143, Combined Joint Task Force Phoenix,
Office of Military Cooperation, Afghanistan

Embedded with Afghan National Army Commandos
23 January 2005

For gallantry in action while deployed in support of Operation Enduring Freedom as an Embedded Trainer and Marine Advisor for the Afghan National Army Commandos and active member of Special Forces Operational Detachment Alpha 143, Combined Joint Task Force Phoenix, Office of Military Cooperation–Afghanistan. Captain Cillessen's courage under fire, and sound leadership in combat were exemplified when his element was subjected to an intense enemy ambush. After the lead vehicle was disabled due to a volley of rocket-propelled grenades and machine gun fire he quickly directed the beleaguered column to initiate immediate action in response. Further, he subjected himself to a hailstorm of enemy fire on multiple occasions to suppress enemy fighting positions with his M-203 grenade launcher, while the remainder of his convoy found covered fighting positions. After realizing that one of the Afghan National Army Soldiers was seriously wounded, Captain Cillessen risked his life, moving under intense fire to render aid. His actions rallied both the Marines and Afghan Soldiers for whom he was responsible. Captain Cillessen's performance of duty is in keeping with the finest traditions of military service and reflects great credit upon himself, the United States Central Command, and the United States Marine Corps.[1]

Silver Star Citation

ON 20 APRIL 2007 Capt. Brian G. Cillessen, USMC, was awarded the Silver Star medal at the Marine Corps Base Camp Lejeune, North Carolina. As noted in his citation, he was a member of Special Forces Operational Detachment Alpha 143, Combined Joint Force Phoenix Office of Military Cooperation, Afghanistan, while deployed in support of Operation Enduring Freedom. At the time of this assignment he was Company Commander, Charlie Company, 1st Battalion, 8th Marine Regiment, 2nd Marine Division.[2]

Combined Joint Force Phoenix might be relatively unknown to the average reader, since few know what's happening in that forbidding, mountainous country because of the news media's focused coverage of the war in Iraq. Perhaps a short primer on the subject will prove informative.

Immediately after the fall of the Taliban regime in 2001 U.S. soldiers from the 10th Mountain Division began the initial development of the Afghanistan National Army (ANA) as Task Force Phoenix 1. The mission of the Task Force (which is in its fifth rotation) is to train and mentor soldiers of the all-volunteer Afghan National Army. This has involved not only American soldiers, Sailors, Marines and airmen, but also military personnel of thirteen Coalition Partner Nations: Canada, Croatia, France, Germany, Great Britain, Italy, Norway, the Netherlands, Poland, Romania, Slovenia, and Sweden. Thus far, the Coalition forces have successfully assisted in training and equipping nearly thirty-five thousand ANA soldiers. These ANA troops operate in 104 locations throughout Afghanistan. Personnel, Operational Mentor Liaison Teams (OMLTs) and U.S. Embedded Training Teams (ETTs) mentor the ANA in leadership, staff, and support functions, planning, assessing, supporting, and execution of operations and training doctrine, tactics, techniques, and procedures. In addition to training and mentoring the ANA the ETTs and OMLTs provide the ANA access to combat enablers such as close air and fire support, medical evacuation, and quick reaction forces (QRFs).[3]

With the resurgence of the Taliban and their brazen attacks and seizure of territory in southern Afghanistan during the past year Coalition commanders have requested additional troops to stem the growing militant violence. This took on new urgency when, in January 2008, terrorists stormed Kabul's most popular luxury hotel, Hotel Serena, throwing grenades and firing AK-47s at hotel guests despite heavy security. Six people were killed. Among them were two reporters, an American and a Norwegian. Six others were wounded. U.S. military officials recently revealed that three thousand two hundred Marines have been told to prepare for deployment to Afghanistan (Marines slated to deploy: two thousand two hundred Marines of the 24th Marine Expeditionary Unit based in North Carolina and approximately one thousand Marines of the 2nd Battalion, 7th Regiment, based in Twentynine Palms, California). This deployment would increase U.S. forces there to as much as thirty thousand service members. Non-U.S. foreign troops in Afghanistan number twenty-eight thousand.[4]

In January 2005 Captain Cillessen was serving in northeast Afghanistan along with three other U.S. servicemen embedded with the 2nd Company, 1st Battalion, 3rd Brigade of the Afghan National Army Commandos. On 23 January while on patrol with forty-five Afghan soldiers they located several large weapons caches. The Afghanis hired sixty donkeys to carry away the weapons. This discovery stirred the militants from their winter siesta and attacks against the Coalition forces began to increase. In fact several members of the Afghani security forces had recently been killed by a roadside bomb. The tactics used by the enemy were to hit hard and then melt away. Though the local authorities were cooperative that day, they gave Cillessen and the Afghan soldiers the sense that something was about to happen because none of them wanted to talk to Coalition soldiers for very long.

As they began to leave the area with the captured weapons the Afghan commander sent some soldiers ahead of the convoy but their vehicle broke down. "We caught up to them about the time we got ambushed and were in the middle of the kill zone," recalled Cillessen.[5] The Afghan soldiers and four U.S. servicemen were on a road flanked on both sides by steep mountains from which Islamic militants fired volleys of rocket-propelled grenades at the convoy. The Coalition troops and the militants were separated by a river. "The enemy had a well-planned ambush on our egress. They knew exactly where to hit us."[6] When a volley of rocket-propelled grenades and machine-gun fire disabled the lead vehicle in their convoy, Cillessen quickly directed the immediate action of the Afghan soldiers around him in what became a four-hour-long firefight.

"There was no place to take cover," the 1990 New Mexico Military Institute, Roswell, New Mexico, graduate recalled. "We were caught between an incline and a river."[7] The men around Cillessen began to suppress the enemy fire immediately. They changed their established procedures and decided to stay and fight instead of leaving the battlefield when they got the chance. Cillessen recalled, "My initial instinct was to return fire and kill as many of the enemy as possible before they had a chance to withdraw."[8]

"In the first five to ten minutes we felt confident of our fire superiority and our ability to leave the kill zone with only a few casualties," said Cillessen, a 1998 University of Colorado, Boulder, Colorado, graduate.[9] "Usually a firefight would last anywhere from five seconds to five minutes. But as the enemy sustained their fire with no letup, I realized that they were not going away. As the fighting progressed we gradually began to gain fire superiority. It looked like we had things well in hand and then the casualties began to mount. One Afghan soldier was dead and more were wounded."[10] Just as they moved to leave the kill zone, the U.S. and Afghan troops experienced an increased volume of fire from the rear. Cillessen realized that they were now in serious trouble. For a moment he thought there was no way out.

Then an Afghan soldier, Sergeant Abdullah, began directing the Coalition fire. He grabbed Cillessen and led him to the middle of the road. Cillessen remembered thinking to himself, "[H]e can't be serious—he wants me to go where?"[11] But Abdullah led him to a better position where he could fire at the enemy with his M-203 grenade launcher. He could now see all of the enemy. The downside, however, was that there was no cover. That didn't seem to faze Abdullah, which reassured Cillessen. "He looked at me with such an expression of confidence that I thought 'it can't be that bad because he's been fighting his whole life.'"[12]

Cillessen began firing grenades at the enemy as Abdullah patted him on the back, told him where to aim, and said, "Good job, Captain," in broken English.[13] Another Marine who was at the scene later told Cillessen that he seemed to disappear in a cloud of dust and tracers. Cillessen eventually fired some forty grenades until he ran out, all the while taking fire. He was unharmed but Abdullah had been hit in the femoral artery. Cillessen noticed how distraught the Afghan soldiers became and reacted quickly in an attempt to save the sergeant's life. "I put a tourniquet on his leg and applied first aid," explained Cillessen, but it was clear that Abdullah had been mortally wounded.[14] "My hands were burning with blood."[15] At that point Cillessen had to make a decision—continue to try and save Abdullah or get the rest of the Coalition troops out of the kill zone. He laid Abdullah down and told the other Afghan soldiers to get ready to move. "I wished him well and told him I was sorry," said Cillessen.[16]

"Sergeant Abdullah was the bravest one out there. He led his soldiers the way they were supposed to be led. He inspired all of us to fight harder," said Cillessen. "He was truly a heroic soldier."[17]

As they continued to suppress the enemy, Cillessen called in close air support. A Marine and several Afghan soldiers moved one of the disabled vehicles out of the way, allowing the rest to finally get out of the kill zone. "We were still in contact with the militants when we left the battle area," said Cillessen who has deployed four times in his career. "A snowstorm hit the next day. We were there for eight days trying to find the insurgents."[18]

Upon receiving the Silver Star medal, Cillessen said that, while he was honored to receive the award, he thought the bigger picture was being overlooked. He said the work done before the ambush was what really mattered. "We made contact in largely isolated villages and helped the Afghanis participate in elections. A lot of progress was made because they participated in the main effort in many missions. To me this is more than another medal to hang on my chest."[19]

ENDNOTES

1. Silver Star citation, Capt. Brian G. Cillessen, USMC, Department of the Army.

2. LCpl. David A. Weikle, 2nd Marine Division, "Aztec, NM Marine Awarded Silver Star Medal for Actions in Afghanistan," *Marine Corps News*, 27 April 2007.

3. Combined Joint Task Force Phoenix V, "Coalition Forces Information," 14 January 2008, http://phnxv.taskforcephoenix.com/cofor.htm.

4. Ann Scott Tyson, "3,200 Marines to Deploy to Afghanistan in Spring," *Washington* (DC) *Post*, 16 January 2008.

5. Weikle, "Aztec, NM, Marine Awarded Silver Star Medal."

6. Ibid.

7. Ibid.

8. Jeff Schogol, "My Hands Were Burning with Blood," *Stars & Stripes*, 7 June 2007.

9. Weikle, "Aztec, NM, Marine Awarded Silver Star Medal."

10. Ibid.

11. Schogol, "My Hands Were Burning with Blood."

12. Ibid.

13. "Aztec, NM, Marine Awarded Silver Star Medal."

14. Ibid.

15. Schogol, "My Hands Were Burning with Blood."

16. Ibid.

17. Ibid.

18. Ibid.

19. Weikle, "Aztec, NM, Marine Awarded Silver Star Medal."

1st Lt. Stephen J. Boada, USMC

Forward Observer and Forward Air Controller, Kilo Company, 3rd Battalion,
3rd Marines, U.S. Marine Corps Forces, Central Command

Shatagal, Afghanistan
5–9 May 2005

For conspicuous gallantry and intrepidity in action against the enemy while serving as Forward Observer and Forward Air Controller, Company K, 3rd Marines, U.S. Marine Corps Forces, Central Command in support of combined Joint Task-Force 76 and Operation Enduring Freedom from 5 to 9 May 2005. While operating near Shatagal Village, First Lieutenant Boada's platoon received intelligence that Al Qaeda and Associate Movement fighters were setting up an ambush position from which to attack the platoon upon their departure from Shatagal. Despite the barrage of intense enemy fire, he calmly directed the tactical employment of the unit and directed fires from an A-10 aircraft onto enemy positions. During the ensuing firefight, First Lieutenant Boada and members of his squad were wounded. Ignoring his injuries, he continued fearlessly to lead his Marines as they fought off a tenacious enemy while other members of the unit extracted their fallen comrades. As the platoon maneuvered over five kilometers of arduous mountain terrain with the injured Marines, First Lieutenant Boada called for and directed AC-130 aircraft to cover the unit's movement. This action resulted in the destruction of the besieging enemy. Without question, First Lieutenant Boada's tactical acumen in directing these aircraft saved many lives in the platoon as the enemy's ambush positions controlled the high ground through the terrain in which the platoon was conducting its retrograde. By his bold leadership, wise judgment, and complete dedication to duty, First Lieutenant Boada reflected great credit upon himself and upheld the highest traditions of the Marine Corps and the United States Naval Service.[1]

Silver Star Citation

ON 1 FEBRUARY 2006 1st Lt. Stephen J. Boada, fire direction officer, 1st Battalion, 12th Marine Regiment, received a Silver Star medal for his actions in Afghanistan. Boada was the first Marine stationed at the Marine Corps Base, Kaneohe, Hawaii, to be awarded the prestigious medal for service in Iraq or Afghanistan. In addition to receiving the Silver Star he was awarded

the Purple Heart medal. He was genuinely humbled for being so honored. The ceremony was as unpretentious as the first lieutenant credited for saving the lives of men in his platoon. It was sun-up at the regular formation of the 1st Battalion, 12th Marines, when the Silver Star was presented to First Lieutenant Boada. Marines of Kilo Company, 3rd Battalion, 3rd Marines, were there too, since it was what Boada did with them that earned him the nation's third highest medal of valor.

Boada remarked, "I wouldn't be here if it wasn't for them. This is not my day. This is their day."[2] The selfless hero inconspicuously slipped the Silver Star back into its box before receiving the congratulations of his battalion. He noticed promotions and drew out his Kilo Company comrades with every greeting. It was obvious that this was a Marine others trusted and respected.

Boada was attached to the 3rd Battalion, 3rd Marine Regiment, during his Afghanistan deployment. This was the first time for the Bristol, Connecticut, native to be deployed to the war zone and he looked forward to the experience.[3]

Boada was later interviewed by Cpl. Michelle M. Dickson, MCB (Marine Corps Base), Hawaii. Her story of his personal account of the action he engaged in with insurgent fighters was carried in the 10 February 2006 issue of *Marine Corps News*, the 14 June 2006 issue of *Stars and Stripes*, and various websites and periodicals. Excerpts of her interview with the decorated Marine follow. (Note: All remaining quotes are from note 4 in the endnotes segment of this chapter.)

"You always train for the possibility of being deployed. It was good to finally have the opportunity to put that training to use. Even though some of it seemed pointless at the time, there was a good reason for all of it. In what seems like a symphony of chaos, there is organization."[4]

Boada served as a forward observer and forward air controller during his deployment. He was with Kilo Company, 3/3, where he took part in a multitude of successful information operations, patrol, and civil affairs, while also coordinating aircraft and mortar firing in the area.

While moving on a five to seven day patrol operation in eastern Afghanistan, Boada and roughly thirty other Marines set out in a mounted (vehicle) convoy through the Alisheng Valley to hopefully gain information on people who were on their target list. The patrol was only supposed to last during the daytime hours, but this day would be different, and two of the Marines would not be coming back alive.

"We set out at approximately 0700 on a cold and wet morning in a mounted convoy through the Alisheng Valley. As you start to come through the valley, the road eventually ends for vehicles, so we set out on foot. We were trying to get to the end of the valley and as we went along, would stop at villages, consulting elders about certain issues."

While getting closer to the end of the valley, the integrated communications (Icom) scanners that were being used to pick up radio frequencies, began receiving radio traffic that was translated by an interpreter to be enemy forces. The forces were watching the Marines and plotting to ambush them in the valley.

"We could hear them discussing how many of us there were, and how we would never make it out alive. So from there we set up a satellite communications antenna and called back to higher command. We requested close-air support to sweep the hills but the poor weather wouldn't allow it."

The radio traffic continued as the Marines proceeded to move through the valley. They had just stopped when they heard over the radio, "They just passed us. We'll get them on the way back."

"The Marines were getting pretty 'amped' up at that moment and we could recognize two of the voices over the radio to be cell leaders who were responsible for a police station that was rocketed just before we arrived. It was difficult to see anything around us though due to the mountainous terrain. We knew what area the enemy was in, but couldn't pinpoint anything."

At that time, 1st Lt. Sam A. Mote, platoon commander, directed a squad and a 240 Gulf team (beefed up machine-gun team), to go southeast onto a hilltop to scan the area. In a short time they received a call back from the squad that they had spotted ten to twelve individuals across the valley who had automatic weapons and rocket-propelled grenades in their possession. "At the same time we heard a single rifle shot, but the round didn't actually land anywhere near us. We couldn't tell whether it was caused by sniper fire, or whether it was possibly a signal."

The machine-gun team was then directed to engage toward the enemy who was located roughly seven to eight hundred meters away. Seeing this movement, the individuals fled into a ravine up the mountainside. "Our support by fire [SBF] 240 Gulf team remained on the hilltop as we decided to make our way toward the enemy. As we began moving into the draw, a brief firefight broke out, but none of us were injured."

The Marines continued and crossed a river that rose up to their chests. As they began to climb up the hillside they again contacted higher command, which was able to send a section of A-10 Warthogs out to the area. "Cpl. Johnny Polander, a squad leader, was on the radio on the hilltop and he was able to let us know where the individuals were located. At that time

Lance Corporal Kirven, 21, of Richmond, Virginia, a team leader, was able to send a 203 smoke round [canister] to mark the cave that the individuals had entered. We also popped smoke rounds and the SBF did the same thing, using different colored smoke rounds so the aircraft knew our positions as opposed to the cave where the enemy was hiding."

Boada informed the aircraft of the situation on the ground and they proceeded to fire 30-mm cannon shells into the enemy cave, while making three or four passes with 2.75-mm rockets. After every pass, the SBF was again contacted, and they would give any adjustments that would need to be made for the aircraft fire. "When they ran out of ammo, more A-10 Warthogs came out and there were about eight or nine passes made, total. During that time, we could hear the enemy over the radio calling out comments such as, 'That went just by my head.' So, they were indirectly helping us adjust our fire."

When the situation was under control, the Marines began their long trek up the mountainside to assess the situation and check for any enemy that had been killed in action (KIA). Upon reaching the caves, Boada teamed up with Sgt. Robert R. Campbell, a squad leader, and began searching the different caves with other Marines. This was when Marines heard LCpl. Nicolas C. Kirven, identify a dead body. He called out and Cpl. Richard P. Schoener, twenty-two, of Hayes, Louisiana, came down to provide security for a dead check.

"Sergeant Campbell and I were probably only twenty-five meters away when we first heard the bursts from an AK-47 and the screams. The squad began circling toward Kirven and Schoener who were laying on the ground, but the gunfire wouldn't stop and we couldn't tell exactly how many people were firing at us."

Most of the Marines managed to find some cover and Corporal Chinana, a scout-sniper attached to Kilo Company, had a 203 (i.e., an M-203 gun, which is an M-16 with a grenade launcher attached) but wasn't able to fire because the weapon needed at least thirty meters to arm itself and the Marines were too close. Chinana would then attempt to mark the cave with a 203 smoke round, but the round would ricochet, and Chinana would receive a bullet fragment on his scalp line and fall back. "We really didn't have any other option at that point because the Marines were laying so close to the mouth of the cave. I made the call to move up closer so we could see where the fire was coming from and attempt to grab the downed Marines."

Boada popped a smoke grenade as he and Cpl. Troy Arndt, of Palmyra, Pennsylvania, team leader, made their way to a position very close to the

Marines. "The fire was still coming as we popped more smoke and kind of leapfrogged from rock to rock. Corporal Arndt attempted to grab one of the Marines by the sappy plate carrier [slang for the vest that holds the body armor Marines wear], but the gear ripped and he fell. By that time the smoke was clearing up and I grabbed him and we got to cover again."

At this point, Boada said he could reach out and touch the downed Marines because they were so close. He then grabbed a fragmentation grenade and threw it, although fire was still coming. "I ended up repeating the process four times. Corporal Arndt would prep the grenades for me, I would shout 'Cover and fire!' and throw the grenades. Corporal Arndt did some amazing things out there as a young corporal. I hope he gets recognized for something." (Arndt was later awarded the Bronze Star medal with a "V" device for valor.)

At this time, support was being given by Campbell and his Marines while Arndt and Boada were attempting to retrieve the downed Marines. "We had to actually shoot over Arndt's and Boada's heads to cover them," said Campbell. "I admired both of them . . . for their bravery."

Finally, there was silence and no movement in the cave. A corporal made the call to search the cave, which now held only the bodies of dead insurgents. Several attempts were made to save the lives of Schoener and Kirven, but CPR was useless. They were both dead.

"By that time, it was about 1800 and getting dark. We weren't prepared for a night operation and there was a lack of both food and water. We set up a landing zone [LZ] to try to get a medevac [medical evacuation helicopter] for the Marines, but they couldn't send one because of the weather." The Marines were beginning to get frustrated with the whole situation. "They were doing a heck of a job out there, and they had just lost two of their friends. After everything that happened though they still remained focused."

It was at that time that the Marines began to carry their fallen comrades in ponchos. "The Marines tried to buy some donkeys to help carry the Marines but it was no use. They carried the Marines the whole time, about seven miles through mountainous terrain. 'What had started as a three hour patrol, ended as a twenty-two-hour ordeal,' said Campbell. 'It was the worst day of my life.'"

AC-130 support was available and gave the Marines a heads up if there were enemy forces up ahead. The gun ships did engage and neutralize twenty-five enemy fighters who were setting up ambushes in two separate areas. We continued to move throughout the night and arrived back to our vehicles at about 0400 or 0500. The Marines really did a hell of a job out there. They weren't even my Marines, but I know I couldn't have picked a better bunch. The hardest part about the whole deployment was having to leave the Marines I was with that fateful day and return to K-Bay [Kaneohe Bay]. Those men were ready for anything, even Kirven and Schoener. They were two great Marines. . . . I think about what happened out there every day, and will for as long as I live. I think about what we could have done different. What we could have done to have those two Marines walk home with us.

Boada returned to his old unit 1/12 in Hawaii, but felt that he should have gone to Iraq with the Marines of 3/3. "It just didn't feel right and I regret not having the opportunity to deploy with them again. I try to keep in touch with all of the Marines I was with."

Campbell said he feels the award for Boada was a much deserved one. "He is an artillery officer, and the things he did, he didn't have to do. He put himself in harm's way and did everything he could do to try and save those two Marines. We all did everything we could do, and it was truly an honor to work with Lieutenant Boada."

Boada says, when asked, that he has a different opinion about his role in the situation. "The Marines I was with that day deserve the recognition. They all need to be talked about, talked about more than me, they are all amazing."

ENDNOTES

1. Silver Star citation, 1st Lt. Stephen J. Boada, USMC, http://www.homeofheroes.com/valor2/SS/7_GWOT/citations_USMC.html.
2. William Cole, "Marines 'Conspicuous Gallantry' Cited," *Honolulu* (HI) *Advertiser*, 2 February 2006, http://the.honoluluadvertiser.com/article/2006/Feb/02/ln/FP602020337.
3. Ibid.
4. Cpl. Michelle M. Dickson, "Marine Recalls Silver Star Actions," *Marine Corps News*, 10 February 2006.
   (Note: All remaining quotes are from the source in note 4.)

IRAQ (2003–PRESENT)

MSgt. Alan F. Johnson, USMC

Tank Leader, Bravo Company, 3rd Battalion, 4th Marines, Regimental Combat Team 7, 1st Marine Division, I Marine Expeditionary Force

Basra, Iraq
21 March–23 April 2003

The President of the United States takes pleasure in presenting the Silver Star Medal to Alan F. Johnson, Master Sergeant, U.S. Marine Corps, for conspicuous gallantry and intrepidity in action against the enemy while serving as Tank Leader, Company B, Third Battalion, Fourth Marines, Regimental Combat Team 7, FIRST Marine Division, I Marine Expeditionary Force in support of Operation Iraqi Freedom from 21 March to 23 April 2003. Master Sergeant Johnson's calm demeanor and tactical expertise while under fire were crucial for the Company's success during six firefights. With the enemy delivering heavy small arms fire on both flanks of the Company at the Shaibah Airfield, Master Sergeant Johnson directed his gunner's fire by engaging targets with his M-16A2 rifle. Subsequently, he identified a concealed Panhard anti-tank missile carrier and destroyed it with two hand grenades. Identifying a group of Iraqi soldiers who had wounded the Company Commander, he dismounted his vehicle and killed them at close range. He then led an infantry assault into a grove, killing numerous enemy soldiers with his rifle and hand grenades. By his bold leadership, wise judgment, and complete dedication to duty, Master Sergeant Johnson reflected great credit upon himself and upheld the highest traditions of the Marine Corps and the United States Naval Service.[1]

Silver Star Citation

As Marine MSgt. Alan F. Johnson worked on his M1A1 Abrams tank at Tactical Area Coyote in Kuwait prior to the invasion, it is unlikely that he had any idea that his actions in the first days of Operation Iraqi Freedom would earn the first Silver Star of the conflict. Deployed from Twentynine Palms, California, in December 2002, Johnson, a tank leader with Bravo

Company, 1st Tank Battalion, was attached to "The Thundering Third," the 3rd Battalion, 4th Marines, 1st Marine Division. As part of Task Force 34 "Darkside" and RCT-7 (Regimental Combat Team 7), they were among the first troops to cross into Iraq on 21 March 2003.[2]

The battalion's fifteen hundred troops, thirty tanks, and sixty assault amphibious vehicle (amtracs, tracks, or AAVs), supported by 155 Howitzer artillery and Cobra gunships would be at the cusp of the spear in the drive to Baghdad and would be the first Marine unit into that city.[3]

One of the first objectives was Shaibah Airfield, a military installation nineteen miles southwest of Basra. The expectation was that it would be a difficult fight, with intelligence estimates giving the Iraqis a numerical advantage of between 6 to 1 and 8 to 1, but morale was high. The Marines expected their superior weapons and training to give them the advantage. As the battalion commander, Lt. Col. Bryan McCoy confidently predicted, "This is not going to be a fair fight!"[4]

Surprisingly, the Marines met less resistance than anticipated, with large numbers of Iraqis deserting and surrendering, but the 3/4 was still involved with mop-up operations, eliminating small pockets of resistance. During this time Johnson is credited with participating in at least six fire-fights, engaging the enemy with small arms and grenades, dismounting his vehicle to engage and kill insurgents who had wounded his company commander, and leading an infantry assault under fire, actions for which he was awarded the Silver Star, the first of Operation Iraqi Freedom.[5]

"McCoy's Marines" would go on to secure Basra International Airport and bridges across the Shat Al-Basra Canal, then move north to fight at Afak, Diwaniyah and Al-Kut, before arriving in Baghdad to pull down Saddam's statue on 9 April 2003. After participating in stabilization operations, the 3/4 returned to California in May 2003.

The 3/4 was with the 1st Marine Division when the United States launched the invasion of Iraq in March 2003. The unit saw a lot of action, first at Basra, then Diwaniya, Kut, and later in Baghdad. The battalion led the fight for a key bridge over the Dyala Canal, a waterway along the southeast area of Baghdad. This structure was key to allowing the rest of the division to cross into the city. On the way, it lost four men—one to an accident and three to hostile fire.

This was the Marine battalion that helped pull down the statue of Saddam Hussein, effectively marking the end of the fight for Baghdad. The 3rd Battalion, 4th Marines crossed into Iraq and fought at the battle for Basra, took the airport and an Iraqi military garrison, and then headed north.

ENDNOTES

1. Silver Star citation, MSgt. Alan F. Johnson, USMC, http://www.homeofheroes.com/valor2/
   SS/7_GWOT/citations_USMC.html.
2. "3rd Battalion, 4th Marine Regiment," GlobalSecurity.org, http://www.globalsecurity.org/
   military/agency/usmc/3-4.htm.
3. Peter Maass, "Good Kills," *New York* (NY) *Times Magazine*, 20 April 2003.
4. Simon Robinson, "Dispatches from the Front," *Time*, 22 March 2003.
5. John Coopman, "Marines Face Resistance from Iraqi Troops Near Basra," *San Francisco* (CA)
   Chronicle, 22 March 2003.

Sgt. Michael E. Bitz, USMC

2nd Assault Amphibious Battalion, 2nd Marine Division

Battle of An Nasiriyah, Iraq
23–29 March 2003

Sergeant Bitz's vehicle sustained a direct hit from a rocket-propelled grenade, setting it on fire. Aware that there were several casualties on board, he maneuvered his vehicle to the company's defensive perimeter. He immediately assisted in moving the wounded to the casualty collection point. Without an amphibious assault vehicle to command and under unrelenting enemy small-arms and artillery fire, he picked up his rifle and joined a squad of the Third Platoon in a deliberate assault. His efforts substantially aided the platoon and, after the squad sustained several casualties, Sergeant Bitz ignored his own wounds and helped in loading the others onto an evacuation vehicle. Despite receiving unrelenting fire, Sergeant Bitz mounted a different vehicle to provide security for the casualties. While escorting the wounded during movement, Sergeant Bitz was mortally wounded by enemy fire when his vehicle sustained a direct hit from a rocket-propelled grenade.[1]

Excerpt from Silver Star Citation

GySgt. Jason Doran, USMC

Weapons Company, 1st Battalion, 2nd Marines,
Regimental Combat Team 2, Task Force Tarawa

Gunnery Sergeant Doran demonstrated extraordinary valor as he led a rescue team to locate and recover isolated Marines. In order to safely transport Marines who were stranded, he commandeered four additional vehicles. Under constant small arms and rocket-propelled grenade fire, he navigated the convoy and directed combined anti-armor team vehicle's suppressive fires on the enemy. After the stranded Marines were rescued and the convoy was returning to safety, Gunnery Sergeant Doran realized a combined anti-armor team vehicle had been left behind. With total disregard for his own safety, he returned to the last known position of the vehicle and found its crew heavily engaged with the enemy. His vehicle's direct fire halted the enemy attack and allowed the combined anti-armor team vehicle to safely proceed out of the city.[2]

Excerpt from Silver Star Citation

CWO5 David Dunfee, USMC

Gunner, 1st Battalion, 2nd Marines,
Regimental Combat Team 2, Task Force Tarawa

During the assault on enemy defenses in An Nasiriyah, Chief Warrant Officer Dunfee dismounted and moved to an exposed position while under enemy fire in order to determine the composition and disposition of the enemy. He provided the Battalion Command an accurate assessment of the enemy action, recommendations on how to employ organic fires, and he directed fires against enemy positions. As a result, nine enemy T-62 Main Battle Tanks were destroyed.[3]

Excerpt from Silver Star Citation

GySgt. Timothy Haney, USMC

Platoon Sergeant, Combined Anti-Armor Platoon, Weapons Company,
2nd Battalion, 8th Marines, Task Force Tarawa

From 23 to 26 March 2003, Gunnery Sergeant Haney participated in firefights with Iraqi Military and Paramilitary Forces in An Nasiriyah, Iraq. . . . During a direct fire engagement against a heavy machine gun, he dismounted his vehicle to gain awareness of the enemy's positions, exposed himself to enemy fire, and provided higher headquarters with vital situational awareness. On 26 March 2003, while the Battalion's Main Command Operations Center came under attack from two directions, Gunnery Sergeant Haney raced through intense fire to emplace Marines in defensive positions and orient their fires. After an explosion riddled Gunnery Sergeant Haney's body with sixty pieces of shrapnel, he ignored his wounds and continued to transport injured Marines to the Battalion Aid Station. He refused medical attention until everyone else had been treated.[4]

Excerpt from Silver Star Citation

GySgt. Phillip Jordan, USMC

Weapons Platoon Sergeant, Charlie Company, 1st Battalion,
2nd Marines, Task Force Tarawa

After crossing the Saddam Canal and receiving heavy machine gun and mortar fire he directed fire on an enemy mortar position. As the engagement continued he adjusted accurate return mortar fire on the enemy while fearlessly encouraging his Marines in the face of tenacious enemy fire. Despite a withering barrage of enemy fire Gunnery Sergeant Jordan moved across open terrain to re-supply vital mortar ammunition. Upon locating an entrenched enemy machine gun position raking the company's flank he dashed across a fire-stricken road and directed devastating machine gun fire that destroyed the enemy's position. While a mortar crew was displaced to cover the company flank Gunnery Sergeant Jordan continuously carried ammunition eighty meters to and from this new position under enemy fire. After making three trips under a heavy bombardment of mortar and artillery fire, he fell mortally wounded.[5]

Excerpt from Silver Star Citation

1st Lt. Frederick Pokorney, USMC

Headquarters Battery, 1st Battalion, 10th Marines,
2nd Marine Expeditionary Brigade

First Lieutenant Pokorney expertly directed artillery fire to destroy heavily fortified enemy positions that engaged the Company with accurate direct and indirect fire. [His] superb coordination of three artillery missions resulted in the destruction of multiple high pay-off targets, to include enemy machine gun positions that were raking his company's position. Under the heaviest enemy fire of the day, [he] exposed himself to devastating fire while crossing several hundred meters in order to meet with the Fire Support Team Leader. After updating the Fire Support Team Leader on the status of fire missions and additional enemy targets, a volley of enemy bullets, and enemy rocket-propelled grenades hit behind his position, mortally wounding First Lieutenant Pokorney.[6]

Excerpt from Silver Star Citation

THERE ARE CERTAIN NAMES that evoke the rich heritage of the Marine's fighting spirit: Belleau Wood, Iwo Jima, Chosin Reservoir, Khe Sahn. For future generations, the name of An Nasiriyah is certain to be included with these lofty names. It was at An Nasiriyah where the Army's 507th Maintenance Company's Pvt. Jessica Lynch was captured, where Marines braved "Ambush Alley," and where the Marines and the Navy corpsmen of 1st Battalion, 2nd Marines would earn two Navy Crosses and six Silver Stars, with eighteen Marines killed and another forty wounded. The world, riveted on the fate of Lynch, would take little note of the Marines' fierce struggle until later.

Early on the morning of 23 March 2003 the Marines of 1/2 were staged south of An Nasiriyah, waiting for the command to advance into the city. It was the fourth day of the invasion, and Coalition forces had advanced over more than two hundred miles of enemy-held territory in three days, an act unprecedented in history.[7]

The plan was for the Army's V Corps, led by the 3rd Infantry Division, to sweep northwest through the desert to the Karbala Gap then through to Baghdad, while the 1st Marine Expeditionary Force (1 MEF) moved north along Highway 1 through the center to Baghdad, and the 1st (U.K.) Armored Division maneuvered north through the eastern marshlands.

The 2nd Marine Expeditionary Brigade (2 MEB), known as Task Force Tarawa, was charged with capturing the bridges across the Euphrates River at An Nasiriyah, which would clear the way for the rest of the 1st Marine Division to push through to Baghdad. Commanded by Brig. Gen. Richard Natonski, Task Force Tarawa comprised two battalions of the 2nd Marines (1st and 3rd), a battalion of the 6th Marines (2nd), and a battalion of the 8th Marines (2nd), supported by 1/10 Marines (artillery), Alpha Company, 8th Tank Battalion, Marine Air Group (MAG) 29, and companies of assault amphibious vehicle (amtracs, tracks, or AAVs).

An Nasiriyah, whose name means "Christian town," was primarily a Shi'ite city about 370 miles southeast of Baghdad, with a preinvasion population of five hundred thirty thousand. Founded in 1870 as part of the Ottoman Empire, it was captured by British troops during World War I. In addition to agricultural operations, primarily the growing of dates, and its shipbuilding and carpentry industries, it was home to the Iraqi Army's 3rd Corps. An Nasiriyah was the first large population center on the road from Kuwait. Because it was primarily Shi'ite, little resistance was anticipated. Following the 1991 Persian Gulf War, An Nasiriyah had been a center of resistance against Iraqi leader Saddam Hussein when Shi'ite Muslims rebelled. The Marines hoped to find little or no resistance from Iraqi forces there.[8]

The 2nd Marines were given the mission of securing An Nasiriyah's bridges. Lt. Col. Paul Dunahoe's 3rd Battalion (3/2) would relieve the 3rd Infantry Division in securing the western bridges along Highway 1, ten miles west. Lt. Col. Dan Grabowski's 1st Battalion (1/2), with the tanks of the 8th Battalion and AAVs from Alpha Company, 2nd Assault Amphibious Battalion, would move up Highway 7 and secure the eastern bridges across the Euphrates River and Saddam Canal. What worried Grabowski most was the four-kilometer (two and a half–mile) stretch of road between the Euphrates and Saddam Canal bridges. Bordered by buildings set back on both sides, its hundreds of alleys, windows, and rooftops could provide cover for an enemy, which earned it the nickname the Mogadishu Mile. It would later be known as Ambush Alley.[9]

To avoid this built-up area, Alpha Company planned to cross first and secure the Euphrates Bridge. The M1A1 Abrams tanks would follow, but turn east and skirt the eastern edge of the city, moving north to the Saddam Canal Bridge, followed by Bravo Company, then the command element, with Charlie Company in the rear. Each company was transported in twelve AAVs.

It was 3:00 AM and the commanders were making final preparations for the assault, when they stood dumbfounded as an eighteen-vehicle convoy with headlights on sped past their position and drove into An Nasiriyah. It was the ill-fated 507th Maintenance Company: thirty-three cooks, clerks, and mechanics in mostly unarmed service vehicles who missed a turn, got lost, and drove through a sleeping An Nasiriyah. Once through the town, and finally realizing their mistake, Capt. Troy King ordered his column to retrace its path back through the city to Highway 1. Now alerted, Iraqi forces directed intense, accurate fire into the column as it passed back through the city. The lead three vehicles, including Captain King, sped up and out of the kill zone, later to make contact with the tanks of Maj. Bill Peeples' Alpha Company, 8th Tank Battalion. The middle element of five vehicles was engaged and its ten soldiers took up defensive positions and fought off attacks until rescued by tanks and Alpha Company. The third element, made up of heavy vehicles at the rear, were disabled and destroyed with eleven killed and six, including Lynch, taken prisoner.[10]

During the rescue operation, CWO5 David Dunfee, the battalion "Gunner," was with elements of Alpha and Bravo Companies as they advanced on a railroad bridge eight miles south of An Nasiriyah. It was defended by a company of Iraqi tanks and soldiers, but many of the tanks were immobile "pillboxes." Without regard for his own safety, Dunfee dismounted from his vehicle and relayed critical information on the enemy's location and disposition from an exposed position while under intense small-arms fire. He also directed fire, resulting in the destruction of nine T-55 tanks, four of them by TOW (tube-launched, optically tracked, wire-guided) anti-armor missiles.[11] For this and subsequent actions, Dunfee would receive the Silver Star from Maj. Gen. Richard Huck, 2nd Marine Division commander, at a ceremony at Camp Ripper, Al-Asad, Iraq, on 10 March 2005.

The assault was stalled as the battalion waited for the tanks to refuel prior to pressing the attack. At about 1:00 PM the tanks returned and pressed forward toward the southern bridge over the Euphrates. But now the order of battle changed as the Combined Anti-Armor Team (CAAT) and some tanks were the first to reach the Euphrates, and began taking intense fire as they crossed the river. They turned right and headed east, followed by Bravo Company, Grabowski's command tracks, and Humvees. Alpha Company crossed next and set up a defensive perimeter around the bridge. To the rear was Charlie Company in eleven tracks. Track C-209 had become disabled just south at a railroad crossing, and the 3rd Squad of 3rd Platoon scrambled aboard C-210 and C-211.[12]

When Bravo Company and Grabowski's tanks and Humvees turned right, they found themselves in a short firefight with uniformed Iraqi soldiers, but fire by the Abrams tanks quickly destroyed any resistance. After continuing, Bravo reported it was mired in mud and stalled east of An Nasiriyah. Unable to make contact with Grabowski, Capt. Dan Wittnam, Charlie Company commander, was unaware which route Bravo had taken or its disposition. His orders were to take the north bridge, and the most direct route was down the middle of the city. Since most of the tanks were still with Bravo Company, he would have to do it without tank support. He ordered his command down the middle.[13]

C-201 led the way, with LCpl. Edward Castleberry driving, and Sgt. William Schaefer in the turret. Almost immediately, they were engulfed in a barrage of rocket-propelled grenade (RPG) and small-arms fire. Schaefer fired in both directions as they raced along the two and a half–mile stretch, alternating between his machine gun and his grenade launcher. Hostile fire seemed to be coming from every direction. "We saw women shoot at us with RPGs. . . . We saw children shoot at us," recalled the company commander, Capt. Daniel J. Wittnam. "We never saw one person in uniform." Several Iraqis raced into the street to fire RPGs at the column. In one instance Castleberry accelerated, crushing an insurgent under his treads. All targets were engaged as they raced through the city.[14]

Near the rear of the column was Sgt. Michael E. Bitz, 2nd Assault Amphibious Battalion, assigned to Charlie Company and driving C-211.

Described as a "regular guy," he'd enlisted in 1995, and had four kids, two of whom were twins he'd never seen. The track was overloaded with Marines picked up from disabled C-209. The company had advanced north to within a few hundred yards of the Saddam Canal when an explosion rocked C-211, lifting the twenty-eight–ton vehicle into the air. An RPG round had penetrated the right rear, just below the tracks; the explosion filled the troop compartment with shrapnel and set the rucksacks outside the track on fire, filling the air with smoke. Four Marines were wounded, two seriously and two severely. Bitz was able to maintain control of the vehicle and, driving full speed and dodging obstacles, was able to get it safely across the northern bridge before it ground to a stop. The other Charlie Company tracks crossed and set up a defensive perimeter.

The grenade had damaged the rear ramp, trapping the Marines inside. Schaefer from C-201 ran over and yanked open the rear hatch door, and Marines scrambled out from the smoke-filled interior. Bitz exited the vehicle and assisted in getting the wounded out. So did corpsman Luis Fonseca who would be awarded a Navy Cross for his actions in evacuating and treating wounded Marines under fire. Bitz was carrying a wounded Marine under fire when a shell exploded, riddling him with shrapnel. With blood streaming down his face, he continued in assisting Marines to safety. The smoke from the burning track attracted enemy mortar fire, and they soon found their range. They loaded the wounded into Fonseca's AAV (C-212), but it was quickly disabled. Again Fonseca relocated the wounded under fire.

Charlie Company was under heavy fire, both direct and indirect, and Cpl. Randal Rosacker set up his machine gun, providing cover. His father, chief of boat on a Navy submarine, was also serving in Iraq. As Rosacker began to fire, he was cut down by artillery or mortar fire, one of the first Marines to die that day.

With his AAV in flames and no vehicle to command Bitz grabbed his M-16 and joined an infantry platoon. "He could have moved to another [track]," recalled his platoon commander, Capt. Conor Tracy. "Instead, he chose to help the Marines he was with. . . . He just fell in step and joined the infantry." Because the platoon ran low on ammunition, Bitz made repeated trips under fire back and forth to a vehicle three hundred yards distant to replenish their supply. Wounded again, he ignored his wounds to load other wounded Marines onto an evacuation vehicle. Air evacuation was considered, and then rejected as too dangerous, given the volume of fire.[15]

At the same time Marines organized and began returning fire. The Weapons Platoon leader, Lt. Ben Reid, set up his three teams of 60-mm mortars under fire on the east side of the road and began to return fire, targeting Iraqi mortar positions across the canal. The commander of the Iraqi 11th Infantry Division had anticipated an American airborne assault in the open fields north of An Nasiriyah, and had prepared fields of fire on the elevated road north of the canal. The Marines were taking direct and indirect fire from both sides of the road and from An Nasiriyah to the south.[16]

Reid ordered SSgt. Phillip Jordan, his platoon sergeant, to set up the .50-caliber machine guns for close targets. Jordan, a fifteen-year veteran of the Marines, had enlisted at age twenty-seven and had seen service during Operation Desert Storm and in Kosovo. His men called him "Gump," like the movie character Forrest Gump, for his sunny disposition, but there was nothing sunny about him that afternoon. When an enemy machine gun threatened his Marines, Jordan led a team across open terrain under intense fire to take out the position. He ran back and forth under fire to resupply his mortar positions with ammunition.

Also present was 2nd Lt. Frederick E. Pokorney, Charlie Company's Forward Artillery Observer (FAO). He was with Reid's men because he was attempting to call in a strike, and he needed higher ground. At six feet seven inches tall, Pokorney's basketball career looked promising, but an injury resulted in his enlisting in the Marines. He guarded nuclear submarines in Bangor, Maine, before being selected for officers training. After graduating from Oregon State in 2001 with a degree in anthropology, Pokorney was commissioned a Marine second lieutenant. As an artillery officer he could have remained relatively safe at the rear, but he'd chosen duty as an FAO with an infantry company. He'd already been wounded in the right arm as he crossed the canal.

Reid ordered Cpl. Jose Garibay's 3rd mortar team to move south with him to set up a position to fire back into the town. Jordan followed with ammo. There was an explosion just as they were setting up, and the team took a direct hit. Five Marines were killed and another four severely wounded. Among those killed were Gunnery Sergeant Jordan and Lieutenant Pokorney, both of whom would receive posthumous Silver Stars.

Reid, knocked to the ground by the explosion, got to his feet, saw the carnage, and ran to get help for the wounded. An explosion knocked him off his feet a second time, but he rose again and made it north to where Shaefer and others were loading the wounded aboard AAVs. Since enemy fire was too intense for a helicopter medical evacuation (medevac), the wounded would have to be transported south back through Ambush Alley to the battalion aid area. "We had guys bleeding to death," Schaefer recalled.[17]

At almost the same time two A-10 Thunderbolt fighters roared overhead. They'd been called in for a ground support mission by the battalion

Forward Air Controller (FAC). Because of poor communications the aircraft were cleared for targets north of the bridge and were unaware that there were Marines north of the canal. The aircraft engaged Iraqi positions, vehicles, and buildings with eight 500-pound bombs, three Maverick missiles, and several strafing runs with their 30-mm Gatling guns.

But there were also casualties from "friendly fire."[18] In the confusion of battle, events happen almost simultaneously, and recollections differ as to sequence of events and basic facts. The battle of An Nasiriyah is no different. For example, a Marine wounded by an RPG explosion who later died was counted as wounded in some accounts and as killed in others. There is some controversy as to how many were killed, and how much damage was caused by friendly fire. Schaefer frantically raised an American flag over the AAV he was on as they loaded the wounded. One of the wounded, Cpl. Randy Glass, remembered, "The A-10 came down hard and lit the track up. There's no mistake about it!" Another wounded Marine, Cpl. Jared Martin, recalled, "The plane was coming right toward us. The next thing I know I'm feeling a lot of heat in my back." He was wounded in the right knee and left hand. He witnessed Lance Cpl. David Fribley killed by A-10 fire.[19]

The extent of the attack will never be certain. Battalion commander Lieutenant Colonel Grabowski stated, "We suspect they took casualties from that A-10, but we don't know and we can't say that's the case until the investigation is completed. I can't sit here and tell you how many casualties were taken at the north side of the bridge versus how many were on the south side, because it's like herding cats. We're not certain who saw who, who was on what [vehicle] and how many. My sense is that most of our [fatalities] occurred on the southern side of the bridge trying to get those that were wounded back."[20]

It is likely that fire from the A-10s destroyed at least one AAV, including the one in which Bitz rode, killing him and other Marines, and disabled one or two other AAVs, but at least three AAVs (C-206, C-208, and C-201) were able to load up the wounded and set out south back through Ambush Alley toward the Euphrates Bridge where medics waited.

An enemy shell landed between C-206 leading the column and C-208 next in line, caving in the top of C-206 and blowing open its ramp. A second shell made a direct hit on C-208, killing the Marines in the troop compartment. Another shell caused C-201 to strike a telephone pole, disabling the vehicle. Under fire, the Marines dismounted and sought shelter in a nearby house, taking positions at windows and on the roof, fighting off numerous assaults. C-206 continued south, its ramp dragging on the road.

As C-206 was nearing the southern bridge an RPG struck its side, and a second RPG flew through the open ramp and exploded inside.

GySgt. Justin Lehew, Alpha Company's Amphibious Assault Platoon Sergeant, recalled, "The vehicle came to a rolling stop right in front of us, not more than thirty meters away, and I saw the crewmen who were on fire, but still moving. They were hanging out of the hatches or maybe trying to climb out, and the men that were in the back were falling out, and on fire. There were seven to nine [wounded] Marines in there."[21]

Lehew and a corpsman, nineteen-year-old Hospitalman Alex Velasquez, without donning helmets and flak vests or grabbing weapons, ran across open terrain under massive enemy fire to reach the smoldering vehicle's open ramp. He and Velasquez shifted bodies to find Cpl. Matthew Juska trapped beneath a collapsed hatch. As they worked to extract him, they became aware that they were working in a time bomb. One of the RPGs had punctured the AAV's fuel tank; the dead Marines, ammunition, and vehicle interior were soaked in gasoline. One more enemy RPG from the battle still raging around them and the AAV would become a flaming coffin.

With other Marines, they worked forty-five minutes under extremely hazardous conditions to save the trapped Marine. An air evacuation was arranged for Juska and other wounded Marines, and a CH-46 helicopter, piloted by Maj. Eric Garcia of Medium Marine Helicopter Squadron 162, MAG-29, flew into heavy fire for the pick-up. For their actions, Lehew would be awarded the Navy Cross, Garcia the Distinguished Flying Cross, and Velasquez the Bronze Star.

By this time, Major Peeples had returned from refueling his tanks, and they supported Alpha and Bravo Companies as they advanced through Ambush Alley to the northern bridges, reinforcing Charlie Company.

Inside the house, Lance Corporal Castleberry, a wounded and bandaged Corporal Martin, and other Marines protecting the wounded were running low on ammunition. Castleberry and another Marine dashed under heavy fire to the disabled track, and grabbed antitank missiles and ammunition. On the roof Martin and other Marines tried to get the attention of U.S. Cobra helicopter gunships overhead. Finally, they watched as the first of the relief vehicles drove up, a Humvee with, as a Marine later described him, "a grizzled gunnery sergeant from another company . . . with a pump-action shotgun." He assessed the situation then radioed for assistance and told them he'd be back. Shortly afterward, an M1A1 Abrams tank arrived and took away the wounded. The gunnery sergeant returned through heavy fire with four additional Humvees to rescue the remaining Marines. Almost certainly, this was GySgt. Jason Doran, the Operations Chief of Weapons Company, 1st Battalion.

Doran, who had tried to enlist in the Marines at age thirteen, was successful on 19 October 1983 and was close to his twenty-year mark. A veteran of the First Gulf War, he'd seen service at Subic Bay in the Philippines and deployed to the Congo for Operation Guardian Retrieval in May 1997, then helped evacuate 451 Americans from Freetown, Sierra Leone, in June 1997 during Operation Noble Obelisk. Now he was in Iraq.

By all accounts, Doran and his Humvee (nicknamed The Mystery Machine) were all over the battlefield that day, assisting in the rescue of soldiers of the 507th and the battle for the Euphrates Bridge, and driving up Ambush Alley dodging mortars, RPGs, and machine-gun fire. After rescuing the stranded Charlie Company Marines and safely evacuating the area, he returned south in An Nasiriyah again and led two Humvees to locate and rescue under fire a missing CAAT team member left behind. For these and other actions that day, Doran was awarded the Silver Star.[22]

With Alpha Company and Bravo Company reinforcing Charlie Company, the battalion set up defensive positions north of the canal and settled in for the night. Marines of the 2nd Battalion, 8th Marines (2/8) moved up behind 2/1 and secured the southern bridges. With the 2/8 was GySgt. Timothy Haney, a platoon sergeant with the CAAT platoon of the Weapons Company.

Haney, an eighteen-year veteran of the Corps, enlisted in 1986, got out, tried college, then reenlisted in the Marines. During the period of 23 March through 26 March, Haney's CAAT platoon conducted search and destroy missions on Iraqi tanks and armored vehicles, engaging in numerous firefights. It would not be until 29 March that An Nasiriyah would be considered "secure." During two separate firefights, Haney dismounted his vehicle, exposing himself to enemy fire to more accurately determine the enemy's location and provide real-time intelligence to his commanders.

On 26 March the battalion Combat Operations Center (COC) came under fire from multiple Iraqi positions, and Haney moved calmly under intense fire to place his Marines in position and direct return fire. Despite an explosion that peppered his body with sixty shrapnel wounds, Haney refused treatment and ignored his wounds to assist other wounded Marines in getting aid. For his bold leadership, wise judgment, and complete dedication to duty Haney was presented the Silver Star on 6 August 2004.

Meanwhile, the 1st Marine Division advanced on Baghdad, and Regimental Combat Team 1 (RCT-1) passed through An Nasiriyah. The 1st Battalion remained until 3 April setting up checkpoints and roadblocks and expanding the security perimeter, as well as providing medical care and repairing the city's infrastructure (water and electricity).

Task Force Tarawa left An Nasiriyah on 4 April after thirteen days. They secured the highways to the rear of the 1st Marines and the town of Ad Diwaniyah. They pushed into Al-Amarah on 7 April and Al-Kut on 11 April before ending the invasion outside Baghdad. Following a six-month deployment, Task Force Tarawa retrograded to Kuwait on 14 May and departed aboard ATF-E ships on 18 May.[23]

One sad final note: On 14 April 2003 1st Lt. Frederick E. Pokorney was laid to rest with full military honors at Arlington National Cemetery, joining his grandfather, an Air Force colonel, and his great-uncle, an Air Force general. He is the first Marine killed during Operation Iraqi Freedom to be buried at Arlington.

ENDNOTES

1. Silver Star citation (excerpt), Sgt. Michael E. Bitz, USMC, http://www.homeofheroes.com/valor2/SS/7_GWOT/citations_USMC.html.

2. Silver Star citation (excerpt), GySgt. Jason Doran, USMC, http://www.homeofheroes.com/valor2/SS/7_GWOT/citations_USMC.html.

3. Silver Star citation (excerpt), CWO5 David Dunfee, USMC, http://www.homeofheroes.com/valor2/SS/7_GWOT/citations_USMC.html.

4. Silver Star citation (excerpt), GySgt. Timothy Haney, USMC, http://www.homeofheroes.com/valor2/SS/7_GWOT/citations_USMC.html.

5. Silver Star citation (excerpt), GySgt. Phillip Jordan, USMC, http://www.homeofheroes.com/valor2/SS/7_GWOT/citations_USMC.html.

6. Silver Star citation (excerpt), 1st Lt. Frederick Pokorney, USMC, http://www.homeofheroes.com/valor2/SS/7_GWOT/citations_USMC-M.html.

7. Mark C. Brinkley, "March 23rd Is a Day Remembered All Too Well," *Army Times*, 17 March 2004.

8. Richard S. Lowry, *U.S. Marine in Iraq: Operation Iraqi Freedom 2003* (London: Osprey Publishing, 2006).

9. Ibid.

10. "U.S. Army Official Report on 507th Maintenance Company, 23 March 2003, An Nasiriyah, Iraq-Executive Summary," http://www.metavr.com/casestudies/aar507ambush.pdf.

11. Gina Cavallaro, "Leathernecks of 1/2 Ran into a Buzz Saw and the Bloodiest Day of the War," *Marine Corps Times*, 12 May 2003.

12. Lowry, *U.S. Marine in Iraq*.

13. Rich Connell and Robert J. Lopez, "Charlie Company," *Los Angeles* (CA) *Times*, 26 August 2003.

14. Ibid.

15. Laura Bailey, "Marine Killed in '03 Iraq Ambush Earns Military's 3rd Highest Award," *Marine Corps Times*, 3 September 2004.

16. Lowry, *U.S. Marine in Iraq*.

17. Connell and Lopez, "Charlie Company."

18. Richard S. Lowry, "The Battle of An Nasiriyah," http://www.militaryhistoryonline.com/desertstorm/annasiriyah/default.aspx.

19. Connell and Lopez, "Charlie Company."

20. Ibid.

21. Trish Wood, *What Was Asked of Us: An Oral History of the Iraq War by the Soldiers Who Fought It* (New York: Little Brown & Co., 2006).

22. Jason K. Doran, *I Am My Brother's Keeper* (North Topsail Beach, NC: Caisson Press, 2005).

23. Lowry, *U.S. Marine in Iraq.*

LCpl. Robert P. Kerman, USMC

Rifleman, Combined Anti-Armor Platoon, Weapons Company,
3rd Battalion, 5th Marines, 1st Marine Division,
I Marine Expeditionary Force

Highway 1, South of Ad Diwaniyah, Iraq
25 March 2003

The Silver Star is presented to Robert P. Kerman, Lance Corporal, U.S. Marine Corps, for conspicuous gallantry and intrepidity in action against the enemy while serving as Rifleman, Combined Anti-Armor Platoon, Weapons Company, Third Battalion, Fifth Marines, FIRST Marine Division, I Marine Expeditionary Force, on 25 March 2003, in support of Operation Iraqi Freedom. Lance Corporal Kerman exhibited exceptional bravery when the lead elements of the battalion were ambushed with mortars, rocket-propelled grenades, and automatic weapons fire. As the vehicle he was traveling in drove directly into machine gun fire and into a trench line, Lance Corporal Kerman sprang from the vehicle and began assaulting down the enemy occupied trench with two other Marines. As enemy soldiers fired at him, he fearlessly plunged towards them firing his M-16 with lethal accuracy. Continuing to move through the trench he repeatedly came under enemy fire. Each time he would calmly occupy a steady firing position and take well-aimed shots that had devastating effects on the enemy. As the group ran out of ammunition, they pressed forward two hundred to three hundred meters utilizing captured enemy AK-47s. Lance Corporal Kerman showed no regard for his own personal safety, and his actions directly contributed to the successful outcome of the engagement. By his bold leadership, wise judgment, and complete dedication to duty, Lance Corporal Kerman reflected great credit upon himself and upheld the highest traditions of the Marine Corps and the United States Naval Service.[1]

Silver Star Citation

LCpl. Armand E. McCormick, USMC

Rifleman, Combined Anti-Armor Platoon, Weapons Company,
3rd Battalion, 5th Marines, 1st Marine Division,
I Marine Expeditionary Force

The Silver Star is presented to Armand E. McCormick, Lance Corporal, U.S. Marine Corps, for conspicuous gallantry and intrepidity in action against the enemy while serving as Rifleman, Combined Anti-Armor Platoon, Weapons Company, Third Battalion, Fifth Marines, FIRST Marine Division, I Marine Expeditionary Force, in support of Operation Iraqi Freedom on 25 March 2003. Lance Corporal McCormick exhibited exceptional bravery when the lead elements of his battalion were ambushed with mortars, rocket-propelled grenades (RPGs), and automatic weapons fire. Under heavy fire, he fearlessly drove his lightly armored vehicle directly at an enemy machine gun position and purposely crashed it into an occupied trench line. With the initial breach of the enemy defense now gained for his unit, he sprang from the vehicle and began assaulting down the berm and ambush line with two Marines. Taking direct fire, and outnumbered, he pressed forward firing his M-9 pistol at enemy forces. Moving through the trench he repeatedly came under enemy fire, each time calmly taking well-aimed shots. As the group ran low on ammunition, he collected enemy rifles and an RPG and continued to press the attack forward several hundred meters. As a follow on company began to make their entrance into the berm, he returned to his vehicle and backed it out of the trench. Lance Corporal McCormick's courageous and boldly aggressive actions greatly reduced the enemy's ability to inflict casualties on the rest of his battalion. By his bold leadership, wise judgment, and complete dedication to duty, Lance Corporal McCormick reflected great credit upon himself and upheld the highest traditions of the Marine Corps and the United States Naval Service.[2]

Silver Star Citation

As a general rule, the maxim of marching to the sound of the guns is a wise one.

Baron Antoine H. Jomini (1779–1869),
Précis Politique et Militaire de la Campagne de 1815[3]

AS FAR BACK AS NAPOLEONIC TIMES "marching to the sound of the guns" has been used as an idiom implying bold and decisive action. Caught in the kill zone of an ambush on 25 March 2003, Marines of the 3rd Battalion, 5th Marines would update the old maxim by driving to the sound of the guns. Their actions would save the column and merit a Navy Cross and two Silver Stars.

Operation Iraqi Freedom was five days old as the Combined Anti-Armor Team (CAAT) platoon, Weapons Company, 3/5 Marines proceeded north along Highway 1, south of Ad Diwaniyah in a convoy of four M1A1 Abrams tanks followed by seven Humvees, each mounting a .50-caliber machine gun on a topside turret.

In the turret of the lead Humvee, LCpl. Robert "Robbie" Kerman kept watch on the Iraq countryside. Kerman, a native of Klamath Falls, Oregon, left the University of Nevada, Reno, to enlist in the Marines on 12 September 2001, the day after the terrorist attacks of 9/11. He chose to serve in the same unit his father had served in during Vietnam, the 3/5 Marines.

The 3/5 has a distinguished history stretching back to 8 June 1917 when the unit was formed in preparation for World War I. It saw action at Belleau Woods, Vierzy, Meuse-Argonne, St. Mihiel, and Soissons. During World War II, the battalion fought at Guadalcanal, New Guinea, Peleliu, and Okinawa. It saw action in Korea at Pusan, Inchon, Seoul, and the Chosin Reservoir. Vietnam added Chu-Lai, DaNang, Quang Nam, Que Son, and An Hoa to its battle lexicon, and it performed combat operations at Al-Wafrah, Kuwait, during Operation Desert Storm. On 7 February 2003 the 3/5 again answered the call to duty when it deployed from Camp Pendleton, California, for Operation Iraqi Freedom.[4]

Next to Kerman in the turret rode Cpl. Thomas "Tank" Franklin, a highly proficient gunner on the .50 caliber who had been on terminal leave, attending classes in Florida. He extended his enlistment to remain with his unit when they deployed to Kuwait, telling his wife, "Honey, I've got to go."[5]

In the driver's seat, LCpl. Armand E. McCormick steered the Humvee along the partially paved roadway, vigilant for potholes as well as improvised explosive devices (IEDs). A basic rifleman, it was his first time driving a Humvee. The twenty-two-year-old Marine from Mt. Pleasant, Iowa, had been in the unit for three years and had confidence in his platoon leader, 1st Lt. Brian R. Chontosh, who sat beside him in the passenger seat. In the rear of the Humvee Corporal Korte operated the radio.

It was shortly after 5:00 AM as the column proceeded north toward Ad-Diwaniyah, the capital city of Iraq's Al-Qadisiyah Province, with more than four hundred thousand inhabitants. Flanking the road were eight-foot-high artificial berms, set off from the road some twenty-five meters. Uneasy, Chontosh radioed the rest of the column to stay alert. Ahead of the tanks, a white civilian truck loaded with Iraqi civilians caused the tanks to slow, then come to an abrupt halt.

Almost immediately, the column began taking fire from mortars, automatic rifles, and rocket-propelled grenades (RPGs). The tankers buttoned up inside their tanks, but the thin-skinned Humvees did not have that luxury. With the tanks stopped and blocking forward progress, the Humvees were trapped in the kill zone.

Chontosh, in actions that would later merit him the Navy Cross, did what Marine leaders have done throughout its history: he moved to locate the threat and eliminate it. Ordering McCormick to drive off road, he directed them toward a break in the berm. Unsure of the exact location of the insurgent fire, he recalled, "It all boiled down to luck and chance."[6]

As they drove through the narrow opening, the Humvee barely clearing the sides, they began taking machine-gun fire from a bunker to the right. Franklin, an expert on the .50 caliber, was especially proficient at hitting his target from a moving vehicle; he gave a practical demonstration, rapidly dispatching five Iraqi insurgents with devastating accuracy which Chontosh would later describe as amazing.

Chontosh ordered McCormick to drive into a trench filled with enemy fighters. After resupplying Franklin with a can of ammunition, McCormick jumped out and joined Kerman and Chontosh, who had already exited the vehicle. Korte remained on the radio to update the column, and Franklin remained at the .50 pouring fire into the enemy and scattering the resistance.

McCormick recalled, "I jumped out. . . . Tosh and Kerman are running down into the trench. I caught up to them and ran in there too. We ran almost two hundred yards. That's when all hell broke loose. There were guys everywhere. I was just shooting . . . there were people five feet in front of us . . . there was nothing to duck behind."[7]

The three Marines, supported by Franklin's superior marksmanship, engaged a force estimated to have numbered close to two hundred, and Chontosh alone is credited with taking out twenty of the enemy. Out of ammo, the Marines picked up fallen AK-47s and continued the fight. Once the ambush was disrupted, the three quickly withdrew under intense fire to return to their vehicle. At one point, Chontosh, seizing an opportunity, turned a captured RPG on the enemy, scattering an assault. Remounting the vehicle, they rapidly advanced back to the column along Highway 1. "There was absolutely no time to think of anything about what happened. Immediately after that action, tanks were on the radio calling for infantry support. There was no time to think about dying," Chontosh recalled.[8]

The battle lasted about fifteen to twenty-five minutes, depending on accounts, and resulted in thirty Iraqi prisoners—a mixture of regular army and conscripts—with another thirty-five to forty Iraqis killed. An artillery barrage into the desert beyond the roadside berm was aimed at fleeing Iraqis. "They put up a fight for a minute or two and then they started surrendering," said LCpl. Kris Spencer.[9]

Chontosh's leadership, McCormick's driving, Kerman's coolness under fire, and Franklin's marksmanship resulted in clearing two hundred yards of trench and killing and wounding numerous Iraqis, no doubt saving countless Marine lives. The sole Marine fatality was a navy corpsman, HM3 Michael Vann Johnson Jr., from Little Rock, Arkansas, who was working as a Medically Augmented Personnel (MAP) with the Weapons Company, CAAT Platoon, 3/5, assigned to Kilo Company. He was tending an injured Marine when an RPG penetrated the Humvee he was in. It struck him in the head and detonated. Another Marine in the turret, Lance Corporal Quintero, was seriously wounded by shrapnel.[10]

The story of the ambush made national news, and caught the attention of President Bush. Interestingly, what brought attention to the fight was not the story of Chontosh and the crew's valor and audacity in charging into an ambush, but rather was a photograph of LCpl. Marcco Ware carrying a wounded Iraqi soldier to safety after the ambush. Speaking to Marines at Camp Lejeune on 3 April 2003, President Bush called the photo "a picture of the strength and goodness of the U.S. Marines. That is the picture of America. [The] people of the United States are proud of the honorable conduct of our military."[11]

For many in the 3/5 Marines, Ad Diwaniyah was their baptism of fire. They continued to see combat for the remainder of their tour. Some, like Chontosh, would return to Iraq for a second combat tour. McCormick, due to be discharged, extended his enlistment for three months to return to Iraq and remain with his comrades until the end of their tour.

On 6 May 2004, in a ceremony at the Marine Corps Air Ground Combat Center (MCAGCC) at Twentynine Palms, California, the Commandant of the Marine Corps, Gen. Michael W. Hagee and Sgt. Maj. John L. Estrada. UMC, presented Capt. Brian R. Chontosh with the Navy Cross, and presented two corporals, LCpl. Armand E. McCormick and LCpl. Robert P. Kerman, with Silver Stars for "conspicuous gallantry and intrepidity."[12] Cpl. Thomas Franklin received a Navy Commendation medal with "V" for Valor in a separate ceremony.

All three are modest and matter-of-fact about their awards. Perhaps Kerman best summed up the experience: "I was pretty scared at the time, but we knew what we had to do and we did it."[13]

ENDNOTES

1. Silver Star citation, LCpl. Robert P. Kerman, USMC, http://www.homeofheroes.com/valor2/SS/7_GWOT/citations_USMC.html.

2. Silver Star citation, LCpl. Armand E. McCormick, USMC, http://www.homeofheroes.com/valor2/SS/7_GWOT/citations_USMC-M.html.

3. Robert D. Heinl, *Dictionary of Military and Naval Quotations* (Annapolis, MD: Naval Institute Press, 1967).

4. "3rd Battalion, 5th Marine History," http://www.i-mef.usmc.mil/div/5mar/3bn/history.asp.

5. Caspar W. Weinberger and Wyton C. Hall, *Home of the Brave: Honoring the Unsung Heroes in the War on Terror* (New York: Tom Doherty Associates LLC, 2006).

6. Ibid.

7. Ibid.

8. Ibid.

9. John Murphy, "An Ambush by Iraqis Tests Mettle of Marines: Enemy Soldiers Attack Convoy, Pay with Thirty-five Lives," *Baltimore* (MD) *Sun*, 26 March 2003.

10. Christopher Ray Johnston, "Remembrance: Iraq/Afghanistan War Heroes," http://www.iraqwarheroes.com/johnsonm.htm, 4 March 2004.

11. Kathy Lally and Jean Marbella, "In a Flash, Marine in Spotlight," *Baltimore* (MD) *Sun*, 4 April 2003.

12. Jeremy M. Vought, "3/5 Marines Awarded for Heroism," *Marine Corps News*, 13 May 2004 (Story ID #2004514112222).

13. Jeremy M. Vought, "Klamath Falls, Oregon, Marine Receives Silver Star," *Marine Corps News*, May 6, 2004.

CWO2 Thomas F. Parks III, USMC

*Battalion Infantry Weapons Officer, 1st Battalion,
4th Marines, Regimental Combat Team 1,
1st Marine Division, I Marine Expeditionary Force*

Battle at Al-Kut, Iraq
3 April 2003

The Silver Star is presented to Thomas F. Parks, Chief Warrant Officer, U.S. Marine Corps, for conspicuous gallantry and intrepidity in action against the enemy while serving as Battalion Infantry Weapons Officer, First Battalion, Fourth Marines, Regimental Combat Team 1, FIRST Marine Division, I Marine Expeditionary Force in support of Operation Iraqi Freedom on 3 April 2003. When the Battalion's forward command element was engaged by enemy forces with intense small arms and rocket fire, Chief Warrant Officer Parks dismounted to direct the security operations. Exposing himself numerous times to enemy fire, he moved from position to position, encouraging Marines and directing the employment of their fires to neutralize enemy strong-points. During the fighting, Chief Warrant Officer Parks personally dispatched three enemy personnel, including a sniper. Amidst a hail of machine gun and sniper fire, Chief Warrant Officer Parks destroyed an enemy T-55 tank with an AT-4 rocket and proceeded under heavy small arms fire to direct the employment of an American tank. As a result of his orders, the tank was able to destroy several enemy bunkers and strong-points. By his outstanding display of decisive leadership, ultimate courage in the face of heavy enemy fire, and utmost devotion to duty, Chief Warrant Officer Parks reflected great credit upon himself and upheld the highest traditions of the Marine Corps and the United States Naval Service.[1]

Silver Star Citation

THE CITY OF AL-KUT (KUT AL-IMARA) lies on the left bank of the Tigris River, approximately one hundred miles southeast of Baghdad. It is a region rich in agriculture, especially grains, and has been a center of Iraq's carpet trade for centuries. It was the site of a decisive battle between the British and Ottoman forces on 26 September 1915, which the British won. It is the capital of the Wasit Province and had a population of four hundred thousand at the start of the war.

On 3 April 2003 Al-Kut also stood between the 1st Marine Division and Baghdad. Orders were given to capture a critical bridge across the Tigris River. It was the last major bridge needed to access a major built-up highway to Baghdad. Regimental Combat Team 1 (RCT-1) comprised three battalions (1st–3rd) of the 1st Marines, and the 1st Battalion of the 4th Marines (1/4) was tasked with the capture of the bridge.

The 1/4 Marines has a long history that predates World War I, including service in the Dominican Republic and guarding the U.S. mail. They were the original "China Marines," serving there from February 1927 until November 1941, when the entire regiment was deployed to the Philippines. The battalion helped defend Corregidor from December 1941 until May 1942 when it was forced to burn its colors and surrender. On 1 February 1944 a new 1/4 was designated the 1st Raider Battalion and saw action in the battles for Guam and Okinawa. Following occupation duty in Japan and later China the battalion served four years in Vietnam (1965–69) and assisted in tactical operations in both Operation Desert Shield and Operation Desert Storm. Deployed directly to Kuwait in January 2003 as part of Amphibious Task Force West, 1/4 was among the first troops across the Iraqi border, and had already fought engagements near An Nasiriyah and Al-Shatrah as they raced north toward Baghdad.[2]

CWO-2 Thomas F. Parks was a "Gunner," in Marine parlance. Although all Gunners are warrant officers, not all warrant officers are Gunners. There are only fifty-two Gunners in the Marine Corps, one per battalion, and each is a specialist within the infantry field, denoted by the insignia of a bursting bomb. Only the most experienced infantry noncommissioned officers are commissioned as a CWO/Gunner.

Parks earned his experience during a twenty-year career that began at Parris Island, South Carolina, on 26 September 1985. The son of a Marine, born at the Portsmouth Naval Hospital, Kittery, Maine, one of Parks' first assignments was as part of the security force guarding nuclear weapons in Adak, Alaska. "On a clear day, you could see Russia. We were that close!" he recalled.[3] Parks spent his entire career as an Infantry Marine—a grunt. He led the 1st Marine Division to victory in the annual rifle squad competition in 1995 and was named the Marine Corps Drill Instructor of the Year in 1998. He saw combat with the 3/7 in Panama in 1988, and with the 3/9 in Desert Storm and Somalia in 1990 and 1992, respectively. In 2000 he was part of the rescue of the USS *Cole* explosion. He deployed to Kuwait aboard the USS *Peleliu* (LAH-5) late in January 2003 and was assigned to the command element of the 1st battalion, 4th Marines as the battalion weapons officer.[4]

On 3 April Parks was in a forward armored Humvee assigned to protecting the battalion commander as they advanced along Route 7 into the city. "The terrain was such that there was one main road, and it was elevated, with berms on both sides. Off to the left, there were squat, flat, brick buildings, and the area to the right was open. We stopped just outside Al-Kut, and there was a gatehouse to the left, and some arches from which hung an Iraqi flag. The battalion commander, Lt. Col. John Mayer, told me 'Gunner, get the flag.' I got it down, and tossed it in his Humvee."[5]

The column set up security and waited while artillery and Cobra airships prepped the area. "We began taking prisoners as they surrendered. I think they were Republican Guard; they had olive green uniforms. We took some colonels and generals. We thought we'd go right into a fight. We didn't plan on being saddled with prisoners. The Army Psyops [psychological operations] vehicle was behind mine, and I heard them blaring rock 'n' roll over the speakers. I think it was 'Hell's Bells' by ACDC. It was the same thing we did in Panama with [General Manuel] Norriega."[6]

In the interim Parks was ordered to the rear to destroy eight abandoned artillery pieces, which he did using thermite grenades. The unit was ready to advance by the time he returned. The battalion advanced with Charlie Company in the lead, followed by Bravo Company, then Alpha Company, with the command element behind Charlie Company.

When the forward element came under intense small-arm and rocket fire, Parks drove to the front of the fight and dismounted from his Humvee to direct the attack. He killed at least three enemy fighters, one a sniper set to kill a fellow Marine. Under heavy enemy fire he engaged an Iraqi T-55 tank with an AT-4 rocket, running across open terrain to destroy the tank. The action was caught on film by Bob Arnot and an MSNBC crew filming live. He recalled later , "We were getting shot at from all directions, north, east, west and south, taking fire from every direction, every angle. It made no difference where you took cover." Dazed from the backblast of the AT-4 rocket, he was still able to direct the HQ element in returning fire. "My machine-gunner, LCpl. [Carlos] Rochell was awesome. We called him 'Taco.' . . . And my driver, Pfc. Xavier Cobb kept me grounded. He taught me to be twenty, I taught him to be forty."[7]

Parks later exposed himself to enemy fire to direct M1A1 Abrams tanks in destroying several fortified positions. Parks lived up to the battalion motto "Whatever it Takes," but will tell you his priority was simply to accomplish his mission, "to neutralize the threat and protect the battalion commander."[8] The almost-constant fighting took its toll on Parks, and he returned to Pendleton, California, at Easter 2003, where he remained as Division Gunner until his retirement on 1 October 2005.

In recognition of his actions between 20 March and 10 April, Parks was awarded the Silver Star on 25 October 2004 in a ceremony at 1st Marine Division Headquarters, Camp Pendleton, California. Capt. Christopher Martin, who served with Parks in Iraq, recalled a different aspect of the warrior, his compassion. "I remember, in Iraq he went out of his way to help out injured Iraqi civilians. . . . [T]hat speaks volumes on the man."[9]

ENDNOTES

1. Silver Star citation, CWO2 Thomas F. Parks III, USMC, http://www.homeofheroes.com/valor2/SS/7_GWOT/citations_USMC-M.html.
2. "Battalion History, 1st Battalion–4th Marines," www.i-mef.usmc.mil/div/1mar/1bn4/history.asp.
3. Thomas F. Parks III, telephone interview with Scott Baron, 26 June 2007.
4. Ibid.
5. Ibid.
6. Ibid.
7. Ibid.
8. Joseph L. Digirolamo, "In the Highest Tradition," *Leatherneck Magazine*, March 2005.
9. Ibid.

Lt. Gen. James F. Amos presents the Silver Star medal on 12 December 2005 to Capt. Christopher P. Niedziocha, USMC, Battlion Landing Team One Six Anti-Armor Platoon Commander assigned to the 22nd Marine Expeditionary Unit, deployed with Commander, United States Fifth Fleet. (U.S. Marine Corps)

The family of fallen Marine Pfc. Daniel B. McClenney stands proudly with McClenney's Silver Star and bronze bust. (U.S. Marine Corps)

Capt. Brian G. Cillessen, USMC, was awarded the Silver Star medal for actions on 23 January 2005 while serving as an embedded trainer and Marine adviser for the Afghan National Army Commandos. He was a member of Special Forces Operational Detachment 143, Combined Joint Task Force Phoenix, Office of Military Cooperation. (U.S. Marine Corps)

1st Lt. Stephen J. Boada, fire direction officer, 1st Battalion, 12th Marine Regiment, somewhere near the Afghanistan-Pakistan border in early 2005. (U.S. Marine Corps)

CWO David R. Dunfee being presented with the Silver Star medal at Camp Ripper, Al-Asad, Iraq, 10 March 2005 by Maj. Gen. Richard A. Huck, commanding general of the 2nd Marine Division. (U.S. Marine Corps)

CWO2 Thomas F. Parks III, Silver Star recipient. (U.S. Marine Corps)

SSgt. Adam R. Sikes, Silver Star medal recipient. (U.S. Marine Corps)

Sgt. Tim C. Tardif, squad leader for Battalion Landing Team, 3rd Battalion, 1st Marine Regiment, Kilo Company, 3rd Platoon, 1st Squad, conducts a hasty vehicle checkpoint near Karmah during an evening patrol. (U.S. Marine Corps)

Maj. Gen Richard F. Natonski congratulates sniper Sgt. John E. Place after presenting him with a Silver Star. (U.S. Marine Corps)

GySgt. Nick Popaditch speaks to the guests at the MCAGCC Birthday Ball, 9 November 2007, where he was the guest of honor. Joking that speech cards wouldn't be very helpful, Popaditch, who lost his right eye and most of the vision from his left, kept his address short, speaking to the Marines from his heart. (U.S. Marine Corps)

Marine officers Maj. Robert S. Weiler and Capt. Christopher J. Bronzi join forces again after a ceremony at Camp Pendleton, where they both were presented the Silver Star by 1st Marine Division commanding general Maj. Gen. Richard F. Natonski. (U.S. Marine Corps)

1st Lt. Thomas E. Cogan, executive officer for Company E, Battalion Landing Team, 2nd Battalion, 4th Marine Regiment, 31st Marine Expeditionary Unit, poses for a photo after being presented with the Silver Star by Lt. Gen. Robert R. Blackman, commanding general, III Marine Expeditionary Force. (U.S. Marine Corps)

Marine Barracks Washington Sgt. Maj. Michael Watkins stands with Gen. Michael W. Hagee, Commandant of the Marine Corps, during the Silver Star medal award ceremony for Capt. Joshua L. Glover, 28 October 2005. (U.S. Marine Corps)

Cpl. Abraham McCarver, a rifleman with 1st Battalion, 5th Marines, receives a Silver Star medal. (U.S. Marine Corps)

Sgt. Ismael Sagredo is awarded the Silver Star by 1st Lt. Christopher D. Ayres. (U.S. Marine Corps)

Capt. Jason E. Smith, Silver Star recipient. (U.S. Marine Corps)

Sally A. Gannon accepts the Silver Star medal and citation on behalf of Maj. Richard J. Gannon IV. Lt. Col. Mathew A. Lopez, former battalion commander for 3rd Battalion, 7th Marine Regiment, presents the award. (U.S. Marine Corps)

Maj. Gen. Ken Quinlan, USA, Joint Forces Staff College commandant, pins the Silver Star on Lt. Col. Matthew A. Lopez, USMC. (U.S. Marine Corps)

LCpl. Danny S. Santos, a rifleman with the 4th Marine Expeditionary Brigade (Anti-Terrorism), is presented a Silver Star by Lt. Gen. James F. Amos, commanding general of II Marine Expeditionary Force. (U.S. Marine Corps)

LCpl. Thomas R. Adametz receives a Silver Star from Lt. Gen. John A. Sattler, I Marine Expeditionary Force commanding general, in a ceremony at Camp Horno. (U.S. Marine Corps)

Capt. Brian Von Kraus, the commander of Headquarters and Support Company, 1st Battalion, 1st Marine Regiment, Regimental Combat Team 6, recipient of the Silver Star medal, looks over a school reconstruction site as Iraqi men tear down the remnants of the old structure. (U.S. Marine Corps)

1st Lt. Jeffery T. Lee, from Pacolet Mills, South Carolina, receives the Silver Star medal from Maj. Gen. Richard A. Huck. (U.S. Marine Corps)

1st Lt. Elliott L. Ackerman receives the Silver Star from Brig. Gen. Charles M. Gurganus, 2nd Marine Division assistant commander. (U.S. Marine Corps)

Vera Rapicault, widow of Silver Star recipient Capt. Patrick M. Rapicault, is comforted by 1st Marine Division commanding general Maj. Gen. Richard F. Natonski during Captain Rapicault's Silver Star award ceremony at Camp San Mateo. (U.S. Marine Corps)

Lt. Col. Todd S. Desgrosseilliers, recipient of a Silver Star. (U.S. Marine Corps)

Rear Adm. Thomas R. Cullison, USN, Medical Corps commander, Navy Medicine East, and commander of the Naval Medical Center at Portsmouth, Virginia, presents HM2 Juan M. Rubio, USN, with the Silver Star medal during an awards ceremony. (Defense Visual Information Center)

Capt. Jason P. Schauble displays three of the highest decorations within the Department of Defense: the Silver Star, the Bronze Star with a combat "V," and the Meritorious Service Medal. (U.S. Marine Corps)

Lt. Col. Nicholas F. Marano awards the Silver Star to Sgt. Jarred L. Adams at the Marines' camp at Al-Qa'im, Iraq. (U.S. Marine Corps)

The family of Sgt. David N. Wimberg is saluted after being presented with the Silver Star medal on Wimberg's behalf. (U.S. Marine Corps)

1st Lt. David T. Russell, Silver Star recipient. (U.S. Marine Corps)

Cpl. Mark A. Camp, an automatic rifleman with Lima Company, 3rd Battalion, 25th Marine Regiment, receives the Silver Star medal. (U.S. Marine Corps)

1st Lt. Brian M. Stann, Weapons Company commander, 3rd Battalion, 2nd Marines, with his family. (U.S. Marine Corps)

Wyatt L. Waldron (Mendes), a former corporal with Weapons Company, 3rd Battalion, 4th Marine Regiment, receives a Silver Star medal in a company formation at the Combat Center's Camp Wilson. (U.S. Marine Corps)

SSgt. Charles M. Evers, a platoon sergeant with 3rd Battalion, 5th Marine Regiment, Regimental Combat Team 6, was awarded the Silver Star on 23 November 2007. Evers displayed gallant leadership while under enemy fire and overcame continuous assaults by coordinating supporting arms to gain fire superiority in June 2006 in Iraq's Anbar Province. (*Marine Corps Times*)

Capt. Doug Zembiec, the commanding officer of Company E, 2nd Battalion, 1st Marine Regiment, 1st Marine Division, and recipient of the Silver Star medal, gives orders to his men over a radio prior to leaving their secured compound for a short patrol in Fallujah, Iraq, 8 April 2004.

GySgt. Jimmie E. Howard, recipient of the Medal of Honor and the Silver Star. (U.S. Marine Corps)

RMSN Harold B. McIver (standing far right), Silver Star recipient, recovers from his wounds with his crew. (U.S. Navy)

Pfc. Jack William Kelso receives the Silver Star. (U.S. Marine Corps)

Pfc. Herman J. Pizzi is awarded the Silver Star. (U.S. Marine Corps)

Typical "outpost" bunker during the Korean War. (National Archives and Records Administration)

Maj. Thomas M. Sellers, USMCR, killed in action, recipient of the Silver Star posthumously. (Courtesy Sharon McDonald collection)

Kimpo Airfield (K-14), South Korea, home of the U.S. Air Force Fourth Fighter Interceptor Wing, 1953. (National Archives and Records Administration)

Mrs. Thomas M. Sellers and her daughter, Sharon, with Col. Frank C. Croft, USMC, after receiving the Silver Star and Distinguished Flying Cross medals on behalf of Major Sellers. (U.S. Marine Corps)

Lt. Chester W. Nimitz Jr. is congratulated by his father, Adm. Chester W. Nimitz, after Lieutenant Nimitz was presented the Silver Star medal by Vice Adm. A. S. Carpender in 1943. (U.S. Naval Institute Photo Archive, Courtesy Fleet Adm. Chester W. Nimitz).

Lt. Franklin Delano Roosevelt Jr., USNR, executive officer of USS *Mayrant* (DD-402), 1943. (U.S. Navy)

Capt. John Hamilton (the nom de guerre of Hollywood actor Sterling Hayden) was the only Marine movie actor awarded the Silver Star during World War II. (Courtesy Catherine Hayden Collection)

Maj. Gen. Carson A. Roberts, commanding general, Third Marine Air Wing, upgrades Pfc. Guy L. Gabaldon's Silver Star medal to a Navy Cross medal. (U.S. Navy)

Lt. Paul Richard Beauchamp, USNR, Silver Star recipient. (U.S. Navy)

Several Air Group 19 pilots pose on board the USS *Lexington* (CV-16) under the air group's tally of destroyed Japanese aircraft in October 1944. Lieutenant Beauchamp is standing top row right wearing an overseas cap. (U.S. Navy)

One of the valuable low-altitude photographs taken by Lt. Paul Richard Beauchamp of vital power plants on the enemy-held island of Formosa. Arrow denotes large metal tubes running down the mountainside to power plants. (U.S. Navy)

GySgt. Jeffrey E. Bohr Jr., USMC

Company Gunnery Sergeant, Alpha Company, 1st Battalion,
5th Marine Regiment, Regimental Combat Team 5, 1st Marine Division,
I Marine Expeditionary Force

Battle for the Al-A'Zamiyah Presidential Palace, Baghdad, Iraq
10 April 2003

The Silver Star is presented to Jeffrey E. Bohr, Gunnery Sergeant, U.S. Marine Corps, for conspicuous gallantry and intrepidity in action against the enemy while serving as Company Gunnery Sergeant, Company A, First Battalion, Fifth Marine Regiment, Regimental Combat Team 5, FIRST Marine Division, I Marine Expeditionary Force in support of Operation Iraqi Freedom on 10 April 2003. With his company assigned the dangerous mission of seizing a presidential palace in Baghdad and concerned that logistical re-supply might be slow in reaching his comrades once they reached the objective, Gunnery Sergeant Bohr selflessly volunteered to move in his two soft-skinned vehicles with the company's main armored convoy. While moving through narrow streets toward the objective, the convoy took intense small arms and rocket-propelled grenade (RPG) fire. Throughout this movement, Gunnery Sergeant Bohr delivered accurate, effective fire on the enemy while encouraging his Marines and supplying critical information to his company commander. When the lead vehicles of the convoy reached a dead end and were subjected to enemy fire, Gunnery Sergeant Bohr continued to boldly engage the enemy while calmly maneuvering his Marines to safety. Upon learning of a wounded Marine in a forward vehicle, Gunnery Sergeant Bohr immediately coordinated medical treatment and evacuation. Moving to the position of the injured Marine, Gunnery Sergeant Bohr continued to lay down a high volume of suppressive fire, while simultaneously guiding the medical evacuation vehicle, until he was mortally wounded by enemy fire. By his bold leadership, wise judgment, and complete dedication to duty, Gunnery Sergeant Bohr reflected great credit upon himself and upheld the highest traditions of the Marine Corps and the United States Naval Service.[1]

Silver Star Citation

2nd Lt. Nicholas J. Horton, USMC

Third Platoon Commander, Alpha Company, 1st Battalion,
5th Marines, 1st Marine Division, I Marine Expeditionary Force

The Silver Star is presented to Nicholas J. Horton, Second Lieutenant, U.S. Marine Corps, for conspicuous gallantry and intrepidity in action against the enemy while serving as Third Platoon Commander, Alpha Company, First Battalion, Fifth Marines, FIRST Marine Division, I Marine Expeditionary Force in support of Operation Iraqi Freedom on 10 April 2003. While conducting a mission along Route 2 into the heart of downtown Baghdad, Second Lieutenant Horton's Battalion was attacked from both sides of the road. He directed suppressive fire while continuing towards the objective. As Alpha Company attacked through an enemy position it encountered a dead-end and began taking intense rocket-propelled grenades (RPG) and small arms fire. Second Lieutenant Horton directed his platoon to return fire, effectively suppressing the enemy. He subsequently took over navigation for the company and led them out of the kill zone. In a subsequent firefight, his track was hit causing casualties in the troop compartment and setting off the halon system. He quickly calmed the Marines and reoriented their fire to suppress the enemy. Continuing the advance, Third Platoon was tasked with clearing a Mosque. After establishing suppression and a mechanical breach into the complex, Second Lieutenant Horton assessed the situation and requested Second Platoon. Second Lieutenant Horton directed their actions, intermingling them with his own platoon in order to clear the multi-story complex. His assault led to the capture of twenty enemy prisoners of war, fourteen RPGs, numerous machine guns and small arms. He executed the entire action inside the Mosque without physical on-scene guidance from the Company Commander. By his bold leadership, outstanding judgment, and complete dedication to duty, Second Lieutenant Horton reflected great credit upon himself and upheld the highest traditions of the Marine Corps and the United States Naval Service.[2]

Silver Star Citation

AS COALITION TROOPS ENTERED BAGHDAD, expecting the "Mother of All Battles" (which never materialized), a question foremost in many commanders' minds was, "Where is Saddam Hussein?" There were sightings, rumors, and reams of intelligence, but despite intensive efforts to locate him, his location remained unknown. On 7 April 2003, at 7:00 AM local time, seventy tanks and sixty Bradley fighting vehicles swept into the city on the western side of the Tigris and occupied the main presidential palace without resistance. Forces also occupied the old palace after a brief skirmish, but resistance continued in the area and Saddam Hussein continued to elude capture.[3]

On 9 April Saddam Hussein was filmed on Al-Arabia Television walking about in the neighborhood of Al-A'Zamiyah, in northern Baghdad. At the same time U.S. intelligence picked up rumors of his presence in Al-A'Zamiyah. At dawn on 10 April three companies of 1st Battalion, 5th Marines, Alpha, Bravo, and Charlie, were dispatched to capture him. Their mission was to drive deep into central Baghdad on the northeast side of the Tigris River and capture the Al-A'Zamiyah Presidential Palace, where Saddam was rumored to be hiding.[4]

Activated on 25 May 1917 at Quantico, Virginia, the 1st Battalion, 5th Regiment deployed to France in June 1917 and saw action at Aisne, St. Mihiel, Meuse-Argonne, Château-Thierry, Marabache, and Limey. Following occupation duties it returned to Quantico in August 1919. In the 1930s the battalion deployed to Nicaragua; during World War II it participated in campaigns at Guadalcanal, New Guinea, New Britain, Peleliu, and Okinawa. It fought at Pusan, Inchon, and the Chosin Reservoir during the Korean War. Deployed to Vietnam from March 1966 through April 1971, the 1/5 operated from Rung Sat, Chu Lai, Que Son, Phu Loc, Phu Bai, An Hoa, and Da Nang. It participated in Operation Desert Shield and Operation Desert Storm from August 1990 through March 1991, and deployed to Kuwait in support of Operation Iraqi Freedom (OIF) in February 2003, the first of what would be three deployments to Iraq for the 1/5.[5]

The Marines of Alpha Company 1/5 had the reputation of being the best-trained company in the 1/5. Their commander, Capt. Blair Sokol, was a former football player at the Naval Academy. At six feet seven inches tall he was known as a rigid disciplinarian and a fanatic on hard, realistic training who pushed his men to their limits. That rigor would serve them well on 10 April.

The Marines of Alpha Company were among the first troops to enter Iraq; their unit is unofficially credited as being the first major U.S. ground unit to cross the Kuwait-Iraq border, a few miles west of Safwan. Their unit was also the first to suffer a fatality in ground combat. Crossing two strands of razor wire, 1/5 invaded Iraq without incident, met only by abandoned tanks and positions. It proceeded north twenty miles on its mission to secure the petroleum pumping station at the massive Rumaila oil field in Kuwait and southern Iraq before it could be torched by the Iraqis. Although there was little resistance a group of escaping Iraqis in a white SUV pick-up opened fire, striking the 2nd Platoon leader, 1st Lt. Shane Childers, in the gut just below his Kevlar vest. He died within minutes, despite the best efforts of several corpsmen. Childers, a "mustang" who was commissioned from the ranks, was popular among his men. The war was now real for Alpha Company.

After a couple days of guarding the oil field Alpha Company proceeded northward on 25 March, crossing the Euphrates River the following day while fighting 40 mph winds, rain, and mud. They were greeted as liberators at Zubaydah, a town on the south bank of the Tigris, and were welcomed by happy crowds as they closed on Baghdad, experiencing only light resistance, mostly from Islamic fundamentalists and Ba'ath Party officials. "We came here to fight, but everywhere we go, the Iraqis just leave," recalled LCpl. Andrew Morales.[6]

They arrived in Baghdad on 9 April and spent their first night setting up defensive positions at the municipal dump, surrounded by stinking refuse, rusting metal, and mosquitoes. It was a welcome relief when they moved out before dawn the following morning, tasked with capturing the Al-A'Zimayah Presidential Palace.

Traveling with Alpha Company's armored column on its mission was GySgt. Jeffrey E. Bohr Jr., a thirty-nine-year-old Ohio native who had volunteered to accompany the column in two "soft-skinned" Humvees to supervise logistical resupply. A two-decade military veteran, Bohr had enlisted in the U.S. Army in 1982 following his graduation from South Winneshiek High School in Ohio, and parachuted into Grenada as part of the 82nd Airborne. He also served in Panama and Somalia. Following his six-year enlistment, Bohr returned to civilian life, but enlisted in the Marines after only a few months. He served during the first Gulf War. "I think he missed it [the military]," his father, Edward, later recalled.[7]

At first, as the column traveled along a major street lined by crumbling urban buildings, there was quiet but as the streets narrowed the unit suddenly came under intense small-arms and rocket-propelled grenade (RPG) fire. The Marines returned fire as they maneuvered down the streets, but in the darkness and confusion, coupled with the lack of street signs and unfamiliarity with the neighborhood, the column found itself at a bridge across the Tigris. The column was forced to back up, a slow and difficult process complicated by incoming fire. Bohr calmly returned fire and encouraged his Marines as he directed the vehicles while maintaining communication with his commander. During the process of turning the column, Bohr's driver, Cpl. Brandon White, was severely wounded in the wrist, and Bohr called for a medical evacuation (medevac), then laid down suppressing fire as he guided in the evacuation vehicle. He was killed by enemy fire and died on the scene. By all accounts, "Gunny Bohr" was the epitome of the gruff noncommissioned officer who took care of his Marines. His death was met with sadness, shock, and anger. The third platoon commander, 2nd Lt. Nicholas Horton, took over navigation of the company and led the column out of the kill zone.

Alpha Company received word that Bravo and Charlie Companies had taken the palace, and Alpha was redirected to advance a mile north and capture the Shari Al-Imam Al-Azam mosque, another possible Hussein hiding place. With little time for elaborate plans and no intelligence they found the coordinates on a city map and mounted up.[8]

The mosque, a large walled compound, was only approachable from narrow streets barely wide enough for the armored vehicles to clear and requiring reduced speeds. As the column moved they were again engaged by AK-47 and RPG fire from doorways, windows, and rooftops. One tank accompanying Alpha was temporarily disabled by RPG fire and the street was too narrow for the tanks to traverse their guns. Enemy fire intensified and the Marines returned fire, but a number of Marines were wounded and the tracks began taking RPG hits. There was a danger that the Marines would be overwhelmed, and at least one Marine later compared it to a scene in the movie *Blackhawk Down*.

The Marines fought furiously, methodically returning fire. Lieutenant Horton directed suppressing fire and breached the mosque. Requesting the 2nd Platoon, he led both platoons in clearing the mosque, taking twenty prisoners, and capturing a cache of RPGs, small arms, and ammunition. Eventually, tank fire and the support of an A-10 Warthog aircraft proved superior, and enemy fire diminished, allowing the column to withdraw after almost four hours of continuous fighting. They left behind numerous enemy dead and wounded and one disabled track, at a cost of one Marine dead and twenty wounded. The battle would be recalled by its participants as one of the most intense close-range encounters of the war.[9]

Alpha Company returned to the now-secure palace and refitted. Organized resistance ended late in the afternoon of 12 April, but Saddam Hussein would not be located until 13 December 2003, hiding in a hole in a yard at Tikrit. In May 2003 1/5 returned home to Camp Pendleton, California, but returned to Iraq (February–July 2004 and February–September 2005) for Stability and Support Operations (SASO).

On 3 May 2004 Lori Bohr accepted her husband's posthumous Silver Star from Secretary of the Navy Gordon England at a ceremony at Marine

Corps Base (MCB) Camp Pendleton, California. Lieutenant Horton accepted his Silver Star on 28 July 2004.

ENDNOTES

1. Silver Star citation, GySgt. Jeffrey E. Bohr Jr., USMC, http://www.homeofheroes.com/valor2/SS/7_GWOT/citations_USMC.html.
2. Silver Star citation, 2nd Lt. Nicholas J. Horton, USMC, http://www.homeofheroes.com/valor2/SS/7_GWOT/citations_USMC.html.
3. Simon Jeffrey and Rebecca Allison, "U.S. Forces Occupy Palaces: Soldiers in Central Baghdad," *Guardian* (Manchester, UK) *Unlimited*, 7 April 2003.
4. Gordon Dillow and Mark Avery, "The Men of Alpha Company," *Orange County* (CA) *Register*, 20 November 2003.
5. "1st Battalion, 5th Marines History," http://www.i-mef.usmc.mil/DIV/5MAR/1BN/history.asp.
6. Dillow and Avery, "The Men of Alpha Company."
7. Sarah Strandberg, "Ossian Man Killed in Baghdad," *Decorah* (IA) *Newspapers*, 11 April 2003.
8. Dillow and Avery, "The Men of Alpha Company."
9. Ibid.

SSgt. Adam R. Sikes, USMC

*Platoon Sergeant, 1st Platoon, Golf Company, 2nd Battalion,
5th Marines, Regimental Combat Team 5, 1st Marine Division,
I Marine Expeditionary Force*

Battle of At Tarmiyah, Iraq
12 April 2003

The Silver Star is presented to Adam R. Sikes, Staff Sergeant, U.S. Marine Corps, for conspicuous gallantry and intrepidity in action against the enemy while serving as Platoon Sergeant, First Platoon, Company G, Second Battalion, Fifth Marines, Regimental combat Team 5, FIRST Marine Division, I Marine Expeditionary Force in support of Operation Iraqi Freedom on 12 April 2003. During the Battle of At Tarmiyah, Staff Sergeant Sikes' platoon was pinned down by heavy small arms and rocket-propelled grenade fire in the opening moments of the fight. Without orders, Staff Sergeant Sikes quickly rallied two of his squads and set them into position to suppress the enemy and prepare them to counterattack. With the squads in position, Staff Sergeant Sikes charged alone across seventy meters of fire-swept ground to close on the first enemy strongpoint, which he cleared with a grenade and rifle fire. Moving to the roof of a three-story building that was exposed to enemy fire, Staff Sergeant Sikes skillfully adjusted sixty-millimeter mortar rounds into nearby enemy positions. The rounds isolated the town from enemy reinforcement and decimated an enemy position in the nearby tree line. Upon learning that another squad had taken casualties, Staff Sergeant Sikes moved to their position. With wounded Marines in a small compound, cut off by the enemy, Staff Sergeant Sikes signaled an amphibious assault vehicle and directed their evacuation while under a hail of small arms and rocket-propelled grenade fire. By his bold leadership, wise judgment, and complete dedication to duty, Staff Sergeant Sikes reflected great credit upon himself and upheld the highest traditions of the Marine Corps and the United States Naval Service.[1]

Silver Star Citation

Cpl. Timothy C. Tardif, USMC

2nd Squad Leader, 1st Platoon, Golf Company, 2nd Battalion, 5th Marine
Regiment, 1st Marine Division, I Marine Expeditionary Force

The Silver Star is presented to Timothy C. Tardif, Corporal, U.S. Marine
Corps, for conspicuous gallantry and intrepidity in action against the enemy
as Second Squad Leader, First Platoon, Company G, Second Battalion, Fifth
Marine Regiment, FIRST Marine Division, I Marine Expeditionary Force in
support of Operation Iraqi Freedom on 12 April 2003. During the Battle of
At Tarmiyah, Corporal Tardif and his squad reinforced First Platoon, which
was pinned down in a violent enemy crossfire ambush. Immediately assessing the situation, Corporal Tardif directed Marines to return fire into enemy
positions in a town. He identified the location of the enemy and determined
the precise point to assault the enemy. Corporal Tardif charged across a road
under intense small arms and rocket-propelled grenade fire inspiring his
Marines to follow his example. Engaged in an intense close-quarters battle,
he received significant shrapnel wounds from an enemy grenade. Refusing to
be evacuated and disregarding his wounds, Corporal Tardif gallantly led his
squad in an assault on an enemy-held compound. After securing the compound, Corporal Tardif received an order to egress and he led his reinforced
squad in a fighting withdrawal. After moving one hundred fifty meters,
Corporal Tardif collapsed from his wounds, unable to continue fighting.
By his bold leadership, wise judgment, and complete dedication to duty,
Corporal Tardif reflected great credit upon himself and upheld the highest
traditions of the Marine Corps and the United States Naval Service.[2]

Silver Star Citation

> Retreat Hell! We just got here.
> *Captain Lloyd S. Williams, 5th Marines, to retreating French troops*
> *at Belleau Wood, France, 5 June 1918.*[3]

ON 12 APRIL 2003 Marines of 1st Platoon, Golf Company, 2nd Battalion,
5th Marine Regiment were on alert at the University of Baghdad, awaiting
a mission. The Marines had been using the university as an operational base
since entering the city.

The 2/5 Marines' long and distinguished history stretches back to 1 July
1914, when the battalion was activated to help restore order in the

Dominican Republic and Haiti. Active in every war since it saw service at Belleau Wood, the Argonne, Guadalcanal, Pelleliu, Okinawa, Inchon, Chosin Reservoir, Pusan, Hue, Operation Desert Storm, and Operation Iraqi Freedom. It is the most decorated battalion in the Marines, and its motto "Retreat Hell!" well represents its fighting spirit. Instrumental in the liberation of Kuwait, the battalion was among the first troops to cross into Iraq on 20 March 2003. Now, three weeks into the war, after steadily marching northward they were in Baghdad.[4]

That Saturday morning, SSgt. Adam R. Sikes was with the 1st Platoon when Capt. Myle Hammond, Golf Company commander, approached. Sikes, a twenty-seven-year-old native of Lake Zurich, Illinois, had been due to be discharged from the Marines that February but had cancelled plans to attend Georgetown University and reenlisted so he could deploy with his unit. Sikes had always wanted to be a Marine and see combat. "I knew I wanted to go into the Marine Corps because they had the whole mystique about them being the finest, the best. They were always the first ones in, they were the toughest and I wanted to be the basic infantry man. I went in specifically to be a frontline troop. When people think of the Marines, that's what they think of. They think of the guy walking down the street with the rifle. Whether it's a good idea or bad idea, I wanted to be in a fight. Maybe it was a test to prove myself. Maybe it was that young adult idea of doing something exciting. I don't know but that's what I wanted to do. I wanted to be a basic grunt."[5]

Enlisting in the Marines in July 1995 Sikes took boot camp at San Diego, California, followed by advanced infantry training, then Marine Security Guard School. In 1997 Sikes helped evacuate civilians from Albania, and served as a Marine Security Guard in Moscow and Lisbon. He was looking forward to getting out and pursuing a degree in International Relations. That was before 9/11. "When September 11th happened, the whole world changed. And I had done some real world operations and stuff like that. So I'd done the real deal, but not a war. That was the whole reason I had joined. You train and do this stuff all the time, you're getting ready for the inevitable. You don't know when it's coming, but you're just trying to get ready for it. So, ok, now it's coming. So I realized that this is what my grandfather had felt when the Japanese bombed Pearl Harbor and he joined the Navy. Our country was under attack. [I felt] I needed to go to Iraq because I'm a Marine and this is what we do."[6]

Echo and Fox Companies were east searching for prisoners of war (POWs), and Golf Company was on a road to the west in reserve. Battalion wanted to see if a bridge over the Tigris River could support tanks. Golf

Company (Gold 2/5) was ordered to check it out, and 1st Platoon was selected for the mission.

At Tarmiyah, a town approximately thirty kilometers northwest of Baghdad, is located on the west bank of the Tigris River. Its population of ten thousand consisted predominantly of Sunni Muslims loyal to Saddam Hussein. Many military, police, and government officials lived within its limits. Its one main street is intersected by numerous side streets, and the town was of strategic importance because it was the location of a site involved with the enrichment of uranium.[7]

As the four assault amphibious vehicles (AAVs, amtracs, or tracks), carrying three squads of the 1st Platoon as well as attached personnel (twenty-two men in each vehicle), approached At Tarmiyah, the men were struck by the disparity of the landscape. Unkempt high grass along the road bordered modern, high-income homes or clusters of walled-in primitive multistory brick structures.

Captain Hammond sent two AAVs (#201 and #203, carrying the 1st and 3rd Squads) forward and they crossed a bridge spanning the river and took positions on the far side of the bridge just outside the town, while the 2nd Squad and command track remained back in reserve. As the 1st and 3rd Squads' AAVs took up position, the 2nd Squad waited to cross. Cpl. Timothy Tardif, the twenty-two-year-old 2nd Squad leader, watched with his buddy, Cpl. Marco Martinez, the 1st Fire Team leader. Tardif, an Eagle Scout, had enlisted in the Marines in his junior year of high school, where he played football and rugby. He had entered the Marines following graduation. He was already a combat veteran of Afghanistan, and had married his fiancée, Alisha, just prior to deploying to Kuwait. One of the first units into Iraq, the 2/5 had captured the Rumaila oil field in Kuwait and southern Iraq and participated in the rescue of Pvt. Jessica Lynch. They saw action all the way to Baghdad and had been involved in the intense fighting around Baghdad University.[8]

At first, people and cars were everywhere, and there was calm for about ten minutes. Most of the Marines had already dismounted the tracks, some were on security, some were stretching, others were taking chow. "There were quite a few Iraqis, even a traffic jam. Then things changed. What set us off was that within a minute's time all the Iraqis and cars disappeared. This was our only indication that something was coming. I heard about five or six RPGs [rocket-propelled grenades] go off and AK-47 gunfire was everywhere. Two of the RPGs got direct hits on 3rd Squad's track. They'd been waiting for us." The enemy, estimated at company strength, greatly outnumbered the Marine platoon.[9]

One RPG hit the 3rd Squad's track, wounding the .50-caliber gunner in his turret, and seriously wounding the other two crew members. As Sikes recalled, "I have no idea how many came at us, but they were coming at us from all different directions. Two of 'em hit my track. [They] went through the nose of my track, basically through the headlights. Blew the heck out of it. Covered me in dust and smoke. I got peppered with stuff. . . . [We] couldn't cross back over the bridge because we would have been sitting ducks and, likewise, no one could cross over to us."[10] As Lieutenant Mauer, the platoon leader, tried to radio in a fire mission, Sikes began to organize the two squads. He had them take cover and return fire as he sought to locate the threat. Both sides exchanged heavy gunfire for about thirty minutes. Determining that a nearby three-story building posed the greatest threat, Sikes called out for covering fire. "I'm going to the three story building. I'm gonna mark it. Get the guns up."[11]

Charging across seventy meters of open terrain under intense small-arms and RPG fire Sikes entered the town and made it to the side of the building, then ignited a colored smoke canister to mark the location for air support. After using his grenades and rifle to neutralize the threat he went up to the exposed roof of the building to direct mortar fire in on enemy positions. He was alone for twenty to thirty minutes before being joined by an improvised squad. Together, they cleared another three buildings.

On the other side of the bridge 2nd Squad "buttoned-up" and crossed the river, taking a position to the right. They could hear rounds impacting the right side of their AAV, and could hear the whoosh of RPGs. Tardif recalled the terrain as "a built-up road with thick tall grass on either side" and could see muzzle flashes from the roofs of a cluster of seven houses to the right.[12] Unable to contact the platoon leader for direction Tardif made the decision to assault through and neutralize the threat. The tactical situation was less than promising. The houses were surrounded by eight-foot-high adobe walls that would have to be breached. There was little cover. Tardif and Martinez advanced through the grass and crossed the road looking for a position to set up the squad's shoulder-fired multipurpose assault weapon (SMAW), the Marine version of an RPG. The plan was to use the SMAW to blow open the fence and assault inside.

While they were setting up to assault the first house, an Iraqi popped up in the grass and lobbed a grenade. The grenade bounced off Tardif's leg, rolled down the berm, and detonated, knocking Tardif off his feet. His right shin and thigh were exposed to the bone, and he was bleeding profusely, but he had his men apply pressure bandages and refused to be evacuated. Martinez shot the grenade thrower and another man as they fled, then assumed command of the fifteen Marines.

At each house, one fire team would enter and neutralize the fighters inside, while the second fire team remained outside to watch over and kill anyone who followed them inside. At the first house, Martinez with three Marines killed fifteen Fedayeen fighters. One by one, they used the SMAW to blow open the four compounds, killing the insurgents inside. At the fourth compound, Martinez made a sole frontal assault using first a captured RPG, then his M-16 until it ran out of ammunition, and finally a grenade to neutralize a fortified position so that a wounded comrade, LCpl. Paul Gardner, could be safely evacuated. For his actions, Martinez would receive the Navy Cross. But draped over the shoulders of two Marines was Corporal Tardif, who continued to help direct the fighting. "There were about sixteen in each house. They were pretty well organized. We'd go in and they'd rush out the back. I sent a fire team behind the back of the houses to shoot them as they came out. That worked pretty well. We got a lot of kills that way."[13]

In the interim Lieutenant Mauer had advised Sikes that 2nd Squad had wounded, and directed him to respond to their area with the medical evacuation (medevac) track. Mauer wanted them to withdraw because he'd ordered an air strike to level the town. Sikes went forward with Private Levesque and Corporal Ross and made contact with the 2nd Squad. Sikes advised Tardif of the pullout, and Tardif led a fighting withdrawal until he passed out from loss of blood. An expeditious blood transfusion in an evacuation helicopter saved his life. An air strike ended the four and a half–hour battle. Sikes would later recall about Tardif, "He was the unstoppable warrior."[14]

The 2/5 would continue its advance north to Samara before the war ended. Tardif was evacuated to the Army's Regional Medical Center at Landstuhl, Germany, but he convinced a doctor to check him out, borrowed a utility uniform from a corpsman, and hitched a ride aboard an Air Force aircraft back to Iraq. He called his wife and told her, "Honey, I could come home right now, but I'm a Marine. And I have responsibilities. I'm a squad leader and my Marines need me. And I'm going to go back.[15]

On 3 May 2004 in a ceremony at Camp Pendleton, California, Secretary of the Navy Gordon England presented Sergeant Martinez with the Navy Cross, the first award since 1991, and Staff Sergeant Sikes and Corporal Tardif with Silver Stars. Additionally, he presented a posthumous Silver Star to the widow of GySgt. Jeffery E. Bohr Jr. for valor in a separate action.

Upon his return home Martinez left the Marine Corps to attend college. He plans on a degree in psychology and is considering returning to the

Marines as a commissioned officer. Sikes returned to Iraq for a second combat tour in August 2004 and was honorably discharged from the Marines in May 2005. He returned to Georgetown University to work on his degree in International Relations. He currently works at the USMC Center for Advanced Operational Culture Learning at Quantico, Virginia.

Sikes remembers the battle as the most intense firefight in which he ever fought. "We found out later that Saddam Hussein had been in Tarmiyah the previous day, and there were lots of hard-core Ba'athists and Fedayeen present. Maybe that's why they fought so hard."[16] But they were no match for the determined Marines.

At this writing, Tardif is back in Iraq for the third time, his fourth combat tour. Ask him, and he'll tell you he did nothing "heroic" that day. "I just wanted to take care of my squad. I didn't want to quit on them."[17]

ENDNOTES

1. Silver Star citation, SSgt. Adam R. Sikes, USMC, http://www.homeofheroes.com/valor2/ SS/7_GWOT/citations_USMC-M.html.
2. Silver Star citation, Cpl. Timothy C. Tardif, USMC, http://www.homeofheroes.com/valor2/ SS/7_GWOT/citations_USMC-M.html.
3. Robert D. Heinl, *Dictionary of Military and Naval Quotations* (Annapolis, MD: Naval Institute Press, 1967).
4. "2nd Battalion/5th Marines History," http://www.i-mef.usmc.mil/DIV/5MAR/2bn/history. asp.
5. Adam Sikes, telephone interview with Scott Baron, 25 June 2007.
6. Ibid.
7. Valentina Mite, "Iraq; In Town Loyal to Hussein, Residents Unscathed but Feeling the Effects of War," Radio Free Europe/Radio Liberty, 22 May 2003, http://www.globalsecurity. org/wmd/library/news/iraq/2003/05/iraq-030522-rfel-154718.htm.
8. Dr. Craig Bernthal, "No Better Friend, No Worse Enemy," *Private Papers*, 16 February 2005, www.victorhanson.com/articles/bernthal021605.html.
9. Sikes, telephone interview.
10. Ibid.
11. C. C. Kurzeja, "Silver Star," July 2, 2005, http://72.14.253.104/search?q=cache: NVg5IKIvl3sJ:flickaspumoni.blogspot.com/2005/07/silverstar.html+%22Adam+Sikes%22 +Marine&hl=en&ct=clnk&cd=31&gl=us.
12. Bernthal, "No Better Friend, No Worse Enemy."
13. Ibid.
14. Ibid.
15. Rudi Williams, "Marine Corps Commandant Tells Stories of Respect, Heroism," American Forces Press Service, 24 June 2004.
16. Sikes, telephone interview.
17. Laura Bailey, "Marines Awarded Some of Military's Highest Honors for Iraq Bravery," *Marine Corps Times*, 17 May 2004.

Cpl. John E. Place, USMC

Team Leader, Scout-Sniper Platoon, 2nd Battalion 1st Marines,
1st Marine Division, I Marine Expeditionary Force,
U.S. Marine Corps Forces, Central Command

Al-Fallujah, Iraq
18 March–26 April 2004, 18 June 2004

The President of the United States takes pleasure in presenting the Silver Star Medal to John Ethan Place, Corporal, U.S. Marine Corps, for conspicuous gallantry and intrepidity in action against the enemy while serving as Team Leader, Scout Sniper Platoon, Second Battalion, First Marines, FIRST Marine Division, I Marine Expeditionary Force, U.S. Marine Corps Forces, Central Command, Iraq, from March to April 2004 in support of Operation Iraqi Freedom II. On 18 March 2004 while conducting a key leader ride-along, Corporal Place's convoy was attacked by two insurgents. He immediately located and destroyed their position, which enabled the convoy to proceed unharmed. On 26 March 2004 while conducting security patrols, Corporal Place encountered two more insurgents and neutralized their position. During these actions, Corporal Place instilled confidence in his Marines with his calm, collected demeanor under intense combat conditions. On 7 April 2004 Corporal Place coordinated with another company and engaged and eliminated enemy forces while under intense enemy fire. From 11 to 24 April 2004, Corporal Place's keen observation skills ensured his supported rifle company maintained a lethal, long-range response to enemy attacks. On 26 April 2004 an enemy force attacked a company patrol four hundred meters away from friendly lines. Corporal Place disregarded his own safety and left the cover of his defensive position to close with and destroy the enemy. By his steadfast initiative, courageous actions, and exceptional dedication to duty, Corporal Place reflected great credit upon himself and upheld the highest traditions of the Marine Corps and the United States Naval Service.[1]

Silver Star Citation

OCCASIONALLY MEDALS ARE AWARDED for a series of acts over a period of time rather than for a single event. Rarely does an individual at war significantly affect the behavior of the entire enemy. Sgt. John E. Place, a twenty-one-year-old scout-sniper from St. Louis, Missouri, qualifies on both counts for his service in Iraq.

Place had deployed to Iraq in 2003 with Marines of 2/1, as part of the 15th Marine Expeditionary Unit during the initial invasion. As the Army and Marines crossed into Iraq from bases in the Kuwaiti desert in late March 2003, however, troops of the 2/1 went ashore from the USS *Tarawa* and the USS *Rushmore* at the Iraqi port of Umm Qasr. Along with British troops they secured the towns of Umm Qasr and Az Zubayr, before moving north into Al-Nasiriyah. They returned to the United States in June.[2]

He was on his second deployment to Iraq in March 2004, having arrived early in the month to replace the Army's 82nd Airborne in the volatile Al-Anbar region. Assigned as a team leader with the scout-sniper platoon of Echo Company 2/1 he led a sniper team through counterambush attacks and on security patrols. On one occasion, he coordinated fires with an adjoining infantry company and eliminated enemy fighters that threatened his battalion from extreme distances exceeding four hundred meters. By all accounts, he was the living definition of "one shot, one kill."

As noted in his Silver Star citation, when insurgents attacked his convoy while he was conducting a ride-along for key leaders on 18 March 2004, Place located and eliminated them. Again on 26 March two insurgents had the bad judgment to attack his security patrol. It was a fatal error for them!

During one engagement, Place used a corpsman as his spotter. "As a sniper you need a spotter to do your job correctly. My first spotter got shot in his hand, then one of the corpsman stepped up and took position as spotter—he did great things," Place said.[3]

On 7 April during the intense fighting in Al-Fallujah, Place was attached to another company that came under intense enemy fire, coolly dispatching his opponents one by one with his M-40A1 sniper rifle whose 7.62 round could kill or wound insurgents at a distance of one thousand yards. And on 28 April, Place, a hunter from his days as a child, left cover, heedless of his vulnerability from incoming fire, to engage insurgents with deadly accuracy.[4]

On 23 June 2005 at the Marine base at Camp Pendleton, California, 1st Marine Division Commander Gen. Richard Natonski presented newly promoted Sergeant Place with the Silver Star, noting, "He neutralized so many insurgents that Iraqi broadcasters in Iraq pleaded [with] the public to watch for snipers. . . . It's hard to believe an individual would have such an impact on a country."[5]

Place, who returned to Camp Pendleton, California, as a marksmanship instructor, still thinks a lot about his time in Iraq. "You make your peace with it," he said. "We lost a lot of good Marines over there."[6]

ENDNOTES

1. Silver Star citation, Cpl. John E. Place, USMC, http://www.homeofheroes.com/valor2/SS/7_ GWOT/citations_USMC-M.html.

2. Darrin Mortenson, "Marine Unit to Return to Iraq over Weekend," *North County* (San Diego, CA) *Times*, 27 February 2004.

3. Ray Lewis, "Scout-Sniper Honored with Silver Star," *Marine Corps News*, 30 June 2005 (Story ID #200563011057).

4. Ibid.

5. Ibid.

6. Ibid.

Sgt. Leandro F. Baptista, USMC

*Team Leader in 2nd Platoon, Bravo Company, 1st Reconnaissance Battalion,
1st Marine Division, I Marine Expeditionary Force, U.S. Marine Corps
Forces, Central Command*

Al-Fallujah, Iraq
7 April 2004

The President of the United States takes pleasure in presenting the Silver
Star Medal to Leandro F. Baptista, Sergeant, U.S. Marine Corps, for conspicuous gallantry and intrepidity in action against the enemy as a Team Leader
in Second Platoon, Company B, First Reconnaissance Battalion, FIRST
Marine Division, I Marine Expeditionary Force, U.S. Marine Corps Forces,
Central Command in support of Operation Iraqi Freedom on 7 April 2004.
In the Al Anbar Province, Iraq, sixty enemy combatants in fortified positions ambushed Sergeant Baptista's 25-man reconnaissance platoon, wounding six Marines and disabling two vehicles. When the attack commenced,
Sergeant Baptista immediately dismounted his vehicle and led his team to
flank the enemy positions. Avoiding enemy fire, Sergeant Baptista sprinted
across a shallow canal, climbed a ten-foot berm, and charged towards the
enemy. Drawing fire from enemy machine guns, he silenced one emplacement and then continued to press the enemy by hastily forming a three-
man assault team. With disregard for his own safety, he advanced over
another berm under heavy enemy fire. He disarmed an improvised explosive
device, and without hesitation, charged forward uncovering eleven enemy
combatants. He ferociously attacked the surprised enemy, single-handedly
eliminating four insurgents at close range while directing the fire of three
Marines against the remaining seven enemy insurgents. While under fire
from different enemy positions, Sergeant Baptista provided cover for his
team to withdraw safely. By his bold leadership, wise judgment, and complete dedication to duty, Sergeant Baptista reflected great credit upon himself and upheld the highest traditions of the Marine Corps and the United
States Naval Service.[1]

Silver Star Citation

Cpl. Jason M. Lilley, USMC

Rifleman, 2nd Platoon, Bravo Company, 1st Battalion, 5th Marines,
1st Marine Division, I Marine Expeditionary Force,
U.S. Marine Corps Forces, Central Command

The President of the United States takes pleasure in presenting the Silver Star Medal to Jason M. Lilley, Corporal, U.S. Marine Corps, for conspicuous gallantry and intrepidity in action against the enemy as a Rifleman, Second Platoon, Company B, First Battalion, Fifth Marines, FIRST Marine Division, I Marine Expeditionary Force, U.S. Marine Corps Forces, Central Command, in support of Operation Iraqi Freedom II on 7 April 2004. In the Al Anbar Province, Iraq, sixty enemy personnel in fortified positions ambushed Corporal Lilley's twenty-five-man reconnaissance platoon instantly wounding six Marines and disabling two vehicles. When his team executed immediate action to flank the enemy machine gun positions, Corporal Lilley dismounted his vehicle and, while under intense enemy machine gun and small arms fire charged forward across a shallow canal and up to a berm. After disposing two well-armed insurgents attempting to flee for cover, he was ordered to go back over the berm and support the withdrawal of another team. With disregard for his own safety and under withering enemy fire, he assaulted and single-handedly neutralized three more insurgents at point-blank range. The vigorous assault of his hastily formed three-man assault team accounted for the destruction of enemy forces, and saved the lives of six fellow Marines. By his bold leadership, wise judgment, and complete dedication to duty, Corporal Lilley reflected great credit upon himself and upheld the highest traditions of the Marine Corps and the United States Naval Service.[2]

Silver Star Citation

Sgt. Michael A. Mendoza, USMC

Bravo Company, 1st Reconnaissance Battalion, 1st Marine Division,
I Marine Expeditionary Force, U.S. Marine Corps Forces, Central Command

The President of the United States takes pleasure in presenting the Silver Star Medal to Michael A. Mendoza, Sergeant, U.S. Marine Corps, for conspicuous gallantry and intrepidity in action against the enemy while serving with Company B, First Reconnaissance Battalion, FIRST Marine Division, I Marine Expeditionary Force, U.S. Marine Corps Forces, Central Command, in support of Operation Iraqi Freedom. On 7 April 2004 Sergeant Mendoza's platoon was patrolling in the Al Anbar Province when ambushed by the enemy in well-fortified positions. After a rocket-propelled grenade disabled his vehicle, Sergeant Mendoza organized and led five Marines in a charge across an open field, up a ten-foot berm, and across a deep and muddy canal to firing positions within hand grenade range of the enemy. The vigor of this first assault eliminated ten insurgents, while forcing others to retreat. Observing that injured Marines were still under fire in the enemy zone, he continued the assault with complete disregard for his own personal safety. During this assault, his commander fell wounded at his side from an enemy combatant concealed in a nearby trench line who Sergeant Mendoza decisively engaged and neutralized. Unwilling to subject his comrades to further danger, he knelt in the open and signaled Marines to remain where they were while another attended to a wounded officer. Avoiding rocket and machine gun fire directed at him, Sergeant Mendoza held his position until an armored vehicle arrived to evacuate the wounded officer. By his bold leadership, wise judgment, and complete dedication to duty, Sergeant Mendoza reflected great credit upon himself and upheld the highest traditions of the Marine Corps and the United States Naval Service.[3]

Silver Star Citation

Cpl. Evan L. Stafford, USMC

Radio Operator, 2d Platoon, Bravo Company, 1st Reconnaissance Battalion, 1st Marine Division, I Marine Expeditionary Force, U.S. Marine Corps Forces, Central Command

The President of the United States takes pleasure in presenting the Silver Star Medal to Evan L. Stafford, Corporal, U.S. Marine Corps, for conspicuous gallantry and intrepidity in action against the enemy as a Radio Operator, 2d Platoon, Company B, First Reconnaissance Battalion, FIRST Marine Division, I Marine Expeditionary Force, U.S. Marine Corps Forces, Central Command, in support of Operation Iraqi Freedom, on 7 April 2004. In Al Anbar Province, Iraq, Corporal Stafford's platoon was on a patrol when sixty insurgents ambushed them from well-fortified positions. When his team executed immediate action to flank the enemy machine gun positions,

Corporal Stafford dismounted his vehicle and, while under enemy machine gun and small arms fire, charged forward across a shallow canal and up a berm. After silencing the first enemy position, he was ordered to go back over the berm and support the withdrawal of another team. With disregard for his own safety, he assaulted over the berm under withering enemy fire for a second time, and single-handedly neutralized two insurgents at point-blank range. As he pushed forward, he came upon another insurgent preparing to throw a hand grenade, and immediately warned his two teammates to take cover. The enemy grenade exploded without causing injury to his Marines. Corporal Stafford continued to lead the assault, and destroyed the enemy emplacement. Corporal Stafford's personal heroism, indomitable spirit, and heroic devotion to duty were an inspiration to those with whom he served. By his bold leadership, wise judgment, and complete dedication to duty, Corporal Stafford reflected great credit upon himself and upheld the highest traditions of the Marine Corps and the United States Naval Service.[4]

Silver Star Citation

GySgt. Nicholas A. Popaditch, USMC

Tank Platoon Sergeant, 1st Platoon, Charlie Company,
1st Tank Battalion, 2nd Battalion, 1st Marine Regiment,
1st Marine Division, I Marine Expeditionary Force

The President of the United States takes pleasure in presenting the Silver Star Medal to Nicholas A. Popaditch, Gunnery Sergeant, U.S. Marine Corps, for conspicuous gallantry and intrepidity in action against the enemy while serving as Tank Platoon Sergeant, First Platoon, Company C, First Tank Battalion, Second Battalion, First Marine Regiment, FIRST Marine Division, I Marine Expeditionary Force, in support of Operation Iraqi Freedom from 6 to 7 April 2004. While on patrol in the city of Al Fallujah, Iraq, Fox Company came under heavy enemy fire and without hesitation, Gunnery Sergeant Popaditch surged his two tanks into the city to support the Marines under fire. He led his tank section several blocks into the city, drawing enemy fire away from the beleaguered Marines. His decisive actions enabled Fox Company to gain a foothold into the city and evacuate a critically wounded Marine. For several hours, enemy forces engaged his tank section with withering rocket-propelled grenade fire until they were destroyed by accurate machine gun fire.

Acting as the forward observer for an AC-130 gunship, Gunnery Sergeant Popaditch directed fire onto enemy targets effecting their annihilation. With complete disregard for his personal safety, he moved his tank forward to draw the enemy from their covered and concealed positions allowing the AC-130 to engage them. On the morning of 7 April Gunnery Sergeant Popaditch was severely wounded by a rocket-propelled grenade blast while fighting insurgents. Blinded and deafened by the blast, he remained calm and ordered his crew to a medical evacuation site. By his bold leadership, wise judgment, and complete dedication to duty, Gunnery Sergeant Popaditch reflected great credit upon himself and upheld the highest traditions of the Marine Corps and the United States Naval Service.[5]

Silver Star Citation

ON 31 MARCH 2004 insurgents in the city of Al-Fallujah ambushed a convoy of vehicles carrying food supplies. Four armed Americans contracted by Blackwater USA, a private security contractor, were dragged from their vehicle, beaten, and set on fire. Their charred corpses were dragged along the street, following which their remains were hung from the Fallujh Bridge. Photographs of jeering Iraqis desecrating the remains outraged the world, and U.S. military commanders began plans for Operation Vigilant Resolve, a military operation to occupy Al-Fallujah and clear the city of all armed militias. Offensive operations began on the evening of 4 April, when two thousand Marines of the I Marine Expeditionary Force (1 MEF) launched assaults to reestablish security in Al-Fallujah.

Located in the heart of the Sunni Triangle within the Al-Anbar Province of Iraq, Al-Fallujah dates back to Babylonian times. Part of the Ottoman Empire, it was acquired by Britain following the end of World War I, and was the site of an unsuccessful uprising against the British on 12 August 1920. Granted independence in 1932, Iraq was again invaded by Britain in 1941 when it appeared to ally itself with Nazi Germany, and Al-Fallujah was again the site of the Iraqi Army's defeat.[6]

Al-Fallujah was a power base for the Ba'ath Party during the reign of Saddam Hussein, and it was a center of Sunni support for Hussein's government. Known as the City of Mosques, it had a preinvasion population of three hundred fifty thousand, and was largely untouched during the March 2003 invasion. Ironically, the city was almost destroyed by the lawlessness and looting that followed the collapse of the Hussein regime. Order was restored with the arrival of the 82nd Airborne Division on 23 April 2003, but was short lived: a demonstration by Iraqis over U.S. troops' use of a school as a base of operations on 28 April resulted in fifteen Iraqis killed and another fifty-two wounded. Three more were killed in a similar demonstration two days later.[7]

Over the next year Al-Fallujah was the site of numerous acts of defiance against the new Coalition government with frequent attacks on convoys, police stations, and patrols. A convoy carrying senior commander Gen. John Abizaid was attacked on 12 February 2004. In March 2004 prior to the ambush on 31 March, the 82nd Airborne transferred authority over the Al-Anbar Province to the 1 MEF, comprising the 1st Marine Division, 3rd Marine Aircraft Wing, and 1st Marine Logistics Group.

Seven Navy Crosses and thirty Silver Stars would be awarded for combat in Al-Fallujah between 2004 and 2007. Two of those Navy Crosses and five Silver Stars would be awarded for actions that occurred on 7 April 2004.

That hot and sunny April morning twenty-five Marines of 2nd Platoon, Bravo Company, 1st Reconnaissance Battalion (1st Recon), 1st Marine Division, under the command of Capt. Brent Morel, were in the five lead Humvees of a convoy, escorting fifteen Humvees and seven-ton trucks on a resupply mission to a forward operating base (FOB) located along Route Boston. Once complete, they would break off and hunt for enemy mortar teams.[8]

Unlike their captain, many of the men were already combat veterans of Iraqi Freedom I, and all were volunteers, first to the Marines, then to the infantry, and finally for reconnaissance training. Considered the elite of the Corps and equal to Army Special Forces, Navy SEALS (Naval Special Warfare Combat Advisory Element), and Air Force Pararescue, Reconnaissance Marines receive advanced marksmanship and small-unit training, and can attend a variety of specialized schools (airborne, combat diver, SERE [survival, evasion, resistance, escape], Pathfinder, sniper, and others). Their primary mission is to "plan, coordinate, and conduct amphibious reconnaissance, ground reconnaissance and surveillance to observe, identify, and report enemy activity, and collect other information of military significance."[9]

The history of the 1st Recon dates back to Guadalcanal. It also participated in Operation Desert Storm, but was deactivated in 1992. It was reactivated by the Commandant of the Marine Corps (CMC), Gen. James L. Jones on 5 July 2000 to revitalize Marine Corps reconnaissance. The battalion was deployed to Iraq and arrived at the Udairi Range in Kuwait on 28 February 2004 for two weeks of training prior to movement to their area of operation (AO). The advance party deployed to FOB Al-Fallujah on

7 and 10 March 2004, with the battalion arriving in Al-Fallujah and com-
mencing operations on 16 March.[10]

It was about 4:00 PM and Cpl. James Wright in the lead Humvee
looked out on fields bisected by palm trees and irrigation canals. Later,
he remembered thinking that the terrain was ideal for an ambush. The
road was elevated and exposed and bordered on both sides by a series of
chest-high earthen walls, which were bordered by ditches that ran parallel to the road. In addition, the neighborhood was known to be unfriendly.
Suddenly a rocket-propelled grenade (RPG) struck the door where Wright
sat, wounding all five Marines inside and disabling the vehicle. Despite having lost both hands, Wright remained conscious and calm, directing his
Marines in applying a tourniquet, then acting as a spotter in identifying
enemy positions. Cpl. Shawn Talbert, standing behind Wright at the roof
machine gun was riddled below the knees with shrapnel, and the team
leader, Sgt. Eric Kochner, had had his right arm and elbow shattered. The
driver replaced Talbert at the roof gun, and Kochner drove the crippled
vehicle out of the kill zone.[11]

Approximately forty to sixty insurgents had opened up on the convoy from fortified positions with mortars, RPGs, and machine guns. The
two lead Humvees took the brunt of the attack. The platoon commander,
Captain Morel, was in the second vehicle in company with Sgt. Willie
Copeland and Sgt. Michael A. Mendoza. Morel ordered his vehicle to take a
position between the convoy and the insurgents, but the vehicle was swiftly
disabled by heavy machine-gun and mortar fire. Concurrently, GySgt. Dan
Griego ordered two trailing Humvees up a dirt road to flank the insurgent
positions. With those Marines was Sgt. Leandro Baptista. His expectation
was that Morel's element would set up a base of fire while his element
would roll the flank of the enemy's primary positions.[12]

Caught in the kill zone Morel chose to advance on the enemy, followed
by Copeland, Mendoza, Sgt. Dan Lalota, and LCpl. Maurice Scott, with the
intention of assaulting through the ambush. Under heavy fire Morel and
his Marines fought their way across open fields, over ten-foot berms, and
through a chest-high canal, engaging the enemy at close range with grenades and rifle fire. They engaged one position, killing ten insurgents, then
continued to advance to reach the last berm. Pausing momentarily, Morel
said, "Cover me. We're assaulting through." When Lalota asked, "You want
us to assault through?" Morel confirmed, and Lalota said, "Roger that."[13]

As Morel crested that last obstacle, he was struck by enemy fire. The
round entered his left armpit and punctured both lungs. Mendoza was
knocked off his feet by an RPG explosion and went down, but recovered to

kill Morel's attacker. Scott, a former Army Ranger, reached Morel first, and dragged him to a shallow, eighteen-inch culvert, the only available cover. Then while Scott and Mendoza worked on the wounded officer, Copeland and Lalota returned suppressing fire, all the time in the open and under fire. For their actions, Morel and Copeland would be awarded the Navy Cross, Morel's posthumously, and Mendoza the Silver Star.

Cpl. Evan L. Stafford and Cpl. Jason M. Lilley had also advanced across the canal and assaulted over the berm to kill two insurgents in a fortified position. Both were combat veterans, having deployed to Iraq for the invasion in 2003. Ordered back over the berm to support the withdrawal of another team, they again assaulted over the berm to kill three additional insurgents at close range, one preparing to throw a hand grenade at other Marines. Like Mendoza, Stafford and Lilley were awarded Silver Stars for their actions.

At about this time Baptista had advanced on the enemy and knocked out a gun emplacement, then with three other Marines maneuvered along the insurgents' main line of fire; there were approximately thirty insurgents in dug-in positions. Outnumbered but undeterred, Baptista led his team forward, first assaulting and eliminating eleven insurgents concealed in some bushes. Baptista, a trained sniper, was credited with five kills. He also disarmed an improvised explosive device (IED) as the team came under fire.[14]

Griego, also a sniper, was busy eliminating four insurgents and disabling two vehicles. Surprised by Morel's rapid, aggressive assault, and fearing a deadly crossfire, Griego recalled Baptista, who provided covering fire as his Marines withdrew.

Copeland, Mendoza, and the others remained with Morel in the open until he could be evacuated (medevaced) in an armored Humvee. Then, supported by two Super-Cobra helicopters and reinforced by a quick reaction force (QRF) from 3rd Platoon, Bravo Company, Griego, now in command, oversaw the elimination of the remaining insurgents. Ultimately, thirty insurgents were killed in an action that cost one Marine, Captain Morel. The Marines of 1st Recon proved that even ambushed by an entrenched enemy twice its size, determined Marines could seize the day and prevail.[15]

Elsewhere in Al-Fallujah that April morning two M1A1 Abrams tanks of 1st Platoon, Charlie Company, 1st Tank Battalion battled in the northwest section of the city, in support of Fox Company, 2/1 Marines. In the cupola of Charlie 1-4, codenamed Red-4 but named Bone Crusher by her crew, sat GySgt. Nicholas A. Popaditch, the platoon sergeant and tank commander. His gunner, Cpl. Ryan Chambers, his loader, LCpl. Alex Hernandez, and the driver, LCpl. Christopher Frias, all anxious to see action, were getting their fill. Protecting his flank was Sgt. Herierto Escamilla in Red-3.[16]

The 1st Tank had arrived in Al-Fallujah and taken over from the Army in mid-March, and there had been only light contacts with the insurgents. Popaditch's platoon had just returned from a three-day mission and had been looking forward to some rest when news of the attack at the Fallujah Bridge and the desecrations reached his crew while they were eating chow. Back only an hour, they were ordered to prepare to move out.

The first couple of days of the offensive were uneventful with his tanks performing mostly reconnaissance and probing missions, coming into light contact with the insurgents. The morning of 6 April orders arrived to support Fox Company, which had had contact with the insurgents the previous night. Now, despite insurgent threats to "turn Fallujah into a graveyard for Americans,"[17] Popaditch and his Marines were hoping for an opportunity to fight the insurgents, who had so far been elusive.

Popaditch was no stranger to combat. A native of Hammond, Indiana, who had enlisted in the Marines on 6 May 1986, he went to tanks following boot camp in San Diego, California. Except for a three-year assignment as a drill instructor, that is where he had remained. He deployed to Kuwait with Bravo Company, 1st Tank Battalion during the Gulf War, returning to marry his fiancée on 9 April 1991. He again deployed to Iraq with Bravo Company for Operation Iraqi Freedom in March 2003.

On his twelfth wedding anniversary, 9 April 2003, Popaditch earned international attention when his photograph appeared on the front page of the world's newspapers. Weeks earlier, Popaditch and his tanks had rolled into Iraq from Kuwait and had battled their way north to Baghdad, in support of the 3rd Battalion 4th Marines. Now, as he sat in the cupola of his tank Carnivore, parked in Paradise Square, he watched as jubilant Iraqis toppled a forty-foot statue of Saddam Hussein. The Associated Press photo depicted Popaditch enjoying a cigar as the statue fell in the background, and the photo came to symbolize the liberation of Baghdad. It also earned Popaditch the sobriquet "Cigar Marine."

Popaditch and Bravo Company returned to the United States aboard the USS *Boxer* (LHD-4) at the end of their deployment, arriving at Camp Pendleton, California, on 25 July 2003. He soon volunteered to redeploy back to Iraq in September 2003 with a different tank company. He had been outraged by the insurgents' desecration of the bodies of American contractors on 31 March 2004, and was anxious for an opportunity to go after those responsible. In early April his section of two tanks was positioned in the center of a defensive line facing buildings on the outskirts of

Al-Fallujah. Despite almost thirty-six hours of constant operation, he felt the intensity and motivation of his Marines.[18]

At about midday on 6 April one of Fox Company's security patrols was ambushed, taking a casualty. They took cover, returned fire, and called for support. After consulting with Fox Company's Commander, the order was given, "Roll tanks." The two tanks, Popaditch in the lead and Escamilla covering the flank, passed through the patrol and advanced into the city, supported by infantry from Fox Company's 2nd Platoon. Eager to engage the enemy, Popaditch sometimes outpaced his infantry support as he sought an enemy as eager to engage him as he was them. "There was no reason or coordination to their attacks. They would pop out of buildings or doorways and take a shot at my tank. Usually their RPG shot wouldn't hit, but always my tank machine guns or main gun would!"[19]

Block by block, they worked their way into the city, the infantry working along the rooftops, directing the tank's fire onto targets and providing overwatch. Although hit by RPG rounds twice without damage, the tanks spread carnage on any insurgent foolish enough to attack two sixty-eight-ton Marine Main Battle Tanks. When targets failed to present themselves, Popaditch would put his tank in reverse, feigning a withdrawal. Unable to resist the temptation of one last shot at the retreating machines, the insurgents would expose themselves, usually resulting in their deaths. By late afternoon, ammunition, and fuel were becoming a concern.[20]

They continued to advance along the narrow streets, penetrating farther into the city than any other unit, which Popaditch saw as a good thing. "With no friendly units to the left or right or ahead, there was no need to deconflict fire before I shot," he recalled.[21] Two blocks to the front, Popaditch saw the way blocked by two telephone poles across the entrance to a courtyard. Power lines were strung between the poles, possibly electrified, and there were several sandbagged firing positions within the courtyard. His main gun soon eliminated any threat from the sandbagged positions, but a radio call confirmed that there were no engineering assets available to remove the poles and power lines. Popaditch, his advance stalled, considered his options.

There was an unblocked alley to the right, but there was a fuel tanker truck trailer parked down the alley, and Popaditch suspected this was the route the insurgents wanted him to take. He was too low on main gun ammunition to attempt to knock down the telephone poles, which would be partially successful at best, and could have disastrous consequences. Then another option presented itself.

An AC-130 gunship came on station after dark, and Popaditch drove within one hundred meters of the obstacles (telephone poles, power lines, and tanker truck) to mark them for the gunship, which soon reduced both to rubble. The resulting explosion confirmed Popaditch's suspicions. Leaving the infantry secured in two buildings, the tanks and gunship continued operations throughout the night and into the morning of 7 April, inflicting heavy casualties on the enemy. "The insurgents had very poor night vision and could easily be caught in the open at night. Due to the rotor wash of the gunship, they often didn't hear the tank coming until the first burst of my machine guns."[22]

At 4:00 AM their ammunition almost completely exhausted, the two tanks withdrew to where the infantry was entrenched to await resupply. Popaditch and his crew hunkered down to get some sleep, but their rest was disturbed when infantry on the roof killed three insurgents trying to infiltrate up to the tank.

An hour after dawn, ammunition was resupplied when Marines arrived on foot in pairs, carrying ammo crates between them. The volume of RPG fire in the area made resupply by truck hazardous, and by fuel tanker suicidal. The plan was to resupply the other two tanks in the platoon, then have them relieve Popaditch's section, so they could upload ammo and fuel safely in the rear. In the interim, Popaditch's Marines assumed a defensive posture. "The enemy in Fallujah had the ability to move unarmed as a civilian and conduct reconnaissance . . . the urban environment allowed the enemy the opportunity to get very close to you before he had to commit . . . all you can do is present a tough target."[23]

Like the previous day, insurgents made sporadic attacks on the Marines, now in a defensive position, and the tanks took several RPG hits without damage. Popaditch's relief was delayed when the platoon commander's tank threw a track outside the city. Then a Marine on a rooftop advised that insurgents were massing about three blocks ahead. All were military-aged males and armed with AK-47s. The order was given—"Go get 'em," and Popaditch's tanks sped forward, leaving the infantry behind as they raced the three blocks and caught the insurgents in the open where they had assembled in front of a mosque.

Half tried to flee into the mosque and were cut down, while the others fled around a corner and down a narrow street. Torn between remaining and securing the mosque—almost certainly a staging area and weapons stockpile—or pursuing the insurgents, Popaditch made an easy choice. "I didn't want to give them a chance to dig in and defend so I kept up the pursuit. The street got narrower as we went down it. Soon I could no longer traverse my tank's turret, but I still had two machine guns so I continued."[24]

Passing a small crossroad which was about eight feet wide, Popaditch scanned to his right in time to see an insurgent fire an RPG at the tank from fifty feet away. The rocket hit the side of the turret without any damage. As he swung his .50-caliber over, a second RPG struck his helmet. There was a bright flash of light, then darkness. "I'd been blinded in both eyes and it felt like I'd been hit in the head with a sledgehammer."[25] Not only blinded in both eyes, he lost his hearing and was bleeding heavily from shrapnel wounds. Hernandez was wounded in the left hand, Chambers in the left tricep.

Popaditch's Silver Star citation credits him with "remaining calm as he directed the tank to a medical evacuation site." Popaditch credits his crew. "Corporal Chambers got the tank moving, but he didn't know where we were at. Lance Corporal Hernandez, because of his position up top manning a machine gun, knew the way back, and directed Chambers which way to go. Hernandez' hand was bleeding profusely and he had to drop down to apply a pressure bandage. . . . Lance Corporal Frias took over the direction of the tank. . . . There would be no medevac to where we were at, so my tank had to return to the Fox Company defensive line and Frias knew the way."[26]

Stabilized by corpsmen under mortar fire at Fox Company's position, Popaditch was transported to a surgical unit by Humvee where the remainder of his right eye was removed, then flown to the Landstuhl Regional Medical Center in Germany, arriving less than thirty-six hours after being injured in Iraq. Further medical care would be provided at the Walter Reed Medical Center in Washington, DC, and the Balboa Naval Medical Center at San Diego, California.[27]

Despite a strong desire to remain with the Corps, his injuries proved too extensive, and Gunnery Sergeant Popaditch was honorably discharged from the Marines on 30 June 2005. On 9 November that year, at the Marine Corps' 230th Birthday Ball held at the Marine Corps Air Ground Combat Center at Twentynine Palms, California, Popaditch was awarded the Silver Star for his actions in Al-Fallujah.

He is currently attending university classes to become a teacher. "I never planned to be a teacher. I expected my career in the Marines to last a bit longer. But I'm beginning to get fired up! Platoon Sergeants do a lot of teaching. The important thing to me is to be doing something that counts, something that matters."[28]

On 3 June 2005 Leandro Baptista, now a civilian, was presented his Silver Star by Gen. Richard Natonski, commander of the 1st Marine Division, in a ceremony at Camp Pendleton, California. Now employed by the Glendale California Police Department, Baptista stated, "I really didn't want to make a big thing out of this. Everybody out there should be recognized. Everybody did their part."[29]

On 17 June 2005 Cpl. Jason M. Lilley was presented the Silver Star in a ceremony at Veterans Memorial Park in Wichita, Kansas. Regarding his award he stated, "I just did my job, did what was asked of me, what anyone else would have done in the same situation."[30] His teammate, Cpl. Evan L. Stafford, accepted his medal in a quiet ceremony held in Tampa, Florida, on 8 November 2005.

Sergeant Mendoza was awarded the Silver Star on 9 August 2005 by Maj. Gen. Douglas O'Dell Jr. at the headquarters of 2/24th Marines near his home in Tinely Park, Illinois. Reflecting on his medal, he stated, "I think about my captain a lot, and wish he were still with us. I'd trade my medal in a second to have him back."[31]

Mendoza returned to Iraq for a third deployment, this time as a staff sergeant and Team Chief of a sniper team with 2nd Battalion, 8th Marines. On 3 August 2006 in the city of Karhma, just north of Al-Fallujah, Mendoza was commanding a five-person team when a grenade was thrown into their position. "It was a Hell of a fight. . . . (A) grenade exploded about ten meters from me and hit me under the armpit, the same spot where [Capt.] Brent Morel was hit. I lost my spleen, collapsed both lungs, ruptured my diaphragm and it peppered my stomach and small intestines."[32] Despite his injuries, Mendoza remained in command, radioing for assistance and a medevac, safely withdrawing his team. Discharged from the Marines following the completion of his second enlistment, Mendoza is currently in Iraq for the fourth time, this time as a personal protection specialist (PPS) agent for the State Department. He said he would do it all again, because his Marine brothers would do the same for him.[33]

ENDNOTES

1. Silver Star citation, Sgt. Leandro F. Baptista, USMC. http://www.homeofheroes.com/valor2/SS/7_GWOT/citations_USMC.html.

2. Silver Star citation, Cpl. Jason M. Lilley, USMC. http://www.homeofheroes.com/valor2/SS/7_GWOT/citations_USMC.html.

3. Silver Star citation, Sgt. Michael A. Mendoza, USMC. http://www.homeofheroes.com/valor2/SS/7_GWOT/citations_USMC-M.html.

4. Silver Star citation, Cpl. Evan L. Stafford, USMC. http://www.homeofheroes.com/valor2/SS/7_GWOT/citations_USMC-M.html.

5. Silver Star citation, GySgt. Nicholas A. Popaditch, USMC. http://www.homeofheroes.com/valor2/SS/7_GWOT/citations_USMC-M.html.

6. N. N. E. Bray, *A Paladin of Arabia: The Biography of Brevet Lieut. Col. G. E. Leachman* (London: Unicorn Press, 1936).

7. "Iraqis in Deadly Clash with U.S. Troops," CNN.COM-World, 29 April 2003.

8. Laura Bailey, "Honored with a Bronze Star, Cpl. James Wright Sets His Sights on Healing," *Marine Corps Times*, June 2004.

9. "1st Reconnaissance Battalion," http://www.i-mef.usmc.mil/DIV/1ReconBn/.

10. *Situation Report* 11, no. 1 (Official Newsletter of the 1st Reconnaissance Battalion Association), May 2004.

11. MSgt. James "Eddie" Wright, "In His Own Words," www.Blackfive.Net/main/2005/11/marine_sergeant.html, 19 November 2005.

12. Owen West, "Leadership from the Rear: Proof that Combat Leadership Knows No Traditional Boundaries," *Marine Corps Gazette*, 1 September 2005.

13. Owen West, "Why Would Anyone Volunteer to Be an Infantryman?" *Slate Magazine,* 30 July 2004, http://www.slate.com/id/2104305/entry/2104546/.

14. Matt Zeigler, *Three Block War II: Snipers in the Sky!* (Lincoln, NE: Universe Press, 2006), 162–64.

15. Ibid.

16. Nicholas Popaditch, telephone interview with Scott Baron, 24 September 2007.

17. Matthew C. Burden, *The Blog of War: Front-Line Dispatches in Iraq and Afghanistan* (New York: Simon and Schuster, 2006).

18. Nicholas Popaditch, "Fallujah Fight: In the Words of the Cigar Marine," http://www.leatherneck.com/forums/showthread.php?t=20876.

19. Popaditch, telephone interview.

20. Popaditch, "Fallujah Fight."

21. Popaditch, telephone interview.

22. Ibid.

23. Popaditch, "Fallujah Fight."

24. Popaditch, telephone interview.

25. Ibid.

26. Ibid.

27. Chelsea Carter, "Nick Popaditch Lit Up to Mark the Fall of Baghdad, as Well as his 12th Wedding Anniversary," Associated Press, 10 April 2005.

28. Nicholas Popaditch, telephone interview with Scott Baron, 28 September 2007.

29. Darrin Mortenson, "Marine Sergeant Awarded Silver Star for Charge in Fallujah," *North County* (San Diego, CA) *Times*, 3 June 2005.

30. James Watkins, "The Dogs of War," www.commonties.com/blog/2007/01/23/the-dogs-of-war/.

31. Mike Mendoza, telephone interview with Scott Baron, 4 October 2007.

32. Ibid.

33. Ibid.

Sgt. Maj. James E. Booker, USMC

*Battalion Sergeant Major, 2nd Battalion, 4th Marines,
1st Marine Division, I Marine Expeditionary Force*

Battle for Ar Ramadi, Iraq
6–10 April 2004

Sergeant Major Booker courageously exposed himself to enemy fire while leading Marines and eliminating enemy forces in several battalion engagements. On 31 March 2004 the forward command element came under intense machine gun and rocket-propelled grenade (RPG) fire. With utter disregard for his own safety, Sergeant Major Booker dismounted the vehicle, engaged the enemy and forced their withdrawal. He pursued his attackers down several darkened city streets and mortally wounded a rocket-propelled grenade gunner who was engaging the Command Group. Sergeant Major Booker subsequently led a search that resulted in the arrest and capture of an eight-man cell and several weapons. On 10 April 2004 the forward command element came under fire from insurgents during cordon and search operations. He calmly led a team of Marines in a counterattack, personally clearing several buildings, eliminating one insurgent fighter, and facilitating the evacuation of a severely wounded Marine. Sergeant Major Booker's efforts enabled the forward command element to regain freedom of maneuver and inspired Marines to fearlessly engage the enemy.[1]

Silver Star Citation

Capt. Christopher J. Bronzi, USMC

*Commanding Officer, Golf Company, 2nd Battalion, 4th Marines,
1st Marine Division, I Marine Expeditionary Force*

During heavy fighting in southern Ar Ramadi, Iraq, Captain Bronzi repeatedly exposed himself to intense small arms and rocket-propelled grenade (RPG) fire while personally destroying several enemy fighting positions. His heroic actions led to the elimination of two hundred fifty insurgents during the two-day period. His selflessness and bravery inspired his Marines to engage and destroy an enemy focused on the destruction of coalition forces in the capital city of the Al Anbar province. During a period of extremely heavy fighting on 6 April, Captain Bronzi led a fire team of Marines into the middle of a fire swept street in order to recover the body of a fallen comrade. On 7 April Captain Bronzi and Third Squad, Fourth Platoon, were surrounded and forced to take cover in a nearby building. Isolated and outnumbered, Captain Bronzi moved to the roof in order to best position himself to command and control the Marines of Golf Company, and while under heavy enemy fire coordinated a link-up of his Second and Fourth Platoons. He then led the embattled squad to the designated rendezvous point and eventually to the safety of the company fire base, eradicating the enemy in the process.[2]

Silver Star Citation

2nd Lt. Thomas E. Cogan IV, USMC

Third Platoon Commander, Echo Company, 2nd Battalion, 4th Marines,
1st Marine Division, I Marine Expeditionary Force

On 6 April 2004, Second Platoon was ambushed by enemy forces while moving to reinforce a heavily engaged unit. With total disregard for his own personal safety, Second Lieutenant Cogan led his platoon across a fire-swept field and directed fire, which destroyed insurgent strongholds. On 10 April 2004 while conducting a sweep of suspected insurgent houses, his platoon and the company command element came under withering enemy fire. Though caught in the crossfire, he exposed himself to direct fire in order to cross an open field and position himself to direct fires on the enemy. His actions enabled the company command element to move to safety. After consolidating his platoon, Second Lieutenant Cogan led his men through a fierce, three-hour, house-to-house assault that destroyed remaining enemy forces in his zone of action.[3]

Silver Star Citation

Maj. John D. Harrill III, USMC

Operations Officer, 2nd Battalion, 4th Marine Regiment,
1st Marine Division, I Marine Expeditionary Force

Throughout enemy attacks and offensive operations, he calmly led the battalion command element and coordinated maneuver of the battalion's combat units, while personally neutralizing enemy automatic weapon and rocket-propelled grenade (RPG) fire, resulting in the enemy's defeat. During a major insurgent attack against coalition forces, Major Harrill led the forward command element into the aim point of the enemy attack. Despite constant enemy fire, he focused the combat power of six companies as they battled in eight separate locations over a seven-hour period. Major Harrill's superior tactical acumen enabled the complete destruction of assaulting enemy forces.[4]

Silver Star Citation

Cpl. Eric M. Smith, USMC

Squad Leader, 2nd Platoon, Echo Company, 2nd Battalion,
4th Marine Regiment, 1st Marine Division, I Marine Expeditionary Force

As part of the company's quick reaction force, Corporal Smith's platoon was ordered to move north and reinforce a squad which was under attack. En route, two high-mobility multipurpose-wheeled vehicles were ambushed leaving the platoon commander critically wounded. Under heavy machine gun and rocket-propelled grenade (RPG) fire, Corporal Smith assumed command of the platoon, and led them fifty meters across open ground to covered positions. He then ran back across the fire-swept field to evacuate his platoon commander and his weapons. Employing machine guns and the platoon's seven-ton truck, Corporal Smith coordinated and led a counterattack against the insurgent forces and freed the isolated squad. He coordinated with an Army Bradley Fighting Vehicle Platoon upon their arrival, facilitated the evacuation of casualties and devised the withdrawal plan for all units back to the command post.[5]

Silver Star Citation

Capt. Robert S. Weiler, USMC

Commanding Officer, Weapons Company, 2nd Battalion, 4th Marines,
1st Marine Division, I Marine Expeditionary Force

On 6 April, Captain Weiler led elements of Weapons Company against an enemy force that was attempting to isolate and destroy a squad-sized element of Echo Company. As the column moved east along Route Nova, they were ambushed by enemy forces. Despite the barrage of intense enemy fire, Captain Weiler calmly directed the tactical employment of the unit, leading to relief of the embattled squad and the destruction of the besieging enemy. On 7 April he led the company on a mission to reinforce a unit in contact. As they moved northeast along Route Apple, the column encountered heavy rocket-propelled grenade (RPG) and automatic weapons fire. During the ensuing three-hour firefight, he repeatedly exposed himself to enemy fire to direct the unit's counterattack, personally leading squads as they assaulted enemy firing positions. His courage and leadership were further displayed during Operation Bug Hunt. Heavily engaged by enemy forces over a four-hour period, Captain Weiler continued to fearlessly lead Marines as they destroyed a tenacious enemy.[6]

Silver Star Citation

ON 6 APRIL 2004, in response to Operation Vigilant Resolve—a Coalition offensive that had begun in Al-Fallujah two days earlier—insurgents staged a counteroffensive in Ar Ramadi, the capital of the Al-Anbar Province, hoping to relieve pressure in Al-Fallujah.

A city of approximately four hundred fifty thousand in April 2004, Ar Ramadi is bordered by the Euphrates River to its north and west; its suburbs stretch east and west. With a predominantly Sunni Muslim population, it had been a power base for Saddam Hussein before the war, and was the site of his "Mother of All Battles" speech. Now, it was a center of resistance for the Iraqi insurgency. Although U.S. forces had arrived in April 2003, they had restricted their presence to a handful of small bases, including a former Saddam palace, renamed Camp Blue Diamond, in the north, and a second former Iraqi Army maintenance facility at the south end of Highway 10 christened Combat Outpost. Several smaller outposts were located along Highway 10, the main route through Ar Ramadi, between the two larger outposts. The economic and political hub of the Al-Anbar Province, and located thirty miles west of Al-Fallujah in the heart of the Sunni Triangle, Ar Ramadi is a gateway to Syria and Jordan, which are both sources of recruits for the insurgency.[7]

Following the announcement of the end of major combat operations on 1 May 2003, Ar Ramadi was the headquarters of the Army's 3rd Armored Cavalry Regiment (3rd ACR), part of the 82nd Airborne, and responsible for the western Al-Anbar Province. The 3rd ACR was replaced by the 1st Brigade, 1st Infantry Division in September 2003. Responsibility for Al-Anbar Province was transferred to the 1st Marine Division in March 2004. Assigned to Ar Ramadi were the Marines of 2nd Battalion, 4th Marine Regiment (2/4), the Magnificent Bastards.[8] The battalion dates back to April 1914, when it was activated as part of the 4th Marine Regiment and deployed to Mexico as part of the expeditionary force. It went ashore in the Dominican Republic to put down a revolution in 1916, and remained there until August 1924.

On 4 October 1927 while fighting in China the 2/4 was redesignated the 2nd Battalion, 12th Marines, and a new 2/4 was activated in Shanghai, China, on 18 September 1932. In November 1941 as relations with Japan were deteriorating the 4th Marines were withdrawn to the Philippines, and further withdrawn to the island fortress of Corregidor following the attack on Pearl Harbor in December of that year. Following weeks of bombardment, an amphibious assault on the island in May 1942 resulted in the outnumbered Marines putting up a furious fight before reluctantly surrendering under orders issued by Maj. Gen. Jonathan Wainwright.[9]

The battalion was reactivated on Guadalcanal on 1 February 1944 and saw combat on Guam and Okinawa. Arriving in Vietnam at Chu Lai in May 1965, it participated in Operation Starlight, a regiment-sized amphibious and helicopter assault on fortified positions on the Van Tuong Peninsula. The battle resulted in a decisive defeat of the 1st Viet Cong Regiment, and the battalion's first Medal of Honor, awarded posthumously to Cpl. Joe C. Paul. The battalion engaged in combat operations throughout Vietnam, including Hue and the Tet Offensive before being withdrawn to Okinawa in late 1969.[10]

The battalion deployed to Saudi Arabia in December 1990 as part of Operation Desert Shield and fought as part of the 2nd Marine Division's Task Force Spartan during Operation Desert Storm in Kuwait. It was the last Marine infantry unit withdrawn, arriving back in the United States on 15 May 1991.

On 15 February 2004, the battalion deployed from Camp Pendleton, California, for Iraq. They arrived in Ar Ramadi in March 2004, and were involved in Stability and Support Operations (SASO) with high-profile patrols. One primary mission involved walking along the main highways searching out improvised explosive devices (IEDs), or homemade bombs. Although the population was not overtly hostile, the Marines had taken occasional sniper fire. In the seven months that the previous unit, Charlie Company, 1st Battalion, 124th Infantry of the Florida National Guard were in Ar Ramadi, fifty soldiers had been wounded in action; none was killed. The battalion took its first loss on March 22 when LCpl. Andrew S. Dang of Alpha Company, 1st Combat Engineer Battalion, attached to Echo Company, was struck in the head by an undetonated RPG round.[11]

On 30 March the battalion suffered another casualty when LCpl. William Wiscowiche was killed when insurgents detonated an IED while he was sweeping the road for bombs. The following evening the command element was traveling down the dark and deserted main supply route (Highway 10) when they were engaged by heavy small-arms and RPG fire. Present was the battalion operations officer, Maj. John D. Harrill III, who immediately ordered his vehicle to the side, dismounted, and led four Marines in an assault on enemy positions, personally engaging and destroying a machine-gun position. Then he and battalion Sgt. Maj. James E. Booker pursued fleeing insurgents down several unlighted blocks, killing an RPG gunner. Five days later, they would lead a raid that would capture three high-value insurgent leaders.

Harrill, a thirty-five-year-old Alabama native and son of a Marine lieutenant colonel, had enlisted in 1993, fulfilling a childhood ambition of becoming a Marine. Booker, a twenty-year veteran of the Corps, who had seen service as a scout-sniper, drill sergeant, and reconnaissance Marine, was already a combat veteran from his service with the I Marine Expeditionary Force (1 MEF) during Operation Desert Storm. For these, and subsequent actions, Harrill and Booker would be awarded Silver Star medals.

In the early days of their deployment, the 2/4 encountered only sporadic resistance. The morning of 6 April would change things: insurgents moved through the markets and warned residents to close their shops and stay inside. Residents were told, "Today, we are going to kill Americans."[12]

The battle of Ar Ramadi was actually a series of prepared attacks on Marines throughout the city. Three companies of Marines were engaged in at least eight separate locations across several miles. As Major Harrill recalled, "The city just exploded with thousands of insurgents, and Marines were getting ambushed all over the place. We had Marines fighting house to house all over the city."[13]

In a letter to Marine families the battalion commander, Lt. Col. Paul Kennedy, would describe the fighting as "the hardest (the) battalion faced in over thirty years. Within the blink of an eye, the situation went from relatively calm to a raging storm."[14]

The morning of 6 April started out no different from previous mornings. Three squads of Golf Company departed their base, Combat Outpost, and took separate routes into the city. The plan was to create a presence, make contact with the locals, search out any IEDs recently concealed along the roadway, then link up and stand guard at the government center two miles distant. As they walked through the maze of narrow streets and cinder block buildings painted with anti-American graffiti, they were unsettled by the quiet and absence of people. Then, as SSgt. Damien Rodriguez remembers, "All hell broke loose."[15]

Rodriguez was leading one squad of twelve Marines when he received word that a squad northwest of his position was taking fire. As Rodriguez' squad raced to flank the attackers, they also came under fire from multiple directions. "It seemed like everybody in the neighborhood who had an AK-47, which almost all do, was shooting out the window."[16] Down the street a machine gun opened up, and as the Marines took cover and returned fire, Rodriguez led others in a house-to-house search to clear out any hostiles. They radioed for assistance as they saw insurgents armed with AK-47s and RPGs moving to flank their position.

Capt. Christopher J. Bronzi, Golf Company commander, led additional men into the city to relieve the besieged Marines. "We just kept throwing more Marines into the fight and just kept pushing and pushing. . . . I ultimately wound up echeloning my entire company into the fight."[17] When one of his Marines was killed, Bronzi led a fire team under intense fire to recover the fallen Marine's body. He carried the body to safety to prevent it from falling into enemy hands, no doubt recalling the fate of the four murdered contractors in Al-Fallujah.

According to Bronzi's Silver Star citation, he repeatedly exposed himself to intense enemy small-arms and RPG fire while personally destroying several enemy positions. The firefight lasted almost two hours at the cost of two Marines as Bronzi consolidated his men in a fighting withdrawal to the company firebase.

Earlier that morning at 9:00 AM Echo Company's "Porcupine 1" (the 1st and 3rd Squads of 1st Platoon) under the command of 2nd Lt. Vincent Valdes had departed Combat Outpost on a seven-hour patrol to clear the main supply route (MSR) Michigan (Highway 10) and Route Nova of IEDs. Besides twenty Marines from the rifle squads, two engineers and a corpsman were with Valdes. At 11:00 AM Porky 3-3 (3rd Squad, 3rd Platoon) had deployed for a five-hour security patrol, with Corporal Waechter in command of ten Marines and a corpsman.[18]

At 1:40 PM Capt. Kelly Royer, Echo Company commander, received word that Porky 3-3 was taking fire from the north, and he ordered quick reaction force Bravo (QRF-Bravo) to launch and assist Porky 3-3. QRF-Alpha, which had earlier been ordered to assist Golf Company, radioed to report they were ready to assist 3-3. Royer directed them to proceed, and QRF-Bravo would follow. QRF-Alpha consisted of fourteen Marines and a corpsman under the command of Second Lieutenant Wroblewski, in four Humvees. QRF-Bravo comprised Royer, 2nd Lt. Thomas E. Cogan, 3rd Platoon commander, twenty-six Marines, and two corpsmen, also in four vehicles.

QRF-Alpha and QRF-Bravo linked up at 3-3's position and began a cordon and search operation with Cogan taking Marines to cordon the west side and Wroblewski the east. The vehicles were parked on a frontage road just north of MSR Michigan.

Royer and his Marines searched house to house without uncovering any insurgents or weapons, and were questioning detainees when he was informed by Combat Operations Center (COC) that a scout-sniper team was under attack. It was 2:45 PM.

The four-man team from Echo Company, Headhunter-2, was in position a mile away, adjacent to the Euphrates River. Under the command of Sgt. Romeo Santiago, three corporals, Stayskal, Stanton, and Ferguson, had departed Combat Outpost at 8:30 PM the previous evening on a thirty-three and a half–hour mission. Hidden in the tall grass, they were to set up an observation post (OP) and watch for insurgents planting IEDs along Route Nova.

When they heard the sounds of a firefight, Santiago called it in, but they soon had other concerns as fourteen Iraqis armed with AK-47s and RPGs appeared and advanced on their position in a line formation, which was unusual for insurgents. As they came under fire, the outnumbered Marines radioed for assistance.

Porky-1 was about a mile downriver, waiting for an explosive ordnance demolition (EOD) team to deal with three mortar rounds they had uncovered along the main supply route when they received the call for help. Valdes took ten Marines in the Humvee, and responded toward the snipers' location. They drove into an ambush! "They were waiting for the right time to strike," Valdes said of the insurgents.[19]

Valdes' Marines dismounted and, joined by the sniper team, drove back the insurgents while under mortar and machine-gun fire from the roofs and windows of nearby houses. During the firefight, two Marines (Cpl. Marcus Cherry and Pfc. Benjamin Carmen) were mortally wounded.

Meanwhile, the Marines left behind by Lieutenant Valdes came under heavy attack near Checkpoint 337, and they called for assistance. Royer received the call for help. Originally directed to assist the beleaguered sniper team, Royer learned that the enemy had successfully been repulsed, and he ordered QRF-Alpha and QRF-Bravo to assist Porky-1.

Royer had earlier moved north on foot with Cogan's QRF to investigate some gunfire, leaving Wroblewski's QRF behind with the vehicles to continue the cordon and search. Now he radioed Wroblewski to proceed with the vehicles to Checkpoint 338 (intersection of Route Gypsum and Route Nova) where they would link up and proceed north along Route Nova to Checkpoint 337 and counterattack.

When Royer observed Wroblewski's eight-vehicle convoy moving north on Route Gypsum, he radioed him to stop so that his Marines could load. The first two vehicles continued moving while the remainder halted. As the two vehicles advanced, they found themselves under intense RPG and .50-caliber machine-gun fire, and in the kill zone of a prepared ambush by approximately sixty insurgents.[20]

Fired on from rooftops on both sides of the road, the first Humvee was riddled with gunfire; seven of the eight Marines inside were killed. LCpl. Deshon Otey dismounted and sought cover behind a concrete wall, joined by Marines in the second vehicle. Farther back, Wroblewski halted his column short of the kill zone, and dismounted his Marines, only to come under intense fire from a second prepared ambush by approximately thirty insurgents.

Cpl. Eric M. Smith, a squad leader in the fourth vehicle, dismounted his Marines and located a house to the east with a low brick wall that would provide cover and a position from which to return suppressing fire. Wroblewski stayed with the vehicle to radio the command post and was wounded when a shot passed through the handset he was holding.

"I see that the commander's been hit," Smith recalled. "He's about 75 meters away from me. I'm in an open field, and he's lying in the road next to his vehicle. I saw him lying there and instinct took over. Not only is he my platoon commander, but he's also a very good friend. So I took off."[21]

Calling for a corpsman and without regard for his own safety Smith raced under intense fire to Wroblewski's position, placed two Marines on security with the downed lieutenant and covered the corpsman as he administered aid. He then ordered Wroblewski evacuated and assumed command of the platoon of twenty Marines. He repeated his dash under fire to attempt to use the radio, but it was inoperable. He recovered Wroblewski's helmet and weapon, then again crossed open terrain under intense fire to return to the platoon unscathed.

Smith saw Marines from the first two vehicles in the kill zone fighting off insurgents a couple of hundred meters to the north. As four U.S. Army Bradley fighting vehicles drove through the ambush, engaging insurgents with their .50-caliber machine guns, Smith moved to assist. Leaving a fire team on the roof of a nearby house to provide overwatch, he moved the remainder of his Marines south to link up with a Marine machine-gun team and several seven-ton trucks. With his Marines providing frontal and flank security, the seven-tonners moved north to link with the Army QRF and assault through. Overwhelmed, the enemy began to egress, by any means necessary. After securing the Marine dead and wounded, Smith supervised the withdrawal south to Combat Outpost.

When Royer, accompanying QRF-Bravo, saw QRF-Alpha come under fire, he tried without success to contact Wroblewski, and then ordered Cogan to take his QRF north and begin clearing houses. Cogan led his platoon across several open fields and a road while under heavy fire, several times taking the point to motivate his Marines. Skillfully emplacing a fire-support position, he maneuvered his men until the danger of envelopment caused the insurgents to withdraw from the area.

Knowing that QRF-Alpha was still engaged to the north, Cogan again advanced his QRF across open fields and roads under heavy fire. Unit integrity was severely degraded as men took whatever cover was available. Cogan moved back and forth across the battlefield, creating ad hoc fire teams, and directing their fire to suppress the enemy. After ninety minutes of intense house-to-house fighting, the enemy was destroyed or had withdrawn.[22]

Elsewhere that morning a Weapons Company QRF, under the command of Capt. Robert S. Weiler, came to the aid of an isolated squad from 1st Platoon of Echo Company which was under attack. Weiler's Silver Star citation notes, "As the column moved east along Route Nova, they were ambushed by enemy forces. Despite the barrage of intense enemy fire, Captain Weiler calmly directed the tactical employment of the unit, leading to relief of the embattled squad and the destruction of the besieging enemy."[23] His citation also credits him for subsequent actions on 7 and 10 April.

Twelve Marines were killed and twenty-five wounded on 6 April. There is no certainty as to how many insurgents were killed that day. Since several Marines witnessed enemy dead and wounded being evacuated by taxis and private vehicles, estimates vary. By midnight, the Marines were back at Combat Outpost, to rest and ready their gear for the next day's patrols.

The following day, 7 April, Marines continued operations in Ar Ramadi. In almost a repeat of the previous day, Bronzi was with 3rd Squad, 4th Platoon of Golf Company when they came under intense fire from all directions. Leading his Marines to cover in a nearby house, Bronzi made his way to the exposed roof and coordinated the linkup of his platoons by radio, all the time while under heavy enemy fire.

Hearing the call for assistance from Bronzi, Weiler led a relief column that itself came under attack as they proceeded northeast along Route Apple. Weiler dismounted and supervised the counterattack, beating back the attackers and personally leading squads in direct assaults on enemy positions. Thus began what would become a three-hour firefight as Marines moved house to house to eliminate the enemy. "You could see [Weiler] by his vehicle, giving directions while bullets were flying by his head," Navy Hospital Corpsman 2nd Class Michael Rakebrandt, senior corpsman with Weapons Company recalled. "He never broke a sweat or flinched."[24]

Resistance continued in Ar Ramadi and throughout the Al-Anbar Province. On 10 April the battalion initiated Operation Bug Hunt, a mission to conduct raids at multiple objectives, codenamed Cave, Cavern, and Canyon, in order to kill or capture terrorists.[25]

At dawn, at about 5:30 AM, platoons of Echo Company began to execute a cordon, knock-and-search in their area of operation (AO). Capt. Royer and his headquarters element initially accompanied 3rd platoon, and were in the process of transiting over to join the 2nd platoon when enemy fire broke out and both platoons took cover.

Royer estimated the opposing force to be platoon strength, armed with AK-47s, light and medium machine guns, sniper rifles, hand grenades, and RPGs. Royer said that they were being fired on from the west, east, and south. With the command element pinned down in a shallow irrigation ditch, and 2nd platoon also under fire, Second Lieutenant Cogan led his Marines under fire across meters of open field to direct suppressive fire to relieve the pressure on the headquarters element, allowing them to low-crawl to the edge of the ditch, link up with elements of second platoon, and secure the roof of a nearby house.

At the same time Cogan ordered a squad to the roof of a building to provide overwatch, then maneuvered west with another squad to break through the enemy ambush. According to the Summary of Action for Cogan's Silver Star, "[H]e exposed himself to an extremely heavy volume of automatic weapon fire . . . in order to allow his Marines to reach a covered position in a nearby house.[26] This squad reached the roof and began to lay down an exceptional amount of suppression on the enemy positions.

Continuing to maneuver his Marines across the battlefield to the point that Marines were now providing suppressive fire from the west, southwest, south, southeast, and east, Cogan ordered a fire team to follow him as he maneuvered to completely envelop the enemy. When his element was pinned down, he radioed a nearby armored Army QRF, and coordinated their movement to the ambush site, guiding them in from an exposed position under fire. After an almost three-hour firefight, the enemy was repelled with twenty-six enemy killed, one wounded, and thirteen detainees.

On 9 June 2005 First Lieutenant Cogan was presented the Silver Star by Lt. Gen. Robert R. Blackman, commanding general, III Marine Expeditionary Force, in a ceremony at Camp Hansen, Okinawa, Japan. He credited his Marines, saying, "They never hesitated, and it's because of their hard work and willingness that we were able to push through."[27]

On 13 December 2005 at Camp Pendleton, California, Maj. Gen. Richard F. Natonski, commander of the 1st Marine Division, presented Capt. Christopher J. Bronzi and Maj. Robert S. Weiler with Silver Star medals. Both credited their Marines. Bronzi stated, "I'm very proud of my Marines . . . how they performed. The entire company was in the fight on the first day. That night, they cleaned their weapons, restocked their ammo, and went out the gate the next day for virtually the same scenario." Weiler agreed. "I'm wearing this medal because of the performance of this battalion," he said.[28]

On 17 December 2005 Maj. John Harrill III received the Silver Star from Lt. Col. Paul Kennedy, his former commanding officer at the Richmond Recruiting Station, which Harrill commanded before being transferred to Quantico, Virginia, in 2007. "My actions were the result of the young Marines beside me and their will, their fighting spirit, and their savvy," Harrill said.[29]

Sgt. Eric M. Smith would be the last to receive a Silver Star for combat in Ar Ramadi that April. On 17 February 2006 at the Ellis County, Texas, Veteran's Memorial, Smith, now a civilian, was presented the medal by Brig. Gen. Darrell L. Moore. His company commander, Captain Royer, had recommended the award of a Navy Cross for Smith's actions on April 6 and 10. Acknowledging the honor, Smith stated "I want to make sure everybody here knows that many young men, nineteen, twenty, twenty-one years old, do this on a daily basis. It's not just me. I don't want this to be my day. I didn't do it alone."[30]

The 2/4 returned to Camp Pendleton, California, in September 2004, but would return to Iraq in November 2006 as part of 15th Marine Expeditionary Unit (MEU), operating out of Al-Hadithah. Resistance would continue in Ar Ramadi, and it remained a center of the Iraqi insurgency.

ENDNOTES

1. Silver Star citation, Sgt. Maj. James E. Booker, USMC, http://www.homeofheroes.com/valor2/SS/7_GWOT/citations_USMC.html.
2. Silver Star citation, Capt. Christopher J. Bronzi, USMC, http://www.homeofheroes.com/valor2/SS/7_GWOT/citations_USMC.html.

3. Silver Star citation, 2nd Lt. Thomas E. Cogan IV, USMC, http://www.homeofheroes.com/valor2/SS/7_GWOT/citations_USMC.html.

4. Silver Star citation, Maj. John D. Harrill III, USMC, http://www.homeofheroes.com/valor2/SS/7_GWOT/citations_USMC.html.

5. Silver Star citation, Cpl. Eric M. Smith, USMC, http://www.homeofheroes.com/valor2/SS/7_GWOT/citations_USMC-M.html.

6. Silver Star citation, Capt. Robert S. Weiler, USMC, http://www.homeofheroes.com/valor2/SS/7_GWOT/citations_USMC-M.html.

7. Patrick J. McDonnell, "No Shortage of Fighters in Iraq's Wild West," *Los Angeles* (CA) *Times*, 25 July 2004.

8. White House, "President Bush Announces Major Combat Operations in Iraq Have Ended," Press release, 1 May 2003.

9. "Unit History: 2nd Battalion, 4th Marine Regiment," GlobalSecurity.org, http://www.globalsecurity.org/military/agency/usmc/2-4.htm.

10. Ibid. In total, six Marines of the 2/4 have been awarded Medals of Honor.

11. Capt. Kelly Royer, telephone interview with Scott Baron, 12 August 2007.

12. David Swanson and Joseph Galloway, "Battle at Ramadi," *Philadelphia* (PA) *Inquirer*, 15 August 2004.

13. Shelby Spires, "Silver Star Winner Recalls Amazing White House Visit," *Huntsville* (AL) *Times*, 16 August 2006.

14. Gregg Zoroya, "Fight for Ramadi Exacts Heavy Toll on Marines," *USA Today*, 12 July 2004.

15. Ibid.

16. Ibid.

17. John Hoellwarth, "The Finest Caliber," *Marine Corps Times*, 10 January 2006.

18. Kelly Royer, "Company (E) Commander's After-Action Report for Combat Actions in the Porcupine Area of Operations," 6 April 2004, unpublished.

19. Zoroya, "Fight for Ramadi Exacts Heavy Toll on Marines."

20. Kelly Royer, "Summary of Action: Navy Cross Recommendation for Cpl. Eric M. Smith," unpublished.

21. Chris Vaughn, "Waxahachie Man Awarded Silver Star," *Ft. Worth* (TX) *Star-Telegram*, 17 February 2006.

22. Kelly Royer, "Summary of Action: Silver Star Recommendation for 2nd Lt. Thomas E. Cogan IV," unpublished.

23. Silver Star citation, Capt. Robert S. Weiler.

24. Hoellwarth, "The Finest Caliber."

25. Royer, "Company (E) Commander's After-Action Report."

26. Silver Star citation, 2nd Lt. Thomas E. Cogan IV.

27. Will Lathrop, "Silver Star Awarded to Marine for Actions in Iraq," *Marine Corps News*, 9 June 2005 (Story ID #2005699476).

28. Hoellwarth, "The Finest Caliber."

29. Beth Zimmerman, "Marine Officer Wins Silver Star for Gallantry in Combat in Iraq," *Richmond* (VA) *Times*, 18 December 2005.

30. Vaughn, "Waxahachie Man Awarded Silver Star."

2nd Lt. Bryan D. Diede, USMCR

Pathfinder Platoon Commander, Weapons Company,
1st Light Armored Reconnaissance Battalion, 1st Marine Division,
I Marine Expeditionary Force

Al-Bu Harden, Iraq
8 April 2004

The President of the United States takes pleasure in presenting the Silver Star Medal to 2nd Lt. Bryan D. Diede, U.S. Marine Corps (Reserve), for conspicuous gallantry and intrepidity in action against the enemy while serving as Pathfinder Platoon Commander, Weapons Company, First Light Armored Reconnaissance Battalion, FIRST Marine Division, I Marine Expeditionary Force in support of Operation Iraqi Freedom II on 8 April 2004. Second Lieutenant Diede led a patrol of three Light Armored Vehicles (LAV) tasked with conducting curfew enforcement in Al Bu Harden, Iraq. As the patrol approached the local police station, the trail vehicle was hit by an improvised explosive device (IED) followed by an ambush of rocket-propelled grenade (RPG), machine gun, and small arms fire. The initial barrage killed the gunner of the lead vehicle and rendered it immobile. Second Lieutenant Diede maneuvered his vehicle to a position that allowed enfilading fires on the enemy and reduced the stricken vehicle's vulnerability to further assault. Immediately, his vehicle became the center of the enemy's attention and was engulfed in rocket-propelled grenade and small arms fire resulting in Second Lieutenant Diede sustaining wounds to his hand and face. Ignoring his wounds, he coordinated his platoon's defense and engaged the enemy with his M-240 machine gun until it jammed. He then retrieved his M-4 carbine and continued to return fire from his turret until the enemy fled. Only after consolidating his forces and directing security of the site, did Second Lieutenant Diede allow his wounds to be treated. By his bold leadership, wise judgment, and complete dedication to duty, Second Lieutenant Diede reflected great credit upon himself and upheld the highest traditions of the Marine Corps and the United States Naval Service.[1]

Silver Star Citation

IN APRIL 2004, as violence broke out in Al-Fallujah, Al-Qa'im, Ramadi, and throughout the Al-Anbar Province, even small villages like Al-Bu Harden, a small town two miles from the Syrian border, were not immune.

On the evening of 8 April 2004, Marines of Weapons Company, 1st Light Armored Reconnaissance Battalion, were involved in patrolling the streets for curfew enforcement. The 1st Light Armored Reconnaissance Battalion had redeployed to the Al-Anbar region in February 2004 as part of Regimental Combat Team 7 (RCT-7). The battalion had performed a wide range of critical missions, including patrolling the border with Syria, helping Iraqi border guards string concertina wire along the border, and patrolling with Iraqi police to prevent the infiltration of arms and insurgents.

The battalion, whose history extends back to its formation in May 1985, had seen service conducting screening and counterreconnaissance operations along the Kuwaiti–Saudi Arabian border prior to the Gulf War and was the first Allied Force to enter and liberate Kuwait City on the third day of the ground offensive during Operation Desert Storm.[2]

Later deployments included Los Angeles, California—to assist law enforcement during the riots in May 1992 as part of the Special Purpose Marine Air Ground Task Force Los Angeles—and Afghanistan—in December 2001 as part of the 15th Marine Expeditionary Unit–Special Operations Capable (MEU-SOC) in support of Operation Enduring Freedom. In January 2003 the battalion again deployed to Southwest Asia, this time in support of Operation Iraqi Freedom. They were the first troops to cross into Iraq on 20 March 2003, as part of RCT-5, and were instrumental in securing Baghdad. They then advanced north to secure Saddam Hussein's hometown of Tikrit as part of Task Force Tripoli. Returning to Camp Pendleton, California, in May 2003, they were redeployed the following February.[3]

That evening of 8 April 2004 2nd Lt. Bryan Diede, the Pathfinder platoon commander, led a vehicle patrol of three light armored vehicles (LAV-25) along the dusty streets. The LAV-25 is an all-terrain, all-weather vehicle with night capabilities and mounts a .25-mm gun and two 7.62-mm machine guns, and is highly mobile, and Diede's Marines were highly trained.

Diede, a thirty-year-old from Bismarck, North Dakota, had enlisted in the Marines right after high school. After completing a four-year hitch, he returned to school and earned a degree from the University of North Dakota. After graduating from college he returned to the Marines and earned a commission as an officer.[4]

The patrol was about sixty yards from the Iraqi police station when an improvised explosive device (IED) detonated under the trail vehicle.

Immediately, insurgents riddled the convoy with rocket-propelled grenade (RPG), machine-gun, and small-arms fire, killing the driver and disabling the lead vehicle. The driver, Cpl. Nicholas Dieruf, became the battalion's first fatality since its return to Iraq.[5]

Without hesitation, Diede ordered his vehicle forward under fire to a position where it shielded the disabled vehicle. He then began laying down fire on the insurgents. Diede's vehicle became the focus of insurgent machine-gun fire and a barrage of RPGs. Diede sustained wounds to his hand and face, but he continued to lay down suppressing fire from the turret M-240 machine gun while coordinating his platoon into defensive positions. When the M-240 jammed, he continued firing his M-4 carbine until the insurgents withdrew. He refused medical treatment until his forces were consolidated and a defensive perimeter established.

For his actions that day, Diede was awarded the Silver Star and Purple Heart. Modest as are most recipients, Diede stated that he did nothing that any other Marine would not have done. "It's not about self-preservation. They are fighting over there for their buddies."[6]

Six days later, the 1st Light Armored Reconnaissance (LAR) Battalion was ordered three hundred fifty miles southeast to secure the roads around Baghdad. They then patrolled around Al-Fallujah before returning to the United States in October 2004.

Diede, now a captain, had surgery on his hand in July 2005, then returned to Iraq for a second tour in August 2005. As of July 2007, he was serving as commanding officer of 2nd Battlion, 23rd Marines, a reserve unit out of Las Vegas, Nevada, and Salt Lake City, Utah.

ENDNOTES

1. Silver Star citation, 2nd Lt. Bryan D. Diede, USMCR, http://www.homeofheroes.com/valor2/SS/7_GWOT/citations_USMC.html.
2. "1st Light Armored Infantry Battalion," http://www.imef.usmc.mil/div/1lar/History_start.asp.
3. Ibid.
4. Tom Rafferty, "Decorated Soldier Returning Home," Bismarck (ND) Tribune, 12 May 2006.
5. Ann Barnard, "Forces Try to Keep Focus as Tactics Shift," Boston Globe, 3 May 2004.
6. Rafferty, "Decorated Soldier Returning Home."

LCpl. Mario Atrian Jr., USMC

Machine Gunner, Weapons Company, 3rd Battalion, 7th Marine Regiment,
Regimental Combat Team 7, 1st Marine Division, I Marine Expeditionary
Force, U.S. Marine Corps Forces, Central Command

Husaybah, Iraq
9 April 2004

The President of the United States takes pleasure in presenting the Silver
Star Medal to Mario Atrian Jr., Lance Corporal, U.S. Marine Corps, for
conspicuous gallantry and intrepidity in action against the enemy while
serving as Machine gunner, Weapons Company, Third Battalion, Seventh
Marine Regiment, Regimental Combat Team 7, FIRST Marine Division, I
Marine Expeditionary Force, U.S. Marine Corps Forces, Central Command
in support of Operation Iraqi Freedom II on 9 April 2004. Reinforcing a
friendly unit caught in an enemy ambush, Lance Corporal Atrian demonstrated extraordinary heroism under fire when a numerically superior enemy
force ambushed his unit from multiple positions. After radioing a warning
to his unit, he laid down suppressive fire on multiple enemy positions with
his machine gun. The enemy responded with a fusillade of rocket-propelled
grenade and machine gun fire. Despite being hit in the left arm, Lance
Corporal Atrian continued to provide fire with deadly accuracy on the flank
of the enemy position. He received another volley of rocket-propelled grenade and machine gun fire, wounding him in the right arm and killing his
driver. While bleeding profusely from both arms, Lance Corporal Atrian
valiantly suppressed the enemy while the remainder of his section's vehicles
bounded through the enemy's successive kill zones. He relinquished his
position to receive medical attention only after the enemy ambush had been
broken and his fellow wounded Marines had been treated. By his bold leadership, wise judgment, and complete dedication to duty, Lance Corporal
Atrian reflected great credit upon himself and upheld the highest traditions
of the Marine Corps and the United States Naval Service.[1]

Silver Star Citation

FOLLOWING THE ONSET OF Operation Vigilant Resolve in Al-Fallujah on
4 April 2004, operations were extended into major cities throughout the
Al-Anbar Province, including Ar Ramadi, Al-Qa'im, and Husaybah, as
anti-Iraqi forces became more active.

Located on the south side of the Euphrates River near the Syrian border, Husaybah was and still is a popular border crossing for smugglers. In February 2004 the 3rd Battalion, 7th Marines deployed to Al-Qa'im and took responsibility for the western Al-Anbar Province, including Husaybah.

The 3/7rd Battalion, 7th Marines—called "The Cutting Edge"—was activated just prior to World War II at Guantanamo Bay, Cuba, on 1 January 1941. Assigned to the 1st Marine Division, the 3/7 saw action at Guadalcanal, New Britain, Peleliu, and Okinawa during World War II. Following occupation duty in northern China until 15 April 1946, the battalion was reactivated for the Korean War on 11 September 1950 and saw service at Inchon and the Chosin Reservoir. Marines of the 3/7 participated in the Vietnam War, the Gulf War, and the 2003 Invasion of Iraq, serving in Karbala until September 2003. Now, six months later, Marines of the 3/7 were back in Iraq, patrolling Husaybah.

On the evening of 9 April 2004 LCpl. Mario Atrian Jr. was behind a machine gun in the turret of his Humvee, the trailing vehicle of a three-Humvee convoy into Husaybah to drop off a foot patrol of Marines from Kilo Company, 3/7.[2]

Atrian had enlisted in the Marines on 17 September 2001, but had started preparations to enter the Corps six months earlier. Like many of his generation, he saw military service as an opportunity. "All my buddies were going in the military, and I thought that if I was going to go, I'd go with the best, so I enlisted in the Marines." Following boot camp in San Diego, California, Atrian was trained as an 0351-Assaultman, primarily involved with demolition and antiarmor operations. Since arriving in Iraq for his second tour, he had served primarily as a machine-gunner in an armored Humvee.[3]

The lead Humvee of the convey, armed with an MK-19 40-mm grenade launcher, was followed by a "highback" Humvee carrying the twelve-man patrol designated "Team #2." Atrian's Humvee was armed with an M-240 machine gun and TOW (tube-launched, optically tracked, wire-guided) antitank missiles brought up the rear. The vehicle commander, Staff Sergeant Lochte, sat next to the driver, LCpl. Elias Torrez. In the rear Corporal Dale provided security when the Marines dismounted at 10:00 PM.

Team #2's area of patrol (AOP) was along Diamond Street to a backfield where intelligence reports placed a large weapons stash. Within minutes of the Kilo Company Marines dismounting, the convoy received a radio report of a unit in contact with insurgents at Diamond Street, the patrol's destination.

After advising the foot patrol, the vehicles began a satellite patrol of the sector, driving around the perimeter of their area of operations.

Atrian estimates it was another five minutes until the convoy began taking potshots from the rooftops, where insurgents popped up, took a shot with a rocket-patrolled grenade (RPG), then disappeared. "There were numerous targets and I returned fire where I could and advised the lead truck that we had contact on the right. We began to 'leap frog' sort of a stop-and-go maneuver to avoid enemy fire. The volume of fire increased, and I saw targets on the ground, in doorways, in windows and on the roof. There must have been at least thirty RPG rounds fired. It was on the third leapfrog that they opened up with everything they had."[4]

The insurgents attacked the convoy with RPGs, Russian-made RPKs ("Kalashnikov hand-held machine gun") machine-gun and automatic small-arms fire. The lead Humvee was stopped in the kill zone with two flat tires on the left side, then was clipped in the rear by the second Humvee. Atrian found himself the focus of insurgent fire as he swung his gun back and forth, engaging targets.

"Right in front of my truck, dead ahead, is this guy manning an RPK machine gun targeting me as I'm targeting him, sort of a machine gun duel. He's shooting, I'm shooting, back and forth. The Marines in the lead truck are on the ground. Eventually, I ran out of rounds, and went down to grab another box. That's when I noticed I was bleeding on the left side. . . . I flexed my hand, saw that I had full function, thought 'no big,' grabbed a can of ammo, reloaded the gun, and thought 'I'm back in business.'"

As he returned to the turret, the truck was hit with an RPG. The explosion peppered shrapnel into Atrian's right arm, and started a fire. Undeterred, Atrian resumed the machine gun duel and, after again coming under heavy fire, the dispirited insurgent withdrew. With the loss of their point man, or perhaps having expended their ammunition, the other insurgents retreated.

Atrian remained behind his gun, alert, as calm returned. Only then did he notice that Lance Corporal Torrez had taken a head shot and was critically wounded. When Staff Sergeant Lochte saw that Atrian was wounded, he ordered Dale to replace him in the turret, then arranged air evacuation for Atrian and Torrez. Atrian estimates the action lasted about fifteen minutes, and has no knowledge of how many insurgents were killed, wounded, or captured. Whatever the number, it was not worth the cost. LCpl. Elias Torrez III died in surgery.

Atrian suffered a gunshot to the lower left bicep and shrapnel injuries to his right triceps and began a road to recovery that stretched from the hospital at Camp Al-Asad to Landstuhl, Germany, to San Diego Naval Hospital, arriving in California in May 2004.[5]

Atrian was promoted to corporal, entered the individual ready reserve, and returned home to take a job with the city of Beverly Hills. He intends to work in law enforcement, and is planning on attending junior college in the future.

On 24 February 2006, in a ceremony at the Los Angeles, California, City Hall, Brig. Gen. Darrell Moore, Commanding General of the Mobilization Command, presented Atrian with the Silver Star. Atrian accepted the medal on behalf of all Marines who have served.[6]

Postscript: Five days later, on 14 April 2004, Kilo Company Marines of the 3/7 were involved in an ambush and firefight in Husaybah that left five Marines dead, and earned one of them, Cpl. Jason Dunham, the Medal of Honor when he used his helmet and body to shield other Marines from the blast of a grenade. It was the sixteenth Medal of Honor for the 3/7, and the first—and to date the only—award of a Medal of Honor to a Marine for service in Afgahanistan or Iraq.

ENDNOTES

1. Silver Star citation, LCpl. Mario Atrian Jr., USMC, http://www.homeofheroes.com/valor2/SS/7_GWOT/citations_USMC.html.
2. John Hoellwarth, "Machine Gun Battle Leads to Silver Star for Marine," *Marine Corps Times*, 13 March 2006.
3. Mario Atrian Jr., telephone interview with Scott Baron, 7 October 2007.
4. Ibid.
5. Ibid.
6. Hoellwarth, "Machine Gun Battle Leads to Silver Star for Marine."

SSgt. Jason Navarette, USMC

Explosive Ordnance Demolition Technician,
Combat Service Support Battalion 1, 1st Force Service Support Group,
1st Marine Division, I Marine Expeditionary Force,
U.S. Marine Forces, Central Command

Lutafiyah, Iraq
9 April 2004

For conspicuous gallantry and intrepidity in action against the enemy as Explosive Ordnance Disposal Technician, Combat Service Support Battalion 1, 1st Force Service Support Group, in support of 2d Battalion, 2d Marine Regiment, 1st Marine Division, I Marine Expeditionary Force, U.S. Marine Forces Central Command on 9 April 2004, in support of Operation Iraqi Freedom II. Enemy insurgents ambushed Staff Sergeant Navarette's Explosive Ordnance Disposal Team in the town of Lutafiyah, Iraq. With automatic weapons and rocket-propelled grenades (RPGs) exploding around him, he left the safety of his armored vehicle to engage the enemy. He and his fellow Marines eliminated and severely wounded several insurgents, and the ferocity of their defense held the enemy at bay. Finding themselves greatly outnumbered, they fought their way to the rally point where they realized one vehicle team was pinned down and had been unable to egress from the ambush site. Once again exiting the relative safety of his armored vehicle, he attacked the enemy and was subsequently wounded in the left arm. Ignoring his bleeding and immobilized arm, he continued to engage the enemy until all personnel and vehicles were ready to move. With enemy fire focused on the unit from both sides, he again exited his armored vehicle to provide covering fire as the vehicles began to leave town. His actions inspired fellow Marines to continue to repel the enemy attack, ultimately leading to their safe withdrawal. By his bold leadership, wise judgment, and complete dedication to duty, Staff Sergeant Navarette reflected great credit upon himself and upheld the highest traditions of the Marine Corps and the United States Naval Service.[1]

Silver Star Citation

ON 9 APRIL 2004 SSgt. Steve Reichert, a sniper, and his spotter, Cpl. Winston Tucker, both from Weapons Company, 2nd Battalion, 2nd Marines, were perched atop an oil storage tank on the outskirts of Lutafiyah,

a small town south of Baghdad. They had been there for several days, covering unit movements through Lutafiyah. That morning they were covering a patrol of 2/2 into the town to search for insurgents and to protect Arbaeen pilgrims through the area when they spotted an explosive device planted in a dead animal carcass along the route the patrol would take.[2]

They advised the patrol by radio, then requested an explosive ordnance demolition (EOD) team. A convoy of five Humvees, containing EOD technicians of the Combat Service Support Battalion responded to the scene, but came under intense RPG and automatic weapons fire. Among the technicians was SSgt. Jason Navarette.

Navarette, a twenty-eight-year-old native of Phoenix, Arizona, realized the vulnerability of Humvees to RPG fire. Rather than stay behind cover, he and two other Marines advanced on the insurgents' positions. They began an assault, and, though greatly outnumbered, are credited with neutralizing several insurgent positions.[3]

Although their assault was effective in putting the insurgents on the defensive, the enemy's greater number began having an effect as they took fire from several locations and directions. Navarette's team was nearly encircled when he received orders by radio to return to the rally point. Pushing through the ambush was not an option because of the IEDs planted up the road, so the order was given to retrace their path out of the kill zone. Navarette and his team remounted their vehicle and withdrew out of the city.

Arriving at the rally point, Navarette was advised that one of his Humvees was still pinned down by enemy fire and was unable to withdraw out of the kill zone. Ordering his driver to make a U-turn, Navarette and his Marines, accompanied by two Humvees of security force Marines, drove back into Lutafiyah.[4]

Despite taking a bullet to the left arm at the outskirts of the city, Navarette continued to the ambush site, surprising the insurgents. Again leaving the cover of his Humvee, he laid down cover fire while crouched behind his vehicle. "I remember having to reload, and my hand wasn't doing what it was supposed to."[5] Reloading with his right hand, he continued to pour fire onto his attackers until everyone was ready to withdraw, then provided covering fire until the others were clear.

On 2 December 2005 Navarette, now a gunnery sergeant and instructor at the Navy Explosive Ordnance Disposal School (NAVSCOLEOD) at Eglin Air Force Base, Florida, was presented a Silver Star for his actions in Lutafiyah. Modest about the award, Navarette will only say, "A lot of people I've worked with have done a lot of good things."[6]

ENDNOTES

1. Silver Star citation, SSgt. Jason Navarette, USMC, http://www.homeofheroes.com/valor2/ SS/7_GWOT/citations_USMC-M.html.
2. Leo Shane III, "We Started Making Them Fly off Roofs," *Stars and Stripes*, 14 June 2005.
3. Gidget Fuentes and John Hoellwarth, "Saving Their Buddies, Three Marines Earn Silver Star," *Marine Corps Times*, 12 December 2005.
4. Ibid.
5. Ibid.
6. Ibid.

1st Lt. Joshua L. Glover, USMC

Quick Reaction Force Platoon Commander, 1st Battalion,
5th Marine Regiment, 1st Marine Division, U.S. Marine Corps Forces,
Central Command

Al-Fallujah, Iraq
13 April 2004

The President of the United States takes pleasure in presenting the Silver
Star Medal to Joshua L. Glover, First Lieutenant, U.S. Marine Corps, for con-
spicuous gallantry and intrepidity in action against the enemy while serving
as Quick Reaction Force Platoon Commander, First Battalion, Fifth Marine
Regiment, FIRST Marine Division, U.S. Marine Corps Forces, Central
Command in support of Operation Iraqi Freedom on 13 April 2004. First
Lieutenant Glover's platoon executed a mechanical recovery of a downed
CH-53 helicopter southeast of Al Fallujah, Iraq. After successfully securing the aircraft's classified material, the platoon was attacked by an enemy
platoon-sized element employing machine gun, small arms and rocket-propelled grenade (RPG) fire. Despite coordinated enemy fire, First Lieutenant
Glover skillfully maneuvered his force and assaulted through the ambush to
friendly lines while inflicting numerous enemy casualties. That evening, he
was tasked to recover a destroyed Assault Amphibious Vehicle and rescue a
besieged rifle platoon deep behind enemy lines. While en route, he led an
engagement against a company-sized force along the enemy's main line of
resistance. First Lieutenant Glover repeatedly exposed himself to enemy fire
as he engaged enemy targets at point-blank range while directing the rifle
platoon's relief and coordinating recovery operations.[1]

Silver Star Citation

LCpl. Abraham McCarver, USMC

Rifleman, 2nd Platoon, Bravo Company, 1st Battalion 5th Marines,
1st Marine Division, I Marine Expeditionary Force,
U.S. Marine Corps Forces, Central Command

The President of the United States takes pleasure in presenting the Silver
Star Medal to Abraham McCarver, Lance Corporal, U.S. Marine Corps, for

conspicuous gallantry and intrepidity in action against the enemy while serving as a Rifleman, Second Platoon, Company B, First Battalion, Fifth Marines, FIRST Marine Division, I Marine Expeditionary Force, U.S. Marine Corps Forces, Central Command, in support of Operation Iraqi Freedom II on 13 April 2004. During an attack on enemy forces, the amphibious assault vehicle in which Lance Corporal McCarver and his platoon were riding became disabled by enemy fire, forcing them to take cover in a nearby house. During their movement, Lance Corporal McCarver expertly provided cover fire for the rest of the Marines. Upon reaching the house, it was learned that his platoon commander was severely wounded and still in the burning vehicle. Disregarding his own safety, Lance Corporal McCarver ran through a hail of enemy fire and assisted his platoon sergeant with the rescue. Over the next hour, Lance Corporal McCarver assisted the corpsman in providing first aid, and constantly moved to various locations under fire. With his ammunition supply exhausted, Lance Corporal McCarver collected ammunition from various positions and continued the assault. When the quick reaction force arrived, he secured additional ammunition and provided cover for his Marines to recover the disabled amphibious assault vehicle.[2]

Silver Star Citation

SSgt. Ismael Sagredo, USMC

Platoon Sergeant, 2nd Platoon, Bravo Company, 1st Battalion,
5th Marines, 1st Marine Division, I Marine Expeditionary Force,
U.S. Marine Corps Forces, Central Command

The President of the United States takes pleasure in presenting the Silver Star Medal to Ismael Sagredo, Staff Sergeant, U.S. Marine Corps, for conspicuous gallantry and intrepidity in action against the enemy while serving as Platoon Sergeant, Second Platoon, Company B, First Battalion, Fifth Marines, FIRST Marine Division, I Marine Expeditionary Force, U.S. Marine Corps Forces, Central Command, in support of Operation Iraqi Freedom II on 13 April 2004. Staff Sergeant Sagredo realized the dire nature of the situation when, during an attack on the enemy, elements of the Second Platoon became isolated deep within enemy territory and were forced to abandon their burning amtrac. He then led his Marines to a nearby house. As his fellow Marines provided cover, he exposed himself to fire as he returned to the burning vehicle to evacuate his platoon commander to safety. Despite continuous rocket-propelled grenade and small arms fire, Staff Sergeant Sagredo moved from position to position to establish radio contact with the quick reaction force. His leadership and calm demeanor under fire reassured the Marines and inspired them as they ran low on ammunition. His perseverance was instrumental in gaining radio contact and directing the quick reaction force to his position. Once the reaction force arrived, Staff Sergeant Sagredo moved with complete disregard for his own safety until his platoon commander was evacuated, the amtrac recovered, and all forces moved to safe positions.[3]

Silver Star Citation

Capt. Jason E. Smith, USMC

Company Commander, Bravo Company, 1st Battalion, 5th Marines, Regimental Combat Team 1, 1st Marine Division, I Marine Expeditionary Force U.S. Marine Corps Forces, Central Command

The President of the United States takes pleasure in presenting the Silver Star Medal to Jason E. Smith, Captain, U.S. Marine Corps, for conspicuous gallantry and intrepidity in action against the enemy while serving as Company Commander, Bravo Company, First Battalion, Fifth Marines, Regimental Combat Team 1, FIRST Marine Division, I Marine Expeditionary Force, U.S. Marine Corps Forces, Central Command in support of Operation Iraqi Freedom II on 13 April 2004. Captain Smith led a rescue convoy through Al Fallujah to reach elements of Bravo Company that were surrounded by enemy forces and requiring support to evacuate casualties. Lacking accurate location information, Captain Smith used smoke from a burning amphibious assault vehicle to guide his convoy to the stranded platoon. When the rescue convoy slowed due to increased enemy fire, Captain Smith dismounted his vehicle, raced on foot to the front of the column, and led the convoy to the platoon. Disregarding his own personal safety and while exposed to enemy fire, Captain Smith returned fire and coordinated counter-attacks on enemy militia. As he reached the surrounded platoon, Captain Smith assessed the situation, organized a strong defensive perimeter around the platoon, and supervised the evacuation of casualties. Discovering remains of a deceased Marine inside a disabled vehicle, he ordered tanks to tow the vehicle back to the base camp. Captain Smith then coordinated the unit's withdrawal, traveling on foot at the rear of the column until all Marines crossed friendly lines. Captain Smith's calm demeanor and forceful character bolstered the fighting spirit of his Marines.[4]

Silver Star Citation

ON 10 APRIL 2004, Coalition forces unilaterally suspended offensive military operations in Al-Fallujah, hoping to give the Iraqi Governing Council time to negotiate a settlement with city leaders.[5] Although heavy fighting ceased, insurgents continued to attack Marines in the city, ignoring the cease-fire, and many Marines were skeptical that a cease-fire would be successfully negotiated. Lt. Col. Brennan Byrne, commanding officer for 1st Battalion, 5th Marine Regiment, stated at the time, "The prospect of some city father walking in and making 'Joe Jihadi' give himself up are pretty slim! What is coming is the destruction of anticoalition forces in Al-Fallujah . . . [T]hey have two choices: Submit or die."[6]

While Marines withdrew to the outskirts of the city, attacks on convoys carrying humanitarian relief supplies continued. One convoy was mortared on 9 April. On 12 April a convoy carrying food, water, and blood was delayed, and then rerouted when improvised explosive devices (IEDs) were discovered along its route. A second convoy carrying aid was hit by IEDs and small-arms fire before it reached the city.[7]

The following day, 13 April, elements of 2nd Platoon, Bravo Company, 1/5 Marines were manning an observation post (OP) in three houses in the eastern portion of Al-Fallujah along Route Michigan, an east-west highway that bisected the city, when Capt. Jason Smith, Bravo Company commander, was advised that a convoy of Humvees en route to resupply the position was under attack. Two squads, under the command of the 2nd platoon commander, 1st Lt. Christopher Ayres, mounted into two assault amphibious vehicle (AAVs, amtracs, or tracks) to locate the convoy. The AAVs located the Humvees, transferred the supplies, and headed toward the OP.[8]

It was midafternoon as the two AAVs maneuvered through the narrow streets. They came under attack from a barrage of rocket-propelled grenades (RPGs), which knocked out the radio of one of the AAVs, resulting in their separation as the two AAVs lost contact. One returned toward friendly lines. The other, in unfamiliar terrain and unable to turn around in the narrow streets, drove deeper into hostile neighborhoods.

As bullets ricocheted and RPGs exploded LCpl. Matthew Puckett steered the vehicle through heavy fire, trying to find his way east. In the turret Cpl. Kevin Kolm laid down suppressing fire. They turned a corner to encounter a large group of armed men, estimated at more than several hundred. "I'd never seen so many RPGs," SSgt. Ismael Sagredo recalled. "A lot of them were propped against the walls with extra rounds." The insurgents quickly put them to use.[9]

As Marines opened up with M-16s and machine guns, RPGs began smashing into the vehicle. One pierced the front, seriously wounding the 2nd Platoon commander, 1st Lt. Christopher Ayres, in the leg, and setting the engine on fire. Another struck Kolm, who was in the turret, killing him. Other hits wounded the Marines inside. Swerving south along a route known as "Shithead Alley," Puckett steered through the smoke trying to put as much distance between themselves and the insurgents before the engine gave out, or the fire spread to the stored munitions inside. The engine gave out moments later, in a residential neighborhood.[10]

With Ayres wounded, Sagredo took command and ordered Cpl. Ronnie Garcia to take a team and secure a nearby house. With the engine dead, the ramp was inoperable, requiring the Marines to exit the vehicle one at a time through the hatches, while under fire. The Marines exited the burning vehicle and withdrew into the unoccupied house, with LCpl. Abraham McCarver providing covering fire from an exposed position. He retreated to the house only to discover that Ayres was still trapped in the burning AAV. Heedless of the danger of exploding munitions and heavy enemy fire, McCarver and Sagredo charged to the burning vehicle to rescue their commander, pulling him free and assisting him to the house through heavy enemy fire.[11]

McCarver assisted the corpsman in providing first-aid to eight wounded Marines and in collecting and redistributing a rapidly diminishing supply of ammunition. As insurgents flocked south to join the fight, the Marines found themselves isolated and surrounded. Insurgents threw grenades over the wall and from neighboring rooftops, and fired into the house. The Marines threw back the grenades and returned fire, determined not to fall into enemy hands as they recalled the fate of four U.S. contractors only days earlier and blocks away. Sagredo went to the roof with the radio operator to try to make radio contact with the quick reaction force (QRF), moving from position to position under fire to try to establish contact.[12]

The Bravo Company commander, Capt. Jason Smith, had been at the battalion command post when he learned that elements of his 2nd platoon were surrounded with an urgent casualty who needed immediate evacuation. After returning to the company Command Post (CP) and receiving a situation report, Smith accompanied a rescue convoy of four M1A1 Abrams tanks and six armored Humvees under the command of 1st Lt. Joshua Glover. With no map or global positioning system (GPS), the stranded Marines were unable to give a location and the QRF, made up of elements of the 81-mm mortar and countermechanized platoons navigated toward the south, and the smoke of the burning AAV. Surrounded by twenty-five riflemen on foot, the convoy fought its way block-by-block into the city.

Due to communication difficulties, an Air Force F-15 was only able to make one strafing run. "We were shooting 360 degrees," said Glover, the Mortar Platoon leader and QRF commander. "When we finally saw the [armored personnel carrier], it was a piece of burning metal."[13]

For Glover, it was the second rescue mission of the day. Earlier that day, the 2001 Naval Academy graduate guided his QRF platoon through enemy lines to recover classified material from a downed Air Force MH-53J Pave Low helicopter. The MH-53J is an all-weather, low-level, long-range helicopter used for undetected penetration into denied areas for insertion and extraction of special forces. On his second deployment, Glover successfully recovered the sensitive material, then led his platoon through a coordinated attack to repel an enemy ambush and fight through to friendly lines, losing only one Marine, Pvt. Noah Boye, in the breakout.[14]

Inside the besieged house, Marines could hear the Iraqis shouting, and could see their shadows under the gate. "They were running across our line of fire like we weren't even shooting at them," remembered Cpl. Koreyan Calloway. "It was just like a range," added Cpl. Jacob Palofax. "We were just shooting them down."[15] But ammunition supplies were rapidly being exhausted. At one point, an ambulance pulled up, and fifteen men with RPGs exited and opened fire. A guerilla burst through the gate with an RPG and was shot dead. A second followed, and was wounded. Almost out of ammo, the Marines' position was becoming untenable. Sagredo considered ordering his Marines to withdraw. "It was in my head, we just got to go. Whoever makes it back makes it back. . . . That was the decision I'd have had to make, and I'm glad I didn't have to."[16]

Meanwhile, Smith, frustrated by the lack of communications and the convoy's slow progress, dismounted from his Humvee at the back of the column and raced to the front on foot to lead the convoy south on Route Frank. "It was all very confusing," Smith recalled. "The XO [Executive Officer Lt. Tyler McGaughey] was trying to direct a rescue force in by radio from the CP, but was sending them in error to the coordinates where the resupply was supposed to have taken place. I could see that the burning smoke was way south of that point, but radio communication was jumbled, so I dismounted and ran to the front."[17]

At the intersection with Route Donna, Smith directed the tanks to establish a blocking position facing west while he led the QRF east on Donna. He exposed himself to accurate, sustained automatic weapons fire as he directed an HMG (heavy machine gun) vehicle to suppress an enemy (machine-gun) position.[18]

Smith pulled the tanks from their blocking position and directed the force south on Frank, then west on Cathy, enduring increasing enemy fire as they moved west. "I felt that as long as we kept moving, things would be OK."[19] He continually returned suppressing fire, as he ran exposed from position to position, until he spotted the burning AAV and led the dismounted QRF to form a perimeter around it, then searched for a house to use. "The houses almost all had walls around them so I looked for one with an open gate. I didn't want to have to be messing with a gate out in the open and exposed. I saw a house on the south side of Cathy with a gate open and a body in the gateway. I'd found the right house by luck!"[20]

The Marines inside the house started shouting that they could hear tanks, then Captain Smith came through the gate shouting, "Marines, Marines, friendlies!" Smith's Marines had successfully broken through! After a situation report from Sagredo and arranging for the evacuation of Ayres and Hospital Corpsman Third Class Villegas, Smith ensured suppressive fire to cover the medical Humvee's withdrawal, then turned his attention to the still-burning AAV.

Smith radioed to request an AAV with towing capabilities, but when it arrived he was advised that a heavier piece of equipment would be necessary in order to tow the hulk, and battalion advised there would be a considerable delay before it would arrive on scene. He was authorized to blow up the AAV in place and return to friendly lines, but he rejected that option. Aware that Cpl. Kolm's body remained inside the burning AAV, Smith stated he was prepared to stay all night, or as long as necessary, to tow the AAV. Rather than wait, Smith decided to let the tanks attempt the tow.[21]

A defensive perimeter was established for the hour it took for a tank to hook up to the disabled AAV containing Kolm's remains under the cover of tank and warplane fire. Once ready, McCarver and LCpl. J. Hedrick drove a Humvee in front of the tanks to lead them back to friendly lines while Smith traveled on foot at the rear of the convoy as it withdrew back to friendly territory. Estimates of insurgents killed vary from twenty to one hundred. The next morning just before dawn, AC-130 Spectre gunships launched a punitive raid over a six-block area near the ambush, virtually destroying the area.[22]

On 14 July 2005 at the Naval Air Station Joint Reserve Base at Belle Chase, Louisiana, Major Smith, then an inspector-instructor with the 3rd Battalion, 23rd Marines at Baton Rouge, was presented the Silver Star. He follows in the footsteps of his father, Walter Smith, who received a Distinguished Flying Cross during Vietnam. Commenting on his "valor," Smith commented, "To me, it wasn't an option to leave those guys there."[23]

He is modest about his actions. "I only got the medal because I was the highest ranking guy there. Personally, I'm in awe of Lt. Glover and his Marines. You have to understand, they were already worn out from an earlier action, and depressed over the loss of a Marine, but from start to finish they never faltered, never wavered. Their only concern was getting to the Marines to help them."[24]

On 12 October 2005 Lance Corporal McCarver echoed Captain Smith's sentiments upon receiving the Silver Star at a ceremony at Camp Pendleton, California, when he stated, "There are just some things that needed to be done, and [that] was one of those things." McCarver, who has been out of the Marines since April 2006, plans a career in federal law enforcement.[25]

Two weeks later, on 28 October, the Commandant of the Marine Corps, Gen. Michael W. Hagee, presented Capt. Joshua Glover with the Silver Star at a ceremony held at the Marine Barracks in Washington, DC. Humbly accepting the award, he stated, "I received this award for what we did as a platoon." A three-tour veteran of Iraq, Glover is assigned to HQ-USMC.[26] On 30 November in a ceremony at Camp Pendleton, California, 1st Lt. Christopher Ayres pinned the Silver Star medal to the blouse of GySgt. Ismael Sagredo and thanked him for saving his life. In accepting the award Sagredo stated, "All we did was go in and do our jobs as we were trained while trying to get everyone out alive."[27]

ENDNOTES

1. Silver Star citation, 1st Lt. Joshua L. Glover, USMC, http://www.homeofheroes.com/valor2/SS/7_GWOT/citations_USMC.html.

2. Silver Star citation, LCpl. Abraham McCarver, USMC, http://www.homeofheroes.com/valor2/SS/7_GWOT/citations_USMC-M.html.

3. Silver Star citation, SSgt. Ismael Sagredo, USMC, http://www.homeofheroes.com/valor2/SS/7_GWOT/citations_USMC-M.html.

4. Silver Star citation, Capt. Jason E. Smith, USMC, http://www.homeofheroes.com/valor2/SS/7_GWOT/citations_USMC-M.html.

5. SFC Doug Sample, "Fallujah 'Under Control' as Gunfire Punctuates Cease-Fire," American Forces Press Service, 10 April 2004.

6. GySgt. Mark Oliva, "Marines Suspend Fallujah Offensive, Push Humanitarian Aid," *Marine Corps News*, 13 April 2004.

7. "Attacks on Humanitarian Aid to Fallujah," United States Central Command News Release #04-04-11, 13 April 2004.

8. Maj. Jason Smith, telephone interview with Scott Baron, 29 October 2007.

9. James Hider, "Stranded Marines Fight to Last Bullets," *London* (UK) *Times*, 16 April 2004.

10. Ibid.

11. John W. Sparks, "A Glint of Silver at 23," *The Commercial Appeal* (Memphis, TN), 27 November 2005.

12. Hider, "Stranded Marines Fight to Last Bullets."

13. Pamela Constable, "A Wrong Turn, Chaos and a Rescue," *Washington* (DC) *Post*, 15 April 2004.

14. Gidget Fuentes and John Hoellwarth, "Captain Earns Silver Star for Two Actions in One Day: His Unit Punched Through Enemy Lines on Separate Missions," *Marine Corps Times*, 21 November 2005.

15. Hider, "Stranded Marines Fight to Last Bullets."

16. Ibid.

17. Smith, telephone interview.

18. "Summary of Action: Recommendation for Silver Star, Capt. Jason Smith," unpublished.

19. Smith, telephone interview.

20. Ibid.

21. "Summary of Action: Recommendation for Silver Star, Capt. Jason Smith."

22. Constable, "A Wrong Turn, Chaos and a Rescue."

23. Joe Gyan Jr., "Marine from BR Cited for Bravery," *New Orleans* (LA) *Advocate*, 14 July 2005.

24. Maj. Jason Smith, telephone interview with Scott Baron, 30 December 2007.

25. Ray Lewis, "Camp Pendleton–Based Rifleman Awarded Silver Star," *Marine Corps News*, 13 October 2005 (Story ID #20051013182324).

26. Fuentes and Hoellwarth, "Captain Earns Silver Star for Two Actions in One Day."

27. Patric Floto, "Gunny Gets Silver Star for Gallantry," *Marine Corps Times*, 30 November 2005 (Story ID #2005121173519).

Maj. Richard J. Gannon IV, USMC

Commanding Officer, Lima Company, 3rd Battalion, 7th Marines,
Regimental Combat Team 7, 1st Marine Division, I Marine Expeditionary
Force, U.S. Marine Corps Forces, Central Command

Al-Qa'im, Iraq
April 2004

The President of the United States takes pride in presenting the Silver Star Medal (Posthumously) to Richard J. Gannon IV, Captain, U.S. Marine Corps, for conspicuous gallantry and intrepidity in action against the enemy while serving as Commanding Officer, Company L, Third Battalion, Seventh Marines, Regimental Combat Team 7, FIRST Marine Division, I Marine Expeditionary Force, U.S. Marine Corps Forces, Central Command in support of Operation Iraqi Freedom on 17 April 2004. While Captain Gannon was leading his company to reinforce a besieged sniper observation post, his unit came under intense rocket-propelled grenade, medium machine gun, and small arms fire. His combined anti-armor team countered this attack with a destructive direct assault employing heavy machine gun fire and guided missiles. While Company L assaulted a fortified position, housing an enemy squad-size force, Captain Gannon employed rockets, heavy machine guns, and snipers to support the maneuver of his platoons. The assault section leader was struck by enemy fire and fell mortally wounded during this engagement. While the section leader was evacuated from the street into the cover of a compound courtyard, Captain Gannon continued to press the attack, steadily moving forward to assist the wounded Marine. Maneuvering through the enemy fire, with complete disregard for his own safety, he entered the courtyard to search for the wounded Marine. Upon entering a house, he exchanged small arms fire and grenades with nine Mujahadeen fighters and fell mortally wounded.[1]

Silver Star Citation

Lt. Col. Matthew A. Lopez, USMC

Commanding Officer, 3rd Battalion,
7th Marines Regimental Combat Team 7, I Marine Expeditionary Force,
U.S. Marine Corps Forces, Central Command

The President of the United States takes pleasure in presenting the Silver Star Medal to Matthew A. Lopez, Lieutenant Colonel, U.S. Marine Corps, for conspicuous gallantry and intrepidity in action against the enemy while serving as Commanding Officer, Third Battalion, Seventh Marines, Regimental Combat Team 7, I Marine Expeditionary Force, U.S. Marine Corps Forces, Central Command, in support of Operation Iraqi Freedom II from 14 April to 18 April 2004. While conducting a civil affairs patrol of police stations in the Al Qa'im area, Lieutenant Colonel Lopez' patrol was ambushed by approximately thirty insurgents. Enemy fire tore into his vehicle, striking him in the back and wounding the translator. Disregarding his personal injuries, he returned fire, eliminating several insurgents while directing the maneuver of the patrol's soft-skinned vehicles out of the impact zone. Despite the chaos of the situation, Lieutenant Colonel Lopez remained utterly calm, executing an aerial medical evacuation of a critically wounded Marine. He fearlessly led the pursuit of enemy fighters in the area, destroying sixteen insurgents. After receiving treatment for the bullet wound, he refused evacuation. On 17 April 2004 demonstrating extraordinary combat endurance and command presence, Lieutenant Colonel Lopez led a 48-hour urban assault to destroy an estimated three hundred insurgents in the city. His brilliant action resulted in more than one hundred twenty insurgents confirmed killed, destroying whole insurgent cells and groups, numerous foreign fighters, and the enemy's will to fight. Throughout the battle, he placed himself with lead platoons, assaulting insurgent fortified positions in house-to-house assaults and employing mortars and rotary wing close air support.[2]

Silver Star Citation

LCpl. Danny Santos, USMC

Squad Leader, 3rd Squad, 3rd Platoon Kilo Company, 3rd Battalion, Regimental Combat Team 7, 1st Marine Division, I Marine Expeditionary Force, U.S. Marine Corps Forces, Central Command

The President of the United States takes pleasure in presenting the Silver Star Medal to Danny S. Santos, Lance Corporal, U.S. Marine Corps, for conspicuous gallantry and intrepidity in action against the enemy while serving as Squad Leader, Third Squad, Third Platoon, Kilo Company, Third Battalion, Regimental Combat Team 7, FIRST Marine Division, I Marine

Expeditionary Force, U.S. Marine Corps Forces, Central Command, in support of Operation Iraqi Freedom II on 17 April 2004. Lance Corporal Santos performed heroically during Third Battalion's attack against militia forces when the lead element of Kilo Company came under intense automatic weapon and rocket-propelled grenade fire from multiple enemy strong points arrayed in two-story houses. Despite sustaining serious wounds to his shoulder and stomach, Lance Corporal Santos led his squad against the enemy in order to destroy their fortified positions. As the squad's point man lay wounded in the street, Lance Corporal Santos disregarded his own safety, exposed himself to enemy crossfire and destroyed an enemy position using an AT-4. Under the suppressive fires of his assault man, he dashed into enemy fire and dragged the wounded point man back to the safety of a covered position. Despite his wounds, he remained calm throughout the engagement, consolidated his squad into a defensive position and triaged the wounded. Refusing medical attention until his men were properly treated, he continued to check his squad's position, and engaged the enemy in adjacent buildings and streets.[3]

Silver Star Citation

IN MID-APRIL 2004 the men of 3rd Battalion, 7th Marines were in the middle of their deployment at Al-Qa'im, a border village one mile east of the Syrian border along the Euphrates River. The fighting that began in Fallujah in early April had spread throughout the Al-Anbar Province, to include Al-Qa'im.

The 3/7 was on its second deployment to Iraq, having deployed to Kuwait in January 2003 at which time it participated in the drive north in March and April during the start of Operation Iraqi Freedom (OIF). Following Stability and Support Operations (SASO) in Karbala, the regiment returned stateside in September 2003, but redeployed in late February 2004, dividing the battalion between Al-Karabilah, Al-Qa'im, and Al-Husaybah.[4]

Their mission was to bring stability to the area by building schools, improving roads, fixing sewers, cleaning up debris, restoring lighting, and training the new Iraqi police. Lima Company, augmented by a platoon from Kilo Company, would be at the point of the spear, taking control of an eight-building former trading post in Al-Husaybah, the primary border crossing between Syria and Iraq, while Kilo Company would garrison Al-Karabilah.

Despite the suspension of offensive operations ordered by U.S. Ambassador Paul Bremer on 9 April, the anti-Iraqi and anticoalition forces had remained active in attacking the Marines. Lt. Isaac Moore with Weapons Company recalled, "We had more contact in a week than we did in the entire first phase of the war."[5] Lima Company endured daily bombings and mortar attacks—with twenty such attacks occurring in one single night—and the battalion began taking casualties. On 8 April LCpl. Christopher Wasser of Lima Company was killed and six others wounded by a roadside bomb. The following day, a Kilo Company Marine, LCpl. Elias Torres was killed by a rocket-propelled grenade (RPG) when his convoy was ambushed. Lt. Nathan Rugi, 1st Platoon leader in Lima Company, summed up the change in attitude as he briefed his men: "I won't lose seven Marines in one day. You do whatever you have to do."[6]

At about noon on 14 April Lt. Col. Matthew A. Lopez, 3rd Battalion Commander, was in Al-Karabilah meeting with local police officials when he learned that units were involved in a firefight. Returning to Al-Husaybah on the main east-west highway, Lopez' eight-vehicle convoy was ambushed by intense machine-gun and RPG fire, wounding Lopez in the back, breaking ribs, and wounding five other Marines. Despite his wounds, Lopez returned fire while he directed his soft-skinned vehicles out of the impact area and arranged for the aerial evacuation of a critically wounded Marine. Twenty-five insurgents were killed in the action. He then continued in command leading the effort to pursue the insurgents and relieve the Marines under attack at a forward-base. His wounds went untreated until that evening, and he refused evacuation.[7]

Back in Al-Karabilah SSgt. John Ferguson, acting platoon commander, hearing of the attack on the battalion commander, mounted up his Marines, a squad of fourteen men commanded by Cpl. Jason Dunham. When they were ambushed as they headed west toward Al-Husaybah, the Marines dismounted and continued on foot, splitting into two fire teams. Passing an unpaved alley, they observed seven Iraqi vehicles parked in a file, doors open, engines idling. As Dunham approached the third vehicle, a white Toyota Land Cruiser, the driver lunged out and attacked Dunham, pulling out a hand grenade. Struggling with the insurgent, Dunham used his Kevlar helmet and body to shield other Marines from the blast, and absorbed the blunt of the explosion, undoubtedly saving teammates Pfc. Kelly Miller and LCpl. William Hampton from death or serious injury. Knocked unconscious, Dunham was transported via Landstuhl, Germany, to Bethesda, Maryland, where he died on 22 April. For his unselfish valor, Dunham was awarded the Medal of Honor, the first—and to date the only—Marine to be so honored in Afghanistan or Iraq.[8]

Three days later, on 17 April, an early-morning bomb explosion near the Ba'ath Party Headquarters initiated a fierce two-day battle between Marines and insurgents in Al-Husaybah. When the Marines sent to investigate the explosion were ambushed, a second force was dispatched, and they also came under intense machine-gun and mortar fire. Lopez led his battalion into Al-Husaybah to root out the insurgents, rumored to number more than three hundred. In command of Lima Company was Captain Richard J. Gannon IV.

Gannon, son of a Marine officer veteran of Vietnam and a graduate of Cornell University NROTC (Naval Reserve Officers Training Commission, Marine Option), was commissioned a second lieutenant of Marines on 13 January 1995. He served as a platoon commander with 2/1 and as an instructor at the Naval Academy before being assigned to the 3/7 in May 2002. He participated in major combat operations on the race north to Baghdad in April 2003, then SASO operations in Al-Karbala. Now, on his second deployment, he commanded Lima Company.

As Gannon led his company to relieve a besieged sniper position, they came under intense RPG, medium machine-gun, and small-arms fire from fortified positions. Gannon employed his Combined Anti-Armor Team (CAAT) team on a direct assault. When the assault section leader was mortally wounded in the assault, Gannon arranged for his evacuation to the cover of a courtyard, then led the assault on the house. In the ensuing battle that took place at close range, grenades and small-arms fire was exchanged as Gannon led his Marines into the house. In the gunfight that followed Gannon and four other Marines (Cpl. Christopher Gibson, LCpl. Michael J. Smith, LCpl Ruben Valdez Jr., and LCpl. Gary F. Van Leuven) died fighting nine Mujahadeen in close combat while going to the aid of a wounded Marine. The battle at that point was only ninety minutes old.[9]

Fighting continued throughout the day as more Marines entered Al-Husaybah. Later that afternoon, LCpl. Danny Santos was with the lead elements of Kilo Company, his 3rd Squad southernmost on the left flank of two platoons on line, as they entered the city to reinforce another unit that had been ambushed. There was heavy RPG and automatic weapon fire coming from fortified positions within two-story houses. "We found ourselves in a fight in every street and alley," recalled Capt. Trent Gibson, Kilo Company commander.[10]

Santos' squad divided into two teams to cover more area, and present less of a target as they dodged grenades, RPGs, and small-arms fire. Santos, on his second deployment, was struck by shrapnel in the stomach and shoulder from an explosion. Despite his wounds, he took up an AT-4 (an antitank guided missile) to neutralize a machine-gun position, then ran exposed to enemy fire to drag his wounded point man to cover. Putting his squad into defensive positions, he oversaw the treatment of his wounded while returning suppressive fire onto enemy positions, and refused medical treatment until his Marines were cared for. He then withdrew with his men before accepting medical evacuation. All nine insurgents in the house were eventually killed.[11]

By 3:00 PM the entire battalion was either engaged in combat or taking positions to relieve those who were. The tide began to turn at 4:30 PM when the first Cobra gunships arrived to support the troops on the ground by strafing enemy positions; by 6:00 PM the insurgents were on the run. The Cobras provided fire support throughout the night, centered on insurgent positions near a soccer stadium. As Lieutenant Colonel Lopez stated, "I don't think they expected us to respond with the kind of force that we did."[12]

The fight continued house to house, block by block, over a two-kilometer area until 11:30 PM when having evacuated their wounded, the Marines withdrew to Al-Qa'im with twenty prisoners, leaving one hundred fifty of the enemy dead. Al-Husaybah would remain quiet until June.[13]

The following 15 April, almost a year after his death protecting his Marines, Sally Gannon accepted her husband's posthumous Silver Star and Purple Heart medals in a ceremony at the Marine Corps Air Ground Combat Center, Twentynine Palms, California. Marines in Al-Husaybah provided their own tribute, renaming Camp Al-Husaybah as Camp Gannon.

On 10 August 2005 Lt. Gen. James Amos, Commanding General of 2 Marine Expeditionary Force (2 MEF) presented Santos with the Silver Star in a ceremony at the Littoral Warfare Training Center at Camp Lejeune, North Carolina. Santos, attached to the 4th Marine Expeditionary Brigade was modest about the award, stating, "I was just doing my job. . . . To me, it was simple. Taking care of my Marines.[14]

On 30 September 2005 Lieutenant Colonel Lopez, now a student at the Joint Forces Staff College in Norfolk, Virginia, was presented the Silver Star by Army Maj. Gen. Ken Quinlan, Joint Forces Staff College commandant. Responding to praise for his actions, he responded, "I didn't do anything that any other Marine wouldn't have done."[15]

ENDNOTES

1. Silver Star citation, Capt. Richard J. Gannon IV, USMC, http://www.homeofheroes.com/valor2/SS/7_GWOT/citations_USMC.html.
2. Silver Star citation, Lt. Col. Matthew A. Lopez, USMC, http://www.homeofheroes.com/valor2/SS/7_GWOT/citations_USMC.html.
3. Silver Star citation, LCpl. Danny Santos, USMC, http://www.homeofheroes.com/valor2/SS/7_GWOT/citations_USMC-M.html.
4. "3/7 Heritage: 3rd Battalion, 7th Marines." http://www.i-mef.usmc.mil/div/7mar/3bn.
5. Ron Harris, "Commemorating the Life of a Comrade," St. Louis (MO) Post Dispatch, 13 April 2004.
6. Ibid.
7. Marc Loi, "Marine Officer Receives Silver Star," Marine Corps News, 30 September 2005.
8. Michael Phillips, "In Combat, Marine Puts Theory to Test, Comrades Believe," Wall Street Journal, 25 May 2004.
9. "Biography of Richard J. Gannon IV," http://www.marketingbysignature.com/gannonbio.html.
10. Chris Mazzolini, "Marine Awarded the Military's Highest Combat Medal," Marine Corps News, 11 August 2005.
11. P. B. Brent, "In the Kill Zone: A Pop and a Spurt of Blood," Honolulu (HI) Star Bulletin, 23 May 2004.
12. Ron Harris, "Coordinated Attack in Force Kills 6 Marines at Al-Husaybah," St. Louis (MO) Post Dispatch, 17 April 2004.
13. Matthew R. Jones, "Marines Recount Fierce Battle," Marine Corps News, 15 September 2004 (Story ID #20049209463).
14. Mazzolini, "Marine Awarded the Military's Highest Combat Medal."
15. Loi, "Marine Officer Receives Silver Star."

LCpl. Thomas R. Adametz, USMC

*Rifleman, Echo Company, 2nd Battalion, 1st Marines,
1st Marine Division, I Marine Expeditionary Force,
U.S. Marine Corps Forces, Central Command*

Al-Fallujah, Iraq
26 April 2004

The President of the United States takes pleasure in presenting the Silver Star Medal to Thomas R. Adametz, Lance Corporal, U.S. Marine Corps, for conspicuous gallantry and intrepidity in action against the enemy as a Rifleman, Echo Company, Second Battalion, First Marines, FIRST Marine Division, I Marine Expeditionary Force, U.S. Marine Corps Forces Central Command in support of Operation Iraqi Freedom II on 26 April 2004. Following the seizure of two key buildings along a vital avenue of approach into the company's sector, Lance Corporal Adametz and his squad moved into the northernmost building and provided security for his platoon's position. The enemy's fierce attack of rocket-propelled and hand-thrown grenades onto his platoon's position resulted in four serious and numerous minor casualties. With disregard for his own safety, Lance Corporal Adametz exposed himself to grenade and small arms fire in order to provide suppressive fire facilitating the evacuation of the wounded Marines. Picking up a squad automatic weapon from a wounded Marine, he delivered withering fire on enemy forces twenty-five meters away. Lance Corporal Adametz' aggressive actions and devastating fire were critical in repelling the enemy's attack.[1]

Silver Star Citation

Cpl. Aaron C. Austin, USMC

*Machine Gun Team Leader, Echo Company, 2nd Battalion 1st Marines,
Regimental Combat Team 1, 1st Marine Division, I Marine Expeditionary
Force, U.S. Marine Forces, Central Command*

The President of the United States takes pride in presenting the Silver Star Medal (Posthumously) to Aaron C. Austin, Lance Corporal, U.S. Marine Corps, for conspicuous gallantry and intrepidity in action against the enemy as Machine Gun Team Leader, Company E, Second Battalion, First Marines, Regimental Combat Team 1, FIRST Marine Division, I Marine Expeditionary Force, U.S. Marine Forces Central Command in support of Operation Iraqi Freedom II on 26 April 2004. At 11:00 AM on 26 April, a numerically superior enemy force attacked Lance Corporal Austin's platoon from three different directions. In the first fifteen minutes of the attack the enemy fired dozens of rocket-propelled grenades (RPGs), thousands of machine gun rounds, and then assaulted to within twenty meters of Lance Corporal Austin's position. While throwing grenades and spraying their positions with AK-47 fire, sixteen of his fellow Marines on the rooftop position were wounded, some severely. After ensuring his wounded platoon members received medical treatment, he rallied the few remaining members of his platoon and rushed to the critical rooftop defensive position. Braving withering enemy machine gun and RPG fire, he reached the rooftop and prepared to throw a hand grenade. As he moved into a position from which to throw his grenade, enemy machine gun fire struck Lance Corporal Austin multiple times in the chest. Undaunted by his injuries and with heroic effort, Lance Corporal Austin threw his grenade, which exploded amidst the enemy, halting their furious attack.[2]

Silver Star Citation

LCpl. Carlos Gomez-Perez, USMC

Fire Team Leader, 1st Platoon, Echo Company, 2nd Battalion,
1st Marine Regiment, Regimental Combat Team 1,
1st Marine Division U.S. Marine Corps, Central Command

The President of the United States takes pleasure in presenting the Silver Star Medal to Carlos Gomez-Perez, Lance Corporal, U.S. Marine Corps, for conspicuous gallantry and intrepidity in action against the enemy while serving as Fire Team Leader, First Platoon, Echo Company, Second Battalion, First Marine Regiment, Regimental Combat Team 1, FIRST Marine Division, U.S. Marine Corps, Central Command in support of Operation Iraqi Freedom II on 26 April 2004. While conducting security patrols in Al Fallujah, Iraq, Lance Corporal Gomez-Perez' platoon secured two buildings from which to observe enemy movement. At 11:00 AM a numerically superior enemy force attacked the platoon with rocket-propelled grenades (RPGs) and machine gun fire from three directions. During the first fifteen minutes of the attack, the enemy closed to within twenty meters of the platoon, wounding many Marines on the rooftop position. After ensuring wounded platoon members received medical treatment, Lance Corporal Gomez-Perez rushed to reinforce the critical rooftop position. After enemy fire wounded one of his comrades, Lance Corporal Gomez-Perez courageously exposed himself to enemy fire to move the Marine to safety and was wounded through the right shoulder and cheek during the process. Despite his injuries, he again exposed himself to enemy fire and continued to attack the enemy with grenades and by firing his rifle with his uninjured arm. Lance Corporal Gomez-Perez' fierce defense halted a determined enemy assault and enabled the evacuation of wounded Marines.[3]

Silver Star Citation

DESPITE A UNILATERAL CEASE-FIRE and unremitting attempts to negotiate a settlement, insurgents continued to attack Coalition forces in Al-Fallujah and throughout the Al-Anbar region. By late April, some Marine commanders hoped for a renewed offensive in Al-Fallujah, while diplomats extended the cease-fire even as they warned that time was running out to honor an agreement for the militants to hand over heavy weapons or risk full-scale offensive operations. The hope was that by initiating joint Marine–Iraqi police–Iraqi Civil Defense Corps (ICDC) patrols, Iraqi authority could be restored in Al-Fallujah. The Bush administration was hoping to avoid further urban combat and civilian casualties, with its resulting deterioration of U.S.-Iraqi relations. On Sunday, 25 April, the day the cease-fire was extended, the commander of the 1st Marine Division, Maj. Gen. James N. Mattis, who was responsible for Al-Fallujah and western Iraq stated, "A military solution is not going to be the solution here unless everything else fails."[4]

Before dawn on the morning of 26 April, 2nd platoon of Echo Company, 2nd Battalion, 1st Marine Regiment (2/1) of the 1st Marine Division advanced into the Jolan section of northeast Al-Fallujah to clear some buildings of snipers. They were accompanied by soldiers of the Special Operations Command (SOC), including MSgt. Don Hollenbaugh, Sgt. Maj. Larry Bolvin, and a medic, SSgt. Dan Briggs. The Marines advanced approximately two hundred yards to occupy two houses north and south of an intersection to use as an observation post.[5]

Most of the Marines of Echo Company were on their second deployment and had frequently come under fire patrolling in Al-Fallujah. Three Marines had been killed since the company began operations on 6 April. On

24 April Fox Company had sent in a patrol that surprised the insurgents, killing eleven. Now it was Echo's turn. It was about 5:00 AM when they took up positions in the two buildings to use as observation posts to spot insurgent activity. At dawn, the insurgents began probing the American defenses with rocket-propelled grenades (RPGs) and machine-gun fire.

At about 9:45 AM Marines began taking small-arms fire from three insurgents in the minaret (tower) of the Al-Ma'adhidy mosque. The Marines returned fire, killing one of their attackers. They then ordered those inside to surrender, speaking in Arabic over loudspeakers, but no one came out. They entered, but found only spent ammunition casings on the floor of the minaret. Shortly after the squad returned from searching the mosque, insurgents returned and resumed firing at the Marines. By 11:00 AM the sporadic sniping had transitioned to a full-scale attack by forty to three hundred heavily armed insurgents.[6] The north house occupied by the Marines began taking heavy mortar, RPG, and machine-gun fire from the rooftops of adjacent houses and nearby buildings, including the mosque.[7]

Large numbers of hostiles had surged into the area. "The Iraqis really believed this was a full-on invasion of Fallujah," Hollenbaugh recalled. "There were supposedly truckloads and busloads of people coming to meet us, and here we're just a thirty-five man outfit."[8]

What followed was a three-hour battle in which Marine after Marine demonstrated extraordinary valor in a close-quarters fight with a numerically superior enemy fighting from fortified positions in a neighborhood that was familiar to them. Echo Company commander, Capt. Douglas Zembiec, proudly stated that his men "fought like lions," earning him the title "Lion of Fallujah." Born in Hawaii, the son of an FBI agent, he was a two-time All-American wrestler at the Naval Academy before graduating in 1995. Zembiec was a veteran of Kosovo and led his Marines from the front. He would later be awarded a posthumous Silver Star during his fourth deployment to Iraq for his actions in combat outside Baghdad on 11 May 2007.[9]

In the north house, LCpl. Carlos Gomez-Perez heard two explosions coming from above, and screams from the roof. This was followed by four wounded Marines racing down the stairs from the roof. Grenades exploded on the roof and were thrown into windows wounding other Marines, as machine-gun fire battered against the walls. Gomez-Perez, who entered the United States illegally with his family when he was nine, joined the Marines in 2001 and was among the first Marines to invade Iraq in March 2003. Now a team leader with Echo Company, Gomez-Perez was on his second deployment to Iraq.[10]

Advised that there were seriously wounded Marines in the north house, Briggs, the Special Forces medic, raced forward across the exposed roadway between the two houses to treat and evacuate the wounded. His Distinguished Service Cross citation states that Briggs "repeatedly subjected himself to intense and unrelenting enemy fire in order to provide critical medical attention to severely injured Marines and organize defensive operations." [11] Hollenbaugh stated that Briggs exposed himself to enemy fire no less than six times, firing his sidearm at insurgents as close as twenty-five yards to protect his Marines. [12]

As machine-gun fire ricocheted off the concrete, LCpl. Aaron C. Austin, a machine-gun team leader, raced up the exposed stairway, followed by Gomez-Perez and another Marine, as they made their way to the top and the inadequate protection of low concrete walls flanking the roof. Insurgents on adjacent rooftops made the venture extremely hazardous, as they unleashed a hail of RPGs, grenades, and AK-47 fire from three directions.

Austin, a twenty-one-year-old from Texas, was also on his second deployment. He rallied his Marines in their effort to counterattack and retake the roof and an uncontrolled machine-gun position. "We've got to get back on the roof and get that gun," he called out and charged up the stairs under fire. Gomez-Perez, close behind him, was shot in the cheek. Undeterred, Gomez-Perez provided suppressive fire as Austin moved forward to throw a grenade, but as Austin prepared to throw the grenade, he was struck multiple times in the chest by machine-gun fire. With his last effort, Austin hurled his grenade into the enemy position, neutralizing the threat, before falling unconscious. [13]

Gomez-Perez attempted to pull Austin into cover, and was struck by an armor-piercing round in his shoulder, leaving a fist-sized hole. "All I could see were his legs, so we reached down to pull him back up, but he was heavy in all his gear, so it took a while to drag him [in]." As another Marine administered CPR to Austin, who by then was "white, stiff, and with no pulse," Gomez-Perez provided covering fire, using his uninjured left arm to fire his M-16A4, emptying four magazines and lobbing grenades with his injured arm. His actions kept pressure on the insurgents, allowing the wounded Marines to be evacuated. [14]

1st Sgt. William S. Skiles, aware of the critical need to relieve the platoon of their wounded Marines, led the evacuation Humvees and personnel forward under fire directly to the embattled position, then dismounted and began directing the evacuation of four severely wounded, and several seriously wounded Marines. With him was twenty-year-old Navy corpsman, PO3 Jason Duty, who rushed back and forth under fire to treat and evacuate the wounded. Echo Company Marines said that "Doc" Duty was faster than bullets that day. At least four times, Duty braved heavy fire in the open to assist the wounded to the waiting Humvees.[15]

Duty made it to the roof to assist with moving Austin under fire to the Humvees. "I remember thinking I was in trouble about the third trip because that's when the volume of fire increased a lot," Duty remembered. "When we were loading the last guy, they chucked a hand grenade at our Humvee, and it hit the hood. It rolled off and didn't explode. I think they were trying to throw it in the back where the wounded were being loaded."[16]

Skiles was pouring suppressive fire on enemy positions while coordinating the rescue, handing out additional ammunition and grenades to riflemen, and loading the wounded. Then, while Duty performed CPR on Austin in the back of the Humvee, Skiles maneuvered the Humvee through intense fire and rubble with one hand and fired his rifle with the other to reach the battalion field hospital. Both Duty and Skiles received the Bronze Star medal with combat "V" for Valor for their actions that day.[17]

Inside the house, LCpl. Thomas R. Adametz saw a Marine machinegunner, dazed by a grenade explosion, drop his squad automatic weapon (SAW). Aware that the number of casualties was mounting and the increased danger that their position could be overrun, Adametz left cover to dash outside and recover the abandoned SAW. He began engaging the insurgents from an exposed courtyard within twenty meters of the enemy. When the SAW seized up from overheating, Adametz picked up a second. When that one also seized up, he ran inside for a third, dashing outside to reengage the insurgents. His suppressive fire facilitated the evacuation of his wounded comrades. "There was no shortage of targets," he recalled. "They just kept on coming."[18]

In the south house, Hollenbaugh, Bolvin, and two Marines fought off attacks, engaging targets of opportunity while ducking RPG, grenade, and automatic-weapons fire. They fired on insurgents creeping along the alleys adjacent to their position, and dropped grenades. When a grenade landed on the roof, Hollenbaugh only had time to dive for cover before the explosion, which seriously wounded both Marines, and riddled Bolvin with shrapnel wounds to his arm and ear. Hollenbaugh moved the Marines to cover, patched up Bolvin, then resumed firing on the enemy, moving from position to position as the other Marines were evacuated.[19]

Two hours into the battle, Marines called in M1A1 Abrams tanks and Cobra attack helicopters to provide suppressive fire, knocking out the mosque's minaret, which had been the source of heavy RPG fire. Col. John Coleman, 1 Marine Expeditionary Force (1 MEF) chief of staff, explained to reporters that mosques used as offensive positions are legitimate targets to be engaged when attacked.[20] Although wounded in the leg, Zembiec twice mounted a tank under heavy enemy fire to direct the tank in engaging enemy targets, actions for which he would be awarded the Purple Heart and Bronze Star with combat "V."

Valor continued throughout the battle as the outnumbered Marines refused to give up the initiative. LCpl. John Flores protected the left flank and refused evacuation after being wounded; Gomez-Perez was evacuated under protest only after being ordered to the rear. LCpl. Craig Bell, though wounded in the right side and angered after narrowly escaping death from an exploding grenade, methodically pumped more than one hundred 40-mm rounds from his M-203 grenade launcher at the enemy in the space of an hour. His accurate fire eliminated numerous enemy positions.[21]

On the roof, Hollenbaugh continued to engage the enemy. "I started putting rounds into the building just east of the north house, to the right. [I was skipping] bullets in off the floor and the walls." When he noticed a heavy machine gun firing on the evacuating Marines, "I got him to shut up," Hollenbaugh said. It was only when Zembiec came to the roof and called, "Hey Don, it's time to go," that he realized that all the Marines, both wounded and healthy, had departed, and that he was the last person out.[22] The citation for his Distinguished Service Cross states he was "essential in turning the tide of the enemy's ground force assault" and stated he was "directly responsible for preventing enemy insurgent forces from overrunning the United States Force."[23]

LCpl. Austin died from his wounds, the only Marine fatality that day, and was awarded a posthumous Silver Star which his parents accepted on 22 July 2005. Two months earlier, on 4 May 2005, Lt. Gen. John Sattler, commanding general of 1 MEF presented Adametz with his Silver Star during a ceremony at Camp Pendleton, California. Released from active duty in November 2005, his palms still bear the scars from severe burns sustained while changing red-hot barrels on the SAW under fire.[24]

On 13 April 2006, just short of two years after the battle, Maj. Gen. Richard Natonski, 1st Marine Division commander, presented Gomez-Perez with the Silver Star. Medically retired from the Marines, he currently teaches a two-week self-defense, force protection, and antiterrorism course to deploying Sailors at the 32nd Street Naval Base in San Diego, California. Major Zembiec, Gomez-Perez' former CO, said at the ceremony, "I joined the Corps to serve with men like him."[25]

When American forces withdrew, twenty-five of the thirty-seven men in the fight had been wounded, with one fatality. Eleven of the wounded were evacuated on stretchers.[26] The action yielded two Distinguished Service Crosses, three Silver Stars, numerous Bronze Stars and Purple Hearts, and eight dead insurgents. More than fifty members of Echo Company were cited for valor during the period of 18 March–26 April 2004, with four Marines killed and seventy wounded in action. But uncommon valor was common that day! As Cpl. Howard Lee Hampton observed, "We survived Fallujah because everyone put the Marine next to him ahead of themselves. . . . Everyone did so much more than they had to."[27]

The last day of heavy fighting in Al-Fallujah before the Marines pulled out under the terms of cease-fire was 26 April. On 1 May 2004 U.S. forces withdrew completely from Al-Fallujah, handing over control of the city to the Fallujah Brigade, a paramilitary force made up of former members of the Iraqi army and Saddam Hussein's special security forces. Inept and ineffective, it was disbanded that September, following evidence that some members had been working openly with the insurgents.[28]

ENDNOTES

1. Silver Star citation, LCpl. Thomas R. Adametz, USMC, http://www.homeofheroes.com/valor2/SS/7_GWOT/citations_USMC.html.

2. Silver Star citation, Cpl. Aaron C. Austin, USMC, http://www.homeofheroes.com/valor2/SS/7_GWOT/citations_USMC.html.

3. Silver Star citation, LCpl. Carlos Gomez-Perez, USMC, http://www.homeofheroes.com/valor2/SS/7_GWOT/citations_USMC.html.

4. Rajiv Chandrasekaran and Karl Vick, "U.S. Opts to Delay Fallujah Offensive. Marines, Iraqi Forces Planning Joint Patrols," *Washington* (DC) *Post*, 26 April 2004.

5. Owen Dorell and Gregg Zoroya, "Battle for Fallujah Forged Many Heroes," *USA Today*, 9 November 2006.

6. Estimates vary widely among participants, and no exact count is available.

7. Rick Rogers, "Valor Defined: Marines Confront, Overcome the Crucible of Fallujah," *San Diego* (CA) *Union Tribune*, 31 July 2004.

8. Dorell and Zoroya, "Battle for Fallujah Forged Many Heroes."

9. "Douglas A. Zembiec," Arlington National Cemetery website, www.arlingtoncemetery.net/dazembiec.htm.

10. Steve Liewer, "One 'Resolute Marine,'" *San Diego* (CA) *Union Tribune*, 10 November 2006.

11. SSgt. Dan Briggs, Distinguished Service Cross citation, http://www.homeofheroes.com/valor/02_wot/dsc_briggs.html.

12. Dorell and Zoroya, "Battle for Fallujah Forged Many Heroes."

13. Patrick J. Floto, "Iron Will Earns Marine Silver Star," *Marine Corps News*, 12 April 2006.

14. Ibid.

15. Rogers, "Valor Defined: Marines Confront, Overcome the Crucible of Fallujah."

16. Ibid.

17. Lanessa Arthur, "Senior Enlisted Receives Bronze Star Medal," *Marine Corps News*, 27 January 2006.

18. Ben Murray, "It Just Felt Wrong Not to Pull the Trigger," *Stars and Stripes*, 14 June 2005.

19. Kevin Maurer, "DSC Awarded to SOF Soldier for Fallujah: Fort Bragg Soldier Recalls Battle that Won Him High Honor," Associated Press, 23 June 2005.

20. John Kifner and John F. Burns, "Inside Falluja: A Ceasefire in Name Only," *New York Times*, 26 April 2004.

21. Matt Zeigler, *Three Block War II: Snipers in the Sky!* (Lincoln, NE: Universe Press, 2006), 162–64.

22. Dorell and Zoroya, "Battle for Fallujah Forged Many Heroes."

23. Distinguished Service Cross citation for MSgt. Don Hollenbaugh, http://www.homeofheroes. com/valor2/SS/7_GWOT/citations_USMC.html.

24. Andy J. Hurt, "13th MEU BLT Marine Receives Silver Star for OIF Heroism," *Marine Corps News*, 5 May 2005.

25. Liewer, "One 'Resolute Marine.'"

26. Maurer, "DSC Awarded to SOF Soldier for Fallujah."

27. Rogers, "Valor Defined: Marines Confront, Overcome the Crucible of Fallujah."

28. "Frustrated U.S. Disbands the Fallujah Brigade: Iraq Notebook," *Seattle* (WA) *Times*, 11 September 2004.

LCpl. Benjamin Gonzalez, USMC

Automatic Rifleman, l, 2nd Battalion, 1st Marine Regiment,
1st Marine Division, I Marine Expeditionary Force,
U.S. Marine Corps Forces, Central Command

Al-Fallujah, Iraq
18 June 2004

The President of the United States takes pleasure in presenting the Silver Star Medal to Benjamin Gonzalez, Lance Corporal, U.S. Marine Corps, for conspicuous gallantry and intrepidity in action against the enemy while serving as an Automatic Rifleman, Company F, Second Battalion, First Marine Regiment, FIRST Marine Division, I Marine Expeditionary Force U.S. Marine Corps Forces, Central Command on 18 June 2004, in support of Operation Iraqi Freedom II. Lance Corporal Gonzalez' fire team was manning an observation post at the Saqlawiyah Bridge on the northern outskirts of Al Fallujah, Iraq. His observation post secured a critical bridge for the Coalition Forces' main supply route. At approximately 10:00 AM a motor-cycle-borne insurgent sped by Lance Corporal Gonzalez' observation post and threw a hand grenade into his fighting hole. Unhesitatingly and with total disregard for his own personal safety, Lance Corporal Gonzalez threw himself on his fellow Marine, Private First Class Koczan, shielding him from the blast. When the grenade detonated, Lance Corporal Gonzalez absorbed the blast and sustained serious injuries to his lower body. Private First Class Koczan survived the blast unscathed due to Lance Corporal Gonzalez' heroic and selfless actions that may have saved the life of his fellow Marine and at the very least protected him from life threatening injuries.[1]

Silver Star Citation

FOLLOWING THE END OF Operation Vigilant Resolve on 28 April, and the withdrawal of U.S. forces from Al-Fallujah on 1 May, control of the city was passed to the Fallujah Brigade, which proved spectacularly incapable of maintaining order or restraining the various insurgent groups; some members of the Brigade even collaborated with the insurgents. Attacks on U.S. and Iraqi forces continued, and kidnapping and executions increased as the character of the resistance transitioned from Saddam loyalists to radical Islamist nationalists. One Marine officer at the time commented, "This isn't a cease-fire. It's a chance for them to regroup."[2]

For the Marines of 2nd Battalion, 1st Marines this period involved night patrols, taking control of checkpoints, and keeping supply routes open while enduring sniper fire, mortar attacks, and improvised explosive devices (IEDs). On the evening of 17 June elements of Fox Company moved through Al-Fallujah to the Saqlawiyah Bridge, in the northern part of the city, where they relieved other Marines at an observation post (OP) adjacent to an Iraqi National Guard traffic control checkpoint. The bridge was on a vital supply route; duty rotated between the battalion's companies.[3]

At 9:30 AM the next morning, the fire team commanded by LCpl. Charlie Koczan was relieved, and moved to the side of the road to get some rest. Among the team was LCpl. Benjamin Gonzalez, a twenty-one-year-old rifleman from El Paso who enlisted in the Marines three days after graduating from Riverside High School in June 2002. Like most of his company, he was a veteran of the fighting in Al-Fallujah in April. Now, as Gonzalez readied his gear in the position he shared with three other Marines, he thought about getting some rest and didn't pay attention to the passing traffic. Thus it was that he did not see the motorcycle with two men speed by and toss a grenade into his position.

He heard a metallic clink and looked down to see an enemy grenade land a few feet away. It was an old pineapple-type hand grenade. Despite his Silver Star citation's description of his actions as "Unhesitatingly and with total disregard for his own personal safety," Gonzalez admitted that his first instinct was to dive for cover, but as he saw his team leader Koczan asleep and unaware, he covered him with his own body in a bear hug and braced himself for the explosion. "I remember the concussion. It jerked my body real bad. I screamed out, 'Damn, I'm hit!'"[4]

"I got burned. It broke both of my legs and broke and fractured other parts. It messed up my nerves really bad. I have permanent trauma. I can't feel my feet or move my ankles." Gonzalez recalled, then joked, "It must have been the crappiest grenade ever made because we were all really close. The detonation was one or two feet away from my legs. If it was one of ours, it would have taken us all out."[5]

Koczan woke up unscathed by the explosion, but Cpl. Avery Williams and another Marine were wounded by shrapnel. As Koczan organized a defense, the others worked on Gonzalez, keeping his wounds clean until a corpsman arrived to administer a general anesthetic and arrange for a medical evacuation by helicopter.[6]

He was sent to Bethesda Naval Medical Center by way of Landsthul, Germany, where he said doctors wanted to amputate his legs, but he refused to permit it. After months of bed rest and several surgeries, he is able to walk with the aid of a cane. Temporarily retired in December 2005, he hopes to rejoin the Corps when he is healed.[7]

On 25 March 2006 at a ceremony at the El Paso Marine Training Center, Texas, Gonzalez was presented the Silver Star medal by his former platoon commander, newly promoted Captain William "Wade" Zirkle. With typical modestly, he downplayed his valor stating, "It's part of what we do. I know he would have done the same thing for me."[8]

ENDNOTES

1. Silver Star citation, LCpl. Benjamin Gonzalez, USMC, http://www.homeofheroes.com/valor2/SS/7_GWOT/citations_USMC.html.
2. John Kifner and John F. Burns, "Inside Falluja: A Ceasefire in Name Only," *New York Times*, 26 April 2004.
3. Ben Murray, "It Felt Like my Body Was Burning from the Inside Out," *Stars and Stripes*, 14 June 2006.
4. Steve Liewer, "Marine Sacrificed His Body to Protect a Sleeping Comrade," *San Diego* (CA) *Union Tribune*, 12 November 2006.
5. John Hoellwarth, "Marine Caught in Grenade Blast Gets Silver Star," *Marine Corps Times*, 10 April 2006.
6. Chris Roberts, "Marine Awarded Silver Star," *El Paso* (TX) *Times*, 25 March 2006.
7. Liewer, "Marine Sacrificed his Body to Protect a Sleeping Comrade."
8. Roberts, "Marine Awarded Silver Star."

1st Lt. Brian Von Kraus, USMC

Platoon Commander, 1st Platoon, Alpha Company,
1st Reconnaissance Battalion, 1st Marine Division

Al-Fallujah, Iraq
25 July 2004

The President of the United States takes pleasure in presenting the Silver Star Medal to Brian R. Von Kraus, First Lieutenant, U.S. Marine Corps, for conspicuous gallantry and intrepidity in action against the enemy while serving as Platoon Commander, First Platoon, Alpha Company, First Reconnaissance Battalion, FIRST Marine Division in support of Operation Iraqi Freedom II from 5 April to 1 August 2004. On 25 July 2004, while conducting clandestine Operation Trojan Horse, First Lieutenant Von Kraus' platoon was heavily engaged in a three-sided ambush by a numerically superior enemy force. With enemy 12.7 millimeter machine gun positions raking the long axis of the convoy and disabling vehicles, First Lieutenant Von Kraus displayed exceptional bravery as he dismounted his vehicle and entered the enemy kill zone to aid his three stricken Marines. Engaging the enemy, he heroically led three separate assaults on different enemy strong points, personally destroying insurgents with rifle fire and grenades. Under a fusillade of enemy fire, First Lieutenant Von Kraus rallied his Marines and led them in close quarters combat resulting in seven foreign fighters killed, two foreign fighters captured, and scores of enemy combatants wounded. His exemplary leadership and tenacious fighting spirit inspired all who observed his personal valor and turned the tide of battle in the face of a resolute and fanatical enemy. By his bold leadership, wise judgment and complete dedication to duty, First Lieutenant Von Kraus reflected great credit upon himself and upheld the highest traditions of the Marine Corps and the United States Naval Service.[1]

Silver Star Citation

IT WAS HOPED THAT once the Fallujah Iraqi Brigade took over responsibility for Al-Fallujah following the withdrawal of the Marines on 1 May 2004 that order would be restored to a city at the heart of the insurgency. But results fell far below expectations when the Brigade not only failed to combat the militants, but aided them by surrendering weapons and equipment, going so far as active participation in attacks on Marines.[2]

The situation was exacerbated by the emergence of Abu Musab al-Zarqawi, a Jordanian militant Islamist with ties to Al-Qaeda in Afghanistan. Although attacks on Marines decreased, attacks on foreigners and Iraqi forces increased, and U.S. forces responded with air attacks on suspected insurgent safehouses, including those rumored to harbor al-Zarqawi loyalists. In addition, though, intelligence was gathered on the ground; this was possibly the mission of the Marine's 1st Reconnaissance Battalion during July 2004.

The 1st Reconnaissance Battalion, whose unit history dates back to Guadalcanal, and which participated in conflicts in Korea, Vietnam, and Desert Storm, was on its second deployment to Iraq, having participated in the invasion of Iraq in 2003. They arrived in the Al-Anbar Province in February 2004. Subsequently, two members of the battalion's Bravo Company, Capt. Brent Morel and Sgt. Willie Copeland, earned Navy Crosses—Morel's posthumously—for leading a counterattack after their convoy was ambushed during Operation Vigilant Resolve on 7 April 2004.[3]

On 25 July 2004 1st Lt. Brian Von Kraus was the twenty-seven-year-old commander of 1st Platoon, Alpha Company, 1st Reconnaissance Battalion, assigned to the 1st Marine Division. Von Kraus, whose family name means "recognition of courage," was a championship fencer and Boston College alumni. He enlisted in the Marines upon his graduation in 2000, and now four years later was commanding a fifteen-Marine, five-vehicle patrol south of Al-Fallujah as part of Operation Trojan Horse, a classified operation in the Al-Anbar Province.[4]

The day was hot and clear that Sunday morning as the patrol rolled along the highway on a clandestine mission. For the previous few weeks, his platoon had been practicing counterambush drills, and gathering information, perhaps for an anticipated upcoming return to Al-Fallujah. Possibly sensing something, Von Kraus sent a three-Marine team to conduct a security sweep to the rear of the column. They encountered a group of insurgents setting up an ambush on a concrete overpass and utilizing the element of surprise, engaged the numerically superior group with M-4 carbine and M-203 fire.[5]

Their ambush destroyed, the insurgents (later identified as "foreign fighters") opened fire on the convoy from three sides with 12.7-mm machine guns, raking the axis of the convoy, disabling multiple vehicles, and wounding several Marines. Without hesitation, Von Kraus dismounted his vehicle and, with his platoon sergeant, SSgt. James Treadwell, led Marines into the kill zone to counterattack and come to the aid of his pinned-down Marines.

Details are few, given the classified nature of the mission, but his Silver Star citation credits him with "heroically leading three separate assaults on different enemy strong points" and "personally destroying insurgents with rifle fire and grenades."[6] Leading his Marines in close-quarter combat under intense enemy fire, Von Kraus and his men routed a numerically superior force in a one-hour firefight, killing seven, capturing two, and wounding uncounted others without a death or serious injury to his Marines.[7]

Several of his Marines received awards for their actions that day; awards included two Bronze Stars and several Navy and Marine Corps Commendation medals for Valor. On 8 February 2006 in a ceremony at Camp Pendleton, California, days before shipping out with the 11th Marine Expeditionary Unit (MEU) on his fourth deployment, Von Kraus was presented the Silver Star by Maj. Gen. Richard Natonski, 1st Marine Division commander. Downplaying his own role in the battle, Von Kraus stated, "The mission was a success because the Marines in my platoon kicked ass and followed their training all the way through. This is more like a platoon award than an individual award."[8]

ENDNOTES

1. Silver Star citation, 1st Lt. Brian Von Kraus, USMC, http://www.homeofheroes.com/valor2/SS/7_GWOT/citations_USMC-M.html.
2. Rajiv Chandrasekaran, "Key General Criticizes April Attack in Fallujah: Abrupt Withdrawal Called Vacillation," *Washington* (DC) *Post Foreign Service*, 13 September 2004.
3. James E. Wise and Scott Baron, *The Navy Cross: Extraordinary Heroism in Iraq, Afghanistan, and Other Conflicts* (Annapolis, MD: Naval Institute Press, 2007).
4. Gidget Fuentes, "Platoon Commander Earns a Silver Star," *Marine Corps Times*, 21 February 2006.
5. Patrick J. Floto, "Marine Captain Leaves No Man Behind, Earns Silver Star," *Marine Corps News*, 8 February 2006.
6. Silver Star citation, 1st Lt. Brian Von Kraus.
7. Fuentes, "Platoon Commander Earns a Silver Star."
8. Floto, "Marine Captain Leaves No Man Behind, Earns Silver Star."

Sgt. Yadir G. Reynoso, USMC

3rd Squad Leader, 81-mm Mortar Platoon, Weapons Company,
Battalion Landing Team 1/4, 11th Marine Expeditionary Unit
(Special Operations Capable), I Marine Expeditionary Force,
U.S. Marine Corps Forces, Central Command

An Najaf, Iraq
5 August 2004

The President of the United States takes pride in presenting the Silver Star Medal (Posthumously) to Yadir G. Reynoso, Sergeant, U.S. Marine Corps, for conspicuous gallantry and intrepidity in action against the enemy as 3d Squad Leader, 81 millimeter Mortar Platoon, Weapons Company, Battalion Landing Team 1/4, Eleventh Marine Expeditionary Unit (Special Operations Capable), I Marine Expeditionary Force, U.S. Marine Corps Forces, Central Command, in support of Operation Iraqi Freedom on 5 August 2004. Ordered to clear a 200-meter section of An Najaf cemetery, Sergeant Reynoso's squad engaged a reinforced platoon-sized enemy unit at ranges of ten to thirty meters and was immediately pinned down by a heavy volume of rocket-propelled grenade (RPG) and AK-47 fire. Sergeant Reynoso responded by throwing a fragmentation grenade that eliminated three insurgents. He then directed the fires of an AT-4 rocket team on a pocket of four insurgents, destroying their position and all personnel. While providing suppressive fire against the enemy to enable his squad to withdraw from its position and maneuver against the enemy, Sergeant Reynoso was mortally wounded. Sergeant Reynoso's bold leadership, wise judgment, and unyielding dedication to duty reflected great credit upon him and were in keeping with the highest traditions of the Marine Corps and the United States Naval Service.[1]

Silver Star Citation

LOCATED ONE HUNDRED SIXTY KILOMETERS south of Baghdad, the Islamic holy city of An Najaf dates to biblical times; it is home to the shrine of Imam Ali Ibn Abi Talib, the Prophet Mohammad's cousin and son-in-law, and fourth caliph. A city of more than one half million people, whose low brick buildings stretch across a high plateau, An Najaf is the spiritual center of Shi'ite Islam. It is also the site of one of the world's largest cemeteries.[2]

It is in the An Najaf Cemetery, one of the most revered places in the Muslim world, that a small group of Marines would fight for their lives in close combat with a numerically superior force of insurgents. This encounter initiated weeks of combat between U.S. forces and militia loyal to Muslim cleric Muqtada al-Sadr. Insurgents had been using the cemetery—with its maze of walled mausoleums, narrow pathways, catacombs, and gravestones—to battle Coalition forces in An Najaf since fighting began in April, even engaging in a battle with U.S. tanks there in May 2004.[3]

On 4 August 2004 Marines of 1st Lt. Lamar Breshears' 81-mm Platoon, Weapons Company Battalion Landing Team (BLT) 1/4, 11th Marine Expeditionary Unit, Special Operations Capable (MEU-SOC) received orders to gear up. Since redeploying to Iraq in May 2004, the battalion had been stationed in southern Baghdad and had seen little action. Now they were ordered eighty miles south on reports of well-armed insurgents taking positions in Ali Wahid Cemetery and the gold-domed Imam Ali shrine. In command of the 3rd Squad of the mortar platoon was Sgt. Yadir G. Reynoso, the twenty-seven-year-old son of a Mexican farmworker from the Yakima Valley town of Wapato, Washington.[4]

Reynoso, an eight-year veteran of the Corps, was new to the unit, having arrived just prior to its deployment, but his experience as an instructor at the School of Infantry (SOI), his competency, and his natural ability as a leader soon had him in command of a squad. He was familiar with the results of war, having helped retrieve the bodies of U.S. Sailors killed after the USS *Cole* was attacked by terrorists in Aden, Yemen, in 2000.[5]

The mortar platoon arrived in An Najaf in the early morning; by 7:30 AM they were assisting Iraqi police in fighting off insurgent attacks, continuing throughout the day in blistering hot temperatures. One Marine was wounded, and at one point they secured the site of a downed helicopter that crashed just north of the police station. At approximately 6:00 PM they began taking heavy rocket-propelled grenade (RPG) and small-arms fire from positions within the Ali Wahid section of the vast cemetery. At that point, the decision was made to go in and clear out the insurgents.

The platoon, divided into 1st Section and 2nd Section, advanced cautiously forward into the maze, an extremely hazardous maneuver given that the numerous thick walls limited visibility and the mausoleums and catacombs provided numerous hiding places from which to ambush the Marines. Less than two hundred yards into the burial grounds, the platoon of approximately fifty Marines surprised a much larger force of advancing insurgents. A close-quarters fight ensued for the next forty-five minutes as the two forces engaged each other with rockets, grenades, machine-gun, and small-arms fire at distances of from thirty to one hundred feet.[6]

Breshears received orders to withdraw, and the message was conveyed to 2nd Section. Reynoso with the 1st Section had no radio and did not receive the order, so he chose instead to move forward. Breshears tried to call in artillery support, but the nature of the target, the second-holiest site in Islam which contained the tombs of several prophets, precluded a fire mission for political reasons. Afraid his 1st Section was in danger of being overrun, Breshears advanced alone under fire to relay the order to withdraw, finally reaching their position.

The danger was that a withdrawal would make the Marines vulnerable to enemy fire from three sides. According to an after-action report filed by Breshears, Reynoso rose up and threw a grenade which killed three insurgents, then directed the fire of an AT-4 rocket team on another position, killing another four. This only focused greater enemy fire on his position. Hoping to cover his squad's withdrawal, Reynoso began laying down suppressive fire with his rifle, exposing him to enemy fire; he took mortal wounds to the neck and face. Navy Corpsman HM2 Joshua Bunker rushed from mausoleum to mausoleum under fire to Reynoso's side, but he was too late: Reynoso was dead.

The 1st Section Marines advanced to recover his body, then, under cover of darkness, fought their way back to a road adjoining the border of the cemetery where they rejoined the 2nd Section. Fighting in that portion of the cemetery would continue until the morning of 7 August, when the Marines would withdraw. Two Marines, Sergeant Reynoso and Sgt. Moses Rocha, were killed on 5 August, and two others, Cpl. Roberto Abad and LCpl. Larry Wells, were killed the following day. Fighting in An Najaf continued until late August, when a senior Iraqi cleric, Ayatollah Ali as-Sistani, negotiated an end to the fighting and a withdrawal of insurgents from the cemetery and shrine.[7]

Weapons Company BLT 1/4 participated in operations in Kufa in August, and Operation Phantom Fury in Al-Fallujah in November, before redeploying to Camp Pendleton, California, in February 2005. For his "unyielding dedication to duty," Sergeant Reynoso was awarded the Silver Star. As his platoon commander, Breshears, recalled, "He fought like a true warrior, and he will always have a place in my heart."[8]

ENDNOTES

1. Silver Star citation, Sgt. Yadir G. Reynoso, USMC, http://www.homeofheroes.com/valor2/SS/7_GWOT/citations_USMC-M.html.

2. "Najaf," GlobalSecurity.org, http://www.globalsecurity.org/military/world/iraq/najaf.htm.

3. Hal Bernton, "Courage Amid Chaos: How a Battle Unfolded," *Seattle* (WA) *Times*, 18 September 2004.

4. Ibid.

5. Hal Bernton, "A Small Town Grieves Over One Family's Loss in Iraq," *The Seattle* (WA) *Times*, 12 August 2004.

6. Bernton, "Courage Amid Chaos."

7. "Najaf," GlobalSecurity.org.

8. Bernton, "Courage Amid Chaos."

Operation Phantom Fury

Al-Fallujah, Iraq
7–16 November 2004

IT IS KNOWN BY MANY NAMES: the Second Battle of Fallujah, Operation Phantom Fury, Operation Al-Fajr, or simply the fight for Fallujah. The Department of Defense called it "the heaviest urban combat Marines have been involved in since Hue City in Vietnam in 1968."[1] Iraqi Defense Minister Sheikh Hazem Shaalan called it Operation Al-Fajr (Arabic for "Dawn") because, "God willing, it's going to be a new, happy dawn for the people of Fallujah."[2] To the Marines who fought it, it was one of the hardest-fought campaigns, sure to rank in Marine lore along with other legendary battles.

The failure of U.S. commanders to resolve the issue of Al-Fallujah during Operation Vigilant Resolve in April 2004, and the subsequent failure of the Fallujah Brigade to restore order following the withdrawal of U.S. forces from the city on 1 May, made a second offensive to retake Al-Fallujah inevitable. Following the disbanding of the Fallujah Brigade in early September, U.S. forces began air operations over Al-Fallujah. Weeks of aerial bombing followed in preparation for ground operations. On 7 November, the day before Operation Phantom Fury began, Interim Prime Minister Ayad Allawi declared a sixty-day state of emergency across Iraq because of increased insurgent activity. The Marines' assault on the city was an attempt to regain control of the city from insurgents in preparation for national elections scheduled for January 2005.[3]

The insurgents also had the summer to prepare, building defensive positions, secreting weapons caches throughout the city, and placing improvised explosive devices (IEDs) at likely routes of advance by Coalition forces. U.S. forces would encounter two hundred ten defensive positions in buildings, to include mosques and schools, many connected by tunnels and many of them booby trapped with IEDs. Eventually, they would uncover more than five hundred arms caches and locations used to make car and roadside bombs.[4]

The nature of the opposition was in transition. Hardcore Saddam loyalists were replaced by militant Islamist jihadists. Led by men such as Shi'ite cleric Muqtada al-Sadr and Al-Qaeda leader Abu Musab al-Zarqawi, they were willing to martyr themselves in a holy war while killing as many Americans as possible. The nature of the battle was also changing, with battalion-level maneuvers replaced by squads of twelve Marines, led by eighteen- or nineteen-year-old corporals advancing and engaging an entrenched enemy block by block, house by house, room by room, earning the conflict the nickname "Three Block War."[5]

Broadly stated, the strategy was to seize all entry points into and out of Fallujah, then sweep in from the northeast and push the insurgents south. The downside to the strategy was that because the Coalition was eliminating any chance of escape, they motivated the insurgents to fight harder. Leaflets were dropped urging civilians to leave the city, and most of the city's population of three hundred thousand people left, leaving an estimated two thousand to three thousand hardcore insurgents. Males from fifteen to fifty were prevented by Coalition forces from entering or leaving the city, and a curfew was declared.[6]

The insurgents were expecting the invasion to come from the southeast, due to diversionary probes and thrusts by 3/1 and other units. Then, on the evening of 7 November, Marines of the 3rd Light Armored Reconnaissance (LAR) Battalion and Bravo Company, 1st Battalion 23rd Marines, assisted by the Iraqi 36th Commando Battalion, seized the Jurf Kas Sukr Bridge and a secondary trestle bridge, than advanced to secure Fallujah General Hospital, both to ensure it remained operational and to prevent its use as a sanctuary by insurgents or as a source of propaganda regarding civilian casualties, as had been done the previous April.[7]

The following day, 8 November, units took up positions northeast of Al-Fallujah as thunder from rainstorms as well as from mortars, artillery, and air strikes echoed in the grey skies. Farthest west was Regimental Combat Team 1 (RCT-1) made up of 3/5 Marines with 3/1 Marines to their east, followed by 2nd Battalion, 7th Cavalry, part of the Army's 1st Cavalry Division. Their mission would be to seize the Jolan District, a densely packed neighborhood where resistance was expected to be fierce.

Farther east, RCT-7, made up of 1/8 Marines to the west, and flanked by 1/3 Marines and the Army's 2/2, would take out the volatile Askari district. This would allow Coalition forces to control both ends of Highway 10, the main east-west highway through the city, code-named Phase Line Fran.[8]

The main assault on Al-Fallujah began Monday night as 3/5 led by Kilo Company moved across the railroad berm into the Jolan district, and seized an elevated apartment complex whose eight-story rooftop gave commanders good observation into the contested area. To the east, elements of 1/8 Marines supported by tanks moved south into the Askari district, its first objective a traffic circle just inside the city limits.

1st Lt. Jeffrey T. Lee, USMCR

*Third Platoon Commander, Alpha Company, 2nd Tank Battalion,
Regimental Combat Team 7, 1st Marine Division, I Marine Expeditionary
Force, U.S. Marine Corps Forces, Central Command*

The President of the United States takes pleasure in presenting the
Silver Star Medal to Jeffrey T. Lee, First Lieutenant, U.S. Marine Corps
(Reserve), for conspicuous gallantry and intrepidity in action against
the enemy as Third Platoon Commander, Company A, Second Tank
Battalion, Regimental Combat Team 7, FIRST Marine Division, I Marine
Expeditionary Force, U.S. Marine Corps Forces Central Command in support of Operation Iraqi Freedom II from 8 to 11 November 2004. First
Lieutenant Lee's aggressive leadership and bold decisions provided the
catalyst for the Regiment's success during two major firefights. While
attached to Company C, he destroyed numerous enemy, allowing the
infantry company to take their objective. Operating for more than twelve
hours and desperately low on fuel, he accepted great tactical risk and continued to destroy the enemy. This decision led to the successful taking of
the Battalion's objective. While attached to Company A, Task Force 1/8,
he led an attack south. While eliminating numerous insurgents all around
him, he was shot through his right arm. Refusing medical attention, he
continued to fight the enemy and help Company A achieve success. In
spite of his gunshot wound he pushed the assault two more city blocks to
reach the battalion phase line. At this time, the tank was critically exposed
in a courtyard while the infantry developed positions in the buildings.
He continued to eliminate insurgents who attacked the tenuous infantry position. His aggressiveness and bravery broke the enemy's will, and
were critical to the success of the Company as it attacked into the heart of
the enemy defenses. By his bold leadership, wise judgment, and complete
dedication to duty, First Lieutenant Lee reflected great credit upon himself
and upheld the highest traditions of the Marine Corps and the United
States Naval Service.[9]

Silver Star Citation

2nd Lt. Elliott L. Ackerman, USMCR

Platoon Commander, 1st Platoon, Alpha Company, 1st Battalion,
8th Marines, Regimental Combat Team 7, 1st Marine Division

v

The President of the United States takes pleasure in presenting the Silver Star Medal to Elliott L. Ackerman, Second Lieutenant, U.S. Marine Corps (Reserve), for conspicuous gallantry and intrepidity in action against the enemy while serving as Platoon Commander, First Platoon, Company A, First Battalion, Eighth Marines, Regimental Combat Team 7, FIRST Marine Division in support of Operation Iraqi Freedom II from 10 to 15 November 2004. During a ferocious enemy counter-attack in the insurgent stronghold of Al Fallujah, with complete disregard for his own safety, Second Lieutenant Ackerman twice exposed himself to vicious enemy fire as he pulled wounded Marines out of the open into shelter. When the amphibious tractors sent to evacuate his wounded men could not locate his position, he once again left the safety of his covered position and rushed through a gauntlet of deadly enemy fire to personally direct the amphibious tractors towards his wounded Marines. On 11 November as the battle continued, Second Lieutenant Ackerman recognized the exposed position of his Marines on the rooftops and ordered them to seek cover in the buildings below. Shortly afterwards, he personally assumed the uncovered rooftop position, prompting a hail of deadly fire from the enemy. With rounds impacting all around him, he coolly employed an M240G machine gun to mark targets for supporting tanks, with devastating effects on the enemy. Throughout the battle and despite his own painful shrapnel wounds, he simultaneously directed tank fire, coordinated four separate medical evacuations, and continually attacked with his platoon directly into the heart of the enemy with extreme tenacity. Second Lieutenant Ackerman's bold leadership, personal initiative, and total devotion to duty reflected great credit upon him and were in keeping with the highest traditions of the Marine Corps and the United States Naval Service.[10]

Silver Star Citation

Sgt. Timothy Connors, USMC

3rd Squad Leader, 2nd Platoon, Alpha Company, 1st Battalion,
8th Marine Regiment, Regimental Combat Team 7, 1st Marine Division,
I Marine Expeditionary Force, U.S. Marine Corps Forces,
Central Command

The President of the United States takes pleasure in presenting the Silver Star Medal to Timothy Connors, Corporal, U.S. Marine Corps, for conspicuous gallantry and intrepidity in action against the enemy while serving as Third Squad Leader, Second Platoon, Company A, First Battalion, Eighth Marine Regiment, Regimental Combat Team 7, FIRST Marine Division, I Marine Expeditionary Force, U.S. Marine Corps Forces, Central Command, in support of Operation Iraqi Freedom II from 10 to 15 November 2004. As Second Platoon came under heavy enemy fire from concealed positions on three sides, Corporal Connors effectively directed the fire of the squad as the platoon attempted to move into surrounding buildings for cover. When the squad entered a building for cover, the first Marine in the door was mortally wounded by several enemies who were defending a heavily fortified machine gun position. Corporal Connors and his fellow non-commissioned officers re-entered the building only to be forced back by a tenacious enemy. He directed the use of improvised explosive devices (IEDs) and a shoulder-launched multi-purpose assault weapon to create a secondary breach and eliminate the enemy position. When it was evident the improvised explosive devices and rocket failed to penetrate the enemy stronghold, Corporal Connors led a group of non-commissioned officers of Second Platoon into the enemy stronghold. Under intense enemy machine gun fire and without regard to his own personal safety, Corporal Connors eliminated the enemy with hand grenades and deadly accurate small arms fire at close proximity. By his bold leadership, wise judgment, and complete dedication to duty, Corporal Connors reflected great credit upon himself and upheld the highest traditions of the Marine Corps and the United States Naval Service.[11]

Silver Star Citation

SSgt. Richard Pillsbury, USMC

Platoon Commander with 2nd Platoon, Alpha Company, 1st Battalion,
8th Marines, Regimental Combat Team 7, 1st Marine Division

The President of the United States takes pleasure in presenting the Silver
Star Medal to Richard Pillsbury, Staff Sergeant, U.S. Marine Corps, for
conspicuous gallantry and intrepidity in action against the enemy while
serving as Platoon Commander with Second Platoon, Company A, First
Battalion, Eighth Marines, Regimental Combat Team 7, FIRST Marine
Division, in support of Operation Iraqi Freedom II from 10 November to
10 December 2004. In Fallujah on 10 November after successfully taking the eastern sector of the Mayor's complex and evacuating his Platoon
Commander, Staff Sergeant Pillsbury found himself thrust into the role of
Platoon Commander in what would turn out to be two weeks of intense
house-to-house fighting. Leading with great skill, presence of mind, and
calm effectiveness, he repeatedly directed his Marines and supporting arms
in attacks on many buildings, under heavy enemy fire, and in direct, close
combat. On one tragic occasion during a firefight, an errant 500-pound
bomb landed twenty meters from his building. Although his platoon suffered three casualties, he calmly orchestrated the evacuation while continuing to fight. On 15 November, approximately fifty meters short of the limit
of advance, one of his squads entered a house to clear it. As the squad came
under intense small arms and machine gun fire, one of his Marines was killed.
Realizing that he could easily lose his entire platoon piece by piece if they
continued to enter the house, he utilized the tank main gun to destroy the
house and insurgents. He then orchestrated a heroic entry into the house and
was able to destroy remaining enemy fighters, and retrieve the body of the
fallen Marine. Staff Sergeant Pillsbury's calmness in the face of impending
hardship inspired absolute trust and loyalty from his platoon. By his courageous actions, zealous initiative, and total devotion to duty, Staff Sergeant
Pillsbury reflected great credit upon himself and upheld the highest traditions of the Marine Corps and the United States Naval Service.[12]

Silver Star Citation

AS THE MARINES OF CHARLIE COMPANY 1/8 advanced into the city of
Al-Fallujah the evening of 8 November, they were supported by tanks of
3rd Platoon, Alpha Company, of the 2nd Tank Battalion. It was not a good
start for the platoon commander, 2nd Lt. Jeffrey Lee, a thirty-five-year-old

reservist from South Carolina. Two of his five tanks were out of service—one broken down, the other damaged by a mine—but as the infantry pressed south, Lee's tanks rolled along in support, engaging targets and demolishing obstacles.[13]

What followed were hours of almost-continuous contact, as insurgents fired from fortified positions, slowing the advance until artillery and air strikes by an AC-130H Spectre gunship and F/A-18 jet fighters obliterated all resistance and the first objective was achieved. Lee's tanks had been driving and fighting for twelve straight hours without refueling. "My fuel level was extremely low. I didn't even have a fuel reading anymore. But I had to stay."[14]

After refueling and resupplying, Lee's tanks went back out, this time supporting Alpha Company, 1/8. By the early morning of 9 November, the Army's 2/2 Infantry had pushed into the Askari and Jeghaifi districts and secured the eastern flank as far as Phase Line Fran (Highway 10).[15]

Bravo and Charlie 1/8 opened the way on 8 and 9 November, then fell back to allow Alpha Company to lead the assault into the city center to secure the government complex, where commanders anticipated the fiercest resistance. In the early hours of 10 November Alpha Company in assault amphibious vehicles (AAVs, amtracs, or tracks), with their supporting M1A1 Abrams tanks of 2nd Tanks waited for the order to advance. At precisely 4:00 AM the order came over the radio, "All Avenger stations, this is Avenger 6. We are 'Oscar Mike' [code for on the move]."[16]

For 2nd Platoon leader 2nd Lt. Elliott Ackerman, a twenty-four-year-old from Washington, DC, it was a personal zero hour. Ackerman had joined the platoon at Camp Lejeune, North Carolina, two months prior to its deployment to Iraq, and many of his men were combat veterans. He had graduated first in his class of two hundred twenty at Quantico, Virginia, but training was not in combat. Now, as he sat at the commander's hatch of his AAVC-7A1 assault vehicle, he considered the responsibility of leading forty-six men into combat. Reaching the government complex just before dawn, Ackerman and his Marines dismounted their tracks and moved into the complex on foot. Lee's tanks used their 120-mm main guns to create openings, but the Marines rushed in only to find the complex deserted.[17]

As Ackerman's Marines moved to secure two six-story buildings on the southern side of the complex, they began taking fire from several directions in the densely packed buildings. Driven from the rooftops by snipers in two nearby minarets (towers), Ackerman called in artillery, some of which landed too close for comfort, since their enemies were only one hundred meters distant. The battle continued throughout the day.

At one point Lee, whose tank had been engaging targets all day from an exposed position within the courtyard of the complex, went outside the turret to retrieve additional .50-caliber ammo, and was shot in the right arm. Returning inside, one of his men wrapped the wound in duct tape, and they fought on. It was eight days before he saw a corpsman, and only after being given a direct order by his captain. "There were a lot more important things going on than me. My tank could do a lot more damage to the enemy."[18]

On 14 March 2006 Maj. Gen. Richard Huck, commander of the 2nd Marine Division, presented Lee, newly promoted to First Lieutenant and XO (Executive Officer) of Headquarters and Service Company, 2nd Tank, with the Silver Star. Characteristically modest, Lee stated, "We were trying to free a city. I was just one man in the fight."[19]

In the late afternoon Alpha Company commander Maj. Aaron Cunningham ordered Ackerman to move out after dark and advance forward to a group of buildings south of their position. With their night vision technology, the Marines had a great advantage over the insurgents at night, and the buildings would serve as a forward base of operations for the next day's fight.

In the early hours of 11 November, 2nd Platoon advanced to discover that the jet ordered to clear the building of insurgents had done a good job. The building was demolished. Acting boldly rather than retreat, Ackerman advanced an additional two hundred fifty meters, leaving his unit even more exposed. They took up positions in an abandoned butcher shop, that the Marines had nicknamed the "Candy Store," and waited for daylight.

As dawn broke, Ackerman observed a large group of insurgents unaware of their presence a few dozen meters away. They wore a mix of uniforms and civilian attire, but all were armed and all wore black, the color of martyrdom. After five months of rarely seeing the enemy in the open, the target proved irresistible and Ackerman ordered his men to open fire, killing a large number, but also exposing their position. "From that position that day, we were a little exposed," Ackerman recalled. "Insurgents came out and slowly tried to surround us."[20]

Once located the Marines began taking fire from all sides. LCpl. Matthew Brown was severely wounded in his femoral artery, and was rapidly losing blood. Ackerman called for an AAV to medically evacuate his wounded, but as it approached it took a direct hit to the fuel tank and exploded into flames. Ackerman and Sgt. Adam Banotai ran into the open under fire to flag down an unarmored Humvee, which subsequently evacuated seven Marines.

Ackerman received orders to rejoin the company as it advanced south. At that point, he realized that the only entrance, on the west side, was covered by insurgent fire. Improvising, he had his engineer blow out the east wall and his platoon rejoined the company, moving south along two parallel alleyways. By the time they reached the point where Major Cunningham ordered the company to "stand firm," an additional thirteen platoon members had been wounded by enemy fire, shrapnel from rocket-propelled grenades (RPGs), or from the concussion of supporting armor.[21]

As he regrouped his platoon Ackerman learned that Cpl. William Long's team was trapped with wounded in a building. Again Ackerman, along with Cpl. Carmine Castelli, charged into the open under fire to flag down an AAV, which provided covering fire as the trapped Marines were extracted. Ordering his men off the roof of a building to the safety of windows on the floor below, he replaced them. Then he and Cpl. Ramon Bejarno, a machine-gunner, took turns marking insurgent positions for the supporting tanks using tracer rounds in the M-240G machine gun. By morning, twenty-one of the original forty-six Marines of 2nd Platoon were casualties, but the platoon was credited with breaking the enemy's resistance. Only six Marines in the platoon were not awarded a Purple Heart.

For simultaneously coordinating tank fire, arranging medical evacuations, and leading his platoon's advance, all while wounded by shrapnel, Ackerman was presented the Silver Star on 12 January 2007 by Brig. Gen. Charles Gurganus, at Camp Lejeune, North Carolina. Stating he was just doing his duty as a Marine, Ackerman stated, "You do what you have to do."[22]

For the next two days the platoon advanced at night and ambushed surprised insurgents the next morning, advancing house by house. On 15 November other platoons of Alpha were delayed by uncovered weapons caches, and Alpha again was in the lead, circumstances that would lead to a Silver Star for a second platoon member.

Sgt. Timothy Connors, a twenty-three-year-old squad leader from Braintree, Massachusetts, was leading 3rd Squad in clearing houses when they came under heavy fire from three sides, and he directed his squad to cover in surrounding buildings. As the squad entered a house, the Marine in the lead, LCpl. Travis Desiato, fell mortally wounded by gunfire from a heavily fortified machine-gun position inside and down the hall. Resolved not to allow a Marine to be desecrated as had happened at Mogadishu, Connors entered the foyer with LCpl. Matthew Brown to retrieve Desiato's body, but they were greeted by a hail of gunfire. Following an exchange of grenades, they withdrew to the courtyard just as Cpl. Camillio Aargon killed an insurgent on the roof.[23]

Connors edged down a narrow alley adjacent to the house and fired into a window, spraying the room. When insurgents returned fire, he tossed a stick of C-4 explosives inside, then dashed to the courtyard as the room exploded. When again he was fired on, he tossed in another grenade, killing an insurgent. Under fire, Sergeant Connors and Cpl. Eubaldo Lovato threw additional grenades while dashing for cover.

Connors led Lovato, Aragon, and two other Marines on a third assault, and noticed Desiato's body had been dragged farther in to lure the Marines farther inside. A grenade thrown by one of the Marines rolled back and exploded, temporarily blinding Connors. Revived, he withdrew again and called in a tank that opened a wall with its main gun. At that point, the Marines rushed inside to kill the remaining insurgents and retrieve Desiato's body.[24]

Two additional Marines, LCpl. Bradley Parker and LCpl. William Miller, were killed in the five-hour battle, as were all six insurgents, one of whom was suspected of being al-Zarqawi lieutenant Omar Hadid.

Connors, who had enlisted right out of high school, rejected any notion of heroism when he accepted the Silver Star in April 2006 at a ceremony at the headquarters of 1/25 Marines at Ft. Devons, Massachusetts. "It's a great honor, but I went in there to get the kid out, not to get a medal."[25]

SSgt. Richard Pillsbury, a platoon sergeant who took over 2nd Platoon of Alpha Company on 10 November when his platoon leader was wounded and led the platoon through two weeks of almost constant house-to-house combat, was also recognized with a Silver Star.

Staff Sergeant Pillsbury was already an eight-year veteran of the Army's 82nd Airborne when he enlisted in the Marines in 1994 at the age of twenty-six. Over two weeks, Pillsbury is credited with "repeatedly [directing] his Marines and supporting arms in attacks on many buildings, under heavy enemy fires, and in direct, close combat."[26] When an errant five-hundred-pound bomb landed twenty meters from a building he was in, resulting in three casualties, Pillsbury successfully evacuated the wounded Marines under fire. On another occasion, he risked enemy fire to retrieve a fallen Marine. Valor was not new to Pillsbury, having been awarded a Navy–Marine Corps Commendation medal with "V" for Valor for his actions with the 26th Marine Expeditionary Unit (MEU) in Mosul in 2003.[27]

On 22 November 2006, two years after the events that earned the medal, Pillsbury, now a combat instructor at the Infantry Unit Leaders Course at Camp Lejeune, North Carolina, accepted the Silver Star from Maj. Gen. Walter Gaskin, the 2nd Marine Division commander. Of the medal, he said, "It's very humbling to be put in this position. You don't wear this for yourself; you wear it for those Marines."[28]

Sgt. Chad Cassady, USMC

Scout-Sniper Team Leader, Lima Company, 3rd Battalion,
1st Marine Division, I Marine Expeditionary Force,
U.S. Marine Corps Forces, Central Command

The President of the United States takes pleasure in presenting the Silver Star Medal to Chad Cassady, Sergeant, U.S. Marine Corps, for conspicuous gallantry and intrepidity in action against the enemy while serving as Scout Sniper Team Leader, Company L, 3d Battalion, 1st Marine Division, I Marine Expeditionary Force, U.S. Marine Corps Forces, Central Command, in Al Fallujah, Iraq, in support of Operation Iraqi Freedom II on 9 November 2004. Sergeant Cassady demonstrated extraordinary leadership, undaunted bravery, and tactical expertise in the execution of his duties. During the multiple engagements, he consistently displayed courage under fire through his rapid decision-making and confident actions. Under sustained, heavy, and highly accurate enemy direct and indirect fire he repeatedly exposed himself to save the lives of several wounded Marines who were trapped in the open, pulling them to safety despite his own multiple, serious wounds. Sergeant Cassady refused to accept medical aid until all other wounded Marines were treated. Throughout the intense urban combat, his judgment and tactical proficiency were unrivaled. His presence of mind and physical courage while under fire were inspiring and undoubtedly saved lives. By his bold leadership, resolute determination, and complete dedication to duty, Sergeant Cassady reflected great credit upon himself and upheld the highest traditions of the Marine Corps and the United States Naval Service.[29]

Silver Star Citation

Cpl. Dale Allen Burger Jr., USMC

Squad Leader, India Company, 3rd Battalion,
1st Marine Regiment, Regimental Combat Team 1, 1st Marine Division,
I Marine Expeditionary Force

The President of the United States takes pride in presenting the Silver Star Medal (Posthumously) to Dale Allen Burger Jr., Corporal, U.S. Marine Corps, for conspicuous gallantry and intrepidity in action against the enemy while serving as Squad Leader, Company I, Third Battalion, First

Marine Regiment, Regimental Combat Team 1, FIRST Marine Division, I Marine Expeditionary Force, in support of Operation Iraqi Freedom II from 9 to 14 November 2004. During an intense firefight, Corporal Burger's squad leader was knocked unconscious and suffered a concussion from a rocket-propelled grenade (RPG). Realizing the platoon's attack was losing momentum, Corporal Burger immediately assumed the squad leader's responsibilities and quickly directed his fire teams to establish positions in nearby buildings. Displaying heroic leadership and tactical proficiency, he personally led a team to a rooftop and neutralized several enemy sniper positions with accurate fire, enabling the Platoon to regain critical momentum. Despite withering enemy fire and with total disregard for his personal safety, Corporal Burger employed his M-203 grenade launcher and two AT-4 rockets, eliminating enemy insurgents operating in adjacent buildings. Leading the squad in an assault against a large group of insurgents occupying a building, he was seriously wounded and evacuated. Disregarding his wounds, he volunteered to return to the Platoon three days later. During an ensuing firefight, Corporal Burger encountered three severely wounded Marines inside a house where numerous insurgents were barricaded behind fortified positions. Again disregarding his own safety, and under heavy enemy fire, he charged into the house to recover his fellow Marines. While valiantly returning fire and calling for the wounded Marines, he received enemy fire and fell mortally wounded. By his bold leadership, wise judgment, and complete dedication to duty, Corporal Burger reflected great credit upon himself and upheld the highest traditions of the Marine Corps and the United States Naval Service.[30]

Silver Star Citation

Sgt. Traver D. Pennell, USMC

*Squad Leader, India Company, 3rd Battalion,
1st Marines, Regimental Combat Team 1, 1st Marine Division,
I Marine Expeditionary Force*

For conspicuous gallantry and intrepidity in action against the enemy while serving as Squad Leader, Company I, 3d Battalion, 1st Marines, Regimental Combat Team 1, 1st Marine Division, I Marine Expeditionary Force in support of Operation Iraqi Freedom II on 14 and 15 November 2004. Sergeant Pennell displayed unyielding personal courage while leading his attacking squad through sustained high intensity urban combat in south Al Fallujah, Iraq. As an adjacent squad entered a house occupied by nine fanatical insurgents, the squad came under heavy enemy fire and sustained numerous casualties. Demonstrating great presence of mind, he unhesitatingly led his squad in an assault into the house to assist his fellow Marines. Locating a Marine shot in the face, Sergeant Pennell, under intense grenade and small arms fire, rescued the Marine and carried him to safety. He immediately called for assistance and courageously reentered the house with another Marine. With bullets impacting all around them, Sergeant Pennell directed his Marines to lay down suppressive fire as he searched for the remaining wounded. Immediately, enemy PKM machine gun fire struck Sergeant Pennell's comrade. Ignoring this intense machine gun fire, he proceeded to suppress the enemy with lethally accurate fire of his own, rescue his fellow Marine and carry him to safety. Sergeant Pennell's multiple attacks and accurate fire repeatedly drew the enemy's attention and allowed a supporting attack from an adjacent platoon to clear the house and rescue the remaining wounded. By his bold leadership, wise judgment, and complete dedication to duty, Sergeant Pennell reflected great credit upon himself and upheld the highest traditions of the Marine Corps and the United States Naval Service.[31]

Silver Star Citation

THE MARINES OF RCT-1 BEGAN THEIR ASSAULT on the night of 8 November, as Kilo Company 3/5 moved south into the insurgent stronghold of the Jolan district. Commanded by Lt. Col. Patrick Malay, most were combat veterans of the assault on Baghdad during Operation Iraqi Freedom I. As the 3/5 secured some high-rise apartments on the heights, giving commanders a bird's-eye view of the battlefield, Marines of Capt. Brian Heatherman's Lima Company 3/1 advanced and captured the train station. This allowed engineers to breach railroad tracks, allowing heavy armor (twenty-four M1A1 Abrams tanks and thirty Bradley fighting vehicles of 2/7 Cavalry) to blast open the way into Jolan for the Marines to advance. The terrain into which they advanced was littered with destroyed vehicles and dead insurgents, victims of Marine artillery and air strikes. The Marines braved hit-and-run ambushes, snipers, and improvised explosive devices (IEDs) as they cleared out fortified insurgent positions in close-quarter, house-to-house fighting.[32]

The insurgents' strategy was to let the armor pass through, then ambush the following Marine patrols. On 9 November Lima Company

3/1 was tasked with clearing out those pockets of resistance. Among those walking the rubble strewn streets that morning was Sgt. Chad Cassady. Cassady, a scout-sniper team leader from Saledo, Texas, had enlisted at the age of twenty-six, after having earned a Master's degree in political science from Southwest Texas State University. He declined a commission, preferring instead the experience of an enlisted Marine in an infantry line company. Now as they walked along the narrow streets of Jolan, they began taking mortar fire, and Cassady realized that his group of thirty Marines was being bracketed by two mortars—one falling behind and another falling in front.[33]

One round exploded a few feet from Cassady, knocking him through the door of a courtyard. In the street Cpl. Russell Scott collapsed with a bullet hole in his arm and shrapnel wounds in his leg and buttocks. He was trying to crawl to a nearby building as bullets and mortars fell around him. Cassady lay in the courtyard, shrapnel lodged in his chest and legs, his right lung collapsed, and his liver and kidneys lacerated. Despite his wounds, he pulled himself to his feet, and, bleeding and dazed, stumbled back out into the street. "You can't just lay down. If they stayed out in the street when rounds were coming down, they were going to die."[34]

Under what his citation described as "sustained, heavy, and highly accurate enemy direct and indirect fire," Cassady ran to Scott. "All of a sudden, [Cassady] came flying out of the smoke and dust and grabbed me. He dragged me to the building and then ran back out for the others," Scott recalled. After dragging Scott to safety, he returned for three more Marines, collapsing from loss of blood in the process of rescuing a fourth. He was himself pulled to safety by SSgt. Christian Erlenbush.[35]

Four 3/1 Marines were killed in action that day, three of them from Lima Company.[36] Cassady was immediately airlifted to a hospital in Baghdad, where he was rushed into emergency surgery and his wounds stabilized. While recovering from his wounds, he was encouraged by Col. Willy Buhl, 3/1's battalion commander, to seek a commission. Despite the discomfort of his wounds, Cassady completed both Officer Candidate School (OCS) and Basic School, and at the age of thirty-three became one of the Corps' oldest second lieutenants.

Second Lieutenant Cassady deployed to Iraq for a third time as 2nd platoon commander for Golf Company, 2nd Battalion, 5th Marines. On 4 September 2007. Gen. Peter Pace, chairman of the Joint Chiefs of Staff and himself a former platoon leader of 2nd Platoon during the Tet Offensive in Vietnam, presented Cassady with a ceremonial K-Bar combat knife which he said he presented, "Out of respect for who you are, out of envy for your future time in the Corps and out of envy for your opportunity to lead these Marines."[37]

When presented his Silver Star at Camp Pendleton, California, on 17 October 2007, just after returning from his third deployment, Cassady declined to speak, stating simply, "It was one of those days when Marines were doing what had to be done."[38]

On 13 November Weapons Company 1st Sgt. Bradley Kasal and Cpl. Robert L. Mitchell Jr., a squad leader with Kilo Company 3/1 entered Marine Corps history by leading Marines in multiple assaults on a heavily fortified house to rescue Marines trapped inside, actions that earned both Kasal and Mitchell Navy Crosses. The photo of a wounded Kasal, still gripping his 9-mm pistol while being assisted out of the house, appeared on front pages of the world's newspapers and is certain to become an icon of Marine Corps lore.

Everywhere, Marines were going to extraordinary lengths to secure the city. The fighting intensified as the Marines of RCT-1 pushed south of Highway 10 into the Resala, Nazal, and Jebail districts. On 14 November Marines of India Company were involved in house-to-house operations; these Marines included a squad led by Cpl. Dale Allen Burger Jr., who had assumed command of the squad days earlier when his squad leader was injured by the concussion from an RPG explosion. Leading the squad to positions inside a nearby house, Burger took a team to the roof where, exposed to enemy fire, he employed his M-203 grenade launcher and two AT-4 rockets to eliminate enemy insurgents operating in adjacent buildings. He then led an assault against a larger force of insurgents occupying a building and was seriously wounded, and then evacuated. Three days later he left the hospital to return to his unit, explaining to his mother on the phone, "I'm going back with my men. . . . These are my guys. They need me!"[39]

Burger, the only son of eight children of a Marine wounded in Vietnam, left school to enlist in the Marines at the age of seventeen. After basic training at Parris Island, South Carolina, he was a part of the initial invasion of Iraq in 2003, and had redeployed in May 2004, days after his father was buried at Arlington. Now, only weeks from the end of his enlistment on 3 December, he voluntarily put himself at risk to be with his brothers.[40]

Also on the street was another squad leader, Sgt. Traver D. Pennell, a twenty-eight-year-old from Smyrna, New York. When he heard that a neighboring squad was in contact with insurgents, he rushed to the scene. "I could hear fire. . . . I didn't know if we had it under control."[41] Cpl. Johnny Crougar advised Pennell that there were still Marines trapped inside a house, but thick smoke from grenades, machine guns, and open fires in the tiny house obscured any view inside.

Unhesitatingly, Pennell and Burger charged into the small, smoke-filled rooms, using muzzle blasts to pinpoint the insurgents. They recovered both Marines inside, but Burger took a gunshot wound to the head, and was pulled back behind cover by Pennell. Burger and another Marine, LCpl. Andres Perez, died on the scene. A fourth Marine is working to recover from his wounds.

After seven months, Pennell returned to the United States and was honorably discharged from the Marines in January 2006 after eight years of service. On 1 March 2006 Burger's mother accepted his posthumous Silver Star and Purple Heart in a ceremony at the headquarters of the Marine Detachment, Ft. Devons, Massachusetts. The following 26 April, Pennell, who now trains National Guard Reservists, accepted his Silver Star stating, "The true heroes are the ones who didn't make the plane ride home. . . . I thought I was just doing what anyone else would have done."[42]

Cpl. Kristopher D. Kane, USMC

Squad Automatic Weapon Gunner, 2nd Platoon, Charlie Company, Battalion Landing Team, 1st Battalion, 3rd Marine Regiment, Regimental Combat Team 7, 1st Marine Division, I Marine Expeditionary Force, U.S. Marine Corps Forces, Central Command

The President of the United States takes pleasure in presenting the Silver Star Medal to Kristopher D. Kane, Corporal, U.S. Marine Corps, for conspicuous gallantry and intrepidity in action against the enemy while serving as Squad Automatic Weapon Gunner, Second Platoon, Company C, Battalion Landing Team, First Battalion, Third Marine Regiment, Regimental Combat Team 7, FIRST Marine Division, I Marine Expeditionary Force, U.S. Marine Corps Forces, Central Command, in support of Operation Iraqi Freedom on 10 November 2004. During Operation Al Fajr, insurgent forces engaged a squad from Second Platoon as they moved up the stairs of a house. Responding to a call for assistance, Corporal Kane entered the building amidst a hail of enemy armor piercing rounds fired at him through the ceiling and dodged hand grenades that were tossed down the stairs. When he observed wounded Marines trapped in the enemy line of fire, Corporal Kane immediately positioned himself to provide covering fire for the Marines attempting to pull the wounded to safety all the while remaining dangerously exposed to the enemy's impact zone. He repeatedly thwarted insurgent attempts to fire their machine guns down the stairs at the fellow Marines with accurate and deadly fire from his Squad Automatic Weapon. He held his ground, in the direct line of enemy fire, even as a D-9 armored bulldozer punched a hole in an adjacent wall and the building began collapsing around him. As the last of the wounded were being evacuated, portions of the building fell on top of him, crushing his leg. His heroic actions and selfless devotion inspired all who observed him and were instrumental in the evacuation of Marines needing urgent medical care, and in the destruction of an enemy stronghold. By his bold leadership, wise judgment, and complete dedication to duty, Corporal Kane reflected great credit upon himself and upheld the highest traditions of the Marine Corps and the United States Naval Service.[43]

Silver Star Citation

SSgt. Theodore S. Holder II, USMC

Platoon Sergeant, Light Armored Reconnaissance Company, Battalion Landing Team 1/3, Regimental Combat Team 7, 1st Marine Division, I Marine Expeditionary Force, U.S. Marine Corps Forces, Central Command

The President of the United States takes pride in presenting the Silver Star Medal (Posthumously) to Theodore S. Holder II, Staff Sergeant, U.S. Marine Corps, for conspicuous gallantry and intrepidity in action against the enemy while serving as Platoon Sergeant, Light Armored Reconnaissance Company, Battalion Landing Team 1/3, Regimental Combat Team 7, FIRST Marine Division, I Marine Expeditionary Force, U.S. Marine Corps Forces Central Command in support of Operation Iraqi Freedom on 11 November 2004. While conducting a movement to contact through the city of Al Fallujah, Iraq, Staff Sergeant Holder and his Light Armored Reconnaissance Company was ambushed from the front and right flank. A heavy volume of enemy small arms and rocket- propelled grenade (RPG) fire hit the lead vehicle, severely wounding one of the scouts. With no way for the scouts to remount their vehicle without exposing themselves to a devastating wall of machine gun fire, Staff Sergeant Holder, with complete disregard for his own safety, skillfully maneuvered his vehicle directly into the enemy's line of fire in order to protect them. Even as a burst of machine gun fire hit the turret wounding him, he continued to remain exposed and guide the fires of the gunner onto the enemy positions. As the enemy fire began to concentrate on the vehicle, he continued to fire an M-240G machine gun and control the fires of the vehicle's main gun. As the enemy fire continued to build, he was seriously wounded once again.Despite the severity of his wounds, he continued to man the machine gun and return fire upon the enemy, eventually succumbing to his fatal injuries. By his bold leadership, wise judgment, and complete dedication to duty, Staff Sergeant Holder reflected great credit upon himself and upheld the highest traditions of the Marine Corps and the United States Naval Service.[44]

Silver Star Citation

THE 1/3 MARINES, under the command of Lt. Col. Michael Ramos, was on its first deployment to Iraq, having arrived in country in October 2004. Their introduction to Fallujah had occurred on 30 October when a car bomb killed seven Marines of Bravo Company. With Charlie Company, 1st Light Armored Reconnaissance (LAR) Battalion attached, 1/3 had advanced into Askari on 9 November at a quicker pace than the other battalions, despite heavy resistance.[45]

During the evening and morning of 9–10 November, 1st Lt. Dustin Shumney led the second platoon into a building near the Muhajareen mosque and set up a base of operations. Although commanders anticipated it would take Charlie Company ninety-six hours to achieve their objectives, they completed their mission in only twelve. The next morning, 10 November 2004, they discovered insurgents in an adjacent building. It was the Marine Corps' 229th birthday.

Among the Marines ordered to clear the building was Cpl. Kristopher D. Kane, at twenty-four one of the oldest Marines in the platoon. With seven other Marines, he entered the first floor of the two-story dwelling and immediately came under fire from armor-piercing rounds, grenades, and RPGs, which killed one Marine and wounded six.[46] Unheeding of the intense fire, Kane exposed himself to lay down suppressing fire on the insurgents, at one point placing himself between the insurgents and a corpsman treating the wounded.[47]

First Lieutenant Shumney wrote in his after-action report that Kane's accurate fire kept the insurgents at bay and allowed for the evacuation of wounded Marines. After grenades thrown by Kane only partially eliminated the insurgents, and in order to get to the trapped Marines, Shumney ordered a D-9 bulldozer to punch through a wall of the building to create an evacuation route for the wounded. Kane continued to provide covering fire, even as the building crumbled around him, resulting in a crushed right femur and broken collarbone.[48]

Kane was medically evacuated to Baghdad, then to the United States to recover from his injuries. Prior to deploying, he had re-enlisted and requested assignment as a marksmanship instructor. Shumney, who died with thirty-one members of his platoon in a helicopter accident near the Syrian border on 26 January 2005, was awarded a posthumous Bronze Star.

On 5 May 2006, while assigned as a marksmanship instructor at the Marine Corps Recruit Depot-San Diego, newly promoted Sergeant Kane was presented the Silver Star by Brig. Gen. John Paxton. Perhaps explaining his motivation for charging into enemy fire, he stated, "A really good friend of mine, Lance Cpl. Aaron Pickering, couldn't be found. He was my protégé, so I set out to find him."[49] Pickering and another Charlie Company Marine, Cpl. Theodore Bowling, were killed in action on 10 November 2004.

A second 1/3 Marine to be awarded the Silver Star was SSgt. Theodore "Sam" Holder II, a twenty-seven-year-old Marine from Colorado assigned to the Light Armored Reconnaissance Company, Battalion Landing Team 1/3. A former Marine Security Guard who had protected dignitaries in Prague and Cyprus, he died protecting his fellow Marines on Veterans Day, 11 November.[50]

As insurgents opened fire, the platoon commander Capt. Paul Webber saw bullets impacting into the dirt near a group of dismounted scouts, and he was advised that one of his Marines, Lance Corporal Armendariz, was seriously wounded. Incoming fire began to intensify, and a second Marine, Cpl. Kyle Burns, was mortally wounded by an RPG. Webber ordered Holder forward. With Holder in the turret with his gunner Cpl. Adam Solis beside him, both exposed from the waist up, the eight-wheeled AAV pulled forward to the trapped Marines to provide covering fire. En route, Holder was seriously wounded, but his vehicle continued forward. As the wounded were loaded into another vehicle, he ordered his AAV forward to a position in front of the other vehicle.

"As they're backing out, he pushes forward. So knowing he would take more fire, he still pushed up," Solis later said. "We could have stayed there in the place where we were. We could have stayed there, but he chose to push forward for a few more yards, deeper into the kill box, so we would take more fire."[51]

Holder's AAV became the focus of enemy fire, and Holder was mortally wounded. On 22 July 2006 Webber presented Holder's parents with his posthumous Silver Star and told those present, "It was by far the most courageous act I ever witnessed. . . . He died for his buddies."[52]

Sgt. Jeffrey L. Kirk, USMC

1st Squad Leader, 3rd Platoon, Kilo Company, 3rd Battalion, 5th Marine Regiment, Regimental Combat Team 1, 1st Marine Division, I Marine Expeditionary Force, U.S. Marine Corps Forces, Central Command

The President of the United States takes pride in presenting the Silver Star Medal (Posthumously) to Jeffrey L. Kirk, Sergeant, U.S. Marine Corps, for conspicuous gallantry and intrepidity in action against the enemy while serving as First Squad Leader, Third Platoon, Company K, Third Battalion, Fifth Marine Regiment, Regimental Combat Team 1, FIRST Marine Division, I Marine Expeditionary Force, U.S. Marine Corps Forces, Central Command, in support of Operation Iraqi Freedom on 10 November 2004. While Sergeant Kirk and his squad gained entry into a building, insurgents threw a grenade from a room containing a hardened machine gun position. Sergeant Kirk quickly organized and led Marines from multiple squads across an open courtyard to eliminate the threat. Effective enemy small arms fire forced him and the other Marines to withdraw to a covered position while returning fire with grenades and small arms. Unfazed, Sergeant Kirk re-grouped his men behind cover and attacked the building a second time. Although wounded as he approached the position, he continued to attack by throwing a grenade into the room and then eliminating the enemy machinegunner with a rifle. Enemy fire and grenades again erupted from the same room. Sergeant Kirk and the Marines withdrew once more, throwing grenades in their wake. Refusing medical attention, he remained as the point man and led the Marines in for a third assault on the enemy position. He quickly overwhelmed and destroyed the remaining insurgents, clearing the building to the roof. His extraordinary actions in the face of great danger destroyed a key defensive position and prevented the enemy from inflicting serious casualties on other Marines. By his outstanding display of decisive leadership, unlimited courage in the face of heavy enemy fire, and utmost devotion to duty, Sergeant Kirk reflected great credit upon himself and upheld the highest traditions of the Marine Corps and the United States Naval Service.[53]

Silver Star Citation

SHORTLY AFTER DAWN ON 10 NOVEMBER 2004, the Corps' 229th birthday, Marines of 3/5 began moving into Jolan. The morning and early afternoon were mostly uneventful as they went house by house, uncovering caches of explosives. At about 3:30 PM Kilo Company began taking sniper fire as they crossed an open plaza near a mosque and they determined the source of the fire to be two houses: one of them a block west, the other a block east of the mosque. Supported by tanks, artillery, and covering machine-gun fire, squads were assigned to assault both houses.[54]

As Marines advanced on the western house, they were greeted by a hail of grenades tossed from the window, which wounded two of the Marines with shrapnel. A third Marine was wounded by sniper fire. The Marines responded with grenades of their own, then they rushed the house, killing all four insurgents inside.

With the troops assaulting the eastern house was a twenty-four-year-old from Baton Rouge, Louisiana, Sgt. Jeffrey L. Kirk, a squad leader with Kilo Company, had enlisted in the Marines in 1998, then re-enlisted to become a pistol instructor at Quantico, Virginia, but had requested a transfer to an infantry company following the terrorist attack on 11 September. He was now a sergeant in FAST Company, an antiterrorist security squad, on his second deployment to Iraq.[55]

As the Marines advanced on the eastern house, they were pinned down by sniper fire. Like many of the dwellings in Al-Fallujah, the house was a two-story structure surrounded by a wall with a courtyard in front and a stairway to the roof along its side. Kirk and other Marines "stacked" at the gate while Pfc. Christopher Adlesperger knocked down the gate. As LCpl. Eric Hodges charged through, he was mortally wounded by a hail of machine-gun fire from inside the house. Other Marines charging into the courtyard were also wounded, including a Navy corpsman, Alonso Rogero, who was wounded in the stomach, and LCpl. Ryan Sunnerville, who was wounded in the leg. Despite his own wounds, Adlesperger returned fire at the insurgents twenty feet distant as he helped the two wounded men to the stairway and up to the roof. When insurgents tried to rush his position, he shot them dead. He then used his M-203 grenade launcher to punch holes in the roof so he could fire inside.[56]

The Marines had withdrawn from the courtyard to cover. Kirk regrouped his Marines for a second assault and was wounded in the thigh, but was still able to toss a grenade and take out an insurgent machine-guner with rifle fire before again being forced to withdraw. He refused medical attention for his wounds.

Adlesperger joined Kirk as they prepared for a third assault. After a light armored vehicle 25 (LAV-25) opened a breach in the wall with fire from its 25-mm "Bushmaster" cannon, allowing the Marines to swarm through, any remaining resistance was eliminated. After thirty minutes the battle was over. Two Marines from 3/5 died that day—Hodges and SSgt. Gene Ramierez.

As the other battalions advanced south, 3/5 would remain in Jolan clearing pockets of resistance. They uncovered a torture chamber with five dead bodies shot through the head, what one Marine would later describe as a "hostage slaughterhouse."[57]

Adlesperger would be nominated for a Medal of Honor, and would ultimately be awarded the Navy Cross. Kirk would be nominated for a Silver Star. Neither man would survive to accept the award. Adlesperger would be killed in action clearing a house in Al-Fallujah on 9 December 2004. Three days later on 12 December Kirk would also be killed while assaulting a house to retrieve the body of a fallen Marine.[58]

In March 2007 Kirk's widow, Carly Kirk, was presented with his posthumous Silver Star. During the ceremony she read from one of his letters: "I hope that if I do go, that I went with honor and courage. I hope that I died leading Marines, and not from a random bomb or a sniper. . . . I will regret not being able to hold you again, but there are fine Marines under my charge, and I want to lead them with honor and courage."

Although Al-Fallujah was announced as secure on 16 November 2004, fighting in the city would continue into the next year.

ENDNOTES

1. Jim Garamone, "Scan Eagle Proves Worth in Fallujah Fight," American Forces News Service, 11 January 2005.
2. "U.S. Forces Unleash Phantom Fury to Seize Fallujah," Agence France Presse, 8 November 2004.
3. "Operation Al-Fajr (Dawn), Operation Phantom Fury, [Fallujah]," GlobalSecurity.org, http://www.globalsecurity.org/military/ops/oif-phantom-fury-fallujah.htm.
4. Chris Roberts, "Marine Awarded Silver Star," El Paso (TX) Times, 26 March 2006.
5. Matt Zeigler, Three Block War II: Snipers in the Sky! (Lincoln, NE: Universe Press, 2006), 162–64.
6. "U.S. Forces Unleash Phantom Fury to Seize Fallujah."
7. Zeigler, Three Block War II.
8. Ibid.
9. Silver Star citation, 1st Lt. Jeffrey T. Lee, USMCR, http://www.homeofheroes.com/valor2/SS/7_GWOT/citations_USMC.html.
10. Silver Star citation, 2nd Lt. Elliott L. Ackerman, USMCR, http://www.homeofheroes.com/valor2/SS/7_GWOT/citations_USMC.html.

11. Silver Star citation, Sgt. Timothy Connors, USMC, http://www.homeofheroes.com/valor2/SS/7_GWOT/citations_USMC.html.
12. Silver Star citation, SSgt. Richard Pillsbury, USMC, http://www.homeofheroes.com/valor2/SS/7_GWOT/citations_USMC-M.html.
13. Chris Mazzolini, "Marine Stayed in Fight Despite Hand Wound, Low Fuel in Tank," *Jacksonville* (NC) *Daily News*, 15 March 2006.
14. Zeigler, *Three Block War II*.
15. Ed Marek, "Battle for Fallujah: Our Warfighters Towered in Maturity and Guts," *Talking Proud Magazine*, http://www.talkingproud.us/Military042805B.html.
16. Michael Blanding, "The Opposite of Fear," *Tufts* (University, MA) *Magazine*, Spring 2007.
17. Zeigler, *Three Block War II*.
18. Lucian Friel, "Heroic Platoon Commander Honored with Silver Star," *Marine Corps News*, 17 March 2006.
19. Mazzolini, "Marine Stayed in Fight Despite Hand Wound, Low Fuel in Tank."
20. Demetrio Espinosa, USMC, "1Lt. Elliott Ackerman: Marine Earns Silver Star for Courage Under Fire," *Marine Corps Times*, 16 January 2007.
21. Blanding, "The Opposite of Fear."
22. Espinosa, "1Lt. Elliott Ackerman."
23. James C. Roberts, "Remember Heroes of Fallujah," *Human Events Magazine*, 6 November 2006.
24. Ibid.
25. Rick Collins, "Iraq Hero Accepts Honor Modestly," *The Patriot Ledger* (MA), 1 May 2006.
26. Silver Star citation, SSgt. Richard Pillsbury.
27. Trista Talton, "Lejeune Combat Instructor Receives Silver Star," *Marine Corps Times*, 22 November 2006.
28. Chris Mazzolini, "Calm in a Time of Storm," *Jacksonville* (NC) *Daily News*, 23 November 2006.
29. Silver Star citation, Sgt. Chad Cassady, USMC, http://www.homeofheroes.com/valor2/SS/7_GWOT/citations_USMC.html.
30. Silver Star citation, Cpl. Dale Allen Burger Jr., USMC, http://www.homeofheroes.com/valor2/SS/7_GWOT/citations_USMC.html.
31. Silver Star citation, Sgt. Traver D. Pennell, USMC, http://www.homeofheroes.com/valor2/SS/7_GWOT/citations_USMC-M.html.
32. Zeigler, *Three Block War II*.
33. Tony Perry, "Marine Who Pulled Comrades to Safety Honored," *Los Angeles* (CA) *Times*, 18 October 2007.
34. Michael Hoffman, "Wounded Sergeant Dragged Four Buddies to Safety," *Marine Corps Times*, 28 October 2007.
35. Ibid.
36. Cpl. William C. James, LCpl. Nicholas D. Larson, and LCpl. Nathan R. Wood of Lima Company and LCpl. Juan Segura of Kilo Company.
37. Hoffman, "Wounded Sergeant Dragged Four Buddies to Safety."
38. Perry, "Marine Who Pulled Comrades to Safety Honored."
39. Mary Otto, "Marine's Family Recall His Dedication to Mission," *Washington* (DC) *Post*, 17 November 2004.
40. Andrew Keirn, "Fallen Marine's Heroism Recognized," *Marine Corps News*, 9 March 2006 (Story ID #20063934816).

41. Jessica Fender, "Smyrna Man's Bravery Honored," *Marine Corps News*, 12 September 2006.
42. Ibid.
43. Silver Star citation, Cpl. Kristopher D. Kane, USMC, http://www.homeofheroes.com/valor2/ SS/7_GWOT/citations_USMC-M.html.
44. Silver Star citation, SSgt. Theodore S. "Sam" Holder II, USMC, http://www.homeofheroes. com/valor2/SS/7_GWOT/citations_USMC-M.html.
45. Zeigler, *Three Block War II*.
46. Rusty Baker, "Dallas Marine Wife, Children Presented Posthumous Bronze Star for Husband's Valor in Iraq," *Marine Corps News*, 16 August 2005 (Story ID #2005816163852).
47. Charlie Chavez, "OIF Combat Veteran Awarded Silver Star," *Marine Corps News*, 12 May 2006 (Story ID #2006512163230).
48. Joe Vargo, "The Marines Honor Sgt. Kristopher Kane with a Billboard," *Press Enterprise*, 5 January 2008.
49. Gregg K. Kakesako, "Kaneohe Maine Award Silver Star for Battle Rescue," *Honolulu Star Bulletin*, 21 May 2006.
50. Jim Sheeler, "Remembering the Brave: Littleton Parents to Receive Silver Star for Dying Son's Actions in Iraqi Battle," *Rocky Mountain* (CO) *News*, 22 July 2006.
51. Ibid.
52. Sheeler, "Remembering the Brave."
53. Silver Star citation, Sgt. Jeffrey L. Kirk, USMC, http://www.homeofheroes.com/valor2/SS/ 7_GWOT/citations_USMC.html.
54. Zeigler, *Three Block War II*.
55. Tony Perry, "Slain Marine Is Awarded Silver Star," *Los Angeles* (CA) *Times*, 6 March 2007.
56. Tony Perry, "Marine Hero Knew Only One Way: Straight Ahead," *Los Angeles* (CA) *Times*, 8 October 2006.
57. "Troops Uncover Hostage 'Slaughterhouse,'" 11 November 2004, http://www.theage.com. au/articles/2004/11/11/1100021910341.html?from=storylhs.
58. Teri Figueroa, "Marine Sgt. Jeffrey L. Kirk Posthumously Awarded Silver Star," *North County* (San Diego, CA) *Times*, 5 March 2007.

Capt. Patrick Marc Rapicault, USMC

Company Commander, Weapons Company, 2nd Battalion,
5th Marine Regiment, 1st Marine Division, I Marine Expeditionary Force,
U.S. Marine Corps Forces, Central Command

Ar Ramadi, Iraq
15 November 2004

The President of the United States takes pride in presenting the Silver Star Medal (Posthumously) to Patrick Marc Rapicault, Captain, U.S. Marine Corps, for conspicuous gallantry and intrepidity in action against the enemy while serving as Company Commander, Weapons Company, Second Battalion, Fifth Marine Regiment, FIRST Marine Division, I Marine Expeditionary Force, U.S. Marine Corps Forces, Central Command, in support of Operation Iraqi Freedom, from 24 September to 15 November 2004. Captain Rapicault courageously led his Marines on the streets of Ar Ramadi, Iraq, through fifty firefights and twenty-seven improvised explosive device (IED) ambushes. Always leading from the front, he directed the fire and maneuver of his company with complete disregard for his own personal safety. Despite being the first Marine in the Battalion wounded and his company suffering the heaviest casualties during daily street fighting, Captain Rapicault always displayed an infectious enthusiasm that motivated every Marine to fight hard and recover quickly from battle. On every mission, Captain Rapicault's intuitive and calm combat leadership ensured success on the battlefield, with limited damage to vehicles and friendly casualties. He gallantly gave his life in the cause of freedom. Captain Rapicault's bold leadership, courageous actions, and complete dedication to duty reflected great credit upon him and were in keeping with the highest traditions of the Marine Corps and the United States Naval Service.[1]

Silver Star Citation

MORE IS KNOWN ABOUT CAPT. PATRICK RAPICAULT'S LIFE than the circumstances of his death. The thirty-four-year-old native of Martinique, France, whom his Marines called "Frenchy" because of his thick accent, had grown up in Florida dreaming of becoming a Marine officer.[2]

He enlisted in the Marine Corps Reserve on 24 May 1993 while a student at Delta State University in Mississippi. He went on active duty after graduation and, upon becoming a U.S. citizen in 1995, took steps to earn a commission, graduating from Officer Candidate School (OCS) in 1997. The following year, he graduated first in his class at the U.S. Army Ranger School at Ft. Benning, Georgia. He was by all accounts a motivated, gung-ho Marine.

Rapicault assumed command of Weapons Company, 2nd Battalion, 5th Marines on 24 September 2004 in Ar Ramadi, while the company was in contact with the enemy. Ironically, he was the first Marine in the battalion to be wounded.[3]

He led his Marines through fifty firefights and twenty-seven improvised explosive device (IED) ambushes between 24 September and 15 November, and saw heavy combat in Ar Ramadi in late October, even as U.S. forces were marshalling to invade Al-Fallujah. He is quoted as describing his mission as, "When we get sent out, it's to defend, deter and detect against any kind of terrorist threat."[4]

In November 2004 fighting increased in Ar Ramadi as insurgents tried to relieve pressure on the fighters in Al-Fallujah. On the afternoon of 15 November Rapicault and two of his Marines, Cpl. Mark T. Ryan and Cpl. Lance Thompson, were killed when a suicide bomber drove up and detonated himself next to their position.

Much loved by his men, Rapicault was laid to rest with full military honors at Arlington National Cemetery on 30 November 2004. On 31 January 2006 Maj. Gen. Richard Natonski, commander of the 1st Marine Division, presented Rapicault's widow with his posthumous Silver Star. As his former commander, Lt. Col. Randall P. Newman, remarked, "He is as alive today as the day he died. . . . He is truly the backbone of what the Corps is today."[5]

ENDNOTES

1. Silver Star citation, Capt. Patrick Marc Rapicault, USMC, http://www.homeofheroes.com/valor2/SS/7_GWOT/citations_USMC-M.html.

2. Patrick Marc Rapicault, Arlington National Cemetery website, http://www.arlingtoncemetery.net/pmmrapicault.htm.

3. Ray Lewis, "Marine Officer Posthumously Receives Silver Star," *Marine Corps News*, 2 December 2005, http://www.militaryconnections.com/news_story.cfm?textnewsid=1771.

4. Phil Zabriskie, "Taking the Battle to the Enemy: U.S. and Iraqi Forces Launch High-Risk Probes of the Insurgency in Fallujah and Ramadi," *Time*, 25 October 2004.

5. Lewis, "Marine Officer Posthumously Receives Silver Star."

Maj. Todd S. Desgrosseilliers, USMC

Officer-in-Charge, Task Force Bruno, 3rd Battalion,
5th Marine Regiment, Regimental Combat Team 1,
1st Marine Division, I Marine Expeditionary Force,
U.S. Marine Corps Forces, Central Command

Al-Fallujah, Iraq
12–23 December 2004

The President of the United States takes pleasure in presenting the Silver Star Medal to Todd S. Desgrosseilliers, Major, U.S. Marine Corps, for conspicuous gallantry and intrepidity in action against the enemy while serving as Officer-in-Charge, Task Force Bruno, Third Battalion, Fifth Marine Regiment, Regimental Combat Team 1, FIRST Marine Division, I Marine Expeditionary Force, U.S. Marine Corps Forces, Central Command, in support of Operation Iraqi Freedom II from 12 to 23 December 2004. On 12 December Major Desgrosseilliers was leading Task Force Bruno in clearing operations when several Marines became trapped inside a building by intense enemy fire. During the engagement, an enemy grenade landed in the midst of the Marines. With complete disregard for his own safety, Major Desgrosseilliers shielded them from the explosion with his own body. Ignoring shrapnel wounds, he rallied his Marines and directed grenade, heavy machine gun and tank fire to destroy the fifteen insurgents in the house. On 23 December Task Force Bruno came under heavy enemy fire while conducting operations in hostile territory. Throughout the firefight, he personally cleared several rooms and eliminated insurgents with rifle and grenade fire. When one of the Marines was seriously wounded he exposed himself to direct enemy fire and helped drag him to safety. Despite being wounded again with shrapnel during the firefight, he remained in the open to direct a devastating volume of tank main gunfire until the enemy was destroyed. In this engagement thirty insurgents were killed including key terrorist leadership. By his bold leadership, wise judgment, and complete dedication to duty, Major Desgrosseilliers reflected great credit upon himself and upheld the highest traditions of the Marine Corps and the United States Naval Service.[1]

Silver Star Citation

Sgt. Samuel Guardiola, USMC

Section Leader, Mortar Platoon, Weapons Company, 3rd Battalion,
5th Marine Regiment, Regimental Combat Team 1, 1st Marine Division,
U.S. Marine Corps Forces, Central Command

Al-Fallujah, Iraq
23 December 2004

The President of the United States takes pleasure in presenting the Silver
Star Medal to Samuel Guardiola, Sergeant, U.S. Marine Corps, for con-
spicuous gallantry and intrepidity in action against the enemy as Section
Leader, Mortar Platoon, Weapons Company, Third Battalion, Fifth Marine
Regiment, Regimental Combat Team 1, FIRST Marine Division, U.S.
Marine Corps Forces, Central Command, in support of Operation Iraqi
Freedom on 23 December 2004. While searching for enemy weapons
caches, Sergeant Guardiola's section was ambushed by insurgents occupying well-fortified positions. Realizing that they were trapped in the impact
zone, he exposed himself to intense enemy fire in order to reorganize and
consolidate his Marines. Upon discovering two of his Marines were isolated
inside a building, he gathered an assault force to recover them. Sergeant
Guardiola used the adjacent rooftop to access the building and reach the
Marines inside, while constantly under small arms and grenade fire. Once
inside, he found his fallen comrades and immediately planned their evacuation. As the enemy assaulted with a fragmentation grenade, he covered the
Marines with his own body to shield them from the enemy grenade, which
did not detonate. Despite intense enemy fire, Sergeant Guardiola carried
one fallen Marine down three flights of stairs, clearing rooms along the
way with his 9 millimeter pistol. Although exhausted and dehydrated, he
continued to carry his comrade to the evacuation point. By his bold leadership, wise judgment, and complete dedication to duty, Sergeant Guardiola
reflected great credit upon himself and upheld the highest traditions of the
Marine Corps and the United States Naval Service.[2]

Silver Star Citation

DESPITE THE ANNOUNCEMENT by Central Command on 16 November that American forces had secured the city of Al-Fallujah, there continued to be sporadic instances of insurgent attacks on American and Iraqi forces. The end of open combat did not mean the end of the Marines' mission in Al-Fallujah.[3]

The 3rd Battalion, 5th Marines, which would remain in Al-Fallujah until 24 December, was tasked with collecting documents and weapons from buildings that housed insurgents and searching for arms caches, explosives and materials to build improvised explosive devices (IEDs). To accomplish the mission, the battalion executive officer, Maj. Todd S. Desgrosseilliers, formed Task Force Bruno, a mix of headquarter and infantry Marines who performed room-to-room searches in some of the deadliest neighborhoods in Iraq.[4]

Desgrosseilliers, son of a career Sailor, enlisted in the Marines in 1985 on an impulse while on a cross-country bicycle trip between the University of Maine where he was a student and Seattle, Washington. Sent to Boston University by the Corps, he graduated in 1990 with a Bachelor's degree in history and a commission as a second lieutenant. He attended the Amphibious Warfare School, where he ranked as honor graduate, and the Marine Command and Staff College before being assigned to the 3/5. On the morning of 12 December 2004 he was midway through his second deployment.[5]

As Desgrosseilliers and his Marines followed the rifle companies searching buildings in the volatile Askari neighborhood looking for weapons caches or insurgents that had re-entered the area, Desgrosseilliers heard gunfire coming from one of the houses and raced over with several Marines. Some of his Marines had been moving up the stairs of the two-story house when they were fired on by insurgents inside, trapping his men.

Preparing to enter the house, he heard a thump and looked down to see a grenade at his feet. Without thinking, he pushed his driver and another Marine against the wall, covering their bodies with his. Knocked unconscious briefly from the concussion of the exploding grenade, he regrouped and led his men into the building. "I heard a lot of chanting. It sounded like fifteen to twenty people up there chanting in unison. They started throwing hand grenades down on top of us, and that's where I got wounded the first time."[6]

Despite shrapnel wounds to his leg, Desgrosseilliers led his Marines in a firefight that lasted more than four hours, which was often at close quarters, until the issue was resolved by the arrival of tanks and the deployment by air of five-hundred-pound bombs, killing fifteen insurgents. Several

3/5 Marines were killed on 12 December, including Sgt. Jeffrey Kirk and Cpl. Jason S. Clairday. Sergeant Kirk would be awarded a posthumous Silver Star for his actions in Al-Fallujah in November (see chapter on Sgt. Jeffrey L. Kirk). Corporal Clairday was awarded a posthumous Navy Cross for leading an assault to reach trapped Marines on 12 December. Both Marines were with Kilo Company. Other 3/5 Marines included SSgt. Melvin Blazer, LCpl. Hilario Lopez, and Cpl. Ian Stewart.

Again, on 23 December, Desgrosseilliers answered the call of Marines trapped inside a building in northeast Al-Fallujah, exchanging fire with insurgents. Three Marines were already dead and another wounded when Desgrosseilliers arrived. On his arrival he had no radio communication with 1st Lt. Alfred Butler, the 81-mm platoon commander whose troops were trapped inside the four-story building (including LCpl. Eric Hillenburg, LCpl. James R. Phillips, and Cpl. Raleigh Smith, all of Weapons Company, 3/5 Marines). After ensuring the safe evacuation of the wounded Marine, Desgrosseilliers learned that Butler was trapped inside with four Marines on the second floor.[7] After several unsuccessful attempts to fight through to Butler, Desgrosseilliers pulled his Marines on the ground floor outside, where he was again wounded by shrapnel. As he oversaw the evacuation of the dead Marines, he requested tank support.

In the interim Butler, who had earlier entered the building to evacuate his Marines, had learned of other Marines trapped on the second floor. With Sgt. Samuel Guardiola, a section leader in the mortar platoon, Butler had led Marines to an adjacent building's rooftop, then jumped roof to roof to assault the house with grenades and small-arms fire to reach the trapped Marines and evacuate them to the adjacent rooftop. For his actions, Butler was awarded the Bronze Star medal with "V" for Valor on 19 May 2006.[8]

Upon learning that the trapped Marines had been safely evacuated, Desgrosseilliers hobbled out into the open under fire to communicate with and direct the fire of the tanks that had arrived, since they had no information regarding which buildings contained Marines. As Capt. Robert Bodisch of the 2nd Tank Battalion described it, "It was like a movie, that was the best way to describe it. . . . Bullets were flying in every direction, and grenades were exploding. But Desgrosseilliers was dashing around, ignoring them."[9]

Once the house had been turned to rubble, they advanced about a block to another hot zone. As Marines entered a walled courtyard, an insurgent appeared in the doorway and fired a machine gun at them, knocking down two Marines. As the other Marines backed out and took cover, Desgrosseilliers dashed through the gate into the line of fire. One of the

Marines, protected by his body armor, had only been stunned. That Marine and Desgrosseilliers dragged the other wounded Marine to safety. Then, limping back to the tanks, Desgrosseilliers directed their fire to demolish the house, again assisted by air support. He is credited with the death of another thirty insurgents, including members of the insurgency leadership. All the trapped Marines were recovered, including the three who died. "No Marine is ever left behind," Desgrosseilliers stated. "My goal was to get everyone out of the building without letting the enemy go."[10]

On 13 February 2006 at a ceremony at Camp Lejeune, North Carolina, Desgrosseilliers, now a Lieutenant Colonel and commanding officer of the 3rd Battalion of the 2nd Marine Regiment, was presented the Silver Star by Brig. Gen. Joseph J. McMenamin, 2nd Marine Division assistant division commander. McMenamin declared himself inspired by "a leader with the experience, combat record . . . who is not afraid to lead (men) into battle."[11]

Desgrosseilliers deployed to Iraq for a third time in August 2006, commanding his new battalion at Habbaniyah. His battalion is tasked with setting up outposts between Ar Ramadi in the west and Al-Fallujah in the east, but his priorities remain unchanged: "Protect the Marines and then kill the enemy—pretty much in that order."[12]

ENDNOTES

1. Silver Star citation, Maj. Todd S. Desgrosseilliers, USMC, http://www.homeofheroes.com/valor2/SS/7_GWOT/citations_USMC.html.

2. Silver Star citation, Sgt. Samuel Guardiola, USMC, http://www.homeofheroes.com/valor2/SS/7_GWOT/citations_USMC.html.

3. "Operation al-Fajr (Dawn) Operation Phantom Fury [Fallujah]," GlobalSecurity.org, http://www.globalsecurity.org/military/ops/oif-phantom-fury-fallujah.htm.

4. Elbert Aull, "A Marine with Merit," *Portland* (ME) *Press Herald*, 25 February 2006.

5. Brad Kelly, "Todd Desgrosseilliers Bit the Bullet in Fallujah," *Investors Business Daily*, 22 June 2007.

6. Lt. Col. Todd Desgrosseilliers, Transcript of *Lou Dobbs Tonight* interview, CNN.COM, 14 April 2006. http://transcripts.cnn.com/TRANSCRIPTS/0604/14/ldt.01.html.

7. Kelly, "Todd Desgrosseilliers Bit the Bullet in Fallujah."

8. Mark Sixbey, "Darkhorse Marine Decorated for Valor," *Marine Corps Times*, 20 May 2006.

9. Jay Price, "Marine's Valor Reaps a Reward," *News and Observer* (Raleigh, NC), 11 February 2006.

10. Ibid.

11. Athanasios L. Genos, "Silver Star Awarded to Desgrosseilliers," *Marine Corps News*, 13 February 2006 (Story ID #200621311418).

12. Jay Price, "Marines Make Restraint Their Weapon," *News and Observer* (Raleigh, NC), 19 October 2006.

HM3 Juan M. Rubio, USN

Platoon Corpsman, 4th Platoon, Small Craft Company,
1st Marine Division, I Marine Expeditionary Force,
U.S. Marine Forces, Central Command

Al-Haditha/Euphrates River, Iraq
1 January 2005

The President of the United States takes pleasure in presenting the Silver Star Medal to Juan M. Rubio, Hospital Corpsman Third Class, U.S. Navy, for conspicuous gallantry and intrepidity in action against the enemy while serving as a Platoon Corpsman attached to the 4th Platoon, Small Craft Company, FIRST Marine Division, I Marine Expeditionary Force, U.S. Marine Forces Central Command, in support of Operation Iraqi Freedom on 1 January 2005. During a dismounted patrol along the Euphrates River, 4th Platoon was ambushed in a complex attack by a well-emplaced and determined enemy. As Petty Officer Second Class Rubio and an assault element swept through the ambush site, insurgents detonated an improvised explosive device (IED). Rocket-propelled grenades (RPGs), machine gun, and small arms fire followed immediately after the explosion, wounding three Marines. Realizing the severity of the Marines' wounds, and although bleeding profusely from wounds to his wrist and elbow, Petty Officer Second Class Rubio low-crawled across open terrain, exposing himself to enemy fire to provide triage. Working simultaneously on three urgent surgical casualties, Petty Officer Second Class Rubio coached his fellow Marines who were assisting other casualties as the volume of incoming fire intensified. Upon stabilizing the wounded for casualty evacuation, he directed the Platoon to provide covering fire as he and several Marines began moving the casualties back towards the watercraft. Without regard for his own life, he once again exposed himself to the heavy and accurate enemy fire moving the Marines from the ambush site to the shoreline. By his bold leadership, wise judgment, and complete dedication to duty, Petty Officer Second Class Rubio reflected great credit upon himself and upheld the highest traditions of the United States Naval Service.[1]

Silver Star Citation

ON 1 JANUARY 2005 Marines of 4th Platoon Small Craft Company attached to the 1st Marine Division were patrolling in small craft along the water-

ways adjacent to Al-Haditha Dam, near the hamlet of Haqlaniyah, Iraq. Accompanying 4th Platoon was their Navy corpsman, HM3 Juan M. Rubio, a thirty-two-year-old from San Angelo, Texas.[2]

Rubio was already a veteran of the war on terror. He had been stationed at Bethesda Naval Hospital in Maryland when an airliner was crashed into the Pentagon on 11 September 2001, and he had rushed to the scene to aid the injured. He then departed for Ground Zero in New York City aboard the hospital ship USS *Comfort* to assist with recovery efforts there. When it appeared likely that there would be combat in Iraq, Rubio volunteered for a slot as a corpsman with a Marine infantry unit. He was assigned to 1st Battalion, 2nd Marines. He participated in the invasion and advance on Baghdad, experiencing heavy combat in Nasiriyah.[3]

When he volunteered for a second deployment in 2004, he had a better idea of what to expect, and he requested assignment to the Small Craft Company operating near Al-Fallujah. The unit's commander, Maj. Dan Wittnam, declined more senior corpsmen in favor of Rubio who'd served with him in Iraq in 2003. He assigned Rubio the task of building a Medical Evacuation Team that could operate under fire. Over the next eight months Rubio trained eighteen additional Marines as combat lifesavers. By all accounts a tough instructor, the training paid off the morning of 1 January.[4]

When the platoon's craft came under fire from shore, the platoon commander, Capt. John Kuniholm, ordered the boats to shore. Marines disembarked to locate and eliminate the threat, entering the small village of Haqlaniyah. Rubio was walking behind the radioman, LCpl. Brian Parrello, when Kuniholm shouted a warning to get behind cover. He'd spotted a suspicious-looking five-gallon aluminum can, and knew it was the type of "marker" insurgents used to know when to set off an improvised explosive device (IED).[5]

The warning came too late: an IED detonated as the Marines turned for cover. This was followed by intense small-arms and rocket-propelled grenade (RPG) fire. Rubio and three Marines were wounded. The force of the explosion knocked Parrello into Rubio, knocking Rubio into a wall. The impact briefly knocked him unconscious. He awoke to find himself in the middle of a firefight. Despite the fact that he was bleeding profusely from shrapnel wounds to the arms and legs, Rubio low-crawled across forty meters of open terrain under intense fire to reach Parrello, who had absorbed much of the blast. After stabilizing Parrello as best he could under fire, he dragged him to safety and turned his care over to one of his trained lifesavers.

Again, Rubio left cover to come to the aid of a wounded Marine. This time it was for the platoon commander, Captain Kuniholm, whose right arm had been severed just below the elbow. Rubio applied a tourniquet; then, as his Marines provided covering fire, he dragged Kuniholm to safety, again turning his care over to a trained Marine. Rubio advanced a third time to assist GySgt. Brian Vinciguerra, the platoon sergeant who was severely wounded in the arm and hand from an RPG. He applied another tourniquet.[6]

With their radioman down and no radio contact, two runners returned to the boats and directed the fire of heavier weapons onto the insurgents' locations. This allowed Rubio to direct the treatment and evacuation of the wounded back to the boats. Once the wounded were loaded, the boats sped the one and a half miles upstream to waiting Humvees that transported the wounded to the battalion aid station. Corpsmen worked on the wounded while awaiting the arrival of evacuation helicopters.

Rubio was attempting to return to the battle when a Marine noticed his wounds, turned around, and drove him back to the aid station and a waiting helicopter. En route to the hospital at Al-Asad, he learned that Parrello had lost consciousness and died. At the hospital, Rubio declined being sent home for surgery to remove some of the deeper shrapnel, opting to remain with the Marines, whom he rejoined a day and a half later.[7]

On 27 April 2006 at a ceremony held at the Naval Hospital of the Naval Air Station Corpus Christi, Texas, newly promoted Petty Officer Second Class Rubio was presented a Silver Star to accompany his Purple Heart for his actions in Iraq. Also present was Maj. Gen. Richard Natonski, commanding general of the 1st Marine Division, who stated, "Your actions saved lives and you have set an example for future corpsmen and Marines to emulate."[8] Rubio believes the real hero was Parrello, who took 90 percent of the explosion, shielding Rubio. Accepting the award, he stated, "This is for you, Brother. Thank you for bringing me home."[9]

ENDNOTES

1. Silver Star citation, HM3 Juan M. Rubio, USN, http://www.homeofheroes.com/valor2/SS/7_GWOT/citations_USN.html.
2. Patrick Dickson, "Heroes 2006: Wounded Himself, Corpsman Rushed to Save Comrades After IED Blast," *Stars and Stripes*, 14 June 2006.
3. Jed Graham, "He's a Silver Star of a Sailor," *Investor Business Daily*, 2 March 2007.
4. Ibid.
5. Dickson, "Heroes 2006."
6. Graham, "He's a Silver Star of a Sailor."
7. Dickson, "Heroes 2006."
8. Bill W. Love, "Corpsman Awarded Silver Star for Heroism in Iraq," *Navy News*, 1 May 2006.
9. Ibid.

Capt. Jason P. Schauble, USMC

*Platoon Commander, 4th Platoon, 2nd Force Reconnaissance Company,
1st Marine Division, I Marine Expeditionary Force*

Al-Fallujah/Hit, Iraq
3 January 2005

The President of the United States takes pleasure in presenting the Silver Star Medal to Jason P. Schauble, Captain, U.S. Marine Corps, for conspicuous gallantry and intrepidity in action against the enemy while serving as Platoon Commander, Fourth Platoon, Second Force Reconnaissance Company, FIRST Marine Division, I Marine Expeditionary Force in support of Operation Iraqi Freedom II on 3 January 2005. While conducting a limited-scale raid on a High Value Target deep inside insurgent-controlled territory, Captain Schauble's assault element came under intense fire from small arms and hand grenades. As they entered and attempted to gain a foothold in the farmhouse, one Marine was killed. Losing their initiative, the assault element pulled back to the first room, set up a barricade, and attempted to reorganize for a second assault. Learning a Marine was killed and the assault had stalled, Captain Schauble moved forward to the barricaded position. He immediately assessed the situation and determined the Marines were in danger. With no regard for his personal safety, he threw a flash bang and entered the darkened, second room. Moving to the far wall, he engaged multiple insurgents and attempted to recover the dead Marine. The insurgents focused on Captain Schauble and engaged him at a distance of less than six feet. Moving deeper into the room, he killed two insurgents before being seriously wounded himself. Despite his injuries, he continued to move, drawing the insurgents' fire and allowing his Marines to make entry and kill five insurgents. Though seriously wounded, he held his position until all insurgents were eliminated, risking his life to protect his Marines. By his bold leadership, wise judgment, and complete dedication to duty, Captain Schauble reflected great credit upon himself and upheld the highest traditions of the Marine Corps and the United States Naval Service.[1]

Silver Star Citation

IF THERE IS A THEME to the more than seventy Silver Stars awarded to Marines for valor in Iraq, it is their willingness to brave extreme risk to come to the aid of their fellow Marines, often suffering severe injury or death to protect others.

On 28 July 2006 in a ceremony at Camp Lejeune, North Carolina, Maj. Gen. Dennis Hejlik, commanding general of Marine Corps Special Operations Command, presented Capt. Jason P. Schauble with the Silver Star, a Bronze Star with combat "V" for Valor, and the Meritorious Service medal. "Most of us have led Marines in combat," Hejlik said. "He has just done it exceptionally well."[2]

Schauble, a political science major from Canton, Massachusetts, enlisted in the Marines after graduating from Bates College, Maine, in 1997. He earned the two combat awards while commanding the 4th Platoon, 2nd Force Reconnaissance Company attached to the 1st Marine Division in Iraq.

The 4th Platoon deployed to Al-Asad, Iraq in August 2004. It is the site of an airbase and is located northwest of Ramadi in the Sunni Triangle. Attached to Regimental Combat Team 7 (RCT-7), its focus was primarily on a list of high-value individuals. "Basically, we were trying to disassemble terrorist networks, insurgent networks, trying to take out key insurgent personnel. We were very, very successful," said Lt. Col. Pete Petronzio, commander of 2nd Force Reconnaissance.[3]

That mission was interrupted during October and November 2004 with major combat in Hit and Al-Fallujah. Schauble's Bronze Star citation, for the period of 11 October through 16 November, credits him with coordinating all artillery fire and sniper operations while leading his platoon under fire in several lengthy firefights that resulted in the elimination of fifty insurgents at the cost of twelve Marines wounded.[4]

Another mission the 4th Platoon performed were operations to counter improvised explosive devices (counter-IED operations), which consisted of infiltrating at night into positions along stretches of roadway targeted by IEDs to catch insurgents in the act of deploying them, then remove the threat. But it was on a limited scale raid that Schauble would earn the Silver Star.

On 3 January 2005 in what his Silver Star citation described as "a limited scale raid on a High Value Target deep inside insurgent-controlled territory,"[5] Schauble led his Marines on a raid of a farmhouse. Thermal images from a drone aircraft overhead had revealed at least a dozen insurgents inside, though actual events would reveal the number to be almost twice that number. "Our job was to go into houses at night and kill or capture insurgents."[6]

As an assault team advanced on and entered the farmhouse, they came under intense fire from insurgents in the back room. One of the Marines, Sgt. Thomas Houser, fell mortally wounded, and the other Marines withdrew to barricaded positions in the first room. They were preparing for a second assault when Schauble arrived at their position. He wanted his Marines to withdraw to safety so the farmhouse could be destroyed by larger, vehicle-mounted weapons, but he refused to leave the Marine inside. "I wanted to make sure I got my guy out," Schauble said. "I didn't know if he was wounded or if he had died, but I didn't want to leave him there."[7]

Advancing alone into the darkened room, preceded by a flash-bang grenade, Schauble engaged the insurgents at close quarters—by some accounts from as close as six feet—killing two insurgents, but taking multiple gunshots wounds. Despite his severe bleeding and shock, he continued to engage the insurgents, drawing their focused fire, which allowed his Marines to enter, retrieve the fallen Marine, and kill five additional insurgents.

Schauble's multiple wounds, which included two gunshot wounds to the right hand and four gunshot wounds to both legs, resulted in eight surgeries and more than eighteen months of hospitals and rehabilitation clinics. Only his tactical vest, which took several hits, saved him from death.

Following his return to duty after returning from Iraq, Schauble was instrumental in the creation of the Foreign Military Training Unit (FMTU), serving as its first Future Operations Officer within the Marine Forces Special Operations Command (MarSOC). For his work, he was awarded the Meritorious Service medal, generally associated with more senior Marines.[8]

Schauble medically retired from the Marines at the conclusion of the award ceremony, after nine years of service. "It was a hard day for me," he said. His wife, Melicia, is a former Marine captain and combat engineer who deployed to Iraq between February and June 2003. Of that morning in Iraq, Schauble would only say, "I do what I do because that's what had to be done at the time."[9]

ENDNOTES

1. Silver Star citation, Capt. Jason P. Schauble, USMC, http://www.homeofheroes.com/valor2/SS/7_GWOT/citations_USMC-M.html.
2. Ryan M. Blaich, "Risking His Life for His Marines," *Marine Corps News*, 28 July 2006 (Story ID #200672815916).
3. Evan M. Eagen, "2nd Force Reconnaissance Returns Home," *Marine Corps News*, 21 March 2005 (Story ID #200532184557).
4. Robert Sears, "Area Family Holds Story of Heroism in Iraq," *Thomasville* (AL) *Times*, 28 September 2006.
5. Silver Star citation, Capt. Jason P. Schauble, USMC.
6. Sears, "Area Family Holds Story of Heroism in Iraq."
7. Ibid.
8. Mark C. Brinkley, "Bravery and Brains Earn Marine Captain Three Top Awards," *Marine Corps Times*, 1 August 2006.
9. Blaich, "Risking His Life for His Marines."

Cpl. Jarred L. Adams, USMC

Assistant Team Leader, Scout-Sniper Platoon, 1st Battalion,
7th Marine Regiment, Regimental Combat Team 7, 1st Marine Division,
I Marine Expeditionary Force

Husaybah, Iraq
6 January 2005

The President of the United States takes pleasure in presenting the Silver Star Medal to Jarred L. Adams, Corporal, U.S. Marine Corps, for conspicuous gallantry and intrepidity in action against the enemy while serving as Assistant Team Leader, Scout Sniper Platoon, First Battalion, Seventh Marine Regiment, Regimental Combat Team 7, FIRST Marine Division, I Marine Expeditionary Force, U.S. Marine Corps Forces, Central, in support of Operation Iraqi Freedom on 6 January 2005. In downtown Husaybah, Iraq, Corporal Adams' patrol came under intense enemy fire causing the lead vehicle to crash. He exited the vehicle and began returning fire as fellow Marines attempted to dislodge the vehicle from the wall. After freeing the vehicle and retrograding back to Camp Gannon, the patrol realized one of the vehicles was separated and needed to be located. Re-entering the kill zone again, his vehicle suffered a direct hit from a rocket-propelled grenade (RPG), causing the vehicle to erupt into flames. Corporal Adams exited the vehicle and began to fire on enemy positions. Suffering from multiple shrapnel wounds and burns, he began returning fire on enemy positions while trying to communicate with the Command Post. Realizing that the turret gunner was still inside the burning vehicle, he jumped back inside the burning wreckage, subjecting himself to the imminent threat of exploding friendly munitions from within the vehicle and enemy fire, refusing to depart the area before retrieving the fallen Marine. Freeing the gunner from the turret, and suffering from multiple wounds, he carried the gunner across the intersection under enemy fire while the remaining Marines provided suppressive fire on the enemy threat. By his bold leadership, wise judgment, and complete dedication to duty, Corporal Adams reflected great credit upon himself and upheld the highest traditions of the Marine Corps and the United States Naval Service.[1]

Silver Star Citation

IN AUGUST 2004, Marines of the 1st Battalion, 7th Marines (1/7) deployed to western Iraq in support of Operation Iraqi Freedom II for security operations along the Euphrates River. In the villages of Husaybah, Karabilah, Sadah, Ubaydi, Al-Qa'im, Al-Haditha, and Hit, they performed a variety of missions, including protecting the main supply route (MSR), conducting sweep, cordon, and knock operations, as well as mounted and dismounted urban patrols and border security.[2]

The 1/7 Marines, known as the "First Team," was activated in San Diego in 1921, and saw its first combat at Guadalcanal in World War II. Marine legends Lewis "Chesty" Puller and "Manila John" Basilone were both members of 1/7, with Puller commanding the battalion at Guadalcanal. The 1/7 saw action at Pelilieu and Okinawa, and drew occupation duty in China following the end of that war. The battalion landed at Inchon during the Korean War and was part of the fighting withdrawal from the Chosin Reservoir, with eight Marines earning Medals of Honor (MOH) during the conflict, five posthumously. In its five years of service in Vietnam another three Marines were awarded the MOH. It was the first unit to man defensive positions along the Saudi border during Operation Desert Shield in August 1990, and spearheaded the thrust into Kuwait City during Operation Desert Storm. In addition to service in Mogadishu, Somalia (1992–93), the battalion was among the first Marines across the Kuwaiti border into Iraq on 18 March 2003 and participated in the rapid advance into Baghdad, returning to their base at Twentynine Palms, California, on 5 October 2003. Most unit members were on their second deployment to Iraq in early 2005.

On the evening of 6 January 2005, Marines of the Scout-Sniper Platoon, Weapons Company 1/7 were in Husaybah, a city of fifty thousand on the south side of the Euphrates River, along the border with Syria. The city had already been the site of numerous battles, and a Marine of the third battalion of the 7th, Cpl. Jason Dunham, would be awarded a posthumous Medal of Honor for his actions there April 2004. That rainy evening, a four-Humvee mounted patrol was en route to an intersection known as the "intersection of death," due to frequent sniper fire and improvised explosive devices (IEDs). Their mission was to provide cover as a Marine reconnaissance unit moved through the area. They never reached their assigned position.[3]

It had rained that day, and the streets were slippery as the patrol suddenly came under intense machine-gun and rocket-propelled grenade (RPG) fire. In maneuvering to avoid fire the driver of the lead vehicle lost control, and the vehicle slid into a building. Cpl. Jarred L. Adams, a twenty-two year-old assistant team leader, exited the vehicle and began laying down covering fire with his M-40 sniper rifle. Another Marine from a trailing Humvee, Cpl. Joseph R. Avila, also dismounted to provide security and suppressive fire as other Marines worked under fire to dislodge the trapped vehicle. After freeing the vehicle, the patrol rapidly withdrew. It was only upon their return to Camp Gannon they realized one of their vehicles was missing.[4]

"During the crash, another vehicle had lost its communication ability. No one knew whether they were hit during the incident or returned to base," Avila recalled. "We assumed the worst so we went back in an effort to rescue them." As they re-entered the kill zone, Adams' Humvee, again in the lead, took a direct hit from an RPG. The explosion killed the turret gunner, LCpl. Julio Cisneros, wounded the driver and other Marines, and set the Humvee on fire.[5]

Adams was able to exit the vehicle. He had shrapnel wounds on his left forearm and hands. His right arm was broken and he'd sprained his ankle exiting the vehicle. He had numerous burns from the vehicle being set ablaze. Despite all his injuries, though, he immediately took cover and began returning fire.

The other two Humvees maneuvered past the burning vehicle in the intersection to a secure position down the street and immediately dismounted to engage the enemy. Avila had dismounted next to the blazing vehicle to assist the wounded Marines, running into the open under fire to return a disoriented Marine to cover.

While Sgt. Lance May remained with the two intact vehicles and directed the counterfire on insurgents who were firing from the second floor and rooftops of surrounding buildings, Avila assisted the wounded Marines to the operational vehicles. For their actions, both Avila and May received the Bronze Star medal with "V" for Valor.[6]

As the Marines consolidated, Adams realized that Cisneros' body was still in the burning Humvee. Running on a sprained ankle under fire, Adams returned to re-enter the burning wreckage to retrieve his fallen comrade, ignoring the danger of exploding munitions, flames, and enemy fire to extract and carry Cisneros through the intersection to the waiting vehicles. Mounting the remaining two vehicles, the Marines withdrew back to Camp Gannon. It was only upon his return to camp that Adams sought medical treatment for his wounds.[7]

Adams was sent to Germany to recover from his wounds. He was awarded the Silver Star on 10 June 2006 in a ceremony held at Camp Al-Qa'im, Iraq, while on his third deployment. Newly promoted to sergeant, Adams returned to Twentynine Palms, California, in September 2006 where he reenlisted for another tour, but hopes he won't redeploy to Iraq for awhile. "Three times in four years is enough."[8]

ENDNOTES

1. Silver Star citation, Cpl. Jarred L. Adams, USMC, http://www.homeofheroes.com/valor2/ SS/7_GWOT/citations_USMC.html.

2. "Unit History of the 1/7 Marines," 1st Battalion, 7th Marine Regiment website, http:// www.i-mef.usmc.mil/div/7mar/1bn/

3. Joseph Ditzler, "Marine Modest about His Heroism," *Anchorage* (AK) *Daily News*, 25 June 2006.

4. Michael C. Cifuentes, "Bronze Star Shines after Valiant Fight in Iraq," *Marine Corps News*, 16 December 2005 (Story ID #200616123623).

5. Jeff McDonald, "Bravery? Nope, 'Just Doing His Job,'" *The San Diego* (CA) *Union Tribune*, 12 November 2006.

6. Cifuentes, "Bronze Star Shines after Valiant Fight in Iraq."

7. Antonio Rosas, "Scout-Sniper Serving in Iraq Awarded U.S. Military's Third-Highest Award for Valor," *Marine Corps News*, 10 June 2006.

8. Ditzler, "Marine Modest about His Heroism."

Cpl. Jeffrey W. Schuller Jr., USMCR

Driver, Weapons Company, 3rd Battalion, 25th Marines, Regimental Combat Team 2, 2nd Marine Division, II Marine Expeditionary Force (Forward)

Battles at Al-Haditha, Iraq
Operation Matador: 7–14 May 2005;
Operation New Market: 25–29 May 2005

The Silver Star is presented to Jeffrey W. Schuller, Corporal, U.S. Marine Corps (Reserve), for conspicuous gallantry and intrepidity in action against the enemy while serving as Driver, Weapons Company, Third Battalion, Twenty-Fifth Marines, Regimental Combat Team 2, 2nd Marine Division, II Marine Expeditionary Force (Forward) in support of Operation Iraqi Freedom on 7 May 2005. While conducting a reinforcement mission, enemy forces ambushed Corporal Schuller's platoon using a suicide vehicle-borne improvised explosive device, rocket-propelled grenades (RPG), and automatic weapons. Instantly, eleven of sixteen Marines were killed or wounded and three of four vehicles severely damaged. Finding his vehicle gunner injured, Corporal Schuller manned the damaged turret and placed the M-240G machine gun into action. Under intense fire, he alternated his fires between enemy positions and suppressed the enemy for nearly 40 minutes, enabling his fellow Marines to evacuate casualties and retrieve sensitive gear. Holding his position, Corporal Schuller expended ordnance of every type aboard his vehicle. He then dismounted and carried his vehicle commander through enemy fire to the casualty collection vehicle and then returned to guide his wounded gunner to safety as well. At the casualty collection vehicle, Corporal Schuller redistributed ammunition and continued to attack enemy positions as he accounted for wounded Marines and sensitive gear. He then mounted the casualty vehicle and continued to engage the enemy from the passenger seat as it traveled through the city back to friendly lines. By his undaunted courage, personal initiative, and complete devotion to duty, Corporal Schuller reflected great credit upon himself and upheld the highest traditions of the Marine Corps and the United States Naval Service.[1]

Silver Star Citation

Cpl. Jeff Hunter, USMCR

Squad Leader, 2nd Platoon, Company L, 3rd Battalion, 25th Marines,
Regimental Combat Team 2, 2nd Marine Division,
II Marine Expeditionary Force (Forward)

The President of the United States takes pleasure in presenting the Silver
Star Medal to Jeff Hunter, Corporal, U.S. Marine Corps (Reserve), for con-
spicuous gallantry and intrepidity in action against the enemy while serv-
ing as Squad Leader, 2d Platoon, Company L, Third Battalion, Twenty-
Fifth Marines, Regimental Combat Team 2, SECOND Marine Division,
II Marine Expeditionary Force (Forward), in support of Operation IRAQI
FREEDOM in Al Anbar Province, Iraq, from 25 May to 28 July 2005.
During Operation NEW MARKET, Corporal Hunter's platoon was
ambushed with small arms fire, seriously wounding one Marine. In his
initial attempt to breach the house containing the insurgent ambush,
Corporal Hunter's squad leader was severely wounded. On his own initiative and without regard for his safety, he immediately re-entered the
house engaging four insurgents with his M16A4 rifle at a range of ten
feet and pulled his squad leader to safety. Then acting as squad leader, he
reorganized his Marines and led them into the insurgent position for the
third time, ultimately securing the house with close range small arms fire
and hand grenades which resulted in one enemy neutralized and three captured. Corporal Hunter's actions enabled his company to regain its momentum. On 28 July after an enemy small arms and rocket-propelled grenade
fire attack on an adjacent squad, Corporal Hunter, on his own initiative,
maneuvered his squad forward to assist. He shot two enemies and made two
unsuccessful assaults in the face of enemy AK-47 fire to retrieve a wounded
Marine. Corporal Hunter then ran across a fire-swept street to link up with
an M1A1 tank, guided its fire, and directed it to breach the building. This
action neutralized one insurgent and allowed the extraction of a mortally
wounded Marine. By his bold leadership, wise judgment, and complete
dedication to duty, Corporal Hunter reflected great credit upon himself and
upheld the highest traditions of the Marine Corps and the United States
Naval Service.[2]

Silver Star Citation

Sgt. David N. Wimberg, USMCR

Squad Leader, Lima Company, 3rd Battalion, 25th Marines,
Regimental Combat Team 2, 2nd Marine Division,
II Marine Expeditionary Force (Forward)

The Silver Star is presented to David N. Wimberg, Sergeant, U.S. Marine Corps (Reserve), for conspicuous gallantry and intrepidity in action against the enemy while serving as Squad Leader, Company L, Third Battalion, Twenty-Fifth Marines, Regimental Combat Team 2, 2nd Marine Division, II Marine Expeditionary Force (Forward) during Operation Iraqi Freedom in Al Anbar Province, Iraq, on 25 May 2005. During Operation New Market, while on patrol in the city of Al-Hadithah, an enemy ambush pinned down Sergeant Wimberg and his Company's Command Element in the street. In an attempt to eliminate the source of the ambush, Sergeant Wimberg left his covered position, maneuvered through intense small arms fire, and scaled a wall in order to gain access to the courtyard where the source of fire was originating. Although twice driven back by high volumes of enemy fire, on his third attempt, he opened the gate and allowed his squad to enter. He then provided suppressive fire into insurgent positions in an adjacent house until his fire team was in position. After two failed attempts to breach the front door, and without regard for his own personal safety, Sergeant Wimberg kicked in the door and gained entry to the house. Finding himself face to face with four insurgents armed with AK-47 rifles, Sergeant Wimberg engaged the enemy at close quarters, firing his M-16A4 rifle until he was shot and fell to the ground unconscious. His heroic actions severely wounded one insurgent, stunned the other enemy fighters and created the momentum needed to break the ambush. Many Marines' lives were saved as a result of Sergeant Wimberg's decisive and selfless actions. By his zealous initiative, courage, and total devotion to duty, Sergeant Wimberg reflected great credit upon himself and upheld the highest traditions of the Marine Corps and the United States Naval Service.[3]

Silver Star Citation

AL-HADITHAH DAM is the second largest hydroelectric plant in Iraq, and is located one hundred thirty miles northwest of Baghdad and ten miles north of the town of Al-Hadithah. Afraid that the destruction of the dam would result in flooding the surrounding area, and realizing how critical a steady source of electric power was in preserving Iraq's infrastructure, the dam was seized by U.S. Army Rangers early in the war, on 1 April 2003, and has remained under U.S. control since that time. On 7 May 2005 the dam was garrisoned by the Marines of Weapons Company, 3/25.[4] Marines of the Weapons Company, 3rd Battalion, 25th Marines, as part of Regimental Combat Team 2 (RCT-2) had been involved in Stability and Support Operations (SASO) and training the Iraqi Security Forces (ISF) since their arrival during the first week of March 2005. The weapons company comprised nine Mobile Assault Platoons (MAPs), consisting of three armored Humvees and one six-wheeled seven-ton armored truck. The lead Humvee usually carried the platoon leader, and was armed with an M-240 machine gun. The second Humvee carried an M-2 .50-caliber machine gun, followed by the seven-ton truck. The third Humvee carried another M-240 MG. The nine MAPs of 3/25 were designated "Kabar-1" through "Kabar-9."

Al-Hadithah is a city in the Al-Anbar Province of western Iraq, approximately two hundred forty kilometers northwest of Baghdad. Primarily a farming community situated on the Euphrates River, its population of ninety thousand was predominantly Sunni Muslim. Following the end of the initial assault on Iraq by U.S. and Coalition forces, it had become the site of numerous insurgent actions. Following the assumption of power by the Shi'ite- and Kurdish-dominated transition government, Operation Matador was launched on 7 May 2005 to counter the escalation in insurgent attacks throughout Iraq.[5]

On the morning of 7 May Marines of Weapons Company, 3/25 had returned to Al-Hadithah Dam following a twenty-four hour patrol on the east side of the Euphrates, and were looking forward to some "down" time. It was not to be. As the platoon leader, SSgt. Randall Watkins would later recall, "We had just come off a twenty-four hour patrol on the east side of the Euphrates, the day prior, and that was supposed to be our down day, but a Civil Affairs mission into Al-Hadithah that morning kept us on alert. Then Kabar-1 hit a land mine and we had to go recover their downed vehicle. We only had hours before going back out on another twenty-four hour security mission to the east. . . . Sgt. Cepeda and I heard the mortars hit the dam. He rushed to get the platoon on the trucks and I went to get orders from the Combat Operation Center. . . . By the time I got on the trucks I heard that Kabar-1 was taking fire, [and] that is the main reason we wanted to get out the gate so fast.[6]

Previously, mortar fire from the insurgents had originated from the east bank of the Euphrates, but Kabar-1 was being shelled from positions within the city of Al-Hadithah itself. The Marines were hesitant to fire into the city, in fear of killing innocent civilians.

A quick reaction force (QRF) was quickly assembled from "off-duty" Marines; MAP-7, consisting of sixteen Marines in three Humvees, and a seven-ton truck, accompanied by two M1A1 Abrams tanks, rolled to assist. Among the Marines were two men, Cpl. Jeffrey W. Schuller and LCpl. Todd Corbin, who would distinguish themselves in combat.

Schuller, from Monroeville, Ohio, was a former heavyweight wrestler at Cleveland (OH) State University, and was the third generation from his family to enlist in the Marines to protect America. Unabashedly patriotic, he was a former military policeman who took pride in being part of MAP-7, which was the platoon assigned to protect the battalion commander, Col. Lionel B. Urquhart.[7]

Corbin, also assigned to MAP-7, was a Huron County deputy sheriff from Sandusky, Ohio. A ten-year veteran of law enforcement, he joined the Marine Reserves in 2001. On 7 May he was serving as the driver of the seven-ton truck. Also along on the mission was SSgt. Dan Priestly, the battalion armorer, who had volunteered to accompany the column. At approximately 8:00 PM MAP-7 was ordered to proceed to a pump house in Al-Hadithah itself, six miles distant, and interdict insurgents firing on Marines. SSgt. Randy Watkins commanded the QRF as they rolled out the gate, the two tanks in the lead.

To get to the pump house, the column had to proceed through Al-Hadithah along a road bordered by houses and businesses to the left and the sprawling one-story Al-Hadithah Hospital to the right, then turn into an alley that led to the pump house. It was narrow with lots of alleys and no room to maneuver: the perfect location for an ambush. Because of a global positioning system (GPS) delay, the column passed the turn-off, and found the road ahead blocked by a car. The street was dark and deserted, and the decision was made to turn the column around and retrace their path. This put the tanks at the rear of the column, and Victor-1 (the call sign for Humvees in QRF), carrying LCpl. Lance Graham, LCpl. Stan Mayer, and LCpl. Emanuel Fellousis, at the front.[8]

The turn-around required Marines to dismount to guide and direct the large vehicles. Sgt. Michael Marzano, Sgt. Aaron Cepeda, and the corpsman, HM3 Jeffery Wiener, were dismounted, providing security, when a white Ford van, identified as a suicide vehicle–borne improvised explosive device (SVBIED) sped from an alley and crashed into a wall, exploding directly to the rear of Victor-1. As Corbin remembered, "All Hell broke loose!"[9]

The blast blew the turret of Graham's Humvee thirty feet, instantly killing Graham, as well as Marzano, Cepeda, and Wiener. Two Marines, Watkins and Priestly, were critically wounded, and five others were seriously wounded. Miraculously, Mayer and Fellousis survived the blast, but were injured. Only five Marines remained combat operational. Three of the four vehicles were disabled by the blast. Immediately, rocket-propelled grenade (RPG) and small-arms fire rained down from within Al-Hadithah Hospital. Patients and medical staff were forced to remain as shields while insurgents fired on the Marines from fortified positions.[10]

Corbin maneuvered his truck to provide cover for the wounded Marines, then radioed a situation report to battalion before exiting the vehicle. LCpl. Mark Kalinowski took a shrapnel wound to the wrist, and was replaced in the turret by Schuller, who laid down suppressing fire as Corbin raced into the open under intense fire to retrieve wounded or dead Marines and carry them to safety. Corbin cannot recall how many times he ran into the open to retrieve dead or wounded comrades and carry them back to the truck, but his citation credits him with at least seven, including Watkins and Weiner.

When Schuller exhausted his ammo, Kalinowski handed up Schuller's M-16 with a full magazine, and Schuller fired on targets while Kalinowski loaded a new box of 7.62 ammo. Schuller and Kalinowski provided covering fire, moving back and forth between targets for nearly forty minutes. After the MK-19 (belt-fed grenade launcher) on the seven-ton truck jammed, Schuller was the only gunner left firing. Once out of ammunition, Schuller helped Corbin recover a dead Marine, assisted Kalinowski to the truck, then provided covering fire with an M-16 as the remaining Marines climbed aboard the seven-ton truck.[11]

Exploding ammunition had kept the Marines from recovering Graham's body, but the remaining Marines of MAP-7, living and dead, were aboard the truck, which was the only operational vehicle. Corbin got the vehicle moving despite three flat tires and a shot up radiator. "The whole platoon rolled out in that seven-ton," Schuller said. "It's a testament to Corporal Corbin's knowledge of that vehicle that he kept it running. . . . Corbin was flipping switches the whole time he drove the five miles back to the battalion aid station."[12]

The tanks pushed the debris of the disabled Humvee out of the way to allow the seven-ton truck to depart, then remained on guard over Graham until the arrival of MAP-9 at about 9:00 PM. They recovered Graham's body, and flushed the hospital of insurgents, killing one and capturing another. They then oversaw the evacuation of patients while securing the area.[13]

On 14 May Operation Matador, a weeklong hunt for insurgents, was declared a success. RCT-2 was credited with securing objectives in and around the Euphrates River cities of Karabila, Rumana, and Ubaydi. The operation netted thirty-nine insurgents "of intelligence value" and killed one hundred twenty-five more, at a cost of nine Marines killed and another forty wounded.[14]

The 3/25 remained in Al-Hadithah and was part of Operation New Market (Souk Jadeed), which commenced on 25 May 2005 and was focused on disrupting terrorist activity in Al-Hadithah while maintaining the pressure on insurgents that had begun with Operation Matador. The operation resulted from an increase in insurgent mortar attacks and roadside car bombs in Al-Hadithah following the handover of sovereignty to the new Iraqi government. One thousand Coalition troops, including RCT-2, supported by the ISF, set up check-points and conducted cordon-and-search operations in an effort to locate enemy insurgents and weapons caches.[15]

On the first day of the operation, Marines of Lima Company, 3/25 were walking in column down a road early in the morning, hoping to arrive in the market district before sunrise to achieve the element of surprise. When a Marine shot a threatening stray dog, they began taking fire, the majority coming from a house thirty-five feet away on the left. Yelling, "Cover me," Sgt. David N. Wimberg ran across open terrain to the wall that surrounded the house, followed by a fire team under the command of Cpl. Jeff Hunter. Wimberg scrambled over the wall to the courtyard on the other side.

Wimberg, raised in Louisville, Kentucky, joined the Marines after graduating from Trinity High School in 1999. He served as an infantryman with Echo Company, 2nd Battalion, 7th Marine Regiment in California, Okinawa, and Korea, before enlisting in the reserves once his four-year tour was complete. He was set to leave the reserves when 3/25 was mobilized; Wimberg could not let them go to war without him. Now, he was seeing war up close.[16]

Hunter, from Albuquerque, New Mexico, had been working as an administrative clerk in the reserves, attached to Delta Company, 4th Reconnaissance Battalion, in Albuquerque when he received orders to deploy to Iraq with Lima Company 3/25.

It took Wimberg three tries to get the gate in the wall open, all the time dodging fire from within the house. Finally, he got the gate open and his squad entered and took positions to breach the door of the house. When another squad member was twice unsuccessful in kicking in the door, Wimberg tried and was successful, only to find himself face-to-face with four armed insurgents.

A close-range gun battle ensued, with one insurgent wounded. One shot entered Wimberg's armpit, bypassing his Kevlar vest, fatally wounding him. Hunter grabbed the wounded Wimberg, and dragged him outside to safety, and covered his body with his own as Wimberg wheezed out an order to "frag" the room (that is, to throw in fragmentation grenades). Ordering two of his team to get Wimberg to a corpsman, Hunter took over the squad and organized an assault, securing the house on the third attempt at close range with small arms and grenades, killing the remaining insurgents. "Wimberg's aggressive action broke the ambush and saved Marines' lives," recalled Sgt. Maj. Dan Altieri who was with Wimberg during the fight.[17]

The following day, Marine Maj. Ricardo A. Crocker, a civil affairs officer from Camp Pendleton, California, was killed by an RPG explosion. During one engagement, a laser-guided bomb was dropped during an air strike to level a building to kill insurgents firing on Marines. On 29 May the operation was declared a success and ended. A statement by the Multi-National Force–Iraq reported Operation New Market resulted in the death of "a significant number of terrorists" and that "Iraqi and Coalition forces also seized numerous weapons caches and munitions, including assault rifles, machine guns, rocket-propelled grenades and a buried cache consisting of over three hundred 82-mm high-explosive mortar projectiles."[18]

There are Marines who criticized the operations, saying that the job was left half-done and that insurgents regained control once the Marines withdrew. If the operations were a success, it was short lived. In mid-June 3/25, along with Marines from 3/2, were part of Operation Spear at Karabilah targeting foreign fighters infiltrating into Iraq from Syria.

On 25 July Hunter's platoon was involved with a sweep of small villages west of Baghdad, and the patrol proceeded without incident until Cpl. Andre Williams knocked on a door prior to a search in the town of Cykla. He was wounded when a heavy machine gun fired through the door, beginning what would be a four-hour firefight.

There were an estimated nine insurgents inside in a fortified position, and some of them withdrew to a second house nearby. Hunter moved his squad under fire to the rooftop of a nearby house overlooking the second house, and began to lay down fire. After approximately two hours with no fire coming from the house, they rushed it to find it empty, except for an RPG launcher. To the rear of the house were two small cinder-block buildings that had to be cleared.

Hunter's squad advanced through livestock toward one of the buildings, and his best friend, LCpl. Christopher Lyons, was cut down by AK-47 fire from within. The rest of the squad took cover behind the three-foot-high wall of an unfinished structure. The insurgents fired on the Marines from their fortified position less than fifteen feet away. "It got pretty scary there for a minute," he recalled.[19]

Hunter twice attempted to retrieve Lyons under fire, was driven back, but is credited with shooting two insurgents. He then left cover and dashed across a road under fire to reach an M1A1 Abrams tank. He directed their fire and guided them in breaching the building, allowing Lyons to be safely extracted; Lyons later died of his wounds.

On 1 August six sniper-scouts from HQ Company were ambushed and killed in Al-Hadithah. Two days later, on 3 August, an assault amphibious vehicle (track, or AAV) struck a roadside bomb, killing fourteen Marines from Lima Company. After a seven-month deployment, the 3/25 was rotated home in late September, with forty-six Marines and two Navy Corpsmen having given their "last full measure of devotion." The battalion was deactivated on 3 January 2006.[20]

On 4 July 2006 at battalion headquarters in Oak Park, Ohio, newly promoted Cpl. Todd Corbin and Sgt. Jeffrey W. Schuller were awarded the Navy Cross and Silver Star, respectively. Schuller believes the conflict in Iraq is winnable, and has no patience with those who feel our efforts are not worthwhile. "Leave it better than you found it," says Schuller. "I will punch anyone who says we didn't."[21]

On 20 August 2006, Tricia and Dennis Wimberg accepted their son's posthumous Silver Star during a ceremony at the reserve center in Columbus, Ohio. Commenting on his brother's courage, Michael Wimberg recalled, "He was never looking for a fight, but he never backed down from one either."[22]

On 18 June 2007 Sgt. Jeff Hunter, now in the inactive reserves, was presented the Silver Star at a ceremony at the Albuquerque City Hall. He had promised his friend Lyons that he would take care of his family if anything happened to him. Hunter kept his word. Letters by e-mail progressed to love and marriage, and Bethany Lyons married Hunter in May 2006 and adopted his daughter Ella. They have since had a son, Atticus. He is a student at the city college, and hopes to teach history in high school.[23]

Of his award, Hunter said, "I honestly don't believe I did anything that heroic. . . . I was just doing my job." Sgt. Shawn Bryan, who was with Lima Company with Hunter observed, "He got the Silver Star for what he did, but he did what he did because that's who he is."[24]

ENDNOTES

1. Silver Star citation, Cpl. Jeffrey W. Schuller Jr., USMCR, http://www.homeofheroes.com/valor2/SS/7_GWOT/citations_USMC-M.html.

2. Silver Star citation, Cpl. Jeff Hunter, USMCR, http://www.homeofheroes.com/valor2/SS/7_GWOT/citations_USMC.html.

3. Silver Star citation, Sgt. David N. Wimberg, USMCR, http://www.homeofheroes.com/valor2/SS/7_GWOT/citations_USMC-M.html.

4. Doug Struck, "The Coolest Posting in a Hot War Zone: For Marines Guarding Strategic Dam, Lakeside Quarters Take Edge off Peril," *Washington* (DC) *Post*, 8 August 2004, A-17.

5. Kevin Flower, Kianne Sadeq, and Enes Dulami, "Hunt for Insurgents near Syria Ends: More than 125 Insurgents, Nine Marines Dead," CNN.Com, 14 May 2005, http://www.cnn.com/2005/WORLD/meast/05/14/iraq.main/index.html.

6. Memorial to LCpl. Lance T. Graham, http://www.corpsstories.com.

7. Jacqueline Marino, "Blood Brothers," *Cleveland* (OH) *Magazine*, June 2006.

8. Beth Zimmerman, "Navy Cross, Silver Star Awarded for Actions in Deadly Firefight," *Marine Corps Times*, September 2006.

9. Ibid.

10. "Three Marines, One Sailor killed in Al-Hadithah," www.centcom.mil, 9 May 2005. www.globalsecurity.org/military/library/news/2005/05/05-05-07c.htm.

11. Ibid.

12. Ibid.

13. Marino, "Blood Brothers."

14. Flower et al., "Hunt for Insurgents near Syria Ends."

15. "Operation New Market Kicks Off in Iraq," USMC Press Release #0525-05-0759, 25 May 2005.

16. Jeb Phillips, "Two Lima Company Marines to Receive Awards for Valor," *Columbus* (OH) *Dispatch*, 20 August 2006.

17. Beth Zimmerman, "Citizen Marine Awarded Silver Star," Military.com, 18 June 2007, http://www.military.com/NewsContent/0,13319,142829,00.html?ESRC=eb.nl.

18. "Operation New Market Ends in Al-Hadithah Multi-National Force, Iraq," News Release # A050530c, 29 May 2005.

19. Zimmerman, "Citizen Marine Awarded Silver Star."

20. "3/25th Marines Unit History," http://www.mfr.usmc.mil/4thmardiv/25thMar/3dBn/.

21. Marino, "Blood Brothers."

22. Betsy Vereckey, "Marine Killed in Iraq Buried in Louisville," *Military Times*, 31 May 2005, http://www.militarycity.com/valor/879849.html.

23. Michael Gisick, "Memories of Combat Are Never Far from Former Albuquerque Marine's Thoughts," *Albuquerque* (NM) *Tribune*, 19 June 2007.

24. Zimmerman, "Citizen Marine Awarded Silver Star."

Sgt. Dennis Woullard Jr., USMCR

Radio Chief, 1st Section, 3rd Platoon, Alpha Company,
4th Assault Amphibious Battalion, Regimental Combat Team 2,
2nd Marine Division, II Marine Expeditionary Force (Forward)

Battle of Al-Qa'im, Iraq
Operation Matador: 7–14 May 2005;
Al-Ubaydi: 7 May 2005; Karabilah: 11 May 2005

The Silver Star is presented to Dennis Woullard, Sergeant, U.S. Marine Corps (Reserve), for conspicuous gallantry and intrepidity in action against the enemy while serving as Radio Chief, First Section, Third Platoon, Company A, Fourth Assault Amphibious Battalion, Regimental Combat Team 2, SECOND Marine Division, II Marine Expeditionary Force (Forward) from 8 to 11 May 2005. On 8 May 2005 in Al Ubaydi, Iraq, Sergeant Woullard volunteered to assist an infantry squad conduct clearing operations during Operation Matador. After clearing several residences without incident, and during a breach of a front door, his team was immediately attacked with heavy machine gun and rocket-propelled grenade (RPG) fire from within. Every member of the team was wounded. Despite his wounds, Sergeant Woullard evacuated two Marines from the residence, and then joined in an assault to recover the remaining trapped Marine. Sergeant Woullard repeatedly exposed himself to heavy fire and assaulted into the house. He rescued the trapped Marine shielding him with his body as he carried him to an Assault Amphibious Vehicle (AAV) where he administered first aid until en route to the battalion. On 11 May 2005 near the Syrian border, Sergeant Woullard's AAV was attacked with an improvised explosive device (IED) that killed or injured all seventeen Marines on board. Although again wounded and disoriented from the explosion, Sergeant Woullard struggled to the rear of the vehicle and opened the personnel hatch. With complete disregard for his own safety and exposed to the intense heat and exploding ammunition, he repeatedly returned to the burning vehicle to evacuate the severely wounded Marines. By his superior leadership, unrelenting determination, and total dedication to duty, Sergeant Woullard reflected great credit upon himself and upheld the highest traditions of thve Marine Corps and the United States Naval Service.[1]

Silver Star Citation

LCpl. Mark A. Camp, USMCR

Automatic Rifleman, 1st Platoon, Lima Company, 3rd Battalion,
25th Marines, Regimental Combat Team 2, 2nd Marine Division,
II Marine Expeditionary Force (Forward)

The Silver Star is presented to Mark A. Camp, Lance Corporal, U.S. Marine Corps (Reserve), for conspicuous gallantry and intrepidity in action against the enemy while serving as Automatic Rifleman, First Platoon, Company L, Third Battalion, Twenty Fifth Marines, Regimental Combat Team 2, SECOND Marine Division, II Marine Expeditionary Force (Forward), in support of Operation Iraqi Freedom from 8 to 11 May 2005. During an assault in New Ubaydi, Iraq, an enemy ambush seriously wounded four members of Lance Corporal Camp's squad and trapped two of them in a courtyard. Leaving his covered position, he engaged the enemy at point-blank range with his M-249 machine gun, thereby allowing one injured Marine to be pulled to cover. Lance Corporal Camp then joined a Marine in a frontal assault of the ambush site, forcing two insurgents from the rear of the house and into friendly fire, and permitting the recovery of the injured Marine. As the assault to clear the house continued, armor-piercing rounds were fired from a hidden bunker beneath the floorboards, mortally wounding another Marine. Lance Corporal Camp refused to leave the building without the fallen Marine, and twice braved intense machine gun fire while attempting to recover the fallen Marine's remains. On 11 May an improvised explosive device (IED) destroyed Lance Corporal Camp's amphibious assault vehicle, killing or wounding all seventeen Marines trapped inside the vehicle, only to be thrown out of the vehicle from a secondary explosion. Receiving additional shrapnel wounds, yet undeterred, Lance Corporal Camp returned to the burning vehicle and pulled a Marine to safety. By his bold leadership, wise judgment, and complete dedication to duty, Lance Corporal Camp reflected great credit upon himself and upheld the highest traditions of the Marine Corps and the United States Naval Service.[2]

Silver Star Citation

EARLY IN 2005 MARINE RESERVISTS assigned to the 4th Assault Amphibious Battalion were advised to prepare for deployment overseas to Iraq. The 4th Tracks, a mechanized battalion of the Marine Reserves headquartered at Tampa Bay, Florida, had subordinate units in Virginia, Texas, and Mississippi. Among the activated reservists of Alpha Company was Sgt. Dennis Woullard.

Woullard, a Mississippi native who attended Jackson State University on a football scholarship, and who had been a Biloxi, Mississippi, police officer, enlisted in the Marines on 26 January 1998 and was already a veteran of Iraq, having served at Nasiriyah in the early days of the U.S. invasion.[3] By March 2005, Woullard and the 4th AA Battalion were in Iraq as part of Regimental Combat Team 2 (RCT-2), 2nd Marine Division.

Meanwhile, activated reservists of the 3rd Battalion, 25th Marine Regiment (3/25), a reserve infantry battalion headquartered at Brookpark, Ohio, also arrived in Iraq in early March. Following activation on 4 January 2005, the battalion received predeployment training at the Marine Corps Air Ground Combat Center, Twentynine Palms, California, then deployed to Iraq as part of RCT-2.

Activated on 1 May 1943 at the beginning of World War II, the 25th Marine Regiment saw combat at the battles of Saipan, Tinian, Kwajalein Atoll, and Iwo Jima. Col. Justice Marino Chambers received the Congressional Medal of Honor for his actions as the commander of 3/25 during the battle of Iwo Jima. Deactivated in 1945, the regiment was reactivated as a reserve unit on 1 July 1962 and was called to active service during Operation Desert Storm.

Assigned as an automatic rifleman with 1st Platoon Lima Company 3/25 was LCpl. Mark A. Camp, an Ohio State University student who joined the Marine Reserves in July 2003 seeking direction in his life. Now he and his unit were in the Al-Anbar Province training Iraqi Security Forces (ISF) and conducting Stability and Support Operations (SASO).[4]

Using available intelligence, military commanders determined early in 2005 that in the western portion of the Al-Anbar Province near the border with Syria ancient smuggling routes in the Al-Jazirah desert north of the Euphrates River were being used as staging areas for foreign fighters crossing into Iraq from Syria, and as a pipeline for support to the insurgents.[5]

The decision was made to launch an offensive in early May to eliminate insurgents and foreign fighters in the region. Codenamed Operation Matador (7–14 May 2005), it deployed more than one thousand Marines and Sailors of RCT-2, primarily 3/2 and 3/25, supported by Cobra helicopters and Hornet warplanes, into territory considered an enemy safe haven. There was a secondary goal of capturing or killing Al-Qaeda terrorist leader Abu Musab al-Zarqawi.[6]

On 7 May Sergeant Woullard was with Lima Company 3/25 waiting for engineers of the Army's 814th Multi-Role Bridge Company to finish constructing a pontoon bridge across the Euphrates when they began taking small-arms fire from Ubaydi, a town a mile away. As insurgents began firing at gunships overhead with small-arms fire, mortar rounds began to fall on the Marines, landing near the operation commander's Humvee. The order was given to advance into Ubaydi.

Lima Company 3/25 and a company of 3/2 entered Ubaydi and were immediately engaged by AK-47 fire and rocket-propelled grenades (RPGs) as they advanced through the town, house by house. Most civilians had already fled the village, seeking sanctuary in mosques, schools, and roadside tents leaving only insurgents in Ubaydi, in well-prepared rooftop and basement bunkers. As the Marines searched, they found numerous caches of weapons, ammunition, mortars, remote control triggering devices, and materials to construct improvised explosive devices (IEDs).[7]

Sergeant Woullard accompanied a squad from Lima Company's 1st Platoon, including LCpl. Mark Camp, as they moved to clear the final block in their sector. At the last house, they found a gateway open leading to a house encircled by high walls. The front door was locked, and the Marines took a combat stack position as the Marine in the lead kicked in the door. Machine-gun fire erupted, wounding the first two Marines—one of them fatally. This was followed by an explosion from an RPG fired from within, wounding several others, including Woullard.

"My fire team came under heavy machine-gun fire while we were attempting to clear a house," Woullard recalled. "The house was heavily bunkered and the occupants had no intention of coming out alive, and we were glad to grant them their wish. However, I was shot twice, a grazing wound to my left temple, and one other round that skipped off my back protective armor."[8]

Dazed and nearly unconscious, Woullard crawled to a position of cover and returned fire, then re-entered the residence to evacuate two wounded team members while Camp, GySgt. Chuck Hurley, and other Marines provided covering fire, then joined in a frontal assault to drive two insurgents out the rear of the house, where they were killed. This allowed Woullard to retrieve the remaining wounded and trapped Marine. Shielding the fallen Marine with his own body, he carried him out to an assault amphibious vehicle (AAV, amtrac, or track) where he administered first-aid.

Believing the death of the two killed insurgents ended the threat, Marines re-entered the compound to search. While checking a storage closet under a stairwell, intense machine-gun fire fatally wounded another Marine and the other Marines retreated, but were unable to retrieve their fallen comrade. Suspecting a fortified bunker, they called for tank support as armored vehicles carried the wounded to waiting helicopters. The tank fired seven rounds, igniting a propane tank and causing a fire to partially engulf the house, yet resistance continued as insurgents' armor-piercing rounds penetrated interior and exterior walls, sometimes impacting as far away as houses across the street.

An airstrike at midnight by an F/A-18 Hornet dropped two bombs, one of which missed the target and one of which failed to detonate. The Marines waited out the night under fire. On the morning of 9 May a rocket launcher was set up across the street, and the rockets fired at close range collapsed the walls over the insurgents' position, a crawl space under the floor. Using a Soviet-designed PKM ("Kalashnikov's machine gun, modernized") machine gun with armor-piercing ammunition, the insurgents had fired upward through the concrete floor. Fearing booby traps, the crawl space was not examined and no body count taken, but grenades were dropped into the crawl space as a precaution. After twelve hours, five infantry assaults, a tank attack, an airstrike, and a rocket attack, the fallen Marines were recovered.[9]

Exhausted, Woullard and the Lima Company Marines slept in moving AAVs as they crossed over to the northern side of the Euphrates. They talked quietly, remembering the two Marines killed the previous day. The Marines arrived in several villages only to find that the insurgents, forewarned, seemed to have evaporated into the desert. Unrewarding searches in the deserted villages were broken up by sporadic gunfire and the occasional mortar round.

On 11 May Woullard was among sixteen members of 1st Platoon aboard an AAV in a column of armored vehicles en route for more house searches in the village of Karabilah. In the top hatch, providing security, Camp watched children at play as they rolled along. He recalled later that it suddenly got quiet, a bad sign in Iraq. The blast from the following explosion lifted the forty-nine thousand–pound armored vehicle four feet in the air, knocking Camp back into the vehicle and filling the interior with shrapnel. All seventeen Marines inside were wounded, some fatally. Camp's hands and face were on fire, and only the fact that he'd been wearing goggles saved his eyes. He fought to extinguish his hands and face, and finally succeeded, although he was severely burned.[10]

Woullard, who had been inside the vehicle recalled, "I remember fire and smoke immediately filling the vehicle. I felt around for the door handle and lifted up on it. The rear door swung open and I immediately dove out. I remember fighting through heavy smoke, heat and rounds that were cooking off; still myself and other Marines returned several times to help retrieve Marines from the back of the vehicle."[11]

Camp heard yelling inside the vehicle and recognized it as his friend and fire team member, Pfc. Christopher Dixon. Despite his burns and shrapnel wounds to his right thigh, he crawled back into the burning vehicle to rescue Dixon. "He was my friend," Camp later said. Unable to grab Dixon, he fought for a way to pull him out, and yelled for help. A second explosion knocked him clear of the vehicle, again setting him on fire. He extinguished himself and crawled back into the vehicle, tugging on the now-still Dixon and again yelling for help. Finally, other hands pulled both men free, but it was too late for Dixon.[12]

Camp, Woullard, Hurley, and others repeatedly braved flame, smoke, intense heat, and exploding ammunition to rescue seriously wounded Marines from the rear of the burning track. In the end four Marines were lost: Pfc. Christopher Dixon, 18, of Columbus, Ohio; LCpl. Nick Erdy, 21, of Williamsburg, Ohio; LCpl. Jonathan Grant, 23, of Santa Fe, New Mexico; and LCpl. Jourdan Grez, 24, of Harrisonburg, Virginia. The remainder of the Marines in the track were wounded, many of them seriously. For one squad in Lima Company's 1st Platoon, the casualty rate (killed or wounded) reached 100 percent.

On 20 August 2006, at his unit's reserve center in Columbus, Ohio, the newly promoted Corporal Camp was awarded the Silver Star. He'd spent a month at Brooke Army Medical Center in Texas getting skin grafts for his hands and recovering. He then returned to active duty awaiting a final operation. As to that day in May, he said, "I was just trying to do what I had to do to keep myself and the guy next to me alive."[13]

Woullard was promoted to Staff Sergeant and was presented the Silver Star at a ceremony at Camp Pendleton, California, on 15 November 2006. In April 2006 he was appointed a deputy sheriff with the Los Angeles County, California, Sheriff's Department.

ENDNOTES

1. Silver Star citation, Sgt. Dennis Woullard Jr., USMCR, http://www.homeofheroes.com/valor2/SS/7_GWOT/citations_USMC-M.html.
2. Silver Star citation, LCpl. Mark A. Camp, USMCR, http://www.homeofheroes.com/valor2/SS/7_GWOT/citations_USMC.html.
3. Kerri Webb, "Silver Star Deputy Honored for Heroism in Iraq," *The Compton* (CA) *City Bulletin*, 20 December 2006.
4. Jeb Phillips, "Two Lima Company Marines to Receive Awards for Valor," *Columbus* (OH) *Dispatch*, 20 August 2006.
5. Donna Miles, "Operation Matador Helping Flush Insurgents from Western Iraq," DefenseLINK News, U.S. Department of Defense, 10 May 2005.
6. Ellen Knickmeyer, "They Came Here to Die: Insurgents Hiding under House in Western Iraq Prove Fierce in Hours-Long Fight with Marines," *Washington* (DC) *Post*, 11 May 2005.

7. Ibid.

8. Webb, "Silver Star Deputy Honored for Heroism in Iraq."

9. Ellen Knickmeyer, "Demise of a Hard Fighting Squad: Marines Who Survived Ambush Are Killed, Wounded in Blast," *Washington* (DC) *Post*, 12 May 2005.

10. Phillips, "Two Lima Company Marines to Receive Awards for Valor."

11. Webb, "Silver Star Deputy Honored for Heroism in Iraq."

12. Phillips, "Two Lima Company Marines to Receive Awards for Valor."

13. Mary A. Staes, "Lima 3/25 Awards 2 Silver Stars," *Marine Corps News*, 20 August 2006 (Story ID #200682414838).

1st Lt. David T. Russell, USMC

1st Platoon Commander, Weapons Company, 1st Battalion,
5th Marines, 2nd Brigade Combat Team, 2nd Marine Division,
II Marine Expeditionary Force (Forward)

Ar Ramadi, Iraq
3 May 2005

The President of the United States takes pleasure in presenting the Silver Star Medal to David T. Russell, First Lieutenant, U.S. Marine Corps, for conspicuous gallantry and intrepidity in action against the enemy while serving as First Platoon Commander, Weapons Company, First Battalion, Fifth Marines, Second Brigade Combat Team, SECOND Marine Division, II Marine Expeditionary Force (Forward) in support of Operation Iraqi Freedom on 3 May 2005. While [First] Lieutenant Russell led his platoon in the operation of an entry control point in the city of Ar Ramadi, thirteen insurgents assaulted his position with small arms, machine guns, and grenades. Realizing the gravity of the attack, he ran to assess the situation from the second deck. First Lieutenant Russell quickly identified an insurgent with a machine gun hiding behind a barrier and killed him with one shot. When he discovered that a Marine isolated in a bunker needed ammunition, he raced to supply him by crossing seventy-five meters of open area while under fire from at least six insurgents. First Lieutenant Russell purposefully subjected himself to enemy fire to allow one Marine to maneuver and other Marines to destroy the insurgents. He was then knocked to the ground when an enemy round struck his helmet. Suffering from a concussion and bleeding profusely from wounds to his face and arms, First Lieutenant Russell rushed back to direct the fight and establish accountability. Finding two men missing, he rushed across the open area to retrieve a wounded Iraqi soldier. Despite explosions from more than twelve enemy grenades and a stream of machine gun and small arms fire, he moved across the kill zone to personally direct the battle and kill the enemy. Only after being ordered to accept treatment did he submit. First Lieutenant Russell's bold leadership, wise judgment, and complete dedication to duty reflected great credit upon him and were in keeping with the highest traditions of the Marine Corps and the United States Naval Service.[1]

Silver Star Citation

ON THE MORNING OF 3 MAY 2005 the twenty-five Marines of the 1st Platoon, Weapons Company, 1/5 Marines were busy monitoring traffic at the North Bridge Traffic Control Point, a mandatory detour into an area where cars could be scanned for bombs, nine at a time. An entry control point into the city of Ar Ramadi, it was located at the edge of the city.[2]

In the command and control building, a half-finished two-story palace overlooking the checkpoint, the platoon commander, 1st Lt. David T. Russell, was shaving when he heard a series of explosions, followed by machine-gun fire. Grabbing his gear, he rushed to the second floor to evaluate the situation. Observing an insurgent armed with a machine gun hiding behind cover, Russell eliminated him with one shot from his M-4 carbine.

On the ground floor, as chain link fencing placed over the windows deflected grenades, the platoon sergeant, SSgt. Timothy Cyparski, received a radio call from LCpl. Juan Reyes advising Cyparski that Reyes was running low on ammunition. Reyes was on duty in a hut adjacent to the vehicle inspection area, nicknamed the "suicide bunker," and separated from the checkpoint by seventy-five yards of open ground.[3]

Paraphrasing Gen. George S. Patton's axiom that "The worst plan executed quickly and violently is better than the best plan not executed at all," Russell and Cyparski loaded up all the machine-gun ammunition they could carry and dashed across seventy-five yards of open terrain under intense fire to reach Reyes' position. Their new position allowed them to better build situational awareness and evaluate their situation, because they had had no information on the size of the opposing force. What they observed was that, while the insurgents were heavily armed, they were undisciplined and lacked any leader coordinating the attack, so Russell devised a plan to draw them out.[4]

As Cyparski covered him, Russell advanced into the vehicle search area and, as his citation describes it, "purposefully subjected himself to enemy fire."[5] This drew the fire of the insurgents, revealing their positions to the Marines above. Wounded by shrapnel in the arms and face, Russell rejoined Cyparski at the bunker. But his strategy was working as, one by one, the insurgents were eliminated by Marine marksmanship. "You give a Marine a nice clear target and it's not going to take them long to get rid of them," he stated.[6]

As Russell moved from cover to engage an insurgent with his rifle, he was struck in the head by an AK-47 round that penetrated his helmet and grazed his skull, causing heavy bleeding and a concussion. "It knocked me on my ass," he admitted.[7]

Regaining his senses, Russell continued to direct the fight for several hours until ordered to get medical treatment by the battalion commander. Cyparski took over the platoon for the next three days. At some point in the battle, Russell is credited with dashing across open ground to rescue a wounded Iraqi soldier. At the end of the battle, thirteen insurgents lay dead, with another eight in custody, without the loss of one Marine life.[8]

On 31 March 2006, in a ceremony at 5th Marines headquarters at Camp Pendleton, California, Maj. Gen. Richard Natonski, 1st Marine Division commander, presented Russell with a Silver Star and Cyparski with a Bronze Star with "V" for Valor, his second Bronze Star; he had been awarded an earlier Bronze Star for his actions in Al-Fallujah in the spring of 2004.

Russell, a 2002 Naval Academy graduate who declined medical school to take a position with a line infantry company, said of the award, "Medals are all about being in the wrong place at the wrong time with the right people. . . . They pinned it on me, but the rest of the unit deserves it as much as I do."[9]

ENDNOTES

1. Silver Star citation, 1st Lt. David T. Russell, USMC, http://www.homeofheroes.com/valor2/ SS/7_GWOT/citations_USMC-M.html.
2. Kevin Conley, "A Few Good Medals," GQ Online, http://men.style.com/gq/features/full/ ?id=content_5139.
3. Beth Zimmerman, "Ammo Dash Earns Lieutenant a Silver Star," *Marine Corps Times*, 8 May 2006.
4. Conley, "A Few Good Medals."
5. Silver Star citation, 1st Lt. David T. Russell.
6. Zimmerman, "Ammo Dash Earns Lieutenant a Silver Star."
7. Ibid.
8. Tony Perry, "Two Marines Decorated for Risking Their Lives to Save an Iraqi Soldier," *Los Angeles* (CA) *Times*, 1 April 2006.
9. Mark Walker, "Silver and Bronze Stars Awarded to Weapons Company Marines," *The North County* (San Diego, CA) *Times*, 1 April 2006.

2nd Lt. Brian M. Stann, USMC

2nd Mobile Assault Platoon Leader, Weapons Company 3rd Battalion,
2nd Marines, Regimental Combat Team 2, 2nd Marine Division,
II Marine Expeditionary Force (Forward)

Karabilah, Iraq
14 May 2005

The Silver Star is presented to Brian M. Stann, Second Lieutenant, U.S. Marine Corps, for conspicuous gallantry and intrepidity in action against the enemy as Second Mobile Assault Platoon Leader, Weapons Company, Third Battalion, Second Marines, Regimental Combat Team 2, SECOND Marine Division, II Marine Expeditionary Force (Forward) in support of Operation Iraqi Freedom from 8 May to 14 May 2005. During Operation Matador, Second Lieutenant Stann led his reinforced platoon on an assault through a foreign fighter and Mujahedeen insurgent defense-in-depth to seize the Ramana Bridge north of Karabilah, Iraq. On three separate occasions, he traversed four kilometers of enemy occupied urban terrain in order to maintain his battle position. With each deliberate attack he controlled close air support and the direct fire systems of tanks and heavy machine guns destroying enemy positions along the route. At one point, the enemy massed on his platoon and fired over 30 rocket-propelled grenades (RPGs), machine guns, detonated two improvised explosive devices (IEDs) and attacked the unit with three suicide vehicle borne improvised explosive devices. Second Lieutenant Stann personally directed two casualty evacuations, three vehicle recovery operations and multiple close air support missions under enemy small arms, machine gun and mortar fire in his 360-degree fight. Inspired by his leadership and endurance, Second Lieutenant Stann's platoon held the battle position on the Euphrates River for six days protecting the Task Force flank and isolating foreign fighters and insurgents north of the river. Second Lieutenant Stann's zealous initiative, courageous actions, and exceptional presence of mind reflected great credit upon himself and upheld the highest traditions of the Marine Corps and the United States Naval Service.[1]

Silver Star Citation

ON 9 MARCH 2005 in a change-of-command ceremony at Camp Al-Qa'im, Iraq, Lt. Col. Christopher Woodridge, commanding officer of 1st Battalion, 7th Marine Regiment turned authority over the Al-Qa'im region to Lt. Col. Tim Mundy, commanding the 3rd Battalion, 2nd Marine Regiment. They were tasked with continuing the Stability and Security Operations (SASO) in and around Al-Qa'im, which included assisting the Iraqi Security Forces (ISF) in conducting vehicle searches, individual checkpoints, and cordon-and-knock operations, in which selected areas were isolated and searched. Additionally, the Marines were to interdict foreign fighters infiltrating into Iraq from nearby Syria.[2] The battalion would deploy for seven months, the normal period for an infantry battalion before being rotated stateside. It would not be an easy tour.

The battalion was formed just prior to U.S. entry into World War II on 18 January 1941, in San Diego. Marines of the 3/2 fought at Guadalcanal, Tarawa, Saipan, Tinian, and Okinawa. As part of the 4th Marine Expeditionary Brigade (4 MEB), the battalion deployed in support of Operation Desert Shield and Operation Desert Storm, and participated in operations in Somalia (1994) and Bosnia-Herzegovina (1998). It was deployed to Iraq in February 2003 as part of Operation Iraqi Freedom. Now, 3/2 was back in Iraq for a second time.[3]

A major test came on 11 April at Camp Gannon in Husaybah. Insurgents, utilizing two suicide vehicle–borne improvised explosive devices (SVBIEDs) tried to break through the camp's perimeter. Despite constant heavy small-arms fire, India Company organized a counterattack, destroying the dump truck and fire engine that the insurgents used as rolling bombs. A third SVBIED detonated outside the camp. Insurgent losses were twenty-one dead and fifteen wounded. No Marines were seriously hurt.[4]

On 7 May 2005 Operation Matador was initiated, a large-scale operation aimed at closing smuggling routes and safe houses for foreign fighters entering Iraq along its western border. Intelligence reports indicated that the Ramana area was being used to train and equip insurgents, and anti-Iraqi and anti-Coalition forces had been intimidating the local populace, forestalling stability in the area.[5]

Operation Matador's goal was to clear the area north of the Euphrates River of insurgents. "Nobody had really been north of the river in probably a year," recalled Mundy. "It was just a tough area to get into."[6]

The cities of Karabilah, Ramana, and Ubaydi were believed to be staging areas for insurgent attacks into Bahgdad, Mosul, Fallujah, and Ramadi. That morning, Marines of 3/2 entered Karabilah initiating a fight that would last six days. The result would be a Marine victory and the award of a Silver Star to a young Marine second lieutenant.[7]

2nd Lt. Brian M. Stann, a twenty-five-year-old native of Scranton, Pennsylvania, commanded the 2nd Mobile Assault Platoon (MAP-2) of Weapons Company, 3/2. A former linebacker for the Naval Academy football team, Stann volunteered for Iraq upon graduating from the Academy in 2003. Now, at 5:00 AM on 7 May 2005, he got the word.

A platoon assigned to secure the Ramana Bridge across the Euphrates River, just north of Karabilah, had not yet reached the bridge. It was critical that the bridge be secured to prevent the escape of enemy fighters as American forces swept north of the Euphrates. Stann's platoon was ordered to take the bridge as fast as possible; Stann led his forty-two Marines forward with less than thirty minutes planning.[8]

The two and a half mile–route to the bridge was bordered on both sides by buildings on the edge of the road, which served as potential cover for insurgents. Additionally, there was a ravine where insurgents were expected to be dug in. Earlier units had taken casualties trying to move through the area. MAP-2 went in expecting a fight, and they were not to be disappointed.

Through a hail of mortar rounds, rocket-propelled grenades (RPGs), grenades, machine-gun fire, and detonating improvised explosive devices (IEDs), the platoon fought its way to the bridge and held it in a 360-degree firefight. After being relieved by the platoon originally assigned to take the bridge, they had to fight their way back through the gauntlet. They made it without a fatality, but en route a tank hit a roadside bomb and three wounded Marines had to be evacuated.[9]

The following night, they made their way to the bridge at night without incident to resupply the platoon, but again had to fight their way out. On the third day, MAP-2 was ordered to relieve the platoon guarding the bridge. It would be their fourth time running the gauntlet, and the worst. This time, the insurgents were prepared with a large, well-organized ambush. In addition to mortar fire, RPGs, and AK-47 fire, the Marines had to fight off three SVBIEDs. They killed the drivers of two before they could get close, but a third rammed one of the vehicles, seriously wounding five Marines. They fought on, with Stann leading his Marines while simultaneously calling in air strikes and directing tank fire on enemy positions. Once they arrived at the bridge, they dug in for a stay that would last three more days as they fought off attacks and called in air strikes. By the sixth day, the operation was over; MAP-2 still held the bridge, and resistance had dwindled to the occasional sniper.[10]

The 3/2 later took part in Operation Spear in Karabilah in late June, then Operation Quick Strike at Haqlayniah in early August. Following the completion of its tour, 3/2 returned to the United States in September 2005. The battalion commander, Lieutenant Colonel Mundy is uncertain regarding the number of insurgents killed. "I deliberately avoid thinking about that, because in my opinion, no amount of dead terrorists will equal the loss of one of our guys."[11] Three Marines of 3/2 made the ultimate sacrifice on that day.

On 14 March 2006 2nd Marine Division commander Maj. Gen. Richard Huck presented newly promoted First Lieutenant Stann with the Silver Star in a ceremony at Camp Lejeune, North Carolina. Stann believes the credit and medal belong to his men, and he removed the medal once he'd left the field where the ceremony was held. "You can forget all the other medals," Stann said. "I just wanted the award that said forty-two out of forty-two men came home safely. And we all came home, so mission accomplished."[12]

ENDNOTES

1. Silver Star citation, 2nd Lt. Brian M. Stann, USMC, http://www.homeofheroes.com/valor2/SS/7_GWOT/citations_USMC-M.html.
2. Lucian Friel, "3/2 Marines Assume Authority of Al-Qa'im Region," *Marine Corps News*, 9 March 2005 (Story ID #200532151947).
3. "3/2 Marines Unit History," www.globalsecurity.org/military/agency/usmc/3-2.htm.
4. "Marine Thwarts Car Bomb Attack," *USA Today*, 18 April 2005.
5. Paul L. Croom II, "Wages of War," *San Diego* (CA) *Magazine*, March 2006.
6. Lucian Friel, "3/2 Ends Deployment in Al-Qa'im, Returns to U.S.," *Marine Corps News*, 20 September 2005.
7. Paul L. Croom, II, "Despite Heavy Resistance, U.S. Officials Say Operation Matador Was a Success," *Stars and Stripes*, 16 May 2005.
8. Jay Price, "Tenacity Wins Marine a Medal," *News and Observer* (Raleigh, NC), 11 March 2006.
9. LCpl. Kevin Smith, Lance Cpl. Lawrence R. Philippon and Lance Cpl. Adam J. Crumpler.
10. Price, "Tenacity Wins Marine a Medal."
11. Ibid.
12. Athanasios Genos, "Lieutenant Awarded Silver Star, Credits it to His Marines," *Marine Corps News*, 14 March 2006 (Story ID #200631493313).

Cpl. Wyatt Waldron (Mendes), USMC

Section Leader, Combined Anti-Armor Platoon 1, Weapons Company,
3rd Battalion, 4th Marines, Regimental Combat Team 8,
2nd Marine Division, II Marine Expeditionary Force (Forward)

Al-Fallujah, Iraq
19 June 2005

The President of the United States takes pleasure in presenting the Silver Star Medal to Wyatt Waldron (Mendes), Corporal, U.S. Marine Corps, for conspicuous gallantry and intrepidity in action against the enemy while serving as Section Leader, Combined Anti-Armor Platoon 1, Weapons Company, Third Battalion, Fourth Marines, Regimental Combat Team 8, SECOND Marine Division, II Marine Expeditionary Force (Forward) in support of Operation Iraqi Freedom from 12 January to 31 July 2005. On 19 June 2005 outside Al Fallujah, Iraq, Corporal Waldron's section was attacked by a 50-man coordinated Improvised Explosive Device (IED) and small arms fire ambush. He led his section into the oncoming machine gun fire, gained fire superiority, and ordered a dismounted attack on the flank of the enemy position. Corporal Waldron dismounted his vehicle and personally destroyed two enemy machine gun positions, killing three insurgents. He then killed two more armed insurgents attempting to reinforce an adjoining enemy position. Corporal Waldron's attack broke the enemy's resistance and they began to displace. He then re-mounted his vehicle and led his section in the pursuit of the fleeing enemy. During the pursuit, his platoon killed an additional sixteen insurgents, captured six, and found another six unexploded IEDs at the ambush site. Due to Corporal Waldron's heroism under enemy fire, his unit was able to seize the initiative and defeat a numerically superior enemy force without friendly casualties. Corporal Waldron's zealous initiative, courageous actions, and exceptional dedication to duty reflected great credit upon him and were in keeping with the highest traditions of the Marine Corps and the United States Naval Service.[1]

Silver Star Citation

IT IS REFERRED TO AS THE "FATHER'S DAY MASSACRE," when seventeen Marines routed a numerically superior enemy force in prepared positions, killing thirty insurgents and wounding another thirty without a single

Marine casualty. In the early morning of 19 June 2005 Marines of Combined Anti-Armor Team (CAAT) Platoon 1, Weapons Company, 3rd Battalion, 4th Marine Regiment (3/4 Marines) were returning from a predawn patrol in an agricultural area southwest of central Al-Fallujah.[2]

It was about 5:30 AM as the patrol of four armored Humvees passed through an area bordered by a series of berms, palm trees, and fruit stands, completing a route and area reconnaissance mission prior to a general who was scheduled to pass through the area. Serving as a section leader among the patrol of seventeen Marines was Cpl. Wyatt Waldron.[3]

Waldron, a six feet two inches, 230-pound, twenty-one-year-old from Quartz Hills, California, gave up a football scholarship to San Diego State University to enlist in the Marines on 12 September 2001. Assigned as a machine gunner with the 3/4 Marines—"The Thundering Third"— Waldron was on his third deployment to Iraq in June 2005.[4]

Waldron had been with the 3/4 when it deployed to Kuwait in December 2002. With the attachment of Lima Battery, 3/11 Artillery, Bravo Company, 1st Tanks, Alpha Company, 3rd Tracks, and a platoon of the 1st Engineer Battalion, 3/4 Marines formed Task Force–34, code-named "Darkside." Darkside had crossed the border into Iraq on 21 March 2003. The battalion was part of the advance on Baghdad; they returned to their base at Twentynine Palms, California, in May 2003.[5]

Now, as Waldron observed the absence of activity in the early morning, with fruit stands closed and deserted, his senses went on alert. "Nobody was there," he recalled. Waldron was in the lead vehicle when he spotted an improvised explosive devices (IED) ahead by the roadway. "During route recons you're looking for anything suspicious—spare tires on the road, parked vehicles with nobody in them, stuff that can be used as explosives," Waldron said.[6]

Waldron identified the IED as a 155-mm shell configured into a daisy chain, a string of linked IEDs. Once the convoy entered the kill zone, the IEDs would be detonated to destroy vehicles and kill Marines. Then, as Waldron later put it, "Everything opened up."[7] Suddenly, an IED detonated nearby, and the convoy came under intense AK-47, machine-gun, and rocket-propelled grenades (RPG) fire from berms to the west.

Intuitively sensing from two previous combat tours that the intent of the attackers was to drive them east into a cluster of IEDs, Waldron did the unexpected. "They put all this firepower on this one side," he said. "What do they want us to do? They wanted to push us down this one road. So I did the exact opposite."[8]

Waldron located four heavy machine-gun positions. Then, leaving two Humvees mounted with machine guns to provide covering fire, Waldron led the two remaining Humvees through intense oncoming machine-gun fire in a direct assault on the insurgents' position. What followed was two hours of fire and maneuver, as Waldron's team flanked and eliminated the enemy.

Waldron is credited for leading a dismounted attack in which he personally destroyed two machine-gun positions, killing three insurgents, and with eliminating another two insurgents attempting to reinforce a gun position. Gaining fire superiority over a numerically superior force, Waldron's Marines broke the enemy's spirit and soon had them fleeing. Waldron's section then remounted their vehicles in pursuit, killing an additional seventeen insurgents and capturing six others, as well as uncovering unexploded IEDs.[9]

Waldron, meritoriously promoted to sergeant, remained in Iraq until the 3/4 returned to Twentynine Palms in August 2005. His enlistment complete, he left the Marines the following February. Engaged, and with a baby due in October 2005, he said, "I was blessed enough to go and do three tours in Iraq. Doing a fourth one, I think, would be pressing my luck a little bit."[10]

On 27 July 2006 Waldron, now a civilian, returned to Camp Wilson at Twentynine Palms for the presentation of his Silver Star. He considers it an honor that he was allowed to fight for his country, but denies he did anything extraordinary. "If I hadn't been there, somebody else would have stepped up and done the same thing. . . . Medals aren't won by individuals; they're won by teams."[11]

Now living in southern California and working as a deputy sheriff with the Los Angeles Sheriff's Department, Waldron, who has reverted to using his mother's maiden name of Mendes, described receiving the Silver Star as "really cool." He reflects on the battle by saying, "I guess they hit the wrong CAAT Team on the wrong day."[12]

ENDNOTES

1. Silver Star citation, Cpl. Wyatt Waldron (Mendes), USMC, http://www.homeofheroes.com/valor2/SS/7_GWOT/citations_USMC-M.html.

2. Gidget Fuentes, "'They Hit the Wrong CAAT Team': Leatherneck Earns Silver Star for Role in Ambush Fight," *Marine Corps Times*, 21 August 2006.

3. Christopher Amico, "Valley Marine Wins Silver Star," *Valley Press* (Lancaster, CA), 28 July 2006.

4. Fuentes, "'They Hit the Wrong CAAT Team.'"

5. "3rd Battalion, 4th Marine Regiment," Globalsecurity.org, www.globalsecurity.org/military/agency/usmc/3-4.htm.

6. Keith Matheny, "Gallant Service Has Reward: Now-Retired Marine Receives Third-Highest Honor from Corps," *The Desert Sun* (Palm Springs, CA), 14 August 2006.

7. Fuentes, "'They Hit the Wrong CAAT Team.'"

8. Matheny, "Gallant Service Has Reward."

9. Amico, "Valley Marine Wins Silver Star."

10. Matheny, "Gallant Service Has Reward."

11. Ibid.

12. Fuentes, "'They Hit the Wrong CAAT Team.'"

Cpl. Jeremy L. Stagner, USMC

Casualty Evacuation Driver, Lima Company, 3rd Battalion,
7th Marines, 2d Brigade Combat Team, 2nd Marine Division,
II Marine Expeditionary Force (Forward)

Ar Ramadi, Iraq
1 November 2005

The President of the United States takes pleasure in presenting the Silver Star Medal to Jeremy L. Stagner, Corporal, U.S. Marine Corps, for conspicuous gallantry and intrepidity in action against the enemy while serving as Casualty Evacuation Driver, Company L, Third Battalion, Seventh Marines, 2d Brigade Combat Team, SECOND Marine Division, II Marine Expeditionary Force (Forward) in support of Operation Iraqi Freedom on 1 November 2005. While he was cordoning an Improvised Explosive Device (IED), Corporal Stagner witnessed an explosion caused by a second IED that destroyed an Explosive Ordnance Disposal vehicle. Almost immediately, he saw a Marine emerge from the vehicle covered in flames, and obviously in extreme pain. Completely disoriented, the Marine attempted to put the flames out by flailing his arms wildly. As his attempts progressively failed, he began to run in circles, and cut sharply in different directions, trying to create enough wind force to extinguish the fire. Without hesitation, while he was under enemy small arms and rocket-propelled grenade fire, Corporal Stagner grabbed a fire extinguisher, ran forty meters over open terrain to the burning Marine, and extinguished the fire. Despite secondary explosions from hand grenades and C-4 in the vehicle, as well as continued exposure to enemy fire, he moved the Marine to the casualty evacuation vehicle. Corporal Stagner then located a corpsman and, exposing himself to the enemy a third time, provided suppressive fire to cover the corpsman's sprint to the casualty. His heroic actions were instrumental in preventing the loss of additional lives. By his bold leadership, wise judgment, and complete dedication to duty, Corporal Stagner reflected great credit upon himself and upheld the highest traditions of the Marine Corps and the United States Naval Service.[1]

Silver Star Citation

AS THE REFERENDUM ON Iraq's Constitution approached, violence against American and Iraqi forces increased in the Al-Anbar Province, even as elements of the 2nd Brigade Combat Team (BCT) were deployed throughout the region in Election Support Elements, and Marines in Ar Ramadi found themselves tasked with the dual mission of trying to ensure a safe election while continuing their counterinsurgency operations.[2]

Marine Gen. Peter Pace, who was also Chairman of the Joint Chiefs of Staff, was looking forward to the national elections that were to take place on 15 December. He stated that the upsurge in violence was not unexpected. "As we projected would happen, the insurgents are trying to divert the Iraqi people [to] prevent them from participating in the political process."[3] Pace also stated that while the number of improvised explosive devices (IED) attacks was increasing, the effectiveness was declining due to the increase of vehicle armor plating and a change in tactics.[4]

Even with improved armor and tactics, IEDs continued to cause Marine casualties. On 1 November 2005 Cpl. Jeremy L. Stagner, a casualty evacuation driver with Lima Company 3/7 Marines, was assisting in cordoning off an IED in Ar Ramadi, a city of four hundred thousand in the southwest corner of the Sunni Triangle.

The 3rd Battalion, 7th Marines, nicknamed "The Cutting Edge," had seen action in Guadalcanal Peleliu Okinawa during World War II, Korea, Vietnam, Southwest Asia during Operation Desert Shield and Operation Desert Storm, and in Somalia. It had deployed to Kuwait in January 2003 and had participated in the invasion of Iraq in March–April 2003.

After Stability and Support Operations (SASO) in Karbala, the battalion returned to its base at Twentynine Palms, California, in September 2003. The battalion redeployed to Al-Qa'im in February 2004, with responsibility for Husaybah, near the Syrian border, remaining until September 2004. The battalion had arrived in Ar Ramadi in September 2006 for its third deployment.[5]

Stagner had enlisted in the Marines following the attack on September 11, and had already experienced combat and witnessed the effects of roadside bombs. That morning of 1 November 2005, he was present as a second IED detonated, setting a Humvee containing explosive ordnance demolition (EOD) personnel on fire.

As documented by his Silver Star citation, Stagner grabbed an extinguisher and raced forward to the burning Humvee across forty meters of open terrain while under fire to extinguish a Marine who had exited the vehicle and was on fire. He pulled the wounded man to safety. As small-arms fire and RPGs impacted around him, Stagner, ignoring the exploding munitions in the Humvee as well as devastating enemy fire, dragged the injured man to the evacuation vehicle, then provided covering fire for a corpsman who had advanced to treat the wounded man. His actions were described in his citation as "instrumental in preventing the loss of additional lives."[6] Two service members, Sgt. Daniel Tsue and Navy corpsman HM2 Alan M. Cundanga, were killed in the explosion. Both were members of the 7th Engineer Support Battalion.[7]

Almost a year later, on 9 November 2007, Stagner was presented the Silver Star and a Navy and Marine Corps Achievement medal with combat "V" at a Law Enforcement Awards Banquet at the University of Missouri at St. Joseph where Stagner was attending the police academy. Now a patrolman with the Plattsburg Police in Missouri, Stagner will only say, "If they call me again, I'll go again."[8]

ENDNOTES

1. Silver Star citation, Cpl. Jeremy L. Stagner, USMC, http://www.homeofheroes.com/valor2/SS/7_GWOT/citations_USMC-M.html.

2. Julliet Chelkowski, "Election Support Teams Help Insure Iraqi Vote," *Marine Corps News*, 2 November 2005 (Story ID #2005111225126).

3. Donna Miles, "Surge in IED Attacks Coincides with Iraqi Political Progress," *Marine Corps News*, 1 November 2005.

4. Ibid.

5. "Linage of 3rd Battalion, 7th Marines, 3/7 Marines," http://www.29palms.usmc.mil/fmf/3-7/heritage.asp.

6. Silver Star citation, Cpl. Jeremy L. Stagner, USMC.

7. Lanessa Arthur, "Marines Remember Fallen Shipmates," *Navy Compass* (San Diego, CA) 9 December 2005.

8. *Tower Topics* (newsletter), University of Missouri, 23–29 October 2006.

SSgt. Charles M. Evers, USMC

Platoon Commander, 3rd Platoon, India Company,
3rd Battalion, 5th Marines, Regimental Combat Team 5,
I Marine Expeditionary Force (Forward)

Habbaniyah, Iraq
8–12 June 2006

The President of the United States takes pleasure in presenting the Silver Star Medal to Charles M. Evers, Staff Sergeant, U.S. Marine Corps, for conspicuous gallantry and intrepidity in action against the enemy while serving as Platoon Commander, 3d Platoon, India Company, 3d Battalion, 5th Marines, Regimental Combat Team 5, I Marine Expeditionary Force Forward, in support of Operation Iraqi Freedom from 8 June to 12 June 2006. During this period, Staff Sergeant Evers' beleaguered platoon was attacked by a determined platoon-sized enemy force closing in from three separate directions, attempting to dislodge them from their observation post, and due to his personal example and decisive combat leadership, each attack was decidedly defeated. Staff Sergeant Evers, with complete disregard for his own safety, continuously braved intense enemy machine gun and small arms fire in order to provide an accurate assessment and better direct his platoon's fire. The positions the Marines had deliberately prepared under Staff Sergeant Evers' watchful eye withstood rocket-propelled grenade (RPG) detonations and thousands of enemy machine gun rounds. The enemy's detonation of a suicide vehicle-borne improvised explosive device (IED) did not deter the fighting spirit that Staff Sergeant Evers instilled in his Marines, and they executed their well-rehearsed battle drill to gain fire superiority over the enemy insurgents. His expert use of supporting arms to include close air support and armor broke the back of the tenacious attackers. Staff Sergeant Evers' resolute, decisive action, and refusal to submit to the enemy's will embodies the ethos of a combat leader and ensured the platoon's position would be held. By his bold initiative, undaunted courage, and complete dedication to duty, Staff Sergeant Evers reflected great credit upon himself and upheld the highest traditions of the Marine Corps and the United States Naval Service.[1]

Silver Star Citation

IN JUNE 2006 the 3rd Battalion, 5th Marine Regiment was on its third deployment to Iraq. They had moved west from Al-Fallujah in May and had taken over a new area of operation (AO) in Habbaniyah, a city located between Ar Ramadi and Al-Fallujah, about eighty kilometers west of Baghdad in the Al-Anbar Province. Their mission included patrolling the highway and keeping the routes clear of improvised explosive devices (IEDs), as well as conducting counterinsurgency operations. In addition they assisted in several humanitarian efforts.[2]

Marines of 3rd Platoon, India Company had undoubtedly griped about the harsh training and obsessive attention to detail displayed stateside by their platoon sergeant, SSgt. Charles M. Evers, but that training would pay off in spades during their deployment to Iraq. Tasked with stopping the placement of IEDs along Route Michigan, the main highway west from Baghdad, the Marines of 3/5 established an observation point (OP) in a house in Habbaniyah with a clear view of the road. On 8 June 2006 twenty-three Marines of 3rd Platoon controlled the outpost.[3]

Very little information has been released regarding details of the battle, but on 8 June a force of more than forty insurgents attacked the outpost from three directions, beginning what would be a four-day battle for control of the critical strategic position.

For three days, the Marines endured an almost continuous barrage of small-arms and rocket-propelled grenade (RPG) fire as insurgents attempted to overrun the position, but the Marines, under Evers' leadership, refused to be dislodged. As bullets and shrapnel filled the air, Evers maneuvered under fire from position to position, directing return fire, encouraging his Marines, and assessing the enemy's strength and position. Already on his second deployment, his experience in supervising the construction and placement of defensive positions allowed them to withstand RPG barrages and thousands of small-arms and machine-gun rounds.[4]

On the third day, suicide vehicle–borne improvised explosive devices (SVBIEDs) detonated close to the outpost, but even this did not diminish the Marines' fighting spirit. The same cannot be said for the insurgents after an airstrike called by the Marines the following day.

On 23 November, in an award ceremony in Iraq, the commandant of the Marines, Gen. James Conway, presented Evers with the Silver Star. Regarding the award, Evers only said, "I may have gotten the Silver Star, but the guys with me were the ones who did the job. . . . I'm proud of my Marines."[5]

ENDNOTES

1. Silver Star citation, SSgt. Charles M. Evers, USMC, http://www.homeofheroes.com/valor2/ SS/7_GWOT/citations_USMC.html.

2. Graham Paulsgrove, "LAR Patrols the Streets of Habbaniyah," *Marine Corps News*, 13 June 2006 (Story ID #200661452418).

3. Michael Hoffman, "Silver Star Awarded for Leadership in Battle," *Marine Corps Times*, 6 December 2006.

4. Brian Jones, "3/5 Marine Awarded Silver Star," *Marine Corps News*, 25 November 2007 (Story ID #20071125545).

5. Hoffman, "Silver Star Awarded for Leadership in Battle."

PO2 Marc A. Lee, USN

*Assaulter and Automatic Weapons Gunner, Naval Special Warfare Combat
Advisory Element (SEAL) Team Three, Naval Special Warfare Task Group*

Ar Ramadi, Iraq
8 August 2006

The President of the United States takes pride in presenting the Silver
Star Medal (Posthumously) to Marc A. Lee, Aviation Ordnanceman Second
Class, U.S. Navy, for conspicuous gallantry and intrepidity in action against
the enemy as Assaulter and Automatic Weapons Gunner in SEAL Team
THREE, Naval Special Warfare Task Group Arabian Peninsula in support
of Operation Iraqi Freedom on 2 August 2006. Petty Officer Lee conducted
clearance operations in South-Central Ar Ramadi as a member of a Naval
Special Warfare Combat Advisory element for the Iraqi Army. During the
operation, one element member was wounded by enemy fire. The element
completed the casualty evacuation, regrouped and returned onto the battlefield to continue the fight. Petty Officer Lee and his SEAL element maneuvered to assault an identified enemy position. He, his teammates, Bradley
Fighting Vehicles and Abrams tanks, engaged enemy positions with suppressive fire. During the assault, his team came under heavy enemy fire from
an adjacent building to the north. To protect the lives of his teammates, he
fearlessly exposed himself to direct enemy fire by engaging the enemy with
his machine gun and was mortally wounded in the engagement. His brave
actions in the line of fire saved the lives of many of his teammates. Petty
Officer Lee's courageous leadership, operational skill, and selfless dedication
to duty, reflected great credit upon him and were in keeping with the highest traditions of the United States Naval Service.[1]

Silver Star Citation

FOLLOWING THE NATIONAL ELECTIONS in Iraq on 15 December 2005 Sunni
Arab and secular Shi'ites alleged fraud, holding that the elections were
rigged to favor the main Shi'ite coalition. Demonstrations were followed
by an increase in car bombings and attacks on U.S. and Iraqi officials.

The arrival of the 3/8 Marines to replace the 3/7 in Ar Ramadi in March
2006 coincided with an escalation of violence, with more than two hundred
insurgents killed in the month of April. The violence continued into the

summer of 2006. On 18 June 2006 the 1st Brigade Combat Team (BCT), 1st Armored Division, and the 1st Division of the Iraqi Army launched a joint offensive operation in Ar Ramadi. Hoping to avoid the full-scale onslaught that occurred in Al-Fallujah in November 2004, the plan was to gradually place units of one hundred men in key locations throughout the city to slowly reduce, then eliminate, the insurgents' ability to move freely.[2]

In July 2006 new outposts, both inside and outside the city, were jointly occupied by Iraqi and U.S. forces. By August Ar Ramadi was in a state of virtual anarchy, due to a skilled and well-financed insurgency. The city had no working government, few police, and 40 percent unemployment. Officials were being assassinated with impunity, and a 1st Armored Division officer in Ar Ramadi described it as "the heart of an insurgent hotbed," as mosque loudspeakers were used to exhort Mujaheddin to "kill Americans."[3]

On 2 August 2006 members of the Naval Special Warfare Combat Advisory Element (SEALs) were accompanying U.S. and Iraqi soldiers of the 1st Brigade, 1st Iraqi Division on a clearing operation in South-Central Ar Ramadi. Along on the mission was a member of SEAL Team-5, Aviation Ordnanceman 2nd Class Marc A. Lee.[4]

Lee, a twenty-eight-year-old from Hood River, Oregon, had enlisted in the U.S. Navy in May 2001 with the hope of becoming a SEAL. After boot camp at the Recruit Training Command in Great Lakes, Illinois, Lee was sent to Pensacola, Florida, for training as an aviation ordnanceman. In October 2001 Lee was accepted into Basic Underwater Demolition–SEAL (BUDS) training, a six-month course at the Naval Special Warfare Training Center in Coronado, California, but he dropped out after he contracted pneumonia. Assigned aboard the USS *Dwight D. Eisenhower*, Lee returned to Coronado in March 2004, successfully completed the program in November, and was assigned to SEAL Team-5.[5] He deployed with his team to Iraq in March 2006.

Information on Special Forces Operations is always limited, but an embedded journalist with *Stars and Stripes* in Ar Ramadi reported that as the force advanced, one SEAL was wounded in the face by sniper fire. After evacuating the casualty, the team regrouped to maneuver and assault the insurgent position, described as bunkered and fortified. Supported by Bradley fighting vehicles and Abrams M1A1 tanks, they engaged the enemy with a heavy volume of suppressing fire from an adjacent building to the north. The battle lasted an hour and covered a five-block area.[6]

According to Navy officials, Lee "single-handedly held off enemy fighters as his team rescued a soldier wounded on a rooftop by a sniper."[7] The second SEAL, wounded in the shoulder, was safely evacuated but Lee, who had exposed himself to draw the insurgents' fire, was mortally wounded while providing covering fire. Lee's actions allowed the rest of the team to kill the insurgents.[8]

For his actions, Lee was awarded a posthumous Silver Star, Bronze Star with combat "V" for Valor, and a Purple Heart, making him the first, and to date only, SEAL to be awarded a Silver Star for actions in Iraq. As of August 2006 he was the only SEAL killed in action in Iraq; sixteen SEALS had died as of August 2006 in combat in Afghanistan.[9]

At a memorial service at the Hood River Expo Center, Oregon, six hundred in attendance listened to Lee's words read from one of his last letters home: "I have seen amazing things and sad things. But being in Iraq makes me realize what a great country we have."[10]

ENDNOTES

1. Silver Star citation, PO2 Marc A. Lee, USN. http://www.homeofheroes.com/valor2/SS/ 7_GWOT/citations_USN.html.
2. Ann Scott Tyson, "Troops Fight to Expand Foothold in Ar Ramadi," *Washington* (DC) *Post*, 2 August 2006.
3. Ibid.
4. Gidget Fuentes, "First SEAL Killed in Iraq: Oregon Native Killed in Ar Ramadi Fighting, Two Other SEALs Wounded," *Navy Times*, 7 August 2006.
5. Cheryl Clark, "First SEAL Killed in Iraq," *San Diego* (CA) *Union-Tribune*, 8 August 2006.
6. Gidget Fuentes, "SEAL Earns Posthumous Silver Star," *Navy Times*, 10 August 2006.
7. "Decorated Sailor from Hood River Killed in Iraq," NWCN.com, 5 August 2006. http:// www.nwcn.com/statenews/oregon/stories/NW_080506ORNsailorkilledEL_.7202a27.html.
8. Fuentes, "First SEAL Killed in Iraq."
9. Ibid.
10. "Navy SEAL Remembered at Oregon Service," Associated Press, 27 August 2006, http:// www.signonsandiego.com/news/world/iraq/memorial/20060827-1629-navyseal-service. html.

Capt. John J. McKenna IV, USMCR

3rd Platoon Commander, Bravo Company, 1st Battalion 25th Marines,
Regimental Combat Team 5, I Marine Expeditionary Force (Forward)

Al-Fallujah, Iraq
16 August 2006

The President of the United States takes pride in presenting the Silver Star Medal (Posthumously) to John McKenna IV, Captain, U.S. Marine Corps, for conspicuous gallantry and intrepidity in action while serving as 3d Platoon Commander, Company B, First Battalion, Twenty-Fifth Marines, Regimental Combat Team 5, I Marine Expeditionary Force (Forward), in support of Operation Iraqi Freedom. On 16 August 2006 Captain McKenna was leading 1st Squad on a foot patrol in Al Fallujah, Iraq. As the patrol neared a friendly observation post, it was suddenly ambushed by well concealed insurgents firing sniper rifles, automatic weapons and rocket-propelled grenades (RPGs) from buildings, rooftops and cars to the north, south and east. The point man at the front of the patrol was fatally wounded by the hail of enemy bullets and fell in the middle of the intersection where the fire was most heavily concentrated. Captain McKenna instantly rushed into action, directing the fires of his men and ordering them to employ smoke grenades to obscure the enemy's vision. Ignoring the imminent peril from the heavy incoming fire, Captain McKenna ran into the intersection in an effort to save his downed Marine. Completely exposed to the enemy fire, he calmly knelt next to the stricken Marine to assess his condition. As he began to drag the Marine to a covered position, Captain McKenna was hit by enemy fire and mortally wounded. Captain McKenna gallantly gave his life in an attempt to save one of his Marines. His actions inspired his men to drive the enemy from the battlefield, and served as a true example of the selfless bravery to which all Marine leaders aspire. By his bold leadership, wise judgment, and complete dedication to duty, Captain McKenna reflected great credit upon himself and upheld the highest traditions of the Marine Corps and the United States Naval Service.[1]

Silver Star Citation

ALMOST TWO YEARS AFTER the massive offensive to eliminate the insurgency in Al-Fallujah in November 2004, sniper fire and roadside bombs continued to take American lives and hinder progress in rebuilding the city. In August

2006 insurgents carried out a campaign of assassination and intimidation that claimed the lives of the head of the city council, the deputy police chief, and numerous police and contract workers.[2]

On 16 August 2006 Capt. John J. McKenna IV was leading a patrol on foot in Al-Fallujah as the commander of 3rd Platoon, Bravo Company, 1/25 Marines. A reservist with Fox Company 2/25 Marines, a reserve company from Albany, New York, McKenna had volunteered to return to Iraq with the 1st Battalion. McKenna, thirty, was born on St. Patrick's Day in Brooklyn, New York. He joined the Marines after earning a history degree from Binghamton University and was commissioned into the reserves on 13 June 1998. In June 1999 he reported to the 2nd Marine Air Wing (MAW) as an air defense control officer. He served tours in Uzbekistan and Afghanistan as an air-defense officer, and served a combat tour in Iraq during the invasion in 2003. McKenna left active duty in 2003 but remained in the reserves, assigned to Fox Company, 1/25. In November 2005 he volunteered for a second tour in Iraq; his unit deployed in March 2006.[3]

In February 2005 McKenna had been sworn in as a New York State Trooper, and he knew that remaining in the reserves might interfere with his law enforcement career. Nevertheless, when the request came for volunteers to deploy McKenna signed up, saying that he could not let his Marines go to combat without him.[4]

Now, as the Marines of McKenna's platoon neared a friendly observation post, insurgents opened fire with small arms and rocket-propelled grenades (RPGs) from windows and rooftops from buildings to the north, south, and east. The point man, LCpl. Michael D. Glover, fell mortally wounded in the middle of the intersection. Ordering the employment of smoke grenades to obscure his movements, McKenna dashed into the open and advanced through heavy fire to Glover's position to render aid. He was dragging the wounded Marine to cover when he was mortally wounded by enemy fire.

On 25 August 2006 McKenna was laid to rest at Saratoga National Cemetery in Schuylerville, New York, before hundreds of Marines and law enforcement officers, as bagpipers played "Amazing Grace" and a squad of seven Marines fired a twenty-one gun salute. New York State Police Superintendent Wayne Bennet said simply of McKenna, "He was the picture of a Marine."[5]

ENDNOTES

1. Silver Star citation, Capt. John McKenna IV, USMCR, http://www.homeofheroes.com/valor2/SS/7_GWOT/citations_USMC-M.html.

2. Scott Peterson, "Under Fire: U.S. Marines Hand Off Battered Fallujah," *Christian Science Monitor*, 24 November 2006.

3. Brian Reimers, "New England's Own Marines Gather to Remember Fallen Brothers," *Marine Corps News*, 26 August 2006.

4. David Carus, "Marine's Memory Honored in Brooklyn," Associated Press, http://www.militarycity.com/valor/2050237.html.

5. "In Memorium: Fallen Marine Laid to Rest," TroyRecord.com, http://www.corpsstories.com/memoriam-McKenna.htm.

Maj. Douglas A. Zembiec, USMC

"The Lion of Fallujah," Marine Adviser, Iraq Assistance Group,
Multi-National Corps, Iraq

Baghdad, Iraq
11 May 2007

The President of the United States takes pride in presenting the Silver Star Medal (Posthumously) to Douglas A. Zembiec, Major, U.S. Marine Corps, for conspicuous gallantry and intrepidity in action against the enemy while serving as a Marine Advisor, Iraq Assistance Group, Multi-National Corps, Iraq, in support of Operation Iraqi Freedom on 11 May 2007. Attacking from concealed and fortified positions, an enemy force engaged Major Zembiec's assault team, firing crew-served automatic weapons and various small arms. He boldly moved forward and immediately directed the bulk of his assault team to take cover. Under withering enemy fire, Major Zembiec remained in an exposed, but tactically critical, position in order to provide leadership and direct effective suppressive fire on the enemy combatant positions with his assault team's machine gun. In doing so he received the brunt of the enemy's fire, was struck and succumbed to his wounds. Emboldened by his actions his team and supporting assault force aggressively engaged the enemy combatants. Major Zembiec's quick thinking and timely action to re-orient his team's machine gun enabled the remaining members of his unit to rapidly and accurately engage the primary source of the enemy's fire saving the lives of his comrades. By his bold initiative, undaunted courage, and complete dedication to duty, Major Zembiec reflected great credit upon himself and upheld the highest traditions of the Marine Corps and the United States Naval Service.[1]

Silver Star Citation

THERE ARE CERTAIN INDIVIDUALS who through word or deed ensure themselves a place in history. The lore of the Marine Corps is filled with men who became legends: Presley O'Bannon, Smedley Butler, "Chesty" Puller, and "Manila John" Basilone. Almost certain to join their ranks is Maj. Douglas A. Zembiec, "The Lion of Fallujah."

Zembiec earned his nom de guerre, and a Bronze Star with combat "V" for Valor, for his actions during Operation Vigilant Resolve in

Al-Fallujah during April 2004. As the commander of Echo Company, 2/1 Marines, he led his company during a month of almost continuous combat to wrest control of the city from the insurgents.

In the early morning hours of 26 April 2004 Zembiec's Echo Company took up positions in two houses inside Al-Fallujah's volatile Jolan neighborhood. As they set up observation posts a fierce battle began that was to last three hours. When armor support was called in, Zembiec, although wounded in the leg, raced down from the roof of one of the houses and into the street to direct the tank fire, totally exposed to enemy fire.

As Capt. Edward Solis, 1st Platoon leader recalled, "Doug ran outside amid rocket-propelled grenade [RPG] and machine-gun fire, and [he] jumped up on the tank and pointed with his rifle at where the tank should aim before running back to his position unscathed. The tank hit its target. The jaws of every Marine there had dropped. It was like, 'Did he just do that?' I am a God-fearing man, but he just sort of walked on water that day."[2]

Zembiec's Bronze Star citation credited him with twice coordinating the actions of his Marines from atop a tank, and "inspiring his Marines to aggressively repel the enemy's determined assault."[3] Out of the one hundred fifty Marines in Echo Company, four were killed and seventy were wounded in the month-long action, the largest number of casualties of any rifle company in Iraq. More than fifty members of Echo Company were cited for valor between March and May 2004.[4]

Tony Perry, a reporter embedded with the 2/1 during the battle for Al-Fallujah, described his impressions of Zembiec on their first meeting, 6 April 2004. "A Marine patrol from 2/1 had been fired on as it ventured [into Jolan] and Marines were assembling a retaliatory raid. . . . [C]ontinuous gunfire from insurgents pelted the sides of our vehicles . . . [and] the Marines rushed out the rear hatch and began returning fire. Zembiec was in the lead yelling 'Let's go! Keep it moving, keep it moving.'"[5]

Douglas Zembiec was born at Kealakekua, Hawaii, in April 1973, the son of an FBI agent. He graduated from the U.S. Naval Academy in 1995, where he was twice All-American on the wrestling team. Commissioned a second lieutenant in the Marine Corps, Zembiec led the 2nd Force Reconnaissance Platoon during a one-month deployment to Kosovo in 1999; he deployed to Afghanistan for Operation Enduring Freedom.

Not content with service with the fleet, and losing hope of ever seeing combat, Zembiec had toyed with leaving the Corps for a career with the FBI. His frustration increased in 2003 as he watched the invasion of Baghdad on a television from his posting in Okinawa. When he finally arrived in Iraq in command of an infantry rifle company, he embraced the warrior ethic of bringing the fight to the enemy. Of his fighting spirit, the battalion operations officer, Maj. Joseph Clearfield remarked, "He [went] out every day and created dilemmas for the enemy."[6]

He earned his second nickname, "Unapologetic Warrior," for a series of quotes that appeared in articles in *The Los Angeles* (CA) *Times* and *Wall Street Journal*. He told his Marines, "Killing is not wrong if it's for a purpose . . . [like] to keep your nation free, or to protect your buddy." He called 26 April "the greatest day of my life. I never felt so alive, so exhilarated, so purposeful. There is nothing equal to combat, and there is no greater honor than to lead men into combat." Of his Marines' valor that day, he said, "These young Marines didn't enlist to get money to go to college. They joined the Marines to be part of a legacy. I am completely in awe of their bravery."[7]

Zembiec held his men in high regard and felt privileged to lead them, sentiments that were mutual. While serving under his command, LCpl. Jacob Atkinson recalled, "He led from the front." Sgt. John Ethan Place, who won the Silver Star in Al-Fallujah, stated, "I would die for this man." And Sgt. Maj. William Skiles, Zembiec's first sergeant in Al-Fallujah, said of his commander that there was no one better to go to war with. "He was the Marine that every other Marine wanted to be next to [when] fighting the enemy."[8]

After Al-Fallujah, Zembiec was promoted to major and assigned to Headquarters Battalion, National Capital Region, in Arlington, Virginia. On 11 May 2007 Zembiec was back in Iraq, his fourth combat deployment, serving as an advisor with the Iraq Assistance Group, Multi-National Corps–Iraq. He was killed in action leading a raid in Baghdad.[9] Details of the action remain classified as of this writing, but what is known is that he was killed by small-arms fire while leading an assault on a fortified position, ordering his team to cover while remaining exposed to direct suppressive fire on enemy positions. His "bold initiative, undaunted courage and complete dedication to duty" earned Zembiec a posthumous Silver Star.[10]

A funeral mass was held on 16 May 2007 in the U.S. Naval Academy Chapel at Annapolis, Maryland, the same location where he had recited his marriage vows two years earlier. He was then interred with full military honors at Arlington National Cemetery. In attendance among one thousand mourners were thirty enlisted members of Echo Company who had traveled from all over the world to attend the ceremony. As one Marine officer remarked, "Your men have to follow your orders, they don't have to attend your funeral."[11]

During his eulogy, a friend read from a journal Zembiec kept on leadership, including a quote from Col. George Bristol, one of Zembiec's favorites: "Be a man of principle. Fight for what you believe in. Keep your word. Live with integrity. Be brave. Believe in something bigger than yourself. Serve your country. Teach. Mentor. Give something back to society."[12]

ENDNOTES

1. Silver Star citation, Maj. Douglas A. Zembiec, USMC, http://www.homeofheroes.com/valor2/SS/7_GWOT/citations_USMC-M.html.
2. Andrea F. Siegel, "Comrades Remember a 'Lion,'" *Baltimore* (MD) *Sun*, 15 May 2007.
3. Rick Rogers, "Home of the Brave: Maj. Douglas Zembiec," *San Diego* (CA) *Union Tribune*, 10 November 2006.
4. Ibid.
5. Tony Perry, "The Unapologetic Warrior: In Iraq, a Marine Corps Captain Is Living Out His Heart's Desire," *Los Angeles* (CA) *Times*, 22 August 2004.
6. Ibid.
7. Perry, "The Unapologetic Warrior."
8. Andrea Siegel, "Famed 'Lion of Fallujah' Dies," *Baltimore* (MD) *Sun*, 14 May 2007.
9. Siegel, "Comrades Remember a 'Lion.'"
10. Silver Star citation, Maj. Douglas A Zembiec, USMC.
11. Mark Olivia, "'Lion of Fallujah' Is Laid to Rest," *Marine Corps News*, 19 May 2007.
12. Dan Morse, "Salute to a Memorable Marine," *Washington* (DC) *Post,* 17 May 2007.

VIETNAM WAR (1959–75)

SSgt. Jimmie Howard, USMC

Charlie Company, 1st Reconnaissance Battalion,
1st Marine Division

Hill 488, Chu Lai, Vietnam
16 June 1966

For conspicuous gallantry and intrepidity at the risk of his own life above and beyond the call of duty. GSgt. [then SSgt.] Howard and his 18-man platoon were occupying an observation post deep within enemy-controlled territory. Shortly after midnight a Viet Cong force of estimated battalion size approached the Marines' position and launched a vicious attack with small arms, automatic weapons, and mortar fire. Reacting swiftly and fearlessly in the face of the overwhelming odds, GSgt. Howard skillfully organized his small but determined force into a tight perimeter defense and calmly moved from position to position to direct his men's fire. Throughout the night, during assault after assault, his courageous example and firm leadership inspired and motivated his men to withstand the unrelenting fury of the hostile fire in the seemingly hopeless situation. He constantly shouted encouragement to his men and exhibited imagination and resourcefulness in directing their return fire. When fragments of an enemy grenade wounded him severely and prevented him from moving his legs, he distributed his ammunition to the remaining members of his platoon and proceeded to maintain radio communications and direct air strikes on the enemy with uncanny accuracy. At dawn, despite the fact that five men were killed and all but one wounded, his beleaguered platoon was still in command of its position. When evacuation helicopters approached his position, GSgt. Howard warned them away and called for additional air strikes and directed devastating air and small arms fire against enemy automatic weapons positions in order to make the landing zone as secure as possible. Through his extraordinary courage and resolute fighting spirit, GSgt. Howard was largely responsible for preventing the loss of his entire platoon. His valiant leadership and courageous fighting spirit served to inspire the men of his platoon to heroic endeavor in the face of overwhelming odds, and reflect the highest credit upon GSgt. Howard, the Marine Corps, and the U.S. Naval Service.[1]

Medal of Honor Citation

THIS IS THE STORY of extreme bravery by a small group of Marines and Navy Corpsmen who fought and survived a fierce battle with North Vietnam and Viet Cong forces in August 1966. The Marines and Navy Corpsmen included SSgt. Jimmie E. Howard, USMC; LCpl. Ricardo Binns, USMC; Pfc. Thomas Glawe, USMC; Pfc. Thomas Powles, USMC; Cpl. Jerrald R. Thompson, USMC; Cpl. Robert Martinez, USMC; HM1 Richard Fitzpatrick, USN; LCpl. Daniel Mulvihill, USMC; LCpl. Alcadio Mascarenas, USMC; LCpl. John T. Adams, USMC; Pfc. James McKinney, USMC; Cpl. Raymond Hildreth, USMC; Pfc. Charles Bosley, USMC; HM3 Billie Holmes, USN; LCpl. Ralph Victor, USMC; Pfc. Ignatius Carlisi, USMC; LCpl. William Norman, USMC; and Pfc. Joseph Kosoglow.[2]

The team was led by SSgt. Jimmie Howard, thirty-six, a combat-seasoned Marine who heroically led his men in one of the fiercest encounters with the enemy during the Vietnam War. The battle for Hill 488 was reminiscent of one he had gone through almost fourteen years earlier on another hill, Bunker Hill, in another country, Korea. Howard was awarded the Silver Star medal and the Purple Heart with Gold Star in lieu of a Purple Heart, and the Navy Unit Commendation for his service in Korea. He still bore the scars from shrapnel and a bayonet wound he sustained during that assault on Bunker Hill by hordes of Chinese Communist forces.[3]

Howard's Vietnam team averaged twenty-three years old (the oldest besides Howard was Fitzpatrick, thirty-five, and the youngest was Glawe, eighteen). They were not an elite force going into battle, but—in the end—the team (for its size) became one of the most highly decorated units in American Military history. Of the eighteen men listed above, six Marines were killed and the remainder wounded at least once.[4] Post-battle medals awarded included one Medal of Honor, four Navy Crosses, thirteen Silver Stars, and eighteen Purple Hearts. One Marine officer commented that it was an Alamo—with survivors![5]

In early June of 1966 2nd Army South Vietnamese (ARVN) intelligence reports indicated that the 2nd North Vietnamese Army (NVA) Division with all three regiments, the 3rd NVA, the 21st NVA, and the 1st Viet Cong Regiment had entered the strategic Que Son Valley that straddled the Quang Tin and Quang Nam provinces of the Republic of Vietnam (RVN).

Control of the Que Son Valley was important to both sides and had been the area of operation (AO) for two U.S. military operations (Double Eagle II and Harvest Moon) the preceding December. Bounded by mountains on the north, south, and west, Que Son Valley extended for some twenty-four miles east to west from Route One to Hiep Duc. The valley contained some of the best farmland in Vietnam and was rich in salt deposits. It was considered to be one of the keys to the struggle for I Corps (the military and administrative subdivision that included the five northern provinces of South Vietnam).

Acting on the ARVN reports, Marine Corps commanders decided to commence an extensive reconnaissance campaign between Tam Kay and Hiep Duc. The operation called for the insertion of six teams from the 1st Reconnaissance Battalion and a seventh team from the 1st Force Reconnaissance Company into selected landing zones to determine the extent of the NVA penetration. On 13 June the team led by SSgt. Jimmie Howard was dropped by helicopter into the AO where they made their way to the top of Hill 488 (Nui Vu), a fifteen-hundred-foot elevation that was less than twenty-five yards across at its widest, and slightly concave. The only cover was a large boulder and a few smaller rocks. Howard deployed three Marine teams on each of the finger ridges that descended about fifty yards from the top of the hill. He ordered that if anyone encountered the enemy all were to immediately retreat to the top where the platoon command post (CP) was set up. For the next two days the team reported on heavy enemy activity in the area, and called in air strikes and fire support from an ARVN 105-mm battery positioned seven miles to the south. By 15 June the enemy was aware of the presence of the Marine spotter team; that evening an American Special Forces patrol reported that an enemy battalion was moving toward Hill 488. When the team heard North Vietnamese troops massing at the base of the hill, Howard radioed for artillery support. LCpl. Ricardo Binns sighted something moving in the darkness on the north ridge less than fifteen yards from him and leveled his rifle, firing three shots which found their marks, as he yelled for everyone to get to the top. Shortly after midnight the enemy stormed the hilltop in a three-sided, all-out attack. One of the Navy Corpsman recalled that the enemy forces "were within 20 feet of us. Suddenly there were grenades all over. People started hollering. It seemed everybody got hit at the same time."[6] A fierce battle suddenly burst atop the hill with explosions, muzzle flashes, and tracer fire as the team met the enemy with bayonets and engaged in hand-to-hand combat. Howard radioed his battalion commander, Lt. Col. Arthur J. Sullivan, USMC, that they were under attack and surrounded with no way to escape. He urgently asked that the team be extracted. "You've gotta get us out of here. . . . There are too many of them for my people."[7] Sullivan assured him that support would be on the way. Despite the intensity of the attack, the Marine perimeter held.

By 2:00 AM Marine and Air Force flare planes, helicopters, and attack aircraft arrived overhead. As flares lit up the hill and surrounding area, a Marine yelled, "Look at them all! It's like ants on an anthill."[8] Marine (VMO-6) gunships strafed to within twenty meters of the patrol's perimeter while Marine jets and Huey gunships concentrated their attacks on enemy troops at the base of the hill. At 3:00 AM Marine Air Group (MAG-36) evacuation helicopters arrived to pick up the patrol, but Howard waved them off because of the intense NVA ground fire. He ordered additional air strikes, directing devastating air and small-arms fire to soften up the enemy positions and create a more secure landing zone.

Finally the battle settled into scattered small firefights. The relentless attacks by the array of aircraft overhead and the continued courageous fire from the Marines on top of the hill convinced the enemy that an additional massive assault was too costly. Running low on ammunition, the Marines threw rocks down on enemy troops hoping that they would mistake them for grenades. At this point five Marines had been killed (a sixth would later succumb en route to the base camp at Chu Lai) and each surviving member of the team had been wounded. Sergeant Howard had been hit in the back by a ricochet and his legs were temporarily paralyzed. Though severely wounded he dragged himself about the perimeter, checking on the wounded and the ammunition supply, while encouraging his men and directing their fire.[9]

At first light on 16 June MAG-36 UH-34s escorted by Huey gunships (thirty-six choppers) landed 250 Marines from Charlie Company, 1st Battalion, 5th Marines at the base of the hill. One of the gunships flown by the commanding officer of VMO-6, Maj. William J. Goodsell, was hit by enemy fire and crashed. Major Goodsell later died from injuries suffered in the crash. As the Marines advanced up the hill they fought off scattered enemy resistance; upon reaching the top they found Howard's wounded men who were mostly armed with AK-47s taken from dead North Vietnamese soldiers. When rescued, Howard's surviving team had only eight rounds of ammunition left. The North Vietnamese (3rd NVA Regiment) continued the fight until noon, when they disengaged. The Marines counted forty-two enemy dead and collected nineteen weapons left behind by the North Vietnamese. Charlie Company suffered two dead and two wounded during the rescue operation.[10]

Upon his return to the United States, Howard was assigned duty as Battalion Training Noncommissioned Officer, Service Company, Headquarters and Service Battalion, Marine Corps Recruit Depot, San Diego, California.[11] On 21 August 1967 President Lyndon B. Johnson presented Jimmie Howard with the Medal of Honor. Following the ceremony, Howard commented that the medal belonged more to the fifteen brave Marines and two Navy Corpsmen than himself. He then took the president over to the eleven survivors of his platoon who were present at the ceremony and introduced each one of them to President Johnson.[12]

Jimmie Howard was promoted to gunnery sergeant in August 1968, and retired from the Marine Corps on 31 March 1977. He died on 12 November 1993 at his home in San Diego. He is buried at the Fort Rosecrans National Cemetery near the Marine Corps Recruiting Depot where years before he served as a Marine drill instructor.[13]

ENDNOTES

1. Medal of Honor citation for SSgt. Jimmie Howard, USMC, http://www.homeofheroes.com/moh/citations_1960_vn/howard_jimmie.html.
2. John G. Hubbell and David Reed, "Hill 488: A Fight To Remember," *Readers Digest*, May 1968, 60–66.
3. Force Marine Information Office Release No: 1130–66, CIB III MAF, Da Nang, Vietnam, 19 June 1966.
4. Hubbell and Reed, "Hill 488."
5. "S/Sgt Jimmie Howard," www.homeofheroes.com/profiles/howard_jimmie.html.
6. Jack Shulimson, *U.S. Marines in Vietnam: An Expanding War, 1966* (Washington, DC: U.S. Government Printing Office, 1982), 134.
7. Ibid.
8. *Vietnam* 6, no. 6 (April 1994), 69.
9. Shulimson, *U.S. Marines in Vietnam*.
10. Ibid.
11. "GySgt. Jimmie E. Howard, USMC (Deceased): Vietnam War 1965–1973, Medal of Honor Recipient," Who's Who in Marine Corps History, United States Marine Corps History Division, www.tecom.usmc.mil/HD/Whos_Who/Howard_JE.htm.
12. "S/Sgt Jimmie Howard."
13. "GySgt. Jimmie E. Howard, USMC (Deceased)."

RMSN Harold B. McIver, USN

River Assault Squadron 13, River Assault Division 131/ T-131-7

Ben Tre, Kien Hoa Province, Vietnam
31 March 1969

For conspicuous gallantry and intrepidity in action against the enemy while serving as Radioman and machine gunner on board River Assault Craft T-131-7, a unit of the River Squadron 13, Task Force 117 in the Republic of Vietnam on 31 March 1969. His unit came under direct rocket and automatic weapons fire from the river canal bank with one of the fired rockets striking the craft, detonating and sending shrapnel throughout the well deck and wounding Seaman McIver in the face and hands, while severely wounding a Hospital Corpsman on board in the chest and head. At the very same time, the spreading shrapnel ignited a gasoline storage can causing that part of the boat to catch fire. Without hesitation and disregarding his own wounds Seaman McIver beat out and extinguished the flames and then ignoring the still incoming enemy fire directed his attention to the gravely wounded Hospital Corpsman. While applying first aid to the wounded man, he realized the man had swallowed his tongue and was unable to breathe. After unsuccessfully attempting to pry open the wounded man's jaws, Seaman McIver used a sharp instrument to perform an emergency tracheotomy on the wounded corpsman, allowing him to resume breathing. A medical evacuation helicopter arrived shortly and though still receiving enemy fire and with his own wounds untreated, he assisted the Boat Captain in carrying the wounded man to the aircraft, at which point he refused to be evacuated for treatment of his own injuries, insisting instead on returning to his machine gun and resuming firing on the enemy position. By his undaunted courage, valiant efforts, and total dedication to duty, Seaman McIver reflected great credit upon himself and upheld the highest traditions of the United States Naval Service.[1]

Silver Star Citation

ON 28 FEBRUARY 2005 former RMSN Harold Bruce McIver, USN, was presented the Silver Star in front of the Military Order of the Purple Heart Memorial Monument, located in the Courtyard of the State of Florida Capital building, Tallahassee, Florida. The presentation was made by Lt. Gen. Lawrence Snowden, USMC (Ret.), some thirty years after Radioman

Seaman McIver had battled Viet Cong guerillas on the Giao Hoa Canal of the Mekong Delta, South Vietnam.[2] The story of how McIver finally received his well-deserved award is intriguing. Actually, there were many cases during past American wars where awards recommended for individual heroic action were never processed due to the number of awards submitted, mishandled administrative work, and paperwork that just dropped through the cracks.

Harold Bruce McIver was born on 17 August 1949 in North Wilkesboro, North Carolina. His mother attended Mary Washington College in Fredericksburg, Virginia, and his father attended the Citadel, Charleston, South Carolina, and the University of Virginia. His great grandfather James Jonathan Lucas was one of the first cadets at the Citadel. Lucas was a major in the Confederacy and commanded the battery on Sullivan's Island. His unit fired the first shot on Fort Sumter that began the War Between the States. Also on the McIver side, John McIver was Chief Justice of the South Carolina Supreme Court and signed the secession document when South Carolina seceded from the Union.

McIver spent his youth in Cheraw, South Carolina. In 1960 he moved to Melbourne, Florida, and graduated from high school in 1967. While in high school he played football; during his senior year the team won the state championship. After graduation, and what with the Vietnam War and the draft in high gear he enlisted in the Navy in November 1967, attended boot camp in San Diego in 1968, and was designated as a prospect to attend the U.S. Naval Academy (after U.S. Naval Prep School in Bainbridge, Maryland). After hearing nothing from the Navy regarding possible attendance at the U.S. Navy schools, he became motivated to serve in Vietnam, and volunteered for service in a combat unit. Much to his disappointment, he received orders to Guam. While awaiting word from the Naval Academy, he had been placed on "hold" and assigned to work in the Naval Training Command (NTC) Personnel Center. Personnel at the Center helped him get his orders changed and he was assigned to Naval Inshore Operations Training Center (NIOTC), Mare Island, California, for further training.

At NIOTC he spent eleven weeks intensively training in Riverine Warfare, counterinsurgency, river assault tactics, small-arms, and heavy weapons. At Camp Roberts, California, Roberts was trained in communications and received gunnery training for crews that were assigned to river patrol boats. He also underwent Survival, Evasion, Resistance and Escape (SERE) training at Whidbey Island, Washington.

In March 1969 RMSN Harold Bruce McIver was among a new group of Sailors that arrived in Vietnam to relieve Mobile Riverine Force (MRF) personnel who were finishing their tours. Men were spread out throughout

the four River Assault Squadrons in the III and IV Corps regions of South
Vietnam. The new crew members were distributed from an attrition pool
and began combat operations from the onset. Their long and intense training at NIOTC was quickly put to use, as McIver recalled:

> Our boat crew trained together at Mare Island so as to establish a
> solid unit and camaraderie. We were trained to man a Tango boat,
> an armored Amphibious Assault Craft [ATC] that carried a crew of
> seven men: Boat captain BM1 John Thibadeau, coxswain BM3 Ron
> Smith, two E-3s—Bell and Parker—controlled the port and star-
> board 20-mm cannons [automatic weapons] and the top turret was
> controlled by Pat Watts who operated an MK-19 grenade launcher.
> The MK-19 fired 40-mm grenades at a cyclic rate of 375 to 400
> rounds per minute, giving a practical rate of fire of sixty rounds per
> minute (rapid) and forty rounds per minute (sustained). The weapon
> operated on the blowback principle, which used the chamber pres-
> sure from each fired round to load and re-cock the weapon. The
> MK-19 was able to lob its grenades at a maximum distance of 2,212
> meters, though its effective range for a point target was about 1,500
> meters, since the large rear leaf sight was only graduated to 1,500
> meters. The nearest safe distance to launch the grenade was seventy-
> five meters. In the Well-Deck (lower deck) was engineman EN3 Ted
> Bernbeck and myself as radioman and a 50 cal. machine-gunner. We
> had two VRC-46 radios with the capability of one that interchanged
> code/cards for secret transmissions as well as a PRC-25.
> We arrived in-country in early March and on the 8th reported
> to our base camp, Dong Tam, Kien Hoa Province; the major base
> camp for the Mobile Riverine Force and the 9th Army Infantry
> Division, and assigned to River Assault Squadron 13/ boat: T-
> 131–7. Early patrol operations were conducted in the vicinity of
> Dong Tam, My Tho and Ben Tre. On 24 March we engaged in a
> firefight as we were about to land the 3/60 9th Infantry Division
> and ARVN units on Toi Son Island in the Mekong River. We were
> hit prior to landing the troops and had to call in Cobra and Seawolf
> gunships in addition to fire support from River Assault Boats
> and 155-mm artillery. The area was heavily booby trapped. Even
> though the ambush was suppressed by the gunships, artillery and
> river assault boats, we began to immediately take casualties from
> snipers and an incredible number of mines and booby traps. This
> was my first experience as a crewman aboard a medical evacuation

(medevac) boat, with an E-6 corpsman embarked. One ARVN soldier was killed when the troops were offloaded. The next casualty
was a young 2nd Lt. who had picked up a hand grenade and as he
released the grenade it exploded and blew off part of his hand. In
addition he suffered multiple shrapnel wounds.[3]

On 31 March several riverine craft began an operation just south of Ben
Tre. All was going well until the column began transiting the Giao Hoa
canal. In a flash the Viet Cong launched an intense ambush firefight striking several boats. McIver was wounded by shrapnel from a Viet Cong B-40
rocket that struck his Tango boat (again a designated medevac craft) during
the initial enemy onslaught. The concussion from the rocket blew McIver
against the forward steel ramp, seriously injuring his back. Additionally,
shrapnel ignited a gasoline fire in the Well Deck. Noting that the hospital corpsman who was riding the boat for the operation was also seriously
wounded, McIver instantly prioritized his options. He rushed to the fire
and worked on it until it was suppressed. Then he quickly moved over to
attend to the serious wounds of the corpsman. Realizing that the corpsman's
life was in grave danger due to head and chest wounds, McIver performed
an emergency tracheotomy. Once the corpsman was breathing again and
somewhat stable, McIver helped his boat captain, BM1 John Thibadeau,
load the wounded crew member onto a medevac helicopter. McIver refused
to be medevac'd and returned to his machine gun to aid in suppressing the
ongoing Viet Cong attack.

During the next few days, Thibadeau began the process of recommend-
ing McIver for the Silver Star medal for his heroic actions. Somewhere along
the line the recommendation was lost or improperly processed.[4] More than
thirty years passed before H. Bruce McIver and John Thibadeau found one
another in 2003 after many years of searching. Soon after their meeting,
Thibadeau contacted the Chief of Naval Operations and the Secretary of the
Navy regarding the Silver Star award. The paperwork was reinitiated via
the Chief of Naval Operations office staff.

During those thirty years McIver just knew the corpsman as "Doc"
since he was serving temporary duty on T-131–7 when he was seriously
wounded. This nagged at McIver because he had no idea whether the corpsman had survived.

In April 2003 McIver and another riverine veteran, close friend Michael
A. Harris, traveled to Washington, DC, to peruse the National Archives in
College Park, Maryland, and the Washington Navy Yard, Naval Historical
Center (NHC) Operational Archives. While researching the NHC archives

they found documents pertaining to Vietnam War Riverine operations in which McIver was involved; they also found a key document regarding the 31 March 1969 firefight. It not only detailed McIver's wounds that day, but it also revealed the corpsman's name, HM1 Zeph Lane, and information regarding his next of kin. He recalled what he and Lane had discussed on that fateful morning while transiting the Giao Hoa Canal. Lane had just returned from rest and relaxation (R&R) in Hawaii where he had married his sweetheart, the woman he had been dating for some time. Barbara (Bobbie) Cox Lane had become Zeph Lane's wife just two weeks prior to the day of the ambush.

That evening McIver checked the phonebook and made his first call. Much to his surprise Lane's mother answered. She had bittersweet news for McIver. Lane had survived his serious wounds after medical stops in Dong Tam, Long Binh, Yokosuka (Japan), and finally Bethesda Naval Hospital in Maryland. He subsequently had become a doctor and private pilot. In 1971 Lane had traveled back to Vietnam to help build a medical clinic close to where he had been wounded. This was the good news. The bad news was that Lane had died in the crash of his personal plane in 1985. Lane's widow made the comment that Lane "lived on the edge" all the time.[5] McIver and those who fought in the waterways of Vietnam could well understand this attitude.

During this process McIver found out that his own children were born around the same time as Lane's two daughters, Jamie and Kim. He stays in touch with the family and much closure has come about for all involved. Jamie continues to communicate with McIver in an attempt to learn all she can about her father's service. Jamie credits McIver with saving her father's life. If he had not done what he had done, she and Kim would never have been born.

On 2 July 2004 McIver received a telephone call from Cdr. Leslie Priest, a representative of the secretary of the Navy. He was informed that the secretary, on behalf of the president of the United States, had approved the award for the Silver Star medal thirty-four years after his courageous actions to save his fellow Sailor and boat that day. In his official letter approving the award, Secretary of the Navy Gordon R. England added the following: "[U]pon transfer to the Fleet Reserve or the Fleet Marine Corps Reserve in accordance with references (a) and (b), Radioman Seaman Harold B. McIver will be accorded the benefits of extraordinary heroism."[6]

McIver went on to serve with River Assault Division 131 until late June 1969. He was then transferred to a Naval Advisory role with MACV Naval Advisory Group ATF-212. Later he moved to ATF-211 and worked with River Assault Interdiction Division (RAID) 72 in the U Minh Forest region with the Vietnamese Marine Corps (VNMC) and Vietnamese Navy (VNN).[7] Radioman McIver was discharged from active duty in March 1970 and from the reserves in November 1973. During his Vietnam Riverine service he made 120 combat patrols. While on patrol he was engaged in twenty-five firefights and numerous rocket and mortar attacks. He was wounded during three engagements with the enemy. His personal, unit, and campaign awards include the Silver Star medal, the Bronze Star medal with combat "V," three Purple Heart medals, the Navy Commendation medal with combat "V," the Navy Achievement Medal with combat "V," the Combat Action Ribbon, the Presidential Unit Citation, Navy Unit Commendation with two bronze stars, the Meritorious Unit Commendation with one bronze star, the National Defense Service medal, the Vietnam Combatant–Small Craft Insignia (SCI), the Vietnam Combatant–Craft Crewman (VCCC) Insignia, the Vietnam Service medal with three bronze stars, the RVN Staff Service Medal–2nd Class, the RVN Cross of Gallantry Medal Color with Palm, and the RVN Civil Actions Medal First Class Color, with Palm and the RVN Campaign Medal with 60s Device.[8]

Following his discharge from the Navy McIver attended Brevard Community College and received an AA degree from Tallahassee Community College, transferring to Florida State University in January 1973. He founded Southeastern Realty and Investment Properties in September 1974 specializing in large acreage land tracts, and then began exclusively representing private land owners who had environmentally endangered land that the State of Florida began to purchase. He represented land owners from the Panhandle of West Florida to the Florida Keys and handled in excess of $200 million in land sales to the State of Florida through 1996. H. Bruce "Mac" McIver presently serves as Region IV Commander, Military Order of the Purple Heart, USA, and resides in Tallahassee, Florida.[9]

ENDNOTES

1. Silver Star citation, RMSN Harold B. McIver, USN, http://www.homeofheroes.com/valor2/SS/5_RVN/citations/navy/a.html.
2. H. Bruce McIver, e-mail, 8 January 2008.
3. "H. Bruce McIver Awarded the Silver Star Medal on 2 June 2004 for Heroic Actions on 31 March 1969," http://mrfa.org/McIver.SilverStar.htm.
4. Ibid.
5. H. Bruce McIver, e-mail, 13 September 2007; "H. Bruce McIver Awarded the Silver Star Medal."
6. Secretary of the Navy Letter (Ser NDBDM/0261), 2 July 2004, to Chief of Naval Operations, Subject Recommendation for Silver Star to Radioman Seaman Harold B. McIver, 263-86-2259, USN.
7. Ibid.
8. Michael A. Harris, e-mail, 9 January 2008. Harris is a Riverine Sailor and close friend of McIver.
9. H. Bruce McIver, e-mail, 18 November 2007.

KOREAN WAR (1950–53)

On 25 June 1950 North Korean ground troops crossed the 38th parallel in a full scale invasion of South Korea. Expecting little more than a diplomatic protest the Koreans projected that they would win the war within a few months. However, the United Nations Security Council convened an emergency session; they condemned the North Korean invasion and ordered military sanctions.

President Truman immediately committed U.S. armed forces to the defense of South Korea and delegated the responsibility of what he later referred to as a "police action" to the Joint Chiefs of Staff who appointed Gen. Douglas MacArthur as Commander in Chief Far East, placing the Seventh Fleet under his command. Within three days the invading North Koreans entered the South Korean capital city of Seoul, sending the South Korean army in full retreat. As the invaders continued their march south they were slowed by blown out bridges that the retreating South Korean army had destroyed, forcing the North Koreans to ferry their tanks and artillery across rivers. This pause allowed the landing of American troops, two battalions of the 24th infantry Division, at the port of Pusan on the southeast coast of the peninsula. The American forces joined in the fight and with the strong support of the South Korean army, which was recovering from its initial reverses, slowed the Red drive short of Pusan. In the meantime, the remainder of the 24th infantry and two more divisions came ashore, thus reconstituting the Eighth Army under the command of Gen. Walton H. Walker, who was able to establish what was called the "Pusan Perimeter." Overwhelming allied air superiority and continuous bombardment by American and British warships destroyed bridges, oil refineries, marshaling yards, fuel storage depots, coastal roads, and railroads, all of which hindered the resupply of the North Koreans.

Fierce fighting continued along the Pusan line, but by mid-September the situation began to stabilize. The Allies did not have enough troop strength to break through the perimeter, and the North Koreans began to suffer from lack of supplies and ammunition because of the Allied air and sea offensive. MacArthur had foreseen such a stalemate and recommended that his forces invade the port at Inchon, located just below the 38th parallel and a few miles southwest of Seoul. Though high-ranking officers looked at the venture as too risky because of waterway and land obstacles, MacArthur won over his critics by convincing them that these very factors would make the enemy think that such an operation was impossible. Thus, if he were to be successful, MacArthur's force would have the element of surprise. His assault force consisted of the 1st Marine Division supported by four battalions of South Korean marines to be backed up by the U.S. 7th Infantry Division with five thousand South Korean troops. These divisions formed the X Corps. On 15 September 1950 MacArthur's invasion force landed at Inchon. Although the North Koreans put up fierce resistance they had too few men and were quickly wiped out. A few days later the Marines took Kimpo airfield, the largest air base in Korea, capturing Seoul on the 26th.

The North Korean situation to the south was now dire. They were cut off from all supplies. Though some escaped back north through the mountains, many were killed, and 125,000 were taken prisoners of war. MacArthur was now authorized by the Joint Chiefs to conduct operations north of the 38th parallel and if necessary achieve the destruction of the North Korean armed forces. As his forces moved north, the port city of Wonsan on the east coast fell to the South Korean army and the U.S. Eighth Army captured the city of Pyongyang, the capital of North Korea. Though warned by the Communist Chinese that if the UN forces approached the Yalu River (on the northern border between North Korea and China) they would enter the war, MacArthur and his staff did not take the warning seriously. He sent the Eighth Army northward from Pyongyang and the X Corps north from Hungnam toward the Yalu. The two armies were separated by eighty miles of mountainous terrain. Taking advantage of this open ground between the Eighth Army and the X Corps, the Chinese crossed the border on the evening of 25 November and entered the war with one hundred eighty thousand troops. The Eighth and X Corps began an immediate retreat. The Eighth fell back past Pyongyang, the 38th parallel, and Seoul. Elements of the 1st Marine Division, X Corps reached the Chosin Reservoir and were surrounded by one hundred twenty thousand Chinese. Despite bitter cold weather and treacherous terrain, the Marines held their position using a defense perimeter. Their ensuing withdrawal from the area in bitter cold weather, blinding snow, and under constant attacks by the enemy is considered to be one of the most heroic retreats in the history of warfare. Once back in Pusan the X Corps was merged into the Eighth Army and it established itself on a firm defense line a few miles south of Seoul.[1]

For the next eighteen months, the two adversaries crossed and recrossed the 38th parallel gaining little ground during fierce assaults, the adversaries finally settled along a relatively stable main line of resistance (MLR) while truce talks were conducted (March 1952–July 1953). What fighting occurred during this time were battles around Allied combat outposts that were positioned in front of the main line. This phase of the conflict was called "The Outpost War."

The outposts commanded hills of high ground from which enemy activity could be observed, controlled, and raided. Numerous hill and outpost sites were established along the MLR, which extended across the width of the peninsula. The outposts were controlled by squad- to company-sized units. Forty-four were 1st Marine sector sites positioned along what was called "The Jamestown Line." Some were continuously occupied, others were occupied only at night. The war became a defensive war, a fight for the high ground. Statistics reveal that nearly 40 percent of all Marine Corps casualties in Korea occurred after April 1952. On average there were twenty-seven casualties each day, or more than one per hour. Seventeen hundred Marines died and fourteen Medals of Honor were awarded during the period April 1952 to July 1953. The battles were close-up, often hand-to-hand combat where troops used shovels and fists. The Chinese Communist forces were numerous, brave, strong, and intelligently led. They were a force to be reckoned with.[2]

Two of the many Marines who fought with gallantry in the "Outpost War" were Pvt. Jack William Kelso and Pfc. Herman Pizzi. Their courageous actions, often against an almost overwhelming enemy force, were typical of the many Marines who fought and died during this little-known segment of the Korean War.

Pfc. Jack William Kelso, USMC

India Company, 3rd Battalion, 7th Marines, 1st Marine Division

Outpost Bunker Hill, Korea
13 August 1952

For conspicuous gallantry and intrepidity at the risk of his life above and beyond the call of duty while serving as a rifleman of Company I, in action against enemy aggressor forces. When both the platoon commander and the platoon sergeant became casualties during the defense of a vital outpost against a numerically superior enemy force attacking at night under cover of intense small-arms, grenade and mortar fire, Pfc. Kelso bravely exposed himself to the hail of enemy fire in a determined effort to reorganize the unit and to repel the onrushing attackers. Forced to seek cover, along with four other Marines, in a nearby bunker which immediately came under attack, he unhesitatingly picked up an enemy grenade which landed in the shelter, rushed out into the open and hurled it back to the enemy. Although painfully wounded when the grenade exploded as it left his hand, and again forced to seek the protection of the bunker when the hostile fire became more intensified Pfc. Kelso refused to remain in his position of comparative safety and moved out into the fire-swept area to return the enemy fire, thereby permitting the pinned down Marines in the bunker to escape. Mortally wounded while providing cover fire for his comrades, Pfc. Kelso, by his valiant fighting spirit, aggressive determination, and self-sacrificing efforts in behalf of others, served to inspire all who observed him. His heroic actions sustain and enhance the highest traditions of the U.S. Naval Service. He gallantly gave his life for his country.[3]

Medal of Honor Citation

JACK WILLIAM KELSO was born on 23 January 1934 in Madera, California, and attended grade and high school in Carutherst, California. He worked on his father's farm until he enlisted in the Marine Corps on 15 May 1951.

He completed recruit training in San Diego, California, in July 1951. In September of that year he was ordered from San Diego to Camp Pendleton, California.

In January 1952 he left for Hawaii where he served until April 1952, when he embarked for Korea. On 2 October of that year he was one of forty-seven Marines taking control of Outpost Warsaw, which had been overrun by a company of Chinese soldiers.

Only thirteen of the forty-seven Marines survived the onslaught and returned to the main line of resistance (MLR). Four of the Marines who escaped the night attack owed their lives to the eighteen-year-old Kelso who had been in the Corps less than a year. A few months earlier Kelso had won a Silver Star and earned a Purple Heart for his courageous action at another outpost, Bunker Hill. Kelso was promoted to private first class following this engagement. (The authors were unable to locate Kelso's Silver Star Citation. However, his heroics at Outpost Warsaw in October earned him the Medal of Honor, but cost him his life.)

Pfc. Herman Pizzi, USMC

1st Platoon, 1st Squad of the H-3-7 Marines

Outpost Frisco, Korea
6 October 1952

For conspicuous gallantry and intrepidity in action against the enemy while serving with a Marine infantry company in Korea on 6 October 1952. Serving as a fire team leader, Private First Class Pizzi displayed outstanding courage and devotion to duty during the defense of a forward outpost. Under cover of darkness, the enemy delivered an intense artillery and mortar barrage followed by an assault of infantry troops. Throughout the action, he fearlessly exposed himself to the deadly enemy fire in order to check his men and administer aid to the wounded. Despite his determined efforts, the men of his fire team were killed by the enemy fire and he was severely shaken by concussion. Although his weapon had been destroyed and he was armed with only a knife, he moved from position to position, aiding the wounded Marines. After organizing the few left, he directed the evacuation of the critically wounded Marines to the main line of resistance. While en route to the main line, he was painfully wounded but with grim determination, he continued to the friendly lines where he collapsed from shock and concussion. When he recovered consciousness, he volunteered to lead a rescue party to evacuate the rest of the casualties. Private First Class Pizzi's gallant and courageous actions inspired all who observed him and were in keeping with the highest traditions of the United States Naval Service.[4]

Silver Star Citation

IN THE EARLY EVENING OF 6 OCTOBER 1952, a group of Marines attached to the 1st Marine Division (Reinf) Fleet Marine Force (FMF) gathered to relieve a Marine platoon on Outpost Frisco, a hill six hundred yards in front of the MLR. The relieving detail consisted of a How Company platoon supported by a machine-gun squad.

Passing through a gate (breaks in the wire to permit passage of men) at 7:00 PM the Marines moved down the forward slope of the MLR, crossed a valley, and climbed to the outpost. Each relieving Marine was quickly posted next to the man he was to relieve. Unfortunately, since the size of the outpost was too small for the combined troops and the relieving Marines were not oriented to the established fields of fire, the sites of their Chinese adversaries or the defensive tactics that were being employed, and although they numerically doubled the outpost force, the result was a less-than-effective combined fighting unit. Shortly after they arrived Chinese soldiers swarmed the hill in a furious attack using artillery, mortars, and grenades. The enemy troops had hit the hill at its most venerable time. They had tunneled to within fifty to seventy-five yards of the outpost, taking the Marines completely by surprise. Confusion existed among the defenders since the members of the two platoons did not know each other, thus there was no coordination against the attack and there was no visible leadership. The assault came from three sides and the Marines could not react fast enough to fend off the attackers. Within fifteen minutes after the enemy assault began, Chinese soldiers captured the hill, bayoneting and burp-gunning any Marine they could find. The regiment must have thought that the outpost had been lost to the enemy since friendly proximity fuse artillery shells began targeting the site, not knowing that some Marines remained alive and were desperately attempting to escape back to the MLR.[5]

The American Marine force on Outpost Frisco consisted of one Marine platoon of about fifty-four men; only eight Marines walked off that hill. Pfc. Herman Pizzi was one of them.

Pizzi vividly recalled that night engagement.

> That night is one I will never forget as I thought I would be killed or captured. I would never see my family, my future wife, and my friends. My platoon was assigned to relieve another outfit protecting Outpost Frisco. We jumped off at dusk and encountered no problems in "no man's land." Upon reaching the outpost, my squad leader, Bob Thornton, told me to relieve and protect an area to the left of the Command Post (CP) bunker. When we arrived I asked the other group if this was a hot area. Someone answered "no problem, keep your head down." Then all hell broke loose. We were bombarded with mortar and artillery shells. We dove for cover in the trench and were huddled four in a row. A round came in and killed the three other guys, and wounded me (concussion and broken ribs). All of a sudden I heard bugles blowing, screaming and hollering "death to the Marines." I looked up and the hill was inundated with Chinese. I thought these idiots came up under their own artillery. I told those in my group who were alive that I was going to look for a corpsman as two were shot up pretty bad. I crawled out and saw a bugler sitting on top of the CP bunker. I got off a few rounds, hopefully killing him. But it was a mistake;

I gave away my position and was charged by a couple of the enemy who I shot. More men came so I played dead and hid from them. Again I went from bunker to bunker and gave aid and encouragement to the wounded. I was spotted by a machine gunman, but thankfully he missed. I then went back to my men and one was bleeding badly and others were wounded. I carried one on my back and held up another who could walk. We got him into "no man's land" and were shot at and got caught in the open under an artillery attack. I was wounded slightly again but had the strength to carry and help the others back. During the close-in combat with enemy soldiers my weapon was destroyed and all I had on me was a sheath knife which I had to use twice.[6]

Pizzi served in Korea from February 1952 to March 1953. Wounded three times in combat (awarded three Purple Heart medals, a Bronze Star medal with a combat "V" for Valor, and a Letter of Commendation with a combat V), he saw action on Carson, Reno, Bunker Hill, Detroit, Frisco, and the Hook Outposts. On one occasion he came close to losing his life. Ordered out on patrol, he and three other Marines went to a hut to retrieve their gear. As he picked up his flak jacket, they heard the twang of a grenade handle spinning free. Someone had set a booby trap, removing the pin from the grenade and depressing the handle so that the grenade would detonate when he picked up the flak jacket. They all dove for cover, but took shrapnel. Fortunately, they all escaped with their lives.

Newark, New Jersey–born Pizzi returned to college following the end of his military service. He earned a Bachelor's degree from Seton Hall University. He presently lives in Roseland, New Jersey, with his wife of forty-seven years, Maureen McKenna Pizzi. They have five children and eleven grandchildren as of 2007.[7]

ENDNOTES

1. E. B. Potter, *Sea Power: A Naval History* (Annapolis, MD: Naval Institute Press, 1981), 363–69.
2. Lee Ballenger, *The Outpost War: US Marines in Korea*, Vol. 1 (Washington, DC: Potomac Books, 2000), xvii, xviii, 1–6.
3. Medal of Honor citation for Pfc. Jack William Kelso, USMC, http://www.homeofheroes. com/moh/citations_1950_kc/kelso_jack.html.
4. Silver Star citation, Pfc. Herman Pizzi, USMC, http://www.homeofheroes.com/valor2/SS/3_ Korea/citations/marines/a.html.
5. Ballenger, *The Outpost War*.
6. Herman Pizzi, personal correspondence with James E. Wise Jr., 29 August 2007.
7. Jay Conlan, "A Patriot's Story," *The Essex County* (NJ) *Advisor*, (Summer 2001), www. koreanwar-educator.org/memoirs/pizzi/index.htm.

Maj. Thomas M. Sellers, USMCR

Pilot, F-86 aircraft, 4th Fighter Interceptor Wing, Fifth Air Force

Yalu River, North Korea
20 July 1953

Major Thomas M. Sellers distinguished himself by gallantry in action against an armed enemy of the United Nations as Pilot of an F-86 aircraft, 4th Fighter Interceptor Wing, Fifth Air Force, on 20 July 1953. On that date Major Sellers and his wingman were on an armed reconnaissance mission deep in North Korea when they sighted eight MiG-15s at a low altitude preparing to attack a flight of friendly fighter-bombers. Although the nature of his mission did not require an attack on this numerically superior force, Major Sellers completely disregarded personal safety and immediately unleashed a furious assault on the enemy formation. In the desperate battle that ensued, Major Sellers demonstrated outstanding airmanship and intrepidity in destroying two of the enemy MiGs. Major Sellers continued to divert the enemy attack on the friendly fighter-bombers until his aircraft was struck by enemy gunfire. The skill, daring, and accuracy of his attack insured the successful accomplishment of a vital United Nations bombing effort, and accounted for two enemy aircraft destroyed. By his extraordinary valor in action and unselfish devotion to duty, Major Sellers reflected great credit upon himself, the Far East Air Forces and the United States Air Forces.[1]

Silver Star Citation

ON THE MORNING OF 20 JULY 1953 two pairs of USAF yellow-marked silver F-86 Sabre jets of the 336th Fighter Interceptor squadron, Fourth Fighter Interceptor Wing, lifted off from Kimpo airfield in South Korea headed toward North Korea on an airfield reconnaissance mission. As the swept-wing aircraft climbed to a cruising altitude above thirty thousand feet they slid into a "four-finger" formation. This is an attack formation— still used—developed effectively by the German Luftwaffe during World War II. It is called "four finger" because the formation resembles the fingers of a hand seen from above. Their mission was to count enemy MiGs at four airfields north of the Yalu River.[2]

Although UN aircraft were not supposed to cross the Yalu during air encounters, the policy of "Hot Pursuit" was raised by senior Air Force

Generals in the Far East. Frustrated at not being allowed to pursue MiGs as they escaped to home bases north of the Yalu, they requested clearance for UN fighters to pursue enemy aircraft across the river to determine the location of enemy bases and destroy their aircraft. When the matter reached the desk of the overall commander, Gen. Douglas MacArthur, he initially waffled on the issue but finally agreed and pressed the Joint Chiefs of Staff (JCS) for approval. Though the JCS, the State Department, and the president favored such action, then–Secretary of Defense George Marshall requested that then–Secretary of State Dean Acheson relate this intended action to other UN countries involved in the war. Several opposed such tactics. Since it was not clear if there was a miscommunication between the State and Defense Departments, a misunderstanding among foreign diplomats, or misinterpretation of the policy by Acheson, a "Hot Pursuit" policy was not adopted, and officially the United States forbade the crossing of Chinese and Soviet Union borders. In reality UN fighter pilots more or less ignored the official policy and engaged MiGs in what was called "MiG Alley" (a fifty- by ninety-mile area in the northwest corner of North Korea, bordered in the south by the city of Sinanju and in the north by the Yalu River). Following engagements, UN fighters often pursued MiGs into Manchuria. MiG Alley became the main battle zone for superiority of the air war in Korea.[3]

The four Sabres that flew north on 20 July were led by Texas-born Maj. Thomas M. Sellers, USMCR, who was on ninety days temporary additional duty (TAD) with the Air Force Fourth Fighter Interceptor Wing. He was a highly experienced fighter pilot, having flown one hundred combat missions in Korea while assigned to Marine Fighter Squadron 115, Marine Air Group 33, 1st Marine Air Wing; he flew F9F Panther jet fighters. Before he departed the squadron for TAD with the Air Force, his squadron threw him a "One Hundred Mission" party, during which his commanding officer and Marine air group commander praised him as one of the most outstanding flight leaders with whom they had the pleasure of serving. Sellers wrote home that he was stunned by the compliments given him and commented at the end of his letter, "Never again will I feel as humble and flattered as I did that night."[4] During his tour with VMF-115, Sellers was awarded two Distinguished Flying Crosses and six Air medals.

Sellers' drive to be the best was motivated by his desire to become a regular Marine. As a reserve officer there was no guarantee that he could remain on active duty and reach the twenty-year active service requirement to warrant a pension. He took every opportunity to advance toward his goal, which would mean security for his wife and two daughters. Although he had achieved success as a combat Panther pilot, he knew that his chances to become a regular Marine would be greatly enhanced if he could fly the Sabre, since the Navy and Marine corps were scheduled to receive FJ Fury aircraft, the Navy version of the Sabre. By getting combat experience in the F-86 he would have a leg up on other Navy and Marine Corps pilots. Also, he yearned to down a MiG. If he was ever to realize this goal, it would be while flying a Sabre.[5]

Sellers reported to the Fourth Fighter Interceptor Wing on 28 April 1953 and was assigned to the 336th Fighter-Interceptor Squadron at Kimpo Airfield (K-14) in South Korea. He was excited about his new duty and the men in his squadron, writing home enthusiastically, "[T]hese guys eat, sleep and drink flying, that is chasing MiGs; they never talk about anything else."[6] He was immediately enrolled in ground school to learn about the F-86 Sabre and squadron airborne tactics against MiGs. As he had since his first days in Korea he continued to write his wife at least twice a week to keep her informed of his daily activities and to express his love for his family. On 3 May he flew his first hop in the F-86 and was elated: "It is without a doubt the finest airplane I've ever flown!" His feelings never changed about the aircraft. After several more flights he wrote home, "I like it more and more each time I fly it. I just can't conceive that I travel and climb as fast as I do. At thirty thousand feet it will indicate an easy four hundred knots, that's about one hundred knots faster than the F9F."[7] He flew his first mission on 10 May without encountering any MiGs. Weather permitting, Sabres would conduct daily sweep flights along the south side of the Yalu River hoping the MiGs would rise from several adjacent airfields to do battle.

The airfield at Andong was the major Communist jet fighter base across the river. When the weather was favorable they would often take off in great numbers to attack the Sabres. The MiG performed in many respects as well as the F-86. The difference between the MiG and the Sabres was the dominant flying skill of the American pilots.[8] Often Chinese pilots would attempt evasive maneuvers to escape a Sabre attack, lose control of their aircraft and crash.[9] Numerous Russians flew into combat piloting MiGs with Chinese markings, wearing Chinese flight gear, and speaking Korean to ground controllers. However, it was not long before they resorted to their native language and took directions from their own ground controllers. Such radio talk was heard by American pilots and reported, but command-level and higher-up officials ignored the matter; such a revelation might spark a wider war.[10]

Two weeks later he flew north in perfect weather and overflew Andong and its surrounding fields. At forty thousand feet he could see a large segment of Manchuria. Although they sighted numerous MiGs on the fields, none left their revetments. Sellers continued to obsess about getting a MiG. He wrote his wife, "The experience I get here should go a long way towards getting me integrated into the regular Marine Corps. If I could be lucky enough to get a couple of MiGs—which I doubt will happen—then I would be permitted to join the Regulars . . . I honestly feel we would be better off in many ways if I do stay in the service . . . I'm trying to do what I think is best for us—for you and the children."[11]

Sellers was given his own plane. The Air Force allowed its pilots to name their aircraft, and within a short time the words "Semper Fi" appeared on his plane's fuselage. By the end of May, Sellers had chalked up fourteen missions but still had not fired his guns. The rainy season began and weather predictions indicated that the squadron would be lucky to get fifteen flying days in June. During the night hours, "Bedcheck Charlie," a Communist World War II biplane (Polikarpov Po-2) would harass the field, lobbing bombs at low altitudes. Not much damage was done but pilots lost much needed sleep during these nightly raids.

Boredom and loneliness were constant companions and the arrival of the mail plane became a major event. Beginning in June Sellers began to count the days until he would be relieved and return home. He estimated that as of 9 June he'd have just thirty-nine more shooting days because of weather conditions. Pilots around him were downing MiGs during their missions but he always seemed to be in the wrong place at the wrong time.

On 30 June Sellers flew three missions and finally engaged MiGs as he was leading his group up the Yalu River near Andong. His wingman, 2nd Lt. Albert B. Dickey, USAF, suddenly called, "Hard right turn!" As they turned there were four MiGs diving on them from fifty thousand feet. The MiGs broke their dive and overshot the Sabres. Sellers called a reverse left. As they rolled out the MiGs were right in front of them cruising almost head on at a slight angle to their left but a little above them. It was the first time Sellers had seen MiGs up close and they were an impressive sight, painted a shade of dark green that glistened in the sunlight. Sellers fired at the number three aircraft but missed him, then he turned to number four. At a range of one thousand feet he fired at him; tracers appeared to hit his tail section. The Marine thought he finally had downed a MiG. Checking the gun camera film the next morning, they could see that Sellers had missed the MiG's tail by fifty feet. During the melee it looked like MiGs and Sabres filled the air as the combatants maneuvered and positioned themselves for attack. At one point Sellers caught sight of four more MiGs, all painted black. The number four MiG broke off and started a screaming dive for the field at Andong. Sellers flew after him but couldn't close the five thousand feet between them. Finally, at one thousand five hundred feet altitude and running low on fuel, Sellers broke off and returned to base.[12]

The following morning Sellers and his Sabres, hoping to pull a sneak attack, took off at first light and arrived at MiG Alley at 6:00 AM. They sighted four enemy airfields as they flew almost sixty miles north of the river. Hundreds of MiGs were seen on the ground but not one left its parking area. The Sabres caught a great deal of flak but at six hundred knots they were too elusive for the enemy guns.[13]

As peace talks dragged on there was more and more talk of going home and leaving what some called "this hell hole!" Still the Sabres continued their missions and new aces seemed to be made every shooting day, much to Sellers' frustration. By 14 July he had flown thirty-nine missions and was beginning to wish for home above all else. He planned on being detached on 30 July, spend two days at the K-3 Marine airfield near Pohang, and arrive in Japan on 1 August—homeward bound.[14]

But everything would change. On the flight north on 20 July Sellers and his flight reached the first airfield they were to survey, but because of weather they had to descend below a cloud layer at twenty thousand feet. They completed their reconnaissance of Dagushan Airfield which was located thirty miles west of the mouth of the Yalu River. The Chinese 4th Division was based at the field but poor weather probably kept them from responding to the overflight. Sellers led his Sabres east to a new airfield, Gaijiaba, which as yet was unknown to the Far East Air Force (FEAF). The new air facility was located between Dagushan and Dadonggou. The last airfield along the coastline was Langtuo, at Andong. At the time, a Soviet regiment, the Chinese 17th Division and a night-flying group from the 4th, were stationed at Dadonggou.

As the Sabres arrived over Gaijiaba they began to pick up very heavy flak. During their turning and evasion maneuvers to stay clear of the flak, Sellers and his wingman, 2nd Lt. Albert Dickey, lost their number three and number four pair of Sabres. Just about this time Sellers spotted MiGs taking off from Gaijiaba. Not knowing that he had lost his numbers three and four, Sellers called a "bounce" (attack) and he and Dickey went into a very steep dive and came in behind the MiGs. Sellers opened his speed brakes and slowed in order to keep his rate of closure down thereby giving him a longer shot at the slow-moving aircraft that had just taken off. Dickey was with him when he slid in behind the eighth MiG. It turned slightly to the right as Sellers was shooting at it. It began to burn and he immediately whipped to the left onto another one. The next one exploded in flames as it was hit by the initial firing of Sellers' guns. About that time Dickey spotted two MiGs diving on them from above. He immediately radioed Sellers to "Break left!" and Sellers responded, "Roger, take her left!" [15]

They were about a fourth of the way through the break when a MiG fired on them. At that instant a 37-mm shell hit Sellers' aircraft in the fuselage fuel tank behind the cockpit and exploded. During a later debriefing Dickey stated that it seemed as if the MiG pilot just fired his cannons and never aimed. Dickey went on to say that the plane blew up right in his face and he was positive that Sellers didn't have a chance to get out. When the plane exploded, the wings and fuselage broke apart. Dickey saw the debris of the aircraft hit the ground and he saw no parachute. This all occurred at one thousand feet, too low an altitude for a successful bailout. By this time Dickey was being swarmed by MiGs and eluded them successfully. As he did so he said he saw dark smoke (burning jet fuel pluming skyward) at three sites where Sellers' F-86 and the two MiGs had gone in. All three burning crash sites were on the Manchurian side of the Yalu. Following Sellers' crash a flight of four F-86 aircraft were dispatched immediately to search an area twenty-five kilometers north of Antung, the main Chinese airfield located a short distance from the north shore of the Yalu River. Why the Sabre search team was ordered to conduct their reconnaissance so far to the north is a mystery. Presently, no official documents have been found that ordered such a distant flight. After twenty minutes in the area, the aircraft departed, reporting negative results.[16] Major Sellers was officially listed as missing in action (MIA) on 20 July 1953 and declared killed in action (KIA) on 20 July 1954.[17]

On 4 December 1954 Col. Frank C. Croft, commanding officer of the Marine Corps Air Station, Cherry Point, North Carolina, presented posthumous awards of the Silver Star, and the Distinguished Flying Cross medals to Mrs. Thomas M. Sellers and one of her children, her daughter Sharon, for their late husband and father. Major Sellers had previously been awarded the Purple Heart medal on 24 September 1954.

Since 1953 and the loss of Major Sellers, his family has struggled with discrepancies regarding the shoot down. However, through personal correspondence to Mrs. Sellers by his wingman and visits by Marine Corps and Air Force pilots who were attached to the Fourth Fighter Interceptor Wing at the time, one thing became certain: Tom Sellers did not survive the crash of his aircraft.

It was not until many years later that one of his daughters, Sharon MacDonald, had the opportunity to examine some of her father's records and the letters from Dickey and Capt. Dean Pogreba, USAF (pilot of the third Sabre in the formation) that were in her mother's possession. Her father's sixty-some letters to her mother, which held significant insights into his Korean experiences and that were thought to have been lost during a move in 1970, surfaced in 1996 after Sharon's mother passed away. "I found the letters in the very last chest I was cleaning out. The chest was full of mothballs, and it was six months before the letters had aired out enough to read them." [18] With all of the above material, Sharon MacDonald, a historian by profession, began to search for the coordinates of her father's crash site. She knew that the coordinates in his Silver Star citation were incorrect since they placed his crash site in Korea: "You can stop worrying about our going across the fence into Manchuria—the 5th Air Force has put a stop to it threatening to court martial the next man to shoot down a MiG trying to land on his own field." Although this was an official order, it's hard to believe that it was adhered to, since from 11 July until the end of the war on 27 July, Sabre pilots shot down 34 MiGs. [19] On-scene pilot reports had her father and the two MiGs he shot down crashing north of the Yalu River in Manchuria. Another apparent discrepancy in the citation was the mention of protecting friendly fighter bombers. Correspondence received by her mother from Dickey and Marine Maj. Jack Bolt mentioned airfield reconnaissance as the only mission assigned to the Sellers flight. Sabres did fly numerous fighter escort missions during the war, but not on this particular occasion. Their specific mission was to count enemy aircraft at four airfields north of the Yalu. Also, Sharon MacDonald noticed another glaring discrepancy regarding the crash site listed in her father's Silver Star medal citation. Since all on-scene pilots who witnessed the engagement agreed that Major Sellers crashed north of the Yalu, the USAF identified the crash site as being in Korea. This change in the crash site location was no doubt made by senior military officials since an order had been promulgated that Sabres were not to cross the Yalu in pursuit of MiG aircraft. In her attempt to clarify these and other issues, she worked with Dr. Xiaoming Zhang, Air Force historian at Maxwell Air Force Base. Through correspondence with Dr. Xiaoming Zhang, Air Force historian at Maxwell Air Force Base, it is the authors' opinion that Major Sellers shot down two MiGs that were taking off from Gaijiaba and that, upon being attacked and downed by a MiG, his aircraft crashed near that airfield which was close to the mouth of the Yalu River. Other personnel who assisted Sharon MacDonald in her research were CWO2 Stephen I. Sewell, USA (Ret.), a former NSA employee who monitored enemy aircraft/ground controllers to prevent USAF and USN/ Marine Corps pilots from being shot down during the Vietnam War; A. Hammers, assistant head, USMC Casualty Section and his successor,

Hattie X. Johnson; and Chief Daniel M. Baughman of the Defense POW/ Missing Personnel Office (DPMO).

All of the above personnel and agencies were invaluable in providing Sharon MacDonald with detailed information regarding the battle environment along the Yalu River (especially MiG Alley) where USAF Sabres and enemy MiGs fought for air superiority. There are perhaps other official documents that might further clarify the details of the loss of her father. If so, they remain missing or unavailable because of classification. Still a DPMO 6 March 2007 letter holds promise that the crash site has been narrowed down and DPMO began discussing the case with the Chinese government in January or February 2007. Until such time as permission is received to survey the area of the suspected crash site, MacDonald will continue in her quest to resolve the many uncertainties regarding the truth about the loss of her father. Hopefully, the day will arrive when the crash site is found and Major Sellers' remains can be returned home to his family. Whether Major Seller's crash site will ever be found is uncertain at the time of this writing. There are many unanswered questions regarding the aerial engagement that occurred more than fifty years ago. Surviving witnesses have been difficult to locate. Official documents that might shed light on the matter have not surfaced, perhaps due to classification. In order for DPMO to survey suspected crash sites it will require the permission of the Chinese government. If the United States and China realize closer ties in the years to come, there is the possibility that a survey will be permitted and uncertainties can be resolved.

The authors are indebted to Sharon MacDonald for sharing the wealth of material she has gathered during her quest. She intends to continue, and the authors will keep her in mind as they research material on other projects related to the Korean War. They will especially be attentive to this subject as they review newly unclassified official Korean War documents at the U.S. National Archives in Rockville, Maryland.

ENDNOTES

1. Silver Star citation, Maj. Thomas M. Sellers, USMCR, Sharon MacDonald collection.
2. 2nd Lt. Albert B. Dickey, USAF, letter to Mrs. Thomas Sellers, 27 August 1953; Luftwaffe Fighter Tactics, http://freespace.virgin.net/john.dell/bf109/Bf109tactics.html; Maj. John F. Bolt, USMC, letter to Mrs. Thomas Sellers, 5 August 1953.
3. Kenneth P. Werrell, *Sabres over MiG Alley* (Annapolis, MD: Naval Institute Press, 2005), 126–33.
4. Major Sellers, letter to his wife, 14 April 1953. Major Sellers was awarded his first Distinguished Flying Cross (DFC) in January 1953 and a second DFC the following June during a visit to his former Marine squadron, VMF-115, at K-3 airfield near Pohang, Korea.

He received his first Air Medal award for 29 October 1952 to 5 December 1952, USMC; second award for 6 December 1952 to 12 January 1953, USMC; third award for 13 January 1953 to 17 February 1953, USMC; fourth award for 27 February 1953 to 21 March 1953, USMC; fifth award for period 22 March to 31 March 1953, USMC; sixth award for 2 April 1953 to 10 April 1953, USMC; seventh award for unknown period, Fifth Air Force; eighth award for 10 May 1953 to 12 June 1953, Fifth Air Force.t

5. Letter from Major Sellers, USMCR, to Commandant of the Marine Corps, dated 29 December 1952; letter from Major Sellers, USMCR, to Commandant of the Marine Corps, dated 18 July 1953; letters from Major Sellers to his wife, 27 March 1953, 3 April 1953, 5 April 1953, 9 April 1953.

6. Letter from Major Sellers to his wife, 29 April 1953.

7. Letters from Major Sellers to his wife, 30 April 1953, 4 May 1953.

8. Warren E. Thompson and David R. Mclaren, *MiG Alley: Sabres vs. MiGs over Korea* (North Branch MN: Specialty Press, 2002), 157–64.

9. Werrell, *SABRES over MiG ALLEY*, 140–41.

10. Soviet Pilots in 1950–53 Korean War, http://aeroweb.lucia.it/rap/RAFAQ/SovietAces.html.

11. Letter from Major Sellers to his wife, 13 May 1953.

12. Letter from Major Sellers to his wife, 1 July 1953.

13. Ibid.

14. Letter from Major Sellers to his wife, 14 July 1953.

15. 2nd Lt. Albert B. Dickey, USAF, letter to Mrs. Thomas Sellers, 27 August 1953.

16. Ibid. Major John F. Bolt, USMC, letter to Mrs. Thomas Sellers, 5 August 1953; Capt. Dean A. Pogreba, USAF, letter to Mrs. Thomas Sellers, 3 September 1953.

17. "USMC Casualty Report, Missing and Captured Personnel Unit: Change in status of Major Thomas Sellers, USMCR: from Missing in Action 20 July 1953 to Killed in Action 20 July 1954."

18. Sharon MacDonald, correspondence with James E. Wise Jr., 14 September 2007.

19. Letter from Major Sellers to his wife, 7 July 1953.

WORLD WAR II

Lt. Chester William Nimitz Jr., USN

Torpedo and Gunnery Officer, and Executive Officer, USS Sturgeon

USS *Sturgeon* (SS-187)
24 June 1939–15 January 1943

For conspicuous gallantry and intrepidity as Torpedo and Gunnery Officer and later as Executive Officer of the USS Sturgeon during action against enemy forces since the commencement of hostilities. Largely through Lieutenant Nimitz' capable efforts the Torpedo Armament of the Sturgeon functioned with above average performance. This, together with the skillful operation of the Torpedo Data Computer contributed greatly to the success in the many actions of the Sturgeon with the enemy, which resulted in the sinking or greatly damaging much enemy shipping. Further, during the Third War Patrol, the Sturgeon was ordered to conduct a reconnaissance and rescue of R. A. F. personnel from a small island off the entrance to Tjilatjap, Java, the waters thereto being under enemy control [he] conducted this with two men in a small submarine power boat . . . and definitely determined that the personnel were not there . . . at great risk to his own personal safety.[1]

Excerpt from Silver Star Citation

CHESTER WILLIAM NIMITZ JR. was born in Brooklyn, New York, on 17 February 1915, son of Fleet Admiral (Chester William) Nimitz, USN, and Mrs. (Catherine Vance) Nimitz. He attended Tabor Academy, San Diego (California) High School, and Severn Preparatory Academy, Severna Park, Maryland, before his appointment to the U.S. Naval Academy by President Herbert C. Hoover in 1932. He was graduated and commissioned ensign on 4 June 1936, and through subsequent promotions, attained the rank of captain, to date from 1 September 1954. On 1 August 1957 he was transferred to the retired list and advanced to rear admiral on the basis of combat citations.

After graduation in June 1936, he was assigned to the USS *Indianapolis* (CA-35), and served aboard that cruiser until December 1938. He was then ordered to the submarine base, New London, Connecticut. After completing instruction in submarines, he joined the USS *Sturgeon* (SS-187) in June 1939. He was serving as torpedo and gunnery officer of that submarine when the United States entered World War II on 8 December 1941; he later had duty as her executive officer. For outstanding service aboard the *Sturgeon*, he was awarded the Silver Star medal by his father, then Commander in Chief, Pacific Fleet, at Pearl Harbor, territory of Hawaii, in January 1943.[2] Nimitz was awarded two Silver Star medals while serving on the USS *Sturgeon*. He was awarded a third Silver Star while executive officer of the USS *Bluefish* (SS-222), 6/43 to 11/43, and as commanding officer of the USS *Haddo* (SS-255), 2/44 to 12/44, he was awarded the Navy Cross.

The *Sturgeon* stood out of Pearl Harbor on 10 November 1941, headed for the Philippine Islands, and arrived at Manila Bay on 22 November. She was then attached to SubRon 2, Submarine Division (SubDiv) 22, United States Asiatic Fleet. The *Sturgeon* was moored in Mariveles Bay on 7 December 1941 when the Japanese attacked Pearl Harbor. She put to sea the next afternoon to patrol an area between the Pescadores Islands and Formosa. Though Japanese convoys and individual enemy ships were sighted, the *Sturgeon's* torpedoes missed their mark. After surviving a fierce enemy depth charge attack, she returned to Mariveles Bay on 25 December.

The *Sturgeon* was at sea again on 28 December en route to the Tarakan area off the coast of Borneo. The early days of the patrol yielded no kills though once again enemy ships were sighted but escaped torpedo firing by the submarine. On 26 January the *Sturgeon* sighted a Japanese tanker southwest of Balikpapan and fired a spread from her forward tubes, resulting in a large explosion, after which the ship's screws stopped turning. However, no post-war record could be found of the ship's sinking, though the transport was believed to be heavily damaged. Finally, on 30 March she sank the 842-ton cargo ship *Choko Maru* while patrolling off Makassar City, Borneo. Four days later she sent a 750-ton enemy frigate to the bottom in the same waters. On 1 July 1942 while patrolling an area west of Manila, the *Sturgeon* sank the 7,267-ton transport *Montevideo Maru*. On 5 July she scored hits on a tanker in a convoy northbound from Manila. Her patrol ended on 22 July when she arrived at Fremantle, Australia, for refit.

On 4 September the *Sturgeon* and her veteran crew left port to begin her fifth war patrol in an area between Mono Island and the Shortland Islands in the Solomons group. On 11 July she began patrolling west of Bougainville Island, Papua New Guinea, to intercept enemy shipping between the islands of Rabaul, Buka, and Faisi, all in Papua New Guinea. At 5:36 AM on 1 October, the *Sturgeon* sighted the 8,033-ton aircraft ferry *Katsuragi Maru* off New Britain. The submarine bored in and so did the four torpedoes speeding toward the ship. Three of the torpedoes hit home. Under a smudge of smoke, the aircraft ferry went down. On a flying field somewhere a group of Japanese pilots were grounded for lack of planes.[3]

At the end of her sixth patrol on 4 January 1943, the *Sturgeon* went into the yard for a five-month overhaul. Lieutenant Nimitz was detached from the boat on 15 January, returned to the United States, and reported the following month to the Electric Boat Company, Groton, Connecticut, to assist in fitting out the USS *Bluefish* (SS-222). He joined that submarine when she was commissioned on 24 May 1943 and served as her executive officer, navigator, and assistant approach officer until 17 February 1944. He was awarded a Gold Star in lieu of his third Silver Star medal, "for distinguishing himself by conspicuous heroism and performance of duty during the first and second war patrols of the *Bluefish*."[4] During these two war patrols the boat sank 38,929 tons of enemy shipping while damaging 50,700 tons.[5]

Lieutenant Commander Nimitz assumed command of the USS *Haddo* (SS-255) on 17 February 1944. During the eight months he commanded the submarine, the *Haddo* sank five enemy vessels, which included the 1,540-ton destroyer *Katsuriki*. For heroic services, he was awarded the Navy Cross and a Letter of Commendation with Ribbon from the Commander in Chief, Pacific Fleet. He also received a facsimile of and ribbon for the Navy Unit Commendation awarded the *Haddo*.[6]

Following his departure from the *Haddo*, Commander Nimitz returned to the United States and served in various land-based commands. In 1950 after a month's instruction at the Fleet Sonar School, and with no former destroyer experience, he recommissioned and assumed command of the USS *O'Brien* (DD-725). "For conspicuous gallantry and intrepidity as Commanding Officer of the USS *O'Brien* during engagements between Naval light forces, particularly in the seizure of Wonson, Korea, on 17 July 1951 . . . he was awarded the Bronze Star medal with Combat 'V.'"[7]

Promoted to captain in September 1954, Nimitz assumed command of the USS *Orion* (AS-18), remaining in that command until relieved of all active duty pending his retirement on 1 August 1957. Upon his retirement Captain Nimitz was advanced to Rear Admiral on the basis of his combat citations. He made a second career in the high-tech field, becoming chief executive officer of Perkin-Elmer before retiring in 1980.[8] Admiral Nimitz passed away in Needham, Massachusetts, at the age of eighty-six in January 2002.[9]

ENDNOTES

1. Silver Star citation, Lt. Chester William Nimitz Jr., USN. From the Operational Archives, Naval History Center, Washington, DC.

2. Official Biography of Radm. Chester W. Nimitz Jr. (Operational Archives, Naval History Center, Washington, DC).

3. *Dictionary of American Naval Fighting Ships (DANFS)*, Vol. 6 (Washington, DC: U.S. Government Printing Office, 1969), 660–661; Theodore Roscoe, *United States Submarine Operations in World War II* (Annapolis, MD: Naval Institute Press, 1998).

4. Official Biography of Radm. Chester W. Nimitz Jr.

5. Ibid.

6. Samuel E. Morison, *History of the United States Naval Operations in World War II* (Boston: Little, Brown and Company, 1962), Vol. 3.

7. Official Biography of Radm. Chester W. Nimitz Jr.

8. Ibid.

9. Martin Weil, "Chester Nimitz Jr. Dies, Navy Officer, Executive," *Washington* (DC) *Post*, 7 January 2002.

Lt. Franklin Delano Roosevelt Jr.

USNR, USS Mayrant *(DD-402)*

Harbor of Palermo, Sicily
1 August 1943

For conspicuous gallantry and intrepidity in action while serving on aboard the USS *Mayrant* during a heavy enemy aerial attack on shipping in the harbor of Palermo, Sicily, on the night of 1 August 1943. When bomb fragments and flying shrapnel from exploding ammunition wounded two men on the bridge, partially amputating the leg of one of the men, Lieutenant Commander (then Lieutenant) Roosevelt unhesitatingly went to their assistance, disregarding his own danger in order to administer first aid. During the height of the attack, [he] carried the most critically injured of the men down the ladders from the bridge to the nearest battle station. His cool, courageous initiative in risking his life on behalf of a shipmate was in keeping with the highest traditions of the United States Naval Service.[1]

Silver Star Citation

FRANKLIN DELANO ROOSEVELT JR. was born on Campobello Island, New Brunswick, Canada, on 17 August 1914, son of President Franklin Delano Roosevelt and Mrs. Eleanor Roosevelt. He attended Groton (Connecticut) School, was graduated from Harvard University, Cambridge, Massachusetts (A. B., 1937), and the University of Virginia School of Law in Charlottesville (LLB, 1940). While at Harvard, he was a member of the Naval Reserve Officers' Training Corps Unit; upon graduation was commissioned ensign in the U.S. Naval Reserve, 11 June 1940. He subsequently was promoted to lieutenant (junior grade) on 2 June 1941; lieutenant on 15 June 1942; lieutenant commander on 15 April 1944; and commander on 5 November 1945. He was released to inactive duty on 12 September 1945.

Following his appointment as ensign in the Naval Reserve, he had a brief period of active training duty on board the destroyer USS *Lawrence* (DD-250) during August 1940. In late summer and early fall of 1940 he assisted his father's presidential campaign for re-election. Later that same year he worked as a junior clerk in a Wall Street law firm, and while there passed the New York Bar examination. Between January and March 1941 he was a member of the law firm of Wright, Gordon, Zachary, Parlin, and Cahill.[2]

Called to active Naval Service in April 1941 he joined the USS *Mayrant* (DD-402) and later assumed the duties of executive officer. At the time, the *Mayrant* was operating off Newfoundland escorting transatlantic convoys as far as Iceland. Although the United States was not yet at war, American shipping was being attacked by German U-boats roaming the Atlantic. After joining a convoy from Halifax to Capetown in late October, the ship received news on 8 December of the U.S. entry into the war. For the next several months the *Mayrant* protected convoys transporting British and Canadian troops to South Africa; engaged in North Atlantic convoy duty; and participated in operations in the Denmark Strait in search of the German battleship *Tirpitz*. She also escorted allied convoys on the "suicide run" to the Russian port of Murmansk.[3]

For the next two years, the *Mayrant* conducted antisubmarine duty in eastern Atlantic waters and the Caribbean; participated in Operation Torch and the Allied invasion of North Africa; cruised the North African coast while escorting convoys in the Mediterranean; and, on 14 July 1943, shifted her base of operations northward to Sicily.[4]

Operation Husky, the Allied invasion of Sicily, commenced on 9–10 July and ended on 17 August in an Allied victory. Although the Italian Navy never played a significant role in repulsing the invaders, Allied destroyers hovered near the northern port of Palermo just in case the Italian navy came out. American, British, and Canadian ground forces raced to defeat the Italian army as they retreated to Messina and the Italian mainland. Since Allied air cover was almost nonexistent (British Spitfire aircraft stationed on Malta to the south did not have the range to offer support in this regard), the combatants had to ward off numerous bomber attacks by the German Luftwaffe.[5]

On the morning of 26 July the *Mayrant* was attacked by three German Ju-88 bombers ten miles off the coast of Palermo. The ship was severely damaged and had to be towed into port by the minesweeper USS *Strive* (AM-117) with five dead and eighteen wounded. Less than a week later the Luftwaffe pounced on the city and harbor. Forty-eight German planes had evaded Allied radar and dropped sixty large bombs, which caused massive damage. The *Mayrant*, which was undergoing repairs at the time, was moored alongside the *Strive* that was supplying her with power and keeping her pumped out. Railway cars containing nine hundred tons of ammunition just fifty yards from the moored ships took a direct hit and exploded in a fiery blaze. Both ships endured flying shell fragments over a period of four hours.[6]

On the bridge of the *Mayrant*, Cox. Nuzio Cammarata was severely wounded, suffering the partial loss of one of his legs. Lieutenant Roosevelt immediately applied a tourniquet and carried Cammarata down the ship's ladders and across the bow to *Strive*, where a pharmacist's mate rendered first aid, which saved the Sailor's life. The air raids continued and the ships beat off enemy air attacks without Allied protective air cover. The ship's antiaircraft gunners became expert through abundant experience; in several encounters the Luftwaffe paid dearly in its loss of front-line bombers and experienced air crews.[7]

Detached from the *Mayrant* in January 1944, Roosevelt was ordered to the Submarine Chaser Training Center, Miami, Florida, from February to April of that year, after which he was in charge of fitting out the USS *Ulvert M. Moore* (DE-442). He commanded that destroyer escort from her commissioning on 18 July 1944 until 22 June 1945. He was awarded the Legion of Merit with Combat "V" and was cited as follows:

> For exceptionally meritorious conduct . . . as Commanding Officer of the USS *Ulvert M. Moore* in action against an enemy Japanese submarine in the convoy lanes west of Luzon, Philippine Islands, on 31 January 1945. Suggesting a procedure for tracking underwater craft, (he) quickly regained a lost contact with a hostile submarine and, in a skillful series of depth-charge attacks, succeeded in sinking the enemy craft as evidenced by the debris and oil rising to the surface of the water.[8]

On 30 June 1945 Commander Roosevelt was assigned to the Naval War College, Newport, Rhode Island, and was released from active duty on 12 September 1945. In addition to the Silver star Medal, the Legion of Merit medal with combat "V," and the Purple Heart medal (awarded in enemy action while on board the USS *Mayrant*), Commander Roosevelt was the recipient of the American Defense Service medal, the American Campaign medal, Asiatic-Pacific Campaign medal, European-African-Middle Eastern Campaign medal, and the World War II Victory medal.[9]

Following his release from the Navy, Roosevelt joined a prominent New York law firm. In May of 1949 he was elected a member of the Eighty-first Congress from the Twentieth New York District and was re-elected to the Eighty-second and Eighty-third Congresses. In 1958 he became president of the Roosevelt Automobile Company. In 1963 he was nominated by President Kennedy to be Under Secretary of Commerce; his nomination was approved by the Senate on 20 March 1963.

As his political career waned, Franklin Jr. became increasingly involved in business, importing foreign cars and working in the banking industry.

He also raised cattle on his farm in Dutchess County, New York. After his mother's death in 1962, he served as chairman of the executive committee of the Franklin and Eleanor Roosevelt Institute and as his mother's literary executor. He also worked on the development of the Roosevelt Campobello International Park. Franklin Delano Roosevelt Jr. passed away in 1988.[10]

ENDNOTES

1. Silver Star citation, Lt. Franklin Delano Roosevelt Jr., USNR, Operational Archives, Naval History Center, Washington, DC.
2. Official Biography of Cdr. Franklin D. Roosevelt Jr. (Operational Archives, Naval History Center, Washington, DC).
3. *Dictionary of American Naval Fighting Ships (DANFS)*, Vol. 6 (Washington, DC: U.S. Government Printing Office, 1969), 284.
4. Ibid.
5. Samuel E. Morison, *History of the United States Naval Operations in World War II,* Vol. 9 Part II (Boston: Little, Brown and Company, 1968).
6. Ibid.
7. Ibid.
8. Official Biography of Cdr. Franklin D. Roosevelt Jr., 1.
9. Ibid.
10. Franklin Delano Roosevelt Library, www.nps.gov/archive/elro/glossary/ roosevelt-franklin-jr.html.

Capt. John Hamilton, USMCR

United States Marine Corps Reserve

Mediterranean Theater of Operations
24 December 1943–2 January 1944

John Hamilton, Captain (as of February 1943), United States Marine Corps Reserve, for gallantry in action in the Mediterranean Theater of Operations from 24 December 1943 to 2 January 1944. Captain Hamilton displayed great courage in making hazardous sea voyages in enemy infested waters, and reconnaissances through enemy-held areas. His conduct reflected great credit upon himself and the United States Armed Forces.[1]

Excerpt of Silver Star Citation
Catherine Hayden Collection

Capt. John Hamilton, the nom de guerre of Hollywood actor Sterling Hayden, was the only Marine movie actor who was awarded the Silver Star during World War II. His war story is unique and relatively unknown to the public.

"Something is wrong," wrote the troubled Sterling Hayden in his autobiography.[2] The theme resonates uncomfortably throughout the work, permeating not only the author's periods of dejection but also his triumphs, in seafaring (his first and only lasting love, aside from his abiding bonds with his six children and his third wife, Catherine), acting, and the military. Hayden suffered from lifelong world-weariness: always the seeker, at peace only when on the docks or out at sea.

He first shipped out at the age of sixteen, but he had been ready to go for at least a year, since the day that he, his doting mother, and his stepfather landed in Boothbay Harbor, Maine. Out beyond the boats and the schooners, the sea sparkled endlessly, offering faraway horizons and ever-new possibilities. Hayden was drawn to the harbor as if by a glittering magnet, and rented a rowboat for fifty cents a day after they arrived, making his way out to three abandoned schooners. Clambering onboard, he lost himself in blissful, solitary exploration, imagining himself and his family living here.

Back in the rowboat, Hayden drifted to Tumbler Island, in the middle of the harbor, where he discovered a cottage for sale or rent. He managed to convince his parents that this tiny house, barely heated by a sheet metal stove, was where they needed to spend the winter of 1931–32. The price was right, a deal was struck, and Hayden began one of the happiest years of his childhood.

Hayden visited the local library every day, reading anything he could find about seafaring and ships; he befriended sailmakers and Sailors. His transportation was a small boat that he sailed around the harbor, waving at ships' crews. Friendly, leathered Sailors invited him aboard, where they regaled him with tales of afar. He soaked it all in. Someday, he knew, these would be his exploits.

George Woodruff Walters and Frances Simonson Walters' only child, Sterling Relyea Walter, got a comfortable, if slightly dull, start in a safe, quiet, suburban neighborhood. Each and every two-week summer vacation was spent at Lake Minnewaska in the Catskills. Mr. Walters' work in advertising ensured satisfactory and steady income for the family. Mrs. Walters kept house, tended to their son, and played her Steinway grand piano for hours at a time, to Hayden's delight.

Everything seemed headed for a predictable, if not exactly wild, future for the Walters. But then, after one of many times Hayden misbehaved, this time involving a slingshot and a neighbor's wife driving by in a car, George took his son over his knee in the basement. As Hayden screamed and his father gave full vent to his anger, he suddenly collapsed and never fully recovered. Three months later he died, leaving his son to mourn him for a long time.

Three years after her husband's death, Mrs. Walters married James Watson Hayden. James Hayden had some big deal in the air at the time, and they were all going to get rich and live a life of ease. But deal after deal fell through for Sterling Hayden's stepfather, and the family began a seemingly endless trek. Even though work was scarce at best after the 1929 market crash, Sterling Hayden's mother always managed to make a few dollars by selling cosmetics door to door. But her new husband remained jobless, always hoping his next deal would succeed.

Sent to the Friends School in Washington, D.C. (and hating it, as he did all schools, finally quitting for good after the tenth grade), Sterling Hayden had to leave, with the tuition bill unpaid. Finally his mother and stepfather decided to try their luck up north, where they landed in Boothbay Harbor. In 1932 at age sixteen Sterling Hayden was enrolled at the Wassookeag School in Dexter, Maine, enjoying the experience about as much as he had all his other academic environments. His tales of seafaring interested no one other than a few schoolmates, and his behavior earned him repeated warnings that he'd best shape up. The young Hayden, however, preferred to ship out and run away to Portland, Maine.

In Portland he made his way to the fishing pier and soon learned that there were no jobs for would-be Sailors. He returned to his family, now living in Boston. After unsuccessfully trying to find a city job he ended up searching for work on ships moored at the city docks. He finally was signed on as ship's boy on a large schooner, *Puritan*, which regularly sailed from New London, Connecticut, to San Pedro, California. He was paid ten dollars a month while aboard the ship.

Sterling Hayden worked aboard ships along the East Coast, in 1936 qualifying as first mate on board the schooner, *Yankee*, upon which he made his first round-the-world voyage. Later he worked as mastheadman and then navigator on board various sailing vessels. Hayden cut quite a dashing figure, with his Viking good looks, over six feet tall, sun-bleached hair, and strong. The press compared him to a "movie idol" and New England reporters began to take notice as the "Viking" brought ships in and out of ports. He and fellow Sailor (and artist) Lawrence O'Toole befriended one newspaperman who haunted the docks almost as much as they did, Associated Press reporter Tom Horgan. Hayden was given command of his first ship at the age of twenty-two. He was hired to sail the Ceylon brigantine *Florence C. Robinson* from Gloucester to Tahiti. The newspapers hailed the little ship's departure and her February arrival in Tahiti in 1939. Braving furious storms to get there, the crew of eleven men, including O'Toole, reveled for six months in paradise.

It was the end of 1939. In Europe the German military machine was on the march. In Massachusetts Tom Horgan and Larry O'Toole convinced Sterling Hayden to try Hollywood. Horgan promptly wrote to an agent he knew, and O'Toole accompanied him to New York, where he knew another agent. In the end Hayden signed with Paramount Studios at six hundred dollars a month. He and his mother (his stepfather had long since disappeared) moved to Hollywood.

Paramount immediately groomed Hayden for stardom. He was given acting lessons and was sent to a gym. He got the full treatment and hated it all. He was sent on publicity tours, which he found ridiculous. He even went to the White House, where the president and Mrs. Roosevelt hosted an event for thespians, including Lana Turner, Greer Garson, Gene Kelly, and Danny Kaye, who had contributed their efforts to the 1941 March of Dimes.

His first movie was *Virginia* (1941), in which he played opposite his future first wife, Madeleine Carroll, smitten with his leading lady from the start. Hayden struggled to develop his new acting skills through the summer of 1940. That same year he appeared in *Bahama Passage* (1941), again opposite Carroll, liking the movie industry less all the time.

Hayden wanted to do something real, something that mattered, something for which he could respect himself as a man. Seafaring was hard and so was war. Carroll talked all the time about getting involved in it. Finally, after honestly explaining his feelings as best he could, Sterling Hayden left Paramount on good terms.

In late November 1941 he contacted Col. William "Wild Bill" Donovan, Coordinator of Information (COI). COI, an intelligence-collecting and covert operations agency established by the president, later became the Office of Strategic Services, or OSS, itself the forerunner of the Central Intelligence Agency (CIA). Donovan arranged for Hayden to receive commando and parachute training in Glasgow, Scotland.

After a miserable convoy crossing, he reported to a London Office where no one had expected him or seemed to care that he was there. Nevertheless, after a few days they got him processed and off to Glasgow, where he trained. In March 1942 he jumped out of a Stirling bomber and parachuted into a quarry, where he broke his ankle, tore up his knee, and injured his backbone.

They fixed him up and sent him back to the States, where he married Madeleine Carroll in a lodge in New Hampshire. Like her husband, Carroll was cynical at best about Hollywood and the film industry. She gave up her movie career, joined the American Red Cross, and was sent to Europe.

Hayden wanted to join the Navy and requested a lieutenant's commission and command of a PT boat. Because he lacked even a high school diploma, the Navy countered with an ensign's ranking and no guarantee of a PT boat assignment. So on 26 October 1942, Sterling Hayden enlisted in the Marine Corps and was sent to Parris Island, South Carolina, for boot training.

This was not an easy experience for a movie star, even a reluctant one. It was especially rough for an independent, individualistic, freedom lover who felt at home only on the open seas. But he toughed it out, learned the ropes, and turned out to be a "hell of a good Marine," according to his drill instructor, Pvt. George S. Featherstone, who added, "life as a DI would be a pleasure if all were as good recruits."[3] One of two in his platoon selected for Officer Candidate School after boot training, Hayden spent three weeks as a drill instructor before he left.

Reporting to the Marine Corps School Command at Quantico, Virginia, he was assigned to the twenty-third Officer Candidates Class. Upon his completion, he was commissioned second lieutenant, USMCR, on 21 April 1943. Hayden was a good Marine on the surface, but he loathed the discipline and the fact that he was so easily recognized, which worked against him in the Corps. He and Carroll no longer wanted to be associated with Hollywood; Hayden wanted to be thought of as just another Marine. They went to court to have their last name changed to Hamilton. Hayden changed his first name, too, and by late June 1943 he was legally John Hamilton.

Even so, he felt the by-now familiar urge to get out of the situation he was in, only this time he was wearing a uniform. He'd been working on the problem since before his commissioning, though, and had again reached Colonel Donovan, in charge of the OSS in Washington. John Hamilton asked to be considered for the secret service. Accordingly, when his class members received their orders, most were sent to the Pacific, but Hayden and two others went to the OSS.

Reporting to Temporary Building Q near the Lincoln Memorial, where the OSS was headquartered, Hayden found himself surrounded by a hodge-podge of businessmen, enlisted men, and junior officers from all services. It was the summer of 1943, and the agency was just getting its confused start. Assignments and plans were developed in secrecy from anyone else, but they all had one goal in common: to torment the enemy in every way possible. Eventually, Hayden was ordered to Cairo, Egypt. He was greeted there by a colonel who had no idea that his unit was about to add a new agent, nor what he was supposed to do with him. After several months, the colonel ordered him to Bari, Italy, to lend support to the head of the Yugoslav partisan fighters, Marshal Tito. Tito led a Communist band that was proving to be quite successful in sabotaging German efforts in their occupied country. Hayden's assignment was to set up a partisan base of operations at the port city of Monopoli, south of Bari.

He took command of some four hundred Yugoslav partisans, fifty of them female, and fourteen schooners, six ketches, and two brigantines. Their mission: to transport supplies across the Adriatic Sea to Tito's guerrillas. After running the German blockade out of Italy, they unloaded the supplies, hastily and under cover of darkness, on Vis, a partisan-held island off Dalmatia. Fishing boats then made their treacherous way to the mainland, unloading between Nazi-held beaches. From there, burro trains transported the supplies up into the mountains to the partisans.

Hayden crossed the Adriatic numerous times dropping off arms, ammunition, and agents to partisans in Yugoslavia and Albania. Known as a hard-driving, experienced seafarer, he became popular with the Serbian communist partisans who sailed with him on dangerous night missions. On his return trips he would bring back rescued American airmen and Italian soldiers. In 1944 Hayden and two others parachuted behind enemy lines in Yugoslavia and led several Allied airmen to safety in Italy.

Hayden was entranced by these fierce Yugoslav partisans. He had been intrigued by Communism before, having heard noises about it in Hollywood and along the waterfront in Oakland, California. Now, watching these partisan guerillas, fighters who were tougher and more disciplined than anyone he had ever known, he felt inspired, and wrote long letters to his friends back home about them. It was this experience that played an important role in his later decision to join the American Communist Party.

A much-respected commanding officer, Hayden was awarded the Silver Star for his service during the Balkan tour. His Silver Star medal is presently on display at the CIA museum in Langley, Virginia. His other decorations included the World War II Victory medal; the European-African-Middle Eastern Campaign medal with two bronze stars and a bronze arrowhead (bronze star for participation in the Naples-Foggia campaign, bronze star for action against the enemy in the Balkan countries, bronze arrowhead for parachuting into enemy-held territory); a Letter of Commendation; and the Yugoslav Government Order of Merit medal. These awards were given by the OSS, shrouded at the time in secrecy.

After completing his duties in the Balkans and enjoying thirty days' leave in the States, Hayden flew back to Europe to join an OSS group in Germany. Landing first in Paris, he was ordered instead to the First Army in Belgium, which had just fought the Battle of the Bulge. There, assisted by six technical sergeants who were fluent in German, he followed the troops' advance from Cologne to Marburg in a mostly fruitless search for authentic anti-Nazis. He spent the summer of 1945 making bomb-damage assessments of ports in Germany, Norway, and Denmark.

In September he visited his wife in Paris where the Hamiltons mutually and amicably agreed that they no longer had a relationship. They were divorced in Reno later that year. Hayden was discharged from active duty on 24 December 1945 and remained in the reserves until 1948.

Hayden returned to Hollywood and made a number of movies. Still fascinated by the exploits of his partisan friends from the war, he drifted into the Communist crowd in the film industry and joined the American Communist Party. Within six months he had become disillusioned with the dogmatic, all-knowing atmosphere and canceled his membership. It would come back to haunt him, in the form of the ignominious House Un-American Activities Committee (HUAC). In April 1951 Hayden fully cooperated with the HUAC, including naming names. He immediately and permanently regretted doing so, and joined the effort to abolish the HUAC. After a brief and humiliating hiatus he went on to make many more films. Despite his screen successes, he abhorred the shallowness and glitz of Hollywood and he had mixed feelings, at best, about his acting profession. His second marriage to Betty Ann De Noon ended in divorce after eight rocky years. Sterling Hayden married Catherine Denise McConnell in 1960 and added two more children to the four he fathered while married to De Noon. In 1986 he died at the age of seventy and Catherine, the children, and close friends scattered his ashes off Point Sausalito, over the San Francisco Bay.[4]

ENDNOTES

1. Capt. John Hamilton, USMCR, Official file, Marine Corps Museums and Historical Division, Quantico, VA.
2. Sterling Hayden, *Wanderer* (London: Longmans, Green, 1964).
3. U.S. Marine Corps Division of Public Relations release, 2 December 1942.
4. James E. Wise Jr. and Anne Collier Rehill, *Stars in the Corps,* (Annapolis, MD.: Naval Institute Press, 1999).

Pfc. Guy L. Gabaldon, USMCR

Japanese Interpreter with Headquarters and Service Company,
2nd Marines, 2nd Marine Division

Saipan and Tinian, Marianas Islands
15 June–1 August 1944

For conspicuous gallantry and intrepidity while serving as a Japanese Interpreter with Headquarters and Service Company, 2nd Marines, 2nd Marine Division, during action against enemy Japanese forces on Saipan and Tinian, Marianas Islands, from 15 June to 1 August 1944. Attempting to capture both civilian and military personnel throughout the entire campaign, Private First Class Gabaldon entered enemy positions in caves, pillboxes, buildings and jungle brush and, in the face of direct enemy fire, obtained vital military information and aided in the capture of over one thousand enemy civilians and military personnel. Working alone in front of the lines, he contributed materially to the success of the campaign and, through his efforts, a definite humane treatment of civilian prisoners was insured. His courage and devotion to duty reflect the highest credit upon Private First Class Gabaldon and the United States Naval Service.[1]

Silver Star Citation

Without Saipan and Tinian we couldn't have bombed Japan, the most important factor in getting them to surrender. I guess I was the only Marine on the island who knew the Japanese people. They didn't want to die any more than an American Marine. So my approach was simple. I spoke Japanese, so I went into caves and gave them a long spiel, assuring them they'd be well treated, with food and medical care. Looking back at this now, I laugh about the experience, but I guess that I was in the right place at the right time.[2]

HAVING LIVED WITH A Japanese-American family, Pfc. Guy L. Gabaldon had been befriended by a young Japanese man, George Une, whom he looked upon as a brother. He was torn by the predicament he found himself in. Though during the initial invasion of Saipan he had personally taken out an enemy pillbox that was raining fierce machine-gun fire on his fellow Marines, he later decided to go off into enemy territory and fight the war as he saw it.[3]

Officially attached to the 2nd Marine Division Intelligence, he'd always worked alone and at night. Wearing a baseball cap and dungarees, he would sneak behind enemy lines and search out caves, buildings, or bunkers where enemy soldiers and civilians were hidden and try to entice them to surrender rather than killing them. However, he carried a carbine rifle, a pistol, and ammunition, ready to take lethal action if his plan did not work. Once near a suspected enemy hideout he would yell out that he had a bunch of Marines with him and they were ready to kill them if they did not surrender, all the while promising them that they would be treated with dignity, and that he would make sure that they were taken back to Japan after the war.[4]

At first, Gabaldon captured small groups of enemy troops; however, on a single day in July 1944 he persuaded some eight hundred Japanese soldiers to surrender and follow him back to American lines, earning him the nickname of the "Pied Piper of Saipan."[5] The Silver Star medal originally awarded to Gabaldon for his heroism during World War II was upgraded to a Navy Cross in December 1960. The official Marine Corps news release of the event related how he single-handedly captured well over one thousand enemy troops and civilians. His commanding officer Col. John Schwabe, then an Oregon lawyer, believed that the total exceeded two thousand. Many were never recorded, because regimental facilities could not handle Gabaldon's "army" of POWs.[6]

Born to Pedro and Amada Gabaldon, formerly of New Mexico, on 26 March 1926, Gabaldon became homeless at an early age when his father died suddenly and his mother was confined to a hospital because of health problems. Guy continued to live alone in his family's dilapidated frame house on the east side of Los Angeles. With the country going through the Great Depression of the 1930s Gabaldon survived by stealing food which frequently got him into trouble with the law. Though only five feet four inches in height, he was a tough kid who gave no quarter when fighting others who crossed him. He eventually found a home with a Japanese-American family and became fluent in the Japanese language.[7] Gabaldon enlisted in the Marine Corps Reserve at Los Angeles, California, on 24 March 1943. He was called to active duty on 15 June 1943, at the Recruit Depot, Marine Corps Base, San Diego, California.[8]

Following his enlistment in the Marine Corps at the age of seventeen and his assignment of active duty, the young Marine received his recruit training with the 1st Recruit Battalion, Recruit Depot, San Diego. He joined the school's Battalion, Camp Elliott, in August 1943; that November he was assigned to the Infantry Battalion. He qualified as a mortar crew member, Japanese interpreter, and scout observer during his enlistment.

On 23 December, then-Private Gabaldon, as a member of the 38th Replacement Battalion, embarked and sailed from San Francisco aboard the SS *Young America*, arriving at Pearl Harbor on 30 December 1943. The following month he joined the 2nd Marine Regiment, 2nd Marine Division, Fleet Marine Force; later that month he was promoted to private first class. Following amphibious training at Maui, Hawaii, Gabaldon sailed from Honolulu for Saipan, Mariana Islands.[9]

In carrying out his one-man missions during the Saipan campaign, Gabaldon worked the island from one side to the other, with units of the 2nd, 6th, and 8th Marines and his own division; with the 23rd and 25th Marines of the Fourth Division, even with units of the Army's 27th Infantry Division. Gabaldon breached enemy lines again and again, each time returning with captured enemy soldiers and civilians.[10]

Later, while on a training patrol with the Division's Scout-Observer Section in a Japanese bivouac area, Gabaldon was wounded by machine-gun fire and evacuated to an Army Field Hospital on 25 January 1945. He was awarded the Purple Heart for wounds received in this action. In March 1945 he was evacuated to the United States for further hospitalization at the U.S. Naval Hospital, Santa Margarita Ranch, Oceanside, California. After serving as a Japanese language instructor at the Marine Training Command, Camp Lejeune, North Carolina, Private First Class Gabaldon was honorably discharged from the Marine Corps on 10 November 1945.[11]

Following the end of the war Gabaldon returned to Los Angeles and became involved in various business enterprises, including a furniture store, a fishing operation, and an import-export firm. In June 1957 he appeared as an honored guest on the NBC television show, "This is Your Life." The 1960 movie *Hell to Eternity* told the story of his wartime exploits on the island. Actor Richard Eyer portrayed him as a youngster, and Jeffery Hunter played him as a Marine. That same year his Silver Star was elevated to a Navy Cross, after Gabaldon requested a review by the Board for Correction of Naval Records in Washington, DC. In 1980 he took up residence in Saipan after thirty-five years away, partly because of his interest in seafood export possibilities in the islands. A few years later the House of Representatives of the Northern Marianas designated him an "Honorary Citizen of Saipan."[12] The Pied Piper of Saipan passed away on 4 September 2006 in Old Town, Florida. He was eighty.[13]

ENDNOTES

1. Silver Star citation, Pfc. Guy L. Gabaldon, USMCR, U.S. Marine Corps Museums and History Division, Quantico Marine Corps Base, Quantico, VA.

2. Guy Anselmo Jr., "The Pied Piper of Saipan," *Leatherneck* 66, no. 6 (June 1983), 22.

3. Edward S. Aarons, *Hell to Eternity* (Greenwich, CT: Fawcett Publications, Inc. 1960), 27–30, 57–59.

4. Anselmo Jr., "The Pied Piper of Saipan," 22–23.

5. Ibid.

6. Ibid.

7. Aarons, *Hell to Eternity*, 26–32.

8. Official Biography of Pfc. Guy L. Gabaldon, USMCR, U.S. Marine Corps Museums and History Division, Quantico Marine Corps Base, Quantico, VA, August 1960.

9. Ibid.

10. Aarons, *Hell to Eternity*, 22.

11. Official biography; "Guy Gabaldon Decoration Elevated to Navy Cross," DoD News Release, 20 December 1960.

12. Matt Sedensky, "WWII Hero Dies," http://ksquest.blogspot.com/2006/09/guy-gabaldon-diminutive-world-war-ii.html.

13. Richard Goldstein, "Guy Gabaldon, 80, Hero of Battle of Saipan, Dies," *New York Times,* 4 September 2006.

Lt. Paul Richard Beauchamp, USNR

U.S. Navy Fighter Squadron 19 (VF-19)

The Lake of the Sun and the Moon, Formosa
12 October 1944

For distinguishing himself conspicuously by gallantry and intrepidity in action while participating in aerial flights against enemy forces in September and October 1944. On 12 October 1944 he led a photographic mission, in conjunction with a strike on an important target on the island of Formosa. He searched out and photographed the target in the mountains although the weather conditions made the mission hazardous. When his division was attacked by a superior number of enemy fighters, he assisted in destroying one enemy plane and led his division in driving off the remaining enemy aircraft without failing to complete his mission. Upon return to his carrier, he was immediately launched and aided a strike group in locating and attacking an important power plant and installations. Again on 13 October 1944, he accompanied a strike to the area where he located the target for our bombers by diving his plane through intense antiaircraft fire ahead of them. He then proceeded to photograph airfields and installations at a very low altitude, necessitated by low clouds. In spite of intense antiaircraft fire which continually shook his plane, he obtained valuable photographs. His leadership, courage, and skill were at all times inspiring and in keeping with the highest traditions of the United States Naval Service.[1]

Silver Star Citation

ON 5 NOVEMBER 2007 the authors made a presentation at the Dole Institute of Politics at the University of Kansas (KU) in Lawrence, Kansas. The subject of the presentation was "Military Heroism," which focused mainly on Navy and Marine Corps personnel in Iraq and Afghanistan who had been recipients of the Navy Cross medal. The stories related were taken from a book they had recently coauthored, *The Navy Cross: Extraordinary Heroism in Iraq, Afghanistan, and Other Conflicts.*[2]

Since I had been an NROTC instructor at KU back in the early 1960s, the affair presented a rare opportunity to reunite with many friends we had made during our NROTC assignment. Prior to making the presentation, the Institute held a private dinner for us which included Institute officials and several old friends. Sitting across from me was Paul Beauchamp, a World War II naval aviator, who had been a close friend in promoting the U.S. Navy at KU and in the surrounding community. I noticed during dinner that he Beauchamp wore a Silver Star medal lapel pin on his jacket, and asked him about it. I found his wartime experience to be fascinating and he kindly forwarded me an account of his gallant action while serving aboard the aircraft carrier *Lexington* in October 1944 in the waters off Formosa in the Pacific theater. What follows is his personal recollection of his missions against "Jitsugetsutan" (The Lake of the Sun and the Moon), the main power source for the entire island.

Our briefing by Air Intelligence concerning the coming strike on Formosa (now Taiwan) was not one calculated to ease tension. It seems that the island, some two hundred miles north to south and fifty miles east to west at its widest point, was inhabited by a variety of dangerous obstacles to a successful operation. According to experts, every known species of poisonous reptile was on the island. Most of the crustaceous life in the surrounding seas was also of the poisonous kind. The barren mountains which covered the eastern half of the island ran the length of Formosa and reached a height of seventeen thousand feet. Somewhere in the depths of these bleak, rocky peaks lived tribes of aboriginal headhunters.

At the time, mid-October 1944, the Japanese controlled the island, and Air Intelligence suspected that there were as many as 2,500 planes of the Imperial Japanese Air Force stationed there. It was highly recommended that if at all possible one should try to reach a designated point at sea rather than putting a disabled plane down on the island itself, a rescue submarine being preferable to anything the island had to offer.

I was leader of a division of F6F-5 Grumman Hellcat fighters consisting of four planes. We were the fighter-photographic unit of Fighter Squadron Nineteen (VF-19). My plane and the plane of my section leader were equipped with cameras. This was an innovation in the history of naval aviation.

The army had been experimenting with cameras installed in a modified twin-engine P-38 Lightning fighter. All armament and armor plating had been removed from the fighter plane increasing its maneuverability and maximum airspeed. I was thankful the Navy had seen fit to leave the F6F Hellcat with all of its original armament and added the camera paraphernalia within the body of the aircraft just aft of the pilot's seat. The only effect this three [hundred] to four hundred pounds of equipment had as far as I could see was in the take-off from the carrier and this was easily compensated for if one were an experienced pilot.

My assignment for the strike on Formosa was to find and photograph the main power source of the entire island. This consisted of two power plants located in the foothills of the mountains on the eastern slopes at some three thousand feet of altitude. The western half of the island was flat and completely cultivated with rice and tea fields starting at the coast and reaching far up into the mountains. From the air it seemed as though every square inch of land was taken advantage of. The two power plants were supplied water power by a man-made lake which the Japanese called "Jitsugetsutan," meaning, we were told, "the lake of the sun and the moon." Even though man-made, it was felt that the tremendous earthen dam would be impervious to torpedoes and thus the need for accurate photographs to determine the best method of putting the plants out of action permanently. So my mission was to find the lake and obtain photographs. To help make the operation a success, another division of fighter planes was assigned as protective cover during photographic runs.

The 12th of October 1944 began as every day in enemy waters did. The horrendous blaring sound of "General Quarters" was broadcast throughout the ship just prior to the first signs of dawn—the time most dangerous for the fleet in terms of possible air and submarine attack. The first sound of the Klaxon brought my roommate, Lt. Barney Garbow, and myself to our feet and in less than sixty seconds, we had slipped into socks, shoes, and flight suits and were on our way to the fighter pilot's ready room. Within a matter of minutes, all watertight hatches throughout the ship were made secure and heaven help the poor soul trapped in a water tight compartment for the duration of General Quarters which could last for hours. The penalty for not being at your assigned post during a General Quarters alert was quite severe—but opening a watertight hatch during General Quarters was a court martial offense—and so one sped with all due haste to whatever position assigned to each of the 3,500 men aboard this incredible floating city, the USS *Lexington* (CV-16).

The ready room at this hour had an eerie quality since all lighting in this pre-dawn situation was produced by red bulbs. Should there be an emergency scramble, the eyes of the pilots would be conditioned to the blackness of a pre-dawn take-off by the red lighted interior of the ready room. The next half-hour was devoted to obtaining weather information which was projected on a screen in the manner of a teletype machine. This information, in addition to code letters for the day, were copied on a navigation chart which was stowed under the instrument panel of the Hellcat. Other information pertinent to the day's strike also came down from the control center located high in the island amid-ship on the *Lexington*, the flag ship of Task Force 58. This formidable force of U.S. Navy fighting ships under the command of Admiral Marc A. Mitscher consisted of two carriers of the Essex class (designated CV), four light carriers (designated CVL), four battleships, several heavy and light cruisers, and many, many destroyers and destroyer escorts. We were able to field a strike force of six hundred planes consisting of fighters, torpedo planes, and dive bombers. My specific instructions were to remain with the main strike force that day until we crossed the southern tip of the island. At that time my group of eight Hellcats was to proceed to Lake Jitsugetsutan—photograph the power plants and surrounding terrain and then return directly to the fleet.

The command, "Pilots, man your planes," flashed across the screen, and within seconds the ready room was vacated. Within a few minutes pilots had located their aircraft (Lt. Hutto and I were the only two who always flew the same planes because of the camera installations). Take-off proceeded without mishap; the first twenty or thirty planes were catapulted off the carrier and the remainder made deck launches. (I doubt that any Air Force pilot would have considered a five hundred–foot take-off normal, but to us it was an everyday procedure.)

The fleet was located approximately two hundred miles due east of Formosa and the flight to the island was uneventful. Upon reaching landfall, I signaled my group to follow me and we departed the main strike force. I had plotted my course carefully and since cloud cover soon made observation impossible, I had to depend on my calculations of direction and airspeed to determine the approximate location of the lake.

We were approaching the area of the target with complete cloud cover at approximately five thousand feet. The mountains of this part of Formosa rose to nearly fifteen thousand feet and it was a

beautiful sight to see the peaks rising through the clouds. I did
not fully appreciate the beauty since my task of locating and photographing seemed at best improbable. It was at this point that
a voice in my headset said, "Bogeys, one o'clock high." I believe
that this was my first sighting of the new Japanese fighter which
the U.S. Navy designated *Oscar*. This plane was reputed to be
faster and more maneuverable than the old faithful *Zero*. The two
divisions of Hellcats immediately assumed a fighter plane tactical
position known throughout the Naval Air Corps as the "Thach
Weave." This maneuver which was beautifully simple and yet
complex, enabled the really skilled Navy pilots flying slower but
infinitely tougher planes, to achieve an incredible kill ratio over
faster but more flimsy Japanese aircraft. In the ensuing dog-fight I
had managed a position on the tail of an enemy aircraft just skim-
ming the cloud cover at five thousand feet. I had fired two short
bursts from my six .50-caliber machine guns when much to my
surprise he rolled over on his back and disappeared into the clouds
heading straight down to earth. I knew that in my craft such a
maneuver would require a minimum loss of one thousand feet in
altitude and I believed then and now that his chances of crashing
into the mountains covered by clouds were about 90 percent.

After the disappearance of my adversary I saw that all enemy
aircraft had vanished. Later I learned that two were definitely
destroyed and the remainder, like the one I pursued, took refuge in
the dangerously low cloud cover. With enemy activity dispelled, I
proceeded with the task of finding and photographing the power
plants. I suspected that the enemy aircraft were assigned to protect
the installation since according to my navigation we were over the
target when we were attacked. The cloud cover was complete but
I decided to make several photo sweeps over the area hoping the
cameras would spot something. After completing my photo runs
we climbed to twenty thousand feet and headed back to the fleet.
Landing proceeded without incident. I waited impatiently for
notification that the film had been developed and delivered to the
air intelligence room. The director of air intelligence aboard the
Lexington was a bright lieutenant by the name of Byron "Whizzer"
White (former Yale all-American football player, Rhodes Scholar,
and future U.S. Supreme Court Justice).

The air intelligence room was large and rather bare so we could
spread the hundreds of 8x10 photos in overlapping strips on the

deck. Each was numbered in the sequence taken; having shot them only a few hours previously I could normally lay them out from memory. However, on this occasion every photograph was almost identical, except one. And there by a miracle through a small hole in the cloud cover were visible five large metal tubes running down the mountainside to a barely visible power plant. The information was given to Admiral Mitscher and a strike on the installation was set for the next morning.

The morning of 13 October began as usual with General Quarters and within an hour our strike force of approximately two hundred planes headed for the Lake of the Sun and the Moon, "Jitsugetsutan." Because the slower and heavily loaded bomber planes would expend too much fuel and time climbing to altitude to cross the mountains and reach the target in a direct line from the carrier, our flight would take us to the southern tip of the island circumventing the mountains. To this day I don't know the name of the air group coordinator who was designated to lead this potent strike force. I only know that he was incompetent. Reaching the southern tip of the island we turned north and proceeded toward our target, two hundred strong. Suddenly at least fifty miles from our destination the strike leader gave the signal to attack and wave after wave of bombers unloaded their five hundred and one thousand pound bombs on a small farm pond. I watched in dismay and utter shock as the attack proceeded. When it became time for my division to attack I signaled them to keep joined on me and departed the fiasco. Our four Hellcats headed north climbing to ten thousand feet for more maneuverability in case of attack. The weather was absolutely beautiful with not a cloud in the sight, crystal clear.

As we approached the target area the Lake of the Sun and the Moon shown like a jewel in the morning sun and the two power plants were visible in every detail. The larger plant was supplied by five tremendous pipes coming from the base of the dam and running at least one thousand feet down the mountain to the plant. The smaller plant was fed by two pipes. As we approached, bursts of antiaircraft shells began appearing, but no sign of enemy aircraft. Because of the ideal conditions it took only a few minutes to photograph the installation and visually determine the best approach for bombing runs. The antiaircraft gunners were not very good, for which we were all grateful. When making photographic runs it is imperative to maintain a constant heading, airspeed, and altitude making us an ideal target for a competent antiaircraft gunner. Although the runs took less than five minutes it always seemed like hours and we were greatly relieved when we completed our sweeps and evasive action could begin.

Once again we headed back to the fleet and arrived in time to join the landing operation of the abortive strike. Immediately after being taken aboard it was standard procedure for every pilot to report to air intelligence and give an oral report of his version of the strike. I was very upset by the stupid waste of bombs (I have always wondered what that poor farmer must have thought when the heavens fell in on him that beautiful October morning). At the conclusion of my report I was directed to report to Commander Hugh Winters, the skipper of VF-19 and I told him what had happened.

Forty years after the event at an Air Group 19 reunion, Hugh Winters told me that after my report reached Admiral Mitscher, he called a meeting of his staff which included Commander Jim Flatley and Commander Winters who was also air group commander.

Jim Flatley was already a legend to young naval aviators because of his feats in 1942 and 1943. Along with Jim Thach he had helped develop . . . the "Thach Weave." Mitscher read them my report and then asked for opinions of whether the strike should be repeated since we had to leave the area the following afternoon. Hugh told me that he told Mitscher that it would be a waste of time and bombs if they couldn't find the power plants. Commander Flatley spoke up saying Beauchamp had found it twice—why not let him lead the strike! Unless you had been in the Navy, one can't imagine what an outrageous suggestion that was. The idea that a major strike be led by a young naval reserve officer who had only reached the rank of lieutenant senior grade two months prior to this time would have brought howls of disapproval from Naval Academy men throughout the Navy. But Commander Flatley was very serious and after brief thought Admiral Mitscher directed Commander Winters to bring me to the bridge.

I had seen him from a distance, of course. Even on a ship as large as the *Lexington* anonymity was difficult to achieve. The main control room of the ship is located forward on the topmost part of the superstructure known as the island. In take-off position one could see the familiar baseball cap that he loved to wear as he carefully followed everything going on below his lofty perch. And now here I was in that lofty perch confronting the legend himself. Once again I recounted my story of the strike. After finishing I waited for his reaction. He thought for a moment and then asked if I would lead another strike group which would take off in twenty minutes. Of course I agreed with a show of enthusiasm which truly was not simulated.

Shortly thereafter another strike force of two hundred planes was heading for the southern tip of Formosa, and this time I was the leader. Reaching the island I took a now familiar heading to the target. As we passed over the poor farmer's bombed pond I signaled to my wingman, Commander Winters, who smiled and shook his head in disbelief.

As we approached the target it was evident that the crystal clear condition of the morning was rapidly changing to a broken cloud condition and that optimum bombing runs were no longer possible. The ideal run for safety and lowest-level bomb release was to come down the mountain side like a skier about five hundred feet above the ground, release bombs at about one thousand feet and continue the run across the low-level plains, the bombing going from east to west.

Because of the rapidly developing cloud cover it was necessary to make our runs from west to east, forcing bomb releases at least 3,500 feet above ground. As we came into position I nosed over into a diving attack and soon had all six guns blazing into the larger power plant. As my altimeter reached six thousand feet I released my five hundred–pound bomb and pulled up at full power climbing up the side of the mountain. Upon regaining altitude, the skipper once more assumed his position as lead plane and I became his wingman. The next five to ten minutes we watched while wave after wave of fighters and bombers made their runs and the scene below disappeared in smoke, debris, and dust created by exploding bombs. Confident that we had destroyed the two power plants, we headed back to the task force and a jubilant scene was repeated in all the carrier ready rooms. According to our reports to air intelligence, all bombs were direct hits and both buildings and water-carrying pipes down the mountainside were destroyed.

I had one last mission to perform and that was to return to the strike area and photograph the target to assess actual damage and verify verbal reports of those involved in the strike. And so once again on the third and last day of our scheduled operation against Formosa, I led my division for one last look at Lake Jitsugetsutan and the power installations. Once again the air was crystal clear and on this occasion neither enemy aircraft nor antiaircraft fire interrupted our mission. There below we saw the incredible: both power plants and all water tubes were apparently undamaged.

Rather disconsolately I made my photographic runs and taking one last look at the rugged beauty of Formosa we headed back to the fleet. I read many years later that a flight of B-29 Air Force bombers attacked "Jitsugetsutan" in 1945 with no more apparent success that we had, and as far as I know the Lake of Sun and the Moon continues supplying power to the island to this very day.

Paul Beauchamp vividly recalls the trigger point for his interest in aviation. At the age of twelve, he saw the movie *All Quiet on the Western Front*, which convinced him that in wartime he would prefer to be fighting in the air as opposed to the trenches.

Beauchamp signed up for the naval aviation unit (V-12 program) on 14 August 1941, and he was ordered to report for duty on 23 October at the Fairfax Naval Air Station in Kansas City, Kansas. He recalls receiving his initial flight training in vintage World War I aircraft that had very few instruments and no radios. The airstrip was so cluttered with construction equipment that achieving successful landings proved even more difficult than landing on an aircraft carrier. During advanced training he "carrier qualified" on board the sidewheeler *Wolverine,* which operated in Lake Michigan.

After completing flight training, Beauchamp was assigned to the Naval Air Station in Pensacola, Florida, where he served as a flight instructor from July 1942 until November 1943. During this period he got married and found that teaching instruments to student pilots was both appealing and gratifying.

Beauchamp and about twenty of his fellow pilots next moved to the San Diego area where they became part of Naval Air Group 19, a squadron awaiting shipment overseas. On 17 March 1944 they boarded the USS *Intrepid* (CV 11) for transport to Hawaii. After learning to fly the F6F Hellcat aircraft, they were posted to the aircraft carrier *Lexington*.

Beauchamp found that the Hellcat was a vastly superior plane to the F4F Wildcat aircraft he had previously been flying. He praised its speed, its maneuverability, its quick response, and its capacity to serve as an excellent platform for shooting. He and his comrades also appreciated the heavy armor protecting the pilot's seat and back. When fully armed, the Hellcat carried six .50-caliber machine guns, six rockets, and two five-hundred-pound bombs. It accounted for 75 percent of the Japanese aircraft shot down during World War II.

Beauchamp flew fifty combat missions while aboard the *Lexington*. VF-19 was credited with shooting down 167 enemy aircraft. He departed the combat zone on Thanksgiving Day 1944, and he concluded his military service at Atlantic City, from mid-December through 14 August 1945, exactly four years after his initial enlistment. In addition to being awarded the Silver Star medal, Beauchamp also won the Distinguished Flying Cross and two Air medals.

Following his separation from the service Beauchamp worked at a Ford dealership in Topeka, Kansas, then opened his own dealership in Lawrence, Kansas.[3] Eventually, Beauchamp moved back to Topeka and opened up an art gallery. At the age of eighty-seven he still works at the gallery and is surrounded by his family of two children, four grandchildren, and eight great-grandchildren.

ENDNOTES

1. Silver Star citation, Lt. Paul Richard Beauchamp, USNR, from the Paul Beauchamp collection.
2. James E. Wise Jr., and Scott Baron, *The Navy Cross: Extraordinary Heroism in Iraq, Afghanistan, and Other Conflicts* (Annapolis, MD: Naval Institute Press, 2007); personal conversation between Jim Wise and Paul Beauchamp, 5 November 2007; documents and photographs received by Wise from Beauchamp, 21 November 2007; telephone conversations between Wise and Beauchamp, 26 and 28 November 2007.
3. Richard Beauchamp, son of Paul Beauchamp, telephone conversations with Jim Wise, 29 November 2007.

BIBLIOGRAPHY

"1st Battalion, 5th Marines History." http://www.i-mef.usmc.mil/DIV/ 5MAR/1BN/history.asp.

"1st Light Armored Infantry Battalion." http://www.imef.usmc.mil/div/1lar/ History_start.asp.

"1st Reconnaissance Battalion." http://www.i-mef.usmc.mil/DIV/1ReconBn/.

"2nd Battalion/5th Marines History." http://www.i-mef.usmc.mil/DIV/ 5MAR/2bn/history.asp.

"3rd Battalion, 2nd Marines Unit History." http://www.lejeune.usmc.mil/ 2dmardiv/32/batlineage.

"3rd Battalion, 4th Marine Regiment." Globalsecurity.org, http://www.glo-balsecurity.org/military/agency/usmc/3-4.htm.

"3rd Battalion, 5th Marine History." http://www.i-mef.usmc.mil/div/5mar/ 3bn/history.asp.

"3rd Battalion, 7th Heritage, 3rd Battalion, 7th Marines." http:// www.29palms.usmc.mil/fmf/3-7/heritage.asp.

"3rd Battalion, 25th Marines Unit History." http://www.marforres.usmc. mil/4thmardiv/25thmar/3dbn/History.htm.

"3/2 Marines Unit History." www.globalsecurity.org/military/agency/usmc/ 3-2.htm.

"3/7 Heritage: 3rd Battalion, 7th Marines." http://www.i-mef.usmc.mil/div/ 7mar/3bn.

"3/25th Marines Unit History." http://www.marforres.usmc.mil/4thmardiv/ 25thmar/3dbn/History.htm.

Aarons, Edward S. *Hell to Eternity*. Greenwich, CT: Fawcett Publications, Inc. 1960.

Amico, Christopher. "Valley Marine Wins Silver Star." *Valley Press* (Lancaster, CA), 28 July 2006.

Anselmo, Guy Jr. "The Pied Piper of Saipan." *Leatherneck*, 66, no. 6 (June 1983).

Arlington National Cemetery website. www.arlingtoncemetery.net/dazem-biec.htm.

Army Regulation 600–8-22 (Military Awards). Chapter 3, 25 February 1995, Government Printing Office, Washington, DC.

Arthur, Lanessa. "Marines Remember Fallen Shipmates." *Navy Compass* (San Diego, CA) 9 December 2005.

———. "Senior Enlisted Receives Bronze Star Medal." *Marine Corps News*, 27 January 2006.

Atrian, Mario Jr. Telephone interview with Scott Baron, 7 October 2007.

"Attacks on Humanitarian Aid to Fallujah," United States Central Command News Release #04-04-11, 13 April 2004.

Aull, Elbert. "A Marine with Merit." *Portland* (ME) *Press Herald*, 25 February 2006.

Bailey, Laura. "Honored with a Bronze Star, Cpl. James Wright Sets His Sights on Healing." *Marine Corps Times*, June 2004.

———. "Marine Killed in '03 Iraq Ambush Earns Military's 3rd Highest Award." *Marine Corps Times*, 3 September 2004.

———. "Marines Awarded Some of Military's Highest Honors for Iraq Bravery." *Marine Corps Times*, 17 May 2004.

Baker, Fred W. "Daughter Accepts Silver Star Her World War I Nurse Mother Earned." *Army News Service*, 2 August 2007.

Baker, Rusty. "Dallas Marine Wife, Children Presented Posthumous Bronze Star for Husband's Valor in Iraq." *Marine Corps News*, 16 August 2005 (Story ID #2005816163852).

Ballenger, Lee. *The Outpost War: US Marines in Korea*, Vol. 1. Washington, DC: Potomac Books, 2000.

Barnard, Ann. "Forces Try to Keep Focus as Tactics Shift." *Boston Globe*, 3 May 2004.

"Battalion History, 1st Battalion–4th Marines." www.i-mef.usmc.mil/div/1mar/1bn4/history.asp.

Beauchamp, Paul. Personal conversations with James E. Wise Jr., 5, 26, and 28 November 2007.

Beauchamp, Richard. Telephone conversations with James E. Wise Jr., 29 November 2007.

Bernthal, Dr. Craig. "No Better Friend, No Worse Enemy." *Private Papers*. 16 February 2005. www.victorhanson.com/articles/bernthal021605.html.

Bernton, Hal. "A Small Town Grieves Over One Family's Loss in Iraq." *The Seattle* (WA) *Times*, 12 August 2004.

———. "Courage Amid Chaos: How a Battle Unfolded." *Seattle* (WA) *Times*, 18 September 2004.

Berryman, Sgt. Chris R., USMC. "Captain Awarded for Battlefield Gallantry." *Marine Corps News*, 12 December 2005.

"Biography of Richard J. Gannon Jr." http://www.marketingbysignature.com/gannonbio.html.

Blaich, Ryan M. "Risking His Life for His Marines." *Marine Corps News*, 28 July 2006 (Story ID #200672815916).

Blanding, Michael. "The Opposite of Fear." *Tufts* (University, MA) *Magazine*, Spring 2007.

Bolt, Maj. John F., USMC. Letter to Mrs. Thomas Sellers, 5 August 1953.

Bray, N. N. E. *A Paladin of Arabia: The Biography of Brevet Lieut. Col. G. E. Leachman.* London: Unicorn Press, 1936.

Brent, P. B. "In the Kill Zone: A Pop and a Spurt of Blood." *Honolulu* (HI) *Star Bulletin*, 23 May 2004.

Brinkley, Mark C. "March 23rd Is a Day Remembered All Too Well." *Army Times*, 17 March 2004.

————. "Bravery and Brains Earn Marine Captain Three Top Awards." *Marine Corps Times*, 1 August 2006.

Burden, Matthew C. *The Blog of War: Front-Line Dispatches in Iraq and Afghanistan.* New York: Simon and Schuster, 2006.

Carter, Chelsea. "Nick Popaditch Lit Up to Mark the Fall of Baghdad, as Well as his 12th Wedding Anniversary." Associated Press, 10 April 2005.

Carus, David. "Marine's Memory Honored in Brooklyn." Associated Press, http://www.militarycity.com/valor/2050237.html.

Cavallaro, Gina. "Leathernecks of 1/2 Ran into a Buzz Saw and the Bloodiest Day of the War." *Marine Corps Times*, 12 May 2003.

Chandrasekaran, Rajiv. "Key General Criticizes April Attack in Fallujah: Abrupt Withdrawal Called Vacillation." *Washington* (DC) *Post Foreign Service*, 13 September 2004.

Chandrasekaran, Rajiv, and Karl Vick. "U.S. Opts to Delay Fallujah Offensive. Marines, Iraqi Forces Planning Joint Patrols." *Washington* (DC) *Post*, 26 April 2004.

Chavez, Charlie. "OIF Combat Veteran Awarded Silver Star." *Marine Corps News*, 12 May 2006 (Story ID #200651216323).

Chelkowski, Julliet. "Election Support Teams Help Insure Iraqi Vote." *Marine Corps News*, 2 November 2005 (Story ID #2005111225126).

Cifuentes, Michael C. "Bronze Star Shines after Valiant Fight in Iraq." *Marine Corps News*, 16 December 2005 (Story ID #200616123623).

Clark, Cheryl. "First SEAL Killed in Iraq." *San Diego* (CA) *Union-Tribune*, 8 August 2006.

Cole, William. "Marines 'Conspicuous Gallantry' Cited." *Honolulu* (HI) *Advertiser*, 2 February 2006. http://the.honoluluadvertiser.com/article/2006/Feb/02/ln/FP602020337.

Collins, Rick. "Iraq Hero Accepts Honor Modestly." *The Patriot Ledger* (MA), 1 May 2006.

Combined Joint Task Force Phoenix V. "Coalition Forces Information." 14 January 2008, http://phnxv.taskforcephoenix.com/cofor.htm.

Conlan, Jay. Conlan, "A Patriot's Story." *The Essex County* (NJ) *Advisor*, (Summer 2001). www.koreanwar-educator.org/memoirs/pizzi/index.htm.

Conley, Kevin. "A Few Good Medals." GQ Online, http://men.style.com/gq/features/full/?id=content_5139.

Connell, Rich, and Robert J. Lopez. "Charlie Company." *Los Angeles* (CA) *Times*, 26 August 2003.

Constable, Pamela. "A Wrong Turn, Chaos and a Rescue," *Washington* (DC) *Post*, 15 April 2004.

Coopman, John. "Marines Face Resistance from Iraqi Troops Near Basra." *San Francisco* (CA) *Chronicle*, 22 March 2003.

Croom, Paul L., II. "Wages of War." *San Diego* (CA) *Magazine*, March 2006.

———. "Despite heavy resistance, U.S. Officials Say Operation Matador Was a Success—164 Insurgents Captured or Killed in Offensive near Syrian Border." *Stars and Stripes*, Mideast Edition, Monday, 16 May 2005.

"Decorated Sailor from Hood River Killed in Iraq." NWCN.com, 5 August 2006. http://www.nwcn.com/statenews/oregon/stories/NW_080506ORNsailorkilledEL_.7202a27.html.

Degrosseilliers, Lt. Col. Todd, Transcript of *Lou Dobbs Tonight* interview, CNN.COM, 14 April 2006. http://transcripts.cnn.com/TRANSCRIPTS/0604/14/ldt.01.html.

Dickey, 2nd Lt. Albert B., USAF. Letter to Mrs. Thomas Sellers, 27 August 1953.

Dickson, Cpl. Michelle M., MCB Hawaii. "Marine Recalls Silver Star Actions." *Marine Corps News*, 10 February 2006.

Dickson, Patrick. "Heroes 2006: Wounded Himself, Corpsman Rushed to Save Comrades After IED Blast." *Stars and Stripes*, 14 June 2006.

Dictionary of American Naval Fighting Ships (DANFS), Vol. 6. Washington, DC: U.S. Government Printing Office, 1969.

Digirolamo, Joseph L. "In the Highest Tradition." *Leatherneck Magazine*, March 2005.

Dillow, Gordon, and Mark Avery. "The Men of Alpha Company." *Orange County* (CA) *Register*, 20 November 2003.

Distinguished Service Cross citations. http://www.homeofheroes.com/valor/02_wot/dsc_briggs.html.

Ditzler, Joseph. "Marine Modest about His Heroism." *Anchorage* (AK) *Daily News*, 25 June 2006.

Department of Defense (DoD). "Guy Gabaldon Decoration Elevated to Navy Cross." DoD News Release, 20 December 1960.

Doran, Jason K. *I Am My Brother's Keeper*. North Topsail Beach, NC: Caisson Press, 2005.

Dorell, Owen, and Gregg Zoroya. "Battle for Fallujah Forged Many Heroes." *USA Today*, 9 November 2006.

Eagen, Evan M. "2nd Force Reconnaissance Returns Home." *Marine Corps News*, 21 March 2005 (Story ID #200532184557).

Espinosa, Demetrio, USMC. "1Lt. Elliott Ackerman: Marine Earns Silver Star for Courage Under Fire." *Marine Corps Times*, 16 January 2007.

Fender, Jessica. "Smyrna Man's Bravery Honored." *Marine Corps News*, 12 September 2006.

Figueroa, Teri. "Marine Sgt. Jeffrey L. Kirk Posthumously Awarded Silver Star." *North County* (San Diego, CA) *Times*, 5 March 2007.

Fischer, Staff Sergeant, 6th Marine Corps District. "Marines Present Silver Star, Bronze Bust, to Fallen Comrade's Family." *Marine Corps News*, 13 May 2005.

Floto, Patrick J. "Gunny Gets Silver Star for Gallantry." *Marine Corps Times*, 30 November 2005 (Story ID #2005121173519).

———. "Marine Captain Leaves No Man Behind, Earns Silver Star." *Marine Corps News*, 8 February 2006.

———. "Iron Will Earns Marine Silver Star." *Marine Corps News*, 12 April 2006.

Flower, Kevin, Kianne Sadeq, and Enes Dulami. "Hunt for Insurgents near Syria Ends: More than 125 Insurgents, Nine Marines Dead." CNN.Com, 14 May 2005, http://www.cnn.com/2005/WORLD/meast/05/14/iraq.main/index.html.

Force Marine Information Office Release No: 1130–66, CIB III MAF, Da Nang, Vietnam, 19 June 1966.

Frank, John. "Ambush Ends Marines' Dreams: Two from Lejeune Die in Afghanistan." Newsobserver.com, http://newsobserver.com/news/v-printer/story/1380729p-7504071c.html.

Franklin Delano Roosevelt Library, www.nps.gov/archive/elro/glossary/roosevelt-franklin-jr.html.

Friel, Lucian. "3/2 Marines Assume Authority of Al-Qa'im Region." *Marine Corps News*, 9 March 2005 (Story ID #200532151947).

———. "3/2 Ends Deployment in Al-Qa'im, Returns to U.S." *Marine Corps News*, 20 September 2005.

———. "Heroic Platoon Commander Honored with Silver Star." *Marine Corps News*, 17 March 2006.

———. "Frustrated U.S. Disbands the Fallujah Brigade: Iraq Notebook." *Seattle* (WA) *Times*, 11 September 2004.

Fuentes, Gidget. "Platoon Commander Earns a Silver Star." *Marine Corps Times*, 21 February 2006.

———. "First SEAL Killed in Iraq: Oregon Native Killed in Ar Ramadi Fighting, Two Other SEALs Wounded." *Navy Times*, 7 August 2006.

———. "SEAL Earns Posthumous Silver Star." *Navy Times*, 10 August 2006.

———. "'They Hit the Wrong CAAT Team': Leatherneck Earns Silver Star for Role in Ambush Fight." *Marine Corps Times*, 21 August 2006.

Fuentes, Gidget, and John Hoellwarth. "Captain Earns Silver Star for Two Actions in One Day: His Unit Punched Through Enemy Lines on Separate Missions." *Marine Corps Times*, 21 November 2005.

———. "Saving Their Buddies, Three Marines Earn Silver Star." *Marine Corps Times*, 12 December 2005.

Fulton, Maj. Gen. William B. "Vietnam Studies, Riverine Operations 1966–1969." Washington, DC: Department of the Army, 1997.

Garamone, Jim. "Scan Eagle Proves Worth in Fallujah Fight." American Forces News Service, 11 January 2005.

Genos, Athanasios L. "Silver Star Awarded to Desgrosseilliers." *Marine Corps News*, 13 February 2006 (Story ID #200621311418).

———. "Lieutenant Awarded Silver Star, Credits it to His Marines." *Marine Corps News,* 14 March 2006 (Story ID #200631493313).

Gisick, Michael. "Memories of Combat Are Never Far from Former Albuquerque Marine's Thoughts." *Albuquerque* (NM) *Tribune*, 19 June 2007.

Goldstein, Richard. "Guy Gabaldon, 80, Hero of Battle of Saipan, Dies." *New York Times*, 4 September 2006.

Graham, Jed. "He's a Silver Star of a Sailor." *Investor Business Daily*, 2 March 2007.

Graham, LCpl. Lance T. "Memorial." http://www.corpsstories.com.

"Guy Gabaldon Decoration Elevated to Navy Cross." DoD News Release, 20 December 1960.

"GySgt. Jimmie E. Howard, USMC (Deceased): Vietnam War 1965–1973, Medal of Honor Recipient." Who's Who in Marine Corps History, United States Marine Corps History Division, www.tecom.usmc.mil/HD/Whos_Who/Howard_JE.htm.

Gyan, Joe Jr. "Marine from BR Cited for Bravery." *New Orleans* (LA) *Advocate*, 14 July 2005.

"H. Bruce McIver Awarded the Silver Star Medal on 2 June 2004 for Heroic Actions on 31 March 1969." http://mrfa.org/McIver.SilverStar.htm.

Hamilton, Capt. John, USMCR. Official file, Marine Corps Museums and Historical Division, Quantico, VA.

Hamilton, Capt. John. "Military Record of Captain John Hamilton USMCR." National Personnel Records Center, St. Louis, MO.

Harris, Ron. "Commemorating the Life of a Comrade." *St. Louis* (MO) *Post Dispatch*, 13 April 2004.

———. "Coordinated Attack in Force Kills 6 Marines at Al-Husaybah." *St. Louis* (MO) *Post Dispatch*, 17 April 2004.

Harris, Michael A. (Web master of McIver website). 15 July 2007, 7 December 2007, 18 December 2007, 20 December 2007, 21 December 2007, 30 December 2007, 31 December 2007, 1 January 2008, 4 January 2008, 9 January 2008..

Hastings, Max. *The Korean War*. New York: Simon & Schuster Paperbacks, 1987.

Hayden, Catherine Denise. Interview with James E. Wise Jr., 1997.

Hayden, Sterling. *Wanderer*. London: Longmans, Green, 1964.

Heinl, Robert D. *Dictionary of Military and Naval Quotations*. Annapolis, MD: Naval Institute Press, 1967.

Hider, James. "Stranded Marines Fight to Last Bullets." *London* (UK) *Times*, 16 April 2004.

Hoellwarth, John. "The Finest Caliber." *Marine Corps Times*, 10 January 2006.

———. "Machine Gun Battle Leads to Silver Star for Marine." *Marine Corps Times*, 13 March 2006.

———. "Marine Caught in Grenade Blast Gets Silver Star." *Marine Corps Times*, 10 April 2006.

Hoffman, Michael. "Silver Star Awarded for Leadership in Battle." *Marine Corps Times*, 6 December 2006.

———. "Wounded Sergeant Dragged Four Buddies to Safety." *Marine Corps Times*, 28 October 2007.

Hubbell, John G., and David Reed. "Hill 488: A Fight To Remember." *Readers Digest*, May 1968, 60–66.

Hurt, Andy J. "13th MEU BLT Marine Receives Silver Star for OIF Heroism." *Marine Corps News*, 5 May 2005.

"In Memorium: Fallen Marine Laid to Rest," TroyRecord.com, http://www.corpsstories.com/memoriam-McKenna.htm.

"Iraqis in Deadly Clash with U.S. Troops." CNN.COM-World, 29 April 2003.

Jeffrey, Simon, and Rebecca Allison. "U.S. Forces Occupy Palaces: Soldiers in Central Baghdad." *Guardian* (Manchester, UK) *Unlimited*, 7 April 2003.

Johnston, Christopher Ray. "Remembrance: Iraq/Afghanistan War Heroes." http://www.iraqwarheroes.com/johnsonm.htm.

Jones, Brian. "3/5 Marine Awarded Silver Star." *Marine Corps News*,
    25 November 2007 (Story ID #20071125545).

Jones, Matthew R. "Marines Recount Fierce Battle." *Marine Corps News*,
    15 September 2004 (Story ID #20049209463).

Kakesako, Gregg K. "Kaneohe Maine Award Silver Star for Battle Rescue."
    Honolulu Star Bulletin, 21 May 2006.

Keirn, Andrew. "Fallen Marine's Heroism Recognized." *Marine Corps News*,
    9 March 2006 (Story ID #20063934816).

Kelly, Brad. "Todd Desgrosseilliers Bit the Bullet in Fallujah." *Investors
    Business Daily*, 22 June 2007.

Kelso, Jack Williams. "Who's Who in Marine Corps History: Private Jack
    William Kelso, USMC (Deceased)." United States Marine Corps History
    Division. www.tecom.usmc.mil/HD/Whos_Who/Kelso_JW.htm.

Kifner, John, and John F. Burns. "Inside Falluja: A Ceasefire in Name Only."
    New York Times, 26 April 2004.

Kimmons, Sean. "Americans Will Not Make It out Alive." *Stars and Stripes*
    (Heroes), 14 June 2006.

Knickmeyer, Ellen. "They Came Here to Die: Insurgents Hiding under
    House in Western Iraq Prove Fierce in Hours-Long Fight with Marines."
    Washington (DC) *Post*, 11 May 2005.

———. "Demise of a Hard Fighting Squad: Marines Who Survived Ambush
    Are Killed, Wounded in Blast." *Washington* (DC) *Post*, 12 May 2005.

Kortegaard, B. L. "Counter-Attack, Stalemate." www.rt66.com/~korteng/
    SmallArms/stalemate.htm.

Kurzeja, C. C. "Silver Star for Adam R. Sikes." Flicka Spumoni.
    http://72.14.253.104/search?q=cache:NVg5IKIvl3sJ:
    flickaspumoni.blogspot.com/2005/07/silverstar.
    html+%22Adam+Sikes%22+Marine&hl=en&ct=clnk&cd=31&gl=us.

Lally, Kathy, and Jean Marbella. "In a Flash, Marine in Spotlight." *Baltimore*
    (MD) *Sun*, 4 April 2003.

Lathrop, Will. "Silver Star Awarded to Marine for Actions in Iraq." *Marine
    Corps News*, 9 June 2005 (Story ID #2005699476).

Lewis, Ray. "Scout-Sniper Honored with Silver Star." *Marine Corps News*, 30
    June 2005 (Story ID #200563011057).

———. "Camp Pendleton–Based Rifleman Awarded Silver Star." *Marine
    Corps News*, 13 October 2005 (Story ID #20051013182324).

———. "Marine Officer Posthumously Receives Silver Star." *Marine Corps
    News*, 2 December 2005, http://www.militaryconnections.com/
    news_story.cfm?textnewsid=1771.

Liewer, Steve. "One 'Resolute Marine.'" *San Diego* (CA) *Union Tribune*, 10
    November 2006.

————. "Marine Sacrificed His Body to Protect a Sleeping Comrade." *San Diego* (CA) *Union Tribune*, 12 November 2006.

"Linage of 3rd Battalion, 7th Marines, 3/7 Marines." http://www.29palms. usmc.mil/fmf/3–7/heritage.asp.

Loi, Marc. "Marine Officer Receives Silver Star." *Marine Corps News*, 30 September 2005.

Love, Bill W. "Corpsman Awarded Silver Star for Heroism in Iraq." *Navy News*, 1 May 2006.

Lowry, Richard S. *U.S. Marine in Iraq: Operation Iraqi Freedom 2003*. London: Osprey Publishing, 2006.

————. "The Battle of An Nasiriyah." http://www.militaryhistoryonline. com/desertstorm/annasiriyah/default.aspx.

Lucas, Peter. *The OSS in World War II Albania: Covert Operations and Collaboration with Communists Partisans*. London: McFarland & Company, 2007.

Luftwaffe Fighter Tactics. http://freespace.virgin.net/john.dell/bf109/ Bf109tactics.html.

Maass, Peter. "Good Kills." *New York* (NY) *Times Magazine*, 20 April 2003.

MacDonald, Sharon. Correspondence with James E. Wise Jr., 14 September 2007.

Marek, Ed. "Battle for Fallujah: Our Warfighters Towered in Maturity and Guts." *Talking Proud Magazine*, http://www.talkingproud.us/ Military042805B.html.

"Marine Corps Deaths in the Iraq War." 24 June 2004. http://www.scuttle-butts/smallchow.com/mardeath57bb.html.

"Marine Thwarts Car Bomb Attack." *USA Today*, 18 April 2005.

Marino, Jacqueline. "Blood Brothers." *Cleveland* (OH) *Magazine*, June 2006.

Matheny, Keith. "Gallant Service Has Reward: Now-Retired Marine Receives Third-Highest Honor from Corps." *The Desert Sun* (Palm Springs, CA), 14 August 2006.

Maurer, Kevin. "DSC Awarded to SOF Soldier for Fallujah: Fort Bragg Soldier Recalls Battle that Won Him High Honor." Associated Press, 23 June 2005.

Mazzolini, Chris. "Marine Awarded the Military's Highest Combat Medal." *Marine Corps News*, 11 August 2005.

————. "Marine Stayed in Fight Despite Hand Wound, Low Fuel in Tank." *Jacksonville* (NC) *Daily News*, 15 March 2006.

————. "Calm in a Time of Storm." *Jacksonville* (NC) *Daily News*, 23 November 2006.

McDonald, Jeff. "Bravery? Nope, 'Just Doing His Job.'" *The San Diego* (CA) *Union Tribune*, 12 November 2006.

McDonnell, Patrick J. "No Shortage of Fighters in Iraq's Wild West." *Los Angeles* (CA) *Times*, 25 July 2004.

McIver, H. Bruce "Mac." River Assault Division 13/T-131–7/MACV Naval Advisory Group RAID 72 (ATF-211). http://www.riverinesailor.com/ McIver.htm.

———. "Mac." E-mail correspondence: 13 September 2007, 2 October 2007, 21 October 2007, 22 October 2007, 23 October 2007, 11 November 2007, 18 November 2007, 21 November 2007, 21 December 2007, 31 December 2007, 4 January 2008, 5 January 2008.

Meid, LtCol. Pat, USMC, and Maj. James M. Yingling, USMC. *U.S. Marine Corps Operations in Korea 1950–1953, Vol. 5. Operations in West Korea.* Washington, DC: Historical Division Headquarters, 1972.

Memorial to LCpl. Lance T. Graham. http://www.corpsstories.com/graham-whatwhenwhere1.htm.

Mendoza, Mike. Telephone interview with Scott Baron, 4 October 2007.

Miles, Donna. "Surge in IED Attacks Coincides with Iraqi Political Progress." *Marine Corps News*, 1 November 2005.

———. "Operation Matador Helping Flush Insurgents from Western Iraq." DefenseLINK News, U.S. Department of Defense, 10 May 2005.

Milks, Gunnery Sgt. Keith A., USMC. "Dispatch from Forward Operating Base Ripley." *Marine Corps News*, 9 July 2004.

Mite, Valentina. "Iraq; In Town Loyal to Hussein, Residents Unscathed but Feeling the Effects of War." Radio Free Europe/Radio Liberty, 22 May 2003. http://www.globalsecurity.org/wmd/library/news/iraq/2003/05/ iraq-030522-rfel-154718.htm.

Morison, Samuel E. *History of the United States Naval Operations in World War II,* Vol. 3. Boston: Little, Brown and Company, 1962.

———. *History of the United States Naval Operations in World War II,* Vol. 9, Part II. Boston: Little, Brown and Company, 1968.

Morse, Dan. "Salute to a Memorable Marine." *Washington* (DC) *Post*, 17 May 2007.

Mortenson, Darrin. "Marine Unit to Return to Iraq over Weekend." *North County* (San Diego, CA) *Times*, 27 February 2004.

———. "Marine Sergeant Awarded Silver Star for Charge in Fallujah." *North County* (San Diego, CA) *Times*, 3 June 2005.

Murphy, Edward F. *Korean War Heroes.* Novato, CA: Presidio Press, 1992.

Murphy, John. "An Ambush by Iraqis Tests Mettle of Marines: Enemy Soldiers Attack Convoy, Pay with Thirty-five Lives." *Baltimore* (MD) *Sun*, 26 March 2003.

Murray, Ben. "It Felt Like my Body Was Burning from the Inside Out." *Stars and Stripes*, 14 June 2006.

————. "It Just Felt Wrong Not to Pull the Trigger." *Stars and Stripes*, 14 June 2005.

"Najaf." GlobalSecurity.org, http://www.globalsecurity.org/military/world/iraq/najaf.htm.

"Navy SEAL Remembered at Oregon Service," Associated Press, 27 August 2006, http://www.signonsandiego.com/news/world/iraq/memorial/20060827-1629-navyseal-service.html.

Official Biography of Pfc. Guy L. Gabaldon, USMCR. U.S. Marine Corps Museums and History Division, Quantico Marine Corps Base, Quantico, VA, August 1960.

Official Biography of Edward S. Aarons. Operational Archives, Naval History Center, Washington, DC.

Official Biography of Radm. Chester W. Nimitz Jr. Operational Archives, Naval History Center, Washington, DC.

Official Biography of Cdr. Franklin D. Roosevelt Jr. Operational Archives, Naval History Center, Washington, DC.

Official Newsletter of the First Reconnaissance Battalion Association, *Sitrep* 11, no. 1, May 2004. http://www.1streconbnassociation.org/Patrol%20Rpt%20%205–04.1–1.DOC.

Olivia, GySgt. Mark. "Marines Suspend Fallujah Offensive, Push Humanitarian Aid." *Marine Corps News*, 13 April 2004.

Olivia, Mark. "'Lion of Fallujah' Is Laid to Rest." *Marine Corps News*, 19 May 2007.

"Operation Al-Fajr (Dawn), Operation Phantom Fury, [Fallujah]." GlobalSecurity.org, http://www.globalsecurity.org/military/ops/oif-phantom-fury-fallujah.htm.

"Operation New Market Ends in Al-Hadithah Multi-National Force." Iraq, News Release #A050530c, 29 May 2005.

"Operation New Market Kicks Off in Iraq." USMC Press Release #0525-05-0759, 25 May 2005.

Otto, Mary. "Marine's Family Recall His Dedication to Mission." *Washington* (DC) *Post*, 17 November 2004.

Parks, Thomas F. III. Telephone interview with Scott Baron, 26 June 2007.

Paulsgrove, Graham. "LAR Patrols the Streets of Habbaniyah." *Marine Corps News*, 13 June 2006 (Story ID #200661452418).

Perry, Tony. "The Unapologetic Warrior: In Iraq, a Marine Corps Captain Is Living Out His Heart's Desire." *Los Angeles* (CA) *Times*, 22 August 2004.

————. "Marine Hero Knew Only One Way: Straight Ahead." *Los Angeles* (CA) *Times*, 8 October 2006.

————. "Marine Who Pulled Comrades to Safety Honored." *Los Angeles* (CA) *Times*, 18 October 2007.

————. "Slain Marine Is Awarded Silver Star." *Los Angeles* (CA) *Times*, 6 March 2007.

————. "Two Marines Decorated for Risking Their Lives to Save an Iraqi Soldier." *Los Angeles* (CA) *Times*, 1 April 2006.

Peterson, Scott. "Under Fire: U.S. Marines Hand Off Battered Fallujah." *Christian Science Monitor*, 24 November 2006.

Phillips, Jeb. "Two Lima Company Marines to Receive Awards for Valor." *Columbus* (OH) *Dispatch*, 20 August 2006.

Phillips, Michael. "In Combat, Marine Puts Theory to Test, Comrades Believe." *Wall Street Journal*, 25 May 2004.

Pizzi, Herman. Correspondence with James E. Wise Jr., 29 August 2007.

Pogreba, Capt. Dean A., USAF. Letter to Mrs. Thomas Sellers, 3 September 1953.

Popaditch, Nick. "Fallujah Fight: In the Words of the Cigar Marine." http://www.leatherneck.com/forums/showthread.php?t=20876.

————. Telephone interviews with Scott Baron, 24 and 28 September 2007.

Potter, E. B. *Sea Power: A Naval History*. Annapolis, MD: Naval Institute Press, 1981.

Price, Jay. "Marines Make Restraint Their Weapon." *News and Observer* (Raleigh, NC), 19 October 2006.

————. "Marine's Valor Reaps a Reward." *News and Observer* (Raleigh, NC), 11 February 2006.

————. "Tenacity Wins Marine a Medal." *News and Observer* (Raleigh, NC), 11 March 2006.

Rafferty, Tom. "Decorated Soldier Returning Home." *Bismarck* (ND) *Tribune*, 12 May 2006.

Rapicault, Patrick Marc. Arlington National Cemetery. http://www.arling-toncemetery.net/pmmrapicault.htm.

Reimers, Brian. "New England's Own Marines Gather to Remember Fallen Brothers." *Marine Corps News*, 26 August 2006.

"Riverine Warfare: The U.S. Navy's Operations on Inland Waters." Naval Historical Center (NHC), Washington Navy Yard, Washington, DC. www.history.navy.mil/library/online/riverine.htm.

Roberts, Chris. "Marine Awarded Silver Star." *El Paso* (TX) *Times*, 25 March 2006.

Roberts, James C. "Remember Heroes of Fallujah." *Human Events Magazine*, 6 November 2006.

Robinson, Simon. "Dispatches from the Front." *Time Magazine*, 22 March 2003.

Rogers, Rick. "Valor Defined: Marines Confront, Overcome the Crucible of Fallujah." *San Diego* (CA) *Union Tribune*, 31 July 2004.

————. "Home of the Brave: Maj. Douglas Zembiec." *San Diego* (CA) *Union Tribune*, 10 November 2006.

Rosas, Antonio. "Scout-Sniper Serving in Iraq Awarded U.S. Military's Third-Highest Award for Valor." *Marine Corps News*, 10 June 2006.

Roscoe, Theodore. *United States Submarine Operations in World War II.* Annapolis, MD: Naval Institute Press, 1998.

Royer, Capt. Kelly. Telephone interview with Scott Baron, 12 August 2007.

————. "Summary of Action: Navy Cross Recommendation for Cpl. Eric M. Smith." Unpublished.

————. "Summary of Action: Silver Star Recommendation for 2nd Lt. Thomas E. Cogan IV." Unpublished.

————. "Company (E) Commander's After-Action Report for Combat Actions in the Porcupine Area of Operations," 6 April 2004. Unpublished.

"S/Sgt Jimmie Howard." www.homeofheroes.com/profiles/howard_jimmie. html.

Sample, SFC Doug. "Fallujah 'Under Control' as Gunfire Punctuates Cease-Fire." American Forces Press Service, 10 April 2004.

Schogol, Jeff. "My Hands Were Burning with Blood." *Stars & Stripes*, 7 June 2007.

Sears, Robert. "Area Family Holds Story of Heroism in Iraq." *Thomasville* (AL) *Times*, 28 September 2006.

Sedensky, Matt. "WWII Hero Dies." http://ksquest.blogspot.com/2006/09/guy-gabaldon-diminutive-world-war-ii.html.

Sellers, Maj. Thomas M., USMCR. Letters to his wife, March, April, May, July 1953.

————. Letter to Commandant of the Marine Corps, dated 29 December 1952, subject: Extended active duty billet in the Marine Corps Reserve.

————. Letter to Commandant of the Marine Corps, dated 18 July 1953, subject: Integration into the Regular Marine Corps.

Shane, Leo III. "We Started Making Them Fly off Roofs." *Stars and Stripes*, 14 June 2005.

Sheeler, Jim. "Remembering the Brave: Littleton Parents to Receive Silver Star for Dying Son's Actions in Iraqi Battle." *Rocky Mountain* (CO) *News*, 22 July 2006.

Shulimson, Jack. *U.S. Marines in Vietnam: An Expanding War, 1966.* Washington, DC: History and Museums Division, Headquarters, U.S. Marine Corps, 1982.

Siegel, Andrea. "Famed 'Lion of Fallujah' Dies." *Baltimore* (MD) *Sun*, 14 May 2007.

———. "Comrades Remember a 'Lion.'" *Baltimore* (MD) *Sun*, 15 May 2007.

Sikes, Adam. Telephone interview with Scott Baron, 25 June 2007.

———. "Silver Star for 1st Lt. Stephen J. Boada." The C-Square, 11 February 2006. http://thecsquare.blogspot.com/2006/02/silver-star-for-1st-lt-stephen-j-boada.html.

Silver Star, sec. 3746, title 10, U.S. Code (10 USC 3746). Established by Act of Congress 9 July 1918 (amended by act of 25 July 1963).

Silver Star citations. http://www.homeofheroes.com/valor2/SS/7_GWOT/citations_USMC-M.html.

Silver Star Fact Sheet. Air Force Personnel Center, Randolph AFB.

Simmins, Chuck. "Capt. Christopher P. Niedziocha USMC." *Philadelphia* (PA) *Inquirer*, 14 December 2005.

Situation Report 11, no. 1 (Official Newsletter of the 1st Reconnaissance Battalion Association), May 2004. http://www.1streconbnassociation.org/NL/sitrep2.htm.

Sixbey, Mark. "Darkhorse Marine Decorated for Valor." *Marine Corps Times*, 20 May 2006.

Smith, Maj. Jason. Telephone interviews with Scott Baron, 29 October 2007, 30 December 2007.

Soviet Pilots in 1950–53 Korean War. http://aeroweb.lucia.it/rap/RAFAQ/SovietAces.html.

Sparks, John W. "A Glint of Silver at 23." *The Commercial Appeal* (Memphis, TN), 27 November 2005.

Spires, Shelby. "Silver Star Winner Recalls Amazing White House Visit." *Huntsville* (AL) *Times*, 16 August 2006.

Staes, Mary A. "Lima 3/25 Awards 2 Silver Stars." *Marine Corps News*, 20 August 2006 (Story ID #200682414838).

Strandberg, Sarah. "Ossian Man Killed in Baghdad." *Decorah* (IA) *Newspapers*, 11 April 2003.

Struck, Doug. "The Coolest Posting in a Hot War Zone: For Marines Guarding Strategic Dam, Lakeside Quarters Take Edge off Peril." *Washington* (DC) *Post*, 8 August 2004, A-17.

"Summary of Action: Recommendation for Silver Star, Capt. Jason Smith." Unpublished.

Swanson, David, and Joseph Galloway. "Battle at Ramadi." *Philadelphia* (PA) *Inquirer*, 15 August 2004.

Talton, Trista. "Lejeune Combat Instructor Receives Silver Star." *Marine Corps Times*, 22 November 2006.

TaskForcePhoenix.com. 14 January 2008. http://phnxv.taskforcephoenix.com/cofor.htm.

Thompson, Warren E., and David R. Mclaren. *MiG Alley: Sabres vs. MiGs over Korea.* North Branch MN: Specialty Press, 2002.

"Three Marines, One Sailor killed in Al-Hadithah." www.centcom.mil, 9 May 2005. www.globalsecurity.org/military/library/news/2005/05/ 05-05-07c.htm.

Tower Topics (newsletter), University of Missouri, 23–29 October 2006.

"Troops Uncover Hostage 'Slaughterhouse,'" 11 November 2004. http://www.theage.com.au/articles/2004/11/11/1100021910341. html?from=storylhs.

Tyson, Ann Scott. "3,200 Marines to Deploy to Afghanistan in Spring." *Washington* (DC) *Post,* 16 January 2008, A11.

———. "Troops Fight to Expand Foothold in Ar Ramadi." *Washington* (DC) *Post,* 2 August 2006.

"Unit History: 2nd Battalion, 4th Marine Regiment." GlobalSecurity.org, http://www.globalsecurity.org/military/agency/usmc/2-4.htm.

"Unit History of the 1/7 Marines." 1st Battalion, 7th Marine Regiment website, www.i-mef_usmc.mil/div/7mar/1bn/.

United States Armed Forces Awards, Decorations, Campaign & Service Medals. Institute of Heraldry, United States Army, Government Printing Office, Washington, DC.

"U.S. Army Official Report on 507th Maintenance Company, 23 March 2003, An Nasiriyah, Iraq-Executive Summary." http://www.metavr.com/cas-estudies/aar507ambush.pdf.

"U.S. Forces Unleash Phantom Fury to Seize Fallujah." Agence France Presse, 8 November 2004.

"USMC Casualty Report, Missing and Captured Personnel Unit: Change in Status of Major Thomas Sellers, USMCR: from Missing in Action 20 July 1953 to Killed in Action 20 July 1954."

Vargo, Joe. "The Marines Honor Sgt. Kristopher Kane with a Billboard." *Press Enterprise,* 5 January 2008.

Vaughn, Chris. "Waxahachie Man Awarded Silver Star." *Ft. Worth* (TX) *Star-Telegram,* 17 February 2006.

Vereckey, Betsy. "Marine Killed in Iraq Buried in Louisville." *Military Times,* 31 May 2005, http://www.militarycity.com/valor/879849.html.

Vought, Jeremy M. "3/5 Marines Awarded for Heroism." *Marine Corps News,* 13 May 2004 (Story ID #2004514112222).

———. "Klamath Falls, Oregon, Marine Receives Silver Star." *Marine Corps News,* May 6, 2004.

Walker, Mark. "Silver and Bronze Stars Awarded to Weapons Company Marines." *The North County* (San Diego, CA) *Times,* 1 April 2006.

Watkins, James. "The Dogs of War." www.commonties.com/blog/2007/
01/23/the-dogs-of-war/.

Webb, Kerri. "Silver Star Deputy Honored for Heroism in Iraq." *The Compton
(CA) City Bulletin*, 20 December 2006.

Weikle, LCpl. David A., 2nd Marine Division. "Aztec, NM Marine Awarded
Silver Star Medal for Actions in Afghanistan." *Marine Corps News*,
27 April 2007.

Weil, Martin. "Chester Nimitz Jr. Dies, Navy Officer, Executive." *Washington
(DC) Post*, 7 January 2002.

Weinberger, Caspar W., and Wyton C. Hall. *Home of the Brave: Honoring the
Unsung Heroes in the War on Terror*. New York: Tom Doherty Associates
LLC, 2006.

Werrell, Kenneth P. *Sabres over MiG Alley*. Annapolis, MD: Naval Institute
Press, 2005.

West, Owen. "Leadership from the Rear: Proof that Combat Leadership
Knows No Traditional Boundaries." *Marine Corps Gazette*, 1 September
2005.

———. "Why Would Anyone Volunteer to Be an Infantryman?" *Slate
Magazine*, 30 July 2004. http://www.slate.com/id/2104305/entry/
2104546/.

White House. "President Bush Announces Major Combat Operations in Iraq
Have Ended." Press release, 1 May 2003.

Williams, Rudi. "Marine Corps Commandant Tells Stories of Respect,
Heroism." American Forces Press Service, 24 June 2004.

Wise, James E. Jr., and Baron, Scott. *The Navy Cross: Extraordinary Heroism
in Iraq, Afghanistan, and Other Conflicts*. Annapolis, MD: Naval Institute
Press, 2007.

Wise, James E. Jr., and Anne Collier Rehill. *Stars in the Corps*. Annapolis,
MD: Naval Institute Press, 1999.

Wood, Trish. *What Was Asked of Us: An Oral History of the Iraq War by the
Soldiers Who Fought It*. New York: Little Brown & Co., 2006.

Wright, MSgt. James "Eddie." "In His Own Words." www.Blackfive.Net/
main/2005/11/marine_sergeant.html.

Zabriskie, Phil. "Taking the Battle to the Enemy: U.S. and Iraqi Forces
Launch High-Risk Probes of the Insurgency in Fallujah and Ramadi."
Time, 25 October 2004.

Zeigler, Matt. *Three Block War II: Snipers in the Sky!* Lincoln, NE: Universe
Press, 2006.

Zimmerman, Beth. "Ammo Dash Earns Lieutenant a Silver Star." *Marine
Corps Times*, 8 May 2006.

———. "Citizen Marine Awarded Silver Star." Military.com, 18 June 2007, www.military.com/newscontent/0,13319,142829,00.html?ESRC=eb.nl.

———. "Marine Officer Wins Silver Star for Gallantry in Combat in Iraq." *Richmond* (VA) *Times*, 18 December 2005.

———. "Navy Cross, Silver Star Awarded for Actions in Deadly Firefight." *Marine Corps Times*, September 2006.

———. "Platoon Leader Honored for Pushing Through Ambush." *Marine Corps Times*, 16 January 2006.

Zoroya, Gregg. "Fight for Ramadi Exacts Heavy Toll on Marines." *USA Today*, 12 July 2004.

———. "3,200 Marines to Deploy to Afghanistan in Spring." *Washington* (DC) *Post*, 16 January 2008.

INDEX

ABOUT THE AUTHORS

JAMES E. WISE JR., a former naval aviator, intelligence officer, and Vietnam veteran, retired from the U.S. Navy as a captain. His books include *The Navy Cross, Stars in Blue,* and *U-505: The Final Journey,* among many others. He lives in the Washington, D.C., metropolitan area.

SCOTT BARON, a U.S. Army veteran of the Vietnam War and former law enforcement officer in California, is the author of *They Also Served: Military Biographies of Uncommon Americans* and coauthor, with Wise, of *International Stars at War, Soldiers Lost at Sea, The Navy Cross,* and *Women at War: Iraq, Afghanistan, and Other Conflicts,* all with the Naval Institute Press.